CW01080246

Palgrave Studies in Sport and Politics

Series Editor
Martin Polley
International Centre for Sports History
De Montfort University
Leicester, Leicestershire, UK

Palgrave Studies in Sport and Politics aims to nurture new research, both historical and contemporary, to the complex inter-relationships between sport and politics. The books in this series will range in their focus from the local to the global, and will embody a broad approach to politics, encompassing the ways in which sport has interacted with the state, dissidence, ideology, war, human rights, diplomacy, security, policy, identities, the law, and many other forms of politics. It includes approaches from a range of disciplines, and promotes work by new and established scholars from around the world.

Advisory Board

Dr. Daphné Bolz, University of Normandy—Rouen, France
Dr. Susan Grant, Liverpool John Moores University, UK
Dr. Keiko Ikeda, Hokkaido University, Japan
Dr. Barbara Keys, University of Melbourne, Australia
Dr. Iain Lindsey, Durham University, UK
Dr. Ramon Spaaij, Victoria University, Australia and University of Amsterdam, the Netherlands

More information about this series at
http://www.palgrave.com/gp/series/15061

Bruce Murray · Richard Parry
Jonty Winch
Editors

Cricket and Society in South Africa, 1910–1971

From Union to Isolation

Editors
Bruce Murray
University of the Witwatersrand
Johannesburg, South Africa

Jonty Winch
Reading, UK

Richard Parry
London, UK

ISSN 2365-998X   ISSN 2365-9998   (electronic)
Palgrave Studies in Sport and Politics
ISBN 978-3-319-93607-9   ISBN 978-3-319-93608-6   (eBook)
https://doi.org/10.1007/978-3-319-93608-6

Library of Congress Control Number: 2018947156

Cover illustration: Anti-apartheid protesters sit-in on pitch before match begins in Oxford, UK on July 10 1969. © Photograph by KEYSTONE-FRANCE/Gamma-Rapho via Getty Images

This Palgrave Macmillan imprint is published by the registered company Springer Nature Switzerland AG
The registered company address is: Gewerbestrasse 11, 6330 Cham, Switzerland

FOREWORD

Consider this. When South Africa came into existence as a new country in 1910, two national cricket controlling bodies were in existence. Instead of subsequently following the practice in other countries such as England, Australia, West Indies, India, New Zealand and Pakistan—where the principle of 'one board one country' became established—the game in South Africa splintered spectacularly between the 1920s and the 1950s. At one stage, there were seven different organisations in existence at the same time, all claiming the title 'national' and 'South African'! Operating in the same cities, towns and provinces, each ran their own leagues and provincial competitions for representative teams and each selected their own national sides.

While the rest of the cricket world increasingly rubbed out old dividing lines, South Africa reinforced them until there was a 'white' men's South Africa, a 'white' women's South Africa, a 'coloured' Christian South Africa, a 'Malay' or 'coloured' Muslim South Africa, a 'Bantu' (or 'black African') South Africa, an 'Indian' South Africa, and—in a slight variation of these—an 'inter-race' South Africa.

The acronyms alone were enough to make one dizzy—SACA, SACCB, SACCA, SABCB, SAICU, SACBOC and SARWCA.

Thus, many international readers will be surprised to learn that the segregation and apartheid era whites-only SACA Springboks who played in 172 Tests between 1889 and 1970 did not represent their country in the proper sense, but were only one of seven national teams or 'Springboks'. The Test team stood, not for a single united country, but for the opposite, a national fragmentation, the product of discriminatory socio-economic and political policies throughout these years.

What caused this division in cricket and the tragic waste of human potential and inefficient use of financial resources and public facilities that went with it? How does one explain the creation of this cricketing chessboard properly? The answer is by trying to understand and illuminate the tectonic shifts in society happening below the surface of the game. And this is what *Cricket and Society in South Africa, 1910–1971: From Union to Isolation* sets out to do.

Recently, a reinvented, post-democracy, South Africa gave Australia a drubbing on home soil for the first time since unity in 1991. The events during the course of the Test series again underlined the truism that the game of cricket has always carried meanings greater than the simple impact of leather on willow. While drawing on professed standards of 'fair play' (which the country, incidentally, fails to implement in areas like its immigration policies), Malcolm Turnbull, Prime Minister of Australia, lambasted Australia's ball tampering as 'a shocking disappointment' and a 'disgrace'. When the tsunami of shock and outrage which engulfed 'the Sandpaper Three' (David Warner, Steve Smith and Cameron Bancroft) receded, the central fact remained. Cricket is not just a game, or a sport, it is an institution and a vehicle for ideas, belief and behaviour.

In this book, the authors set out to show that cricket is a quintessential political game, the handmaiden of Empire, and, in South Africa, a barometer of race, class, ethnicity and gender. Also that cricket was a critical factor in the history of segregation in sport. They trace the colour bar over a period of 75 years from the time it was formalised way back in 1894 when the fast-bowler 'Krom' Hendricks was denied an opportunity to represent his country on the first overseas tour to England by the then Cape Prime Minister (Cecil John Rhodes), to 1968 when Basil D'Oliveira, selected as a member of the MCC team to tour South Africa, was rejected by the South African Prime Minister, Johannes Balthazar Vorster, on account of the pigmentation of his skin, effectively ending South Africa's international cricketing contact until the run-up to democracy in the 1990s.

Cricket took root in South Africa following the first British invasion of the Cape in 1795, but in an astonishing reality the country's cricketers have been formally united under a single Cricket South Africa for only 27 out of the 223 years since then. This divided past still bears heavily on the present. Therefore, the editors and authors are to be congratulated for making the effort to explain the development of the game in ways which go beyond the 'elegant cover drive' school of descriptive writing. Understanding the murky history of class, racial and gender oppression in South Africa and where we have come from will enable our cricketers (and cricket lovers worldwide) to understand better also the unique challenges South Africa faces in making concrete its post-democracy goals of creating equal opportunity and inclusive unity on and off the cricket field.

To quote Wally Hammond, writing in South Africa where he passed his final days, 'we can only hope for a happy future if we first learn the lessons of the past'. Hammond's point gains heft from being penned by the hand which directed the most sublime of cover drives, where finesse and grace obscured the mere mechanics of its operation. The authors of *Cricket and Society*, too, have collectively brought their considerable finesse to teasing out various strands of South Africa's cricketing life from Union to isolation. They help uncover still largely unknown facets of this experience, recognise the achievements of players excluded by a racialised male establishment who for so long claimed the game as their own, and demonstrate how cricket was shaped by society and society by cricket.

Neither does *Cricket and Society* ignore the global dimensions. It shows how Rhodes sought to perpetuate his imperial vision and the significance of cricket in this process. Also how the establishment of cricket within the diasporic Indian community in South Africa, with its close ties with the Indian motherland, was a defence against racist state policies. Of course, the decision to engage or not with South Africa was a key issue for the rest of the sporting world. Two great West Indians, Learie Constantine and C. L. R. James, debated the issue in the 1950s, and by the 1960s, the MCC selectors were forced to take a position on the selection of D'Oliveira. The tortuous path leading to the English withdrawal of contact is examined here, and a chapter containing an in-depth investigation on the impact of the D'Oliveira affair and its aftermath on women's cricket touches on often ignored aspects of the game's history as well. As with the racial exclusions of the past, it will take generations to write gendered cricket histories that undo the dangerous Victorian stereotypes propounded by W. G. Grace and his contemporaries that women who played were 'neither cricketers nor ladies'.

Six of the contributors of *Cricket and Society* were involved as well as in putting together a polished predecessor volume, *Empire and*

Cricket (2009), which dealt with the late nineteenth-century and early twentieth-century period. Double thanks are therefore due to Richard Parry, Bruce Murray and Jonty Winch (the editors of this volume) as well as Geoffrey Levett, Goolam Vahed and Dale Slater for their solid research and thoughtful revisionist inputs over a lengthy period. They are joined here by project newcomers Jon Gemmell, Rafaelle Nicholson, Albert Grundlingh and Patrick Ferriday. The originality of the above-mentioned two books lies partly in the fact that they were written by a mainly British-based group of scholars and that they have a flexibility which allows the multiple authors to explore eclectic themes. The works complement other volumes which have recently appeared in South Africa, most notably *Cricket and Conquest* (2016), *Reverse Sweep* (2017) and *Divided Country* (2018), adding critical mass to a grow-ing new literature on the social dimensions of sport in South Africa. As co-author of the first and third of these last-mentioned books—which are volumes 1 and 2 of the four-part series on *The History of South African Cricket Retold* —I wish to thank Dr. Jonty Winch and Dr. Richard Parry in particular for their cooperative approach. Jonty's research on nine-teenth-century establishment cricket was of such a high standard that Krish Reddy, Christopher Merrett and myself invited him to become a co-author of *Cricket and Conquest*. Though our respective projects emerged separately and are different in focus and sometimes in perspec-tives, the resultant works in many respects complement each other.

To conclude, *Cricket and Society* is an important addition to the redis-covery of history as a basis for social transformation. It not only exposes new realities of South African cricket through different eras, but in doing so also helps illuminate the nature of the South African society itself.

Cape Town, South Africa

André Odendaal
Honorary Professor in History
and Heritage Studies
University of the Western Cape

ACKNOWLEDGEMENTS

In the course of producing this publication, we have been greatly helped by a number of cricket writers, archivists, librarians, curators, photographers and followers of the game.

Professor André Odendaal kindly wrote the foreword. He has for some years been at the forefront of the new historiography of South African cricket through taking on lead roles in both chairing the Transformation Monitoring Committee and recording the full history of South African cricket. We have learnt much from being able to work closely with him and appreciate his encouragement and support in the course of this project.

We are grateful to Robin Isherwood who gave us the benefit of his expertise in correcting statistical errors and drawing attention to areas that we had overlooked. His knowledge of South African cricket is legendary, and we were fortunate that he should spend considerable time on the manuscript.

It is equally important to acknowledge the contribution that Dale Slater has made in the course of writing and editing this publication. He could not have been more generous with time, information and advice.

One of the most demanding of all tasks in producing a work involving ten authors is the administration. Bernard Tancred Hall has been a tower of strength throughout in assembling material, maintaining links with everyone, and fielding various problems that have arisen.

We are indebted to the librarians and archivists at the British Library; the National Library of South Africa, Cape Town; the Cullen Library,

University of the Witwatersrand; the Johannesburg Municipal Library; and the MCC Library at Lord's. In addition, Ian Johnstone (through the Zimbabwe Archives) provided invaluable research material in assisting Geoff Levett and Jonty Winch in their chapters that referred to early Rhodesian history.

Carole Cornthwaite and the Women's Cricket Associates allowed Rafaelle Nicholson access to the Women's Cricket Association Archive. Rafaelle also appreciated the help she received from those women who agreed to be interviewed on the period. Giles Ridley kindly offered comment on the Rhodes Scholar cricketers from Rhodesia, and Peter and Graeme Pollock, Don Mackay-Coghill, Mike Procter and Barry Richards were generous with insights about the 'Walk-off' at Newlands.

Rick Smith in Tasmania provided photographs from the collection that he and the late Brian Bassano have built up on South African cricket. We would also like to thank André Odendaal, Giles Ridley, the *Cape Times* and the University of the Witwatersrand for permission to use their photographs.

CONTENTS

Notes on Contributors

Patrick Ferriday has an English Literature degree from the University of East Anglia. He began writing and publishing cricket books in 2012 with *Before the Lights Went Out*, an account of the 1912 Triangular Tournament, which was shortlisted for the Cricket Society Book of the Year Award. He then edited and co-wrote *Masterly Batting* and *Supreme Bowling* which attempted to classify the greatest Test centuries and bowling performances. Since then he has published three more titles, two for David Frith, and his most recent title, *In Tandem*, is a history of great fast-bowling pairs. He lives in Brighton with his wife and two children, and his real job is commentating on horse racing.

Dr. Jon Gemmell is the author of *The Politics of South African Cricket*. He has also edited volumes on Cricket's World Cup and the Globalisation of Cricket. His interest lies in the relationship between politics and cricket, and he has had articles published on South Africa, Ireland, Zimbabwe, Pakistan, Australia and international politics in general. His latest book, *Cricket's Changing Ethos: Nobles, Nationalists and the IPL*, is released on Palgrave Macmillan. Jon writes the occasional contribution on cricket and politics in *The Morning Star* newspaper.

Professor Albert Grundlingh is a graduate of the University of the Free State and was appointed to the University of South Africa in 1973 where he obtained his MA and D Litt et Phil degrees. In 2001, he moved to Stellenbosch University as Head of Department. Grundlingh is the author of and co-author of several books and numerous articles and chapters in books. Many of his publications have appeared in leading international journals. He specialises in social and cultural history with a particular interest in war and society. His major works deal with the Boer collaborators during the Anglo-Boer War of 1899–1902, black South African troops during the First World War, and he would like to think that the book he has written on rugby and South African society is akin to dealing with the phenomenon of war in a different format.

Dr. Geoffrey Levett is a historian who writes on sport and empire in Britain and France in the twentieth century. His doctoral thesis was on sport and imperial culture in the Edwardian period. Previous publications include a chapter on the 1907 South African tour in *Empire and Cricket: The South African Experience 1884–1914* (2009), various scholarly articles on the history of sport, as well as a series of contributions on West Indian cricketers for the *Dictionary of Latin American and Caribbean Biography*.

Professor Bruce Murray is Emeritus Professor of History at the University of the Witwatersrand, Johannesburg, where he lectured from 1970 to 2001, offering courses in British, American and medieval European history. He is the author of *The People's Budget: Lloyd George and Liberal Politics, 1909/10* (1980), and two volumes on the history of Wits University, *Wits: The Early Years* (1982) and *Wits: The 'Open' Years* (1997). He is co-author with Christopher Merrett of *Caught Behind: Race and Politics in Springbok Cricket* (2004) and a contributor to and co-editor of *Empire and Cricket: The South African Experience 1884–1914* (2009).

Dr. Rafaelle Nicholson has recently completed her doctorate at Queen Mary University, London, which focuses on the history of women's cricket in Britain since 1945. Prior to this, she gained a BA in Modern History and Politics at Merton College, Oxford, and an MSt in Women's Studies at Mansfield College, Oxford. She has published articles in *History of Education* and *Women's History Review* and has also written freelance on women's cricket for, among others, ESPNCricinfo and *Wisden*. She is the editor of the women's cricket website, www.crickether. com.

André Odendaal is Honorary Professor in History and Heritage Studies at the University of the Western Cape. After graduating with a Ph.D. from Cambridge, he taught at UWC and was founding director of both the Mayibuye Centre for History and Culture in South Africa at UWC and the Robben Island Museum, the first heritage institution of the new South African democracy. He was then Chief Executive Officer of the Western Province Cricket Association and the successful Cape Cobras professional team. He had previously played first-class cricket in South Africa and England and was the only provincial cricketer designated 'white' to join the non-racial SACOS during the apartheid years. He was an anti-apartheid activist in the UDF, NECC, NSC and ANC and chaired the United Cricket Board of South Africa's Transformation Monitoring Committee from 1998 to 2002. In that year, he received the President's Award for Sport (Silver Class). André has written ten books on the history of the liberation struggle and the social history of sport in South Africa including *Vukani Bantu!* (1984), *The Story of an African Game* (2003) and *The Founders* (2012). He is currently lead writer and project coordinator of *The History of South African Cricket Retold*, a four-volume series, while also serving as writer and research coordinator for the Albie Sachs Trust on constitutionalism and the Rule of Law.

Dr. Richard Parry studied at the University of Natal, Durban and Queen's University, Canada. His Master's thesis was on Rhodes and the Development of Segregation at the Cape (1983), and his Ph.D. tackled informal resistance and the limits of colonial power in Rhodesia (1988). After 15 years in the UK Inland Revenue as an expert in international taxation, he was Head of Global Relations in the Centre for Tax Policy and Administration, at the Paris-based Organisation for Economic Co-operation and Development. He has written variously on culture, sport and resistance to colonialism in Africa, on early South African cricket, and on international taxation. Since 2016, he has divided his time between advising African countries on implementing effective tax systems and writing on South African cricket and social history. He was a contributor to *Empire and Cricket: The South African Experience 1884–1914* (2009).

Dale Slater grew up in the Eastern Cape and studied Politics at the University of Natal, Durban. Living and working in the field of Information and Research in the UK since 1979, he has contributed occasionally to sundry cricket and cricket history titles. He contributed to *Empire and Cricket: The South African experience, 1884–1914* (2009), and his article on 'Dik' Abed was selected by Ramachandra Guha for his anthology of notable cricket writing, *The Picador Book of Cricket* (2001).

A survivor of both cancer and major heart disease, he is retired on health grounds and uses this time writing and researching cricket and social history, and watching his granddaughter play for Surrey. He is currently collecting material for a Reader on South African cricket history and for a piece on the rapidly developing tradition of black South African fast bowlers.

Professor Goolam Vahed is an Associate Professor in History at the University of KwaZulu Natal. He received his Ph.D from Indiana University, Bloomington. His research interests include the history of identity formation, citizenship, ethnicity, migration and transnationalism among Indian South Africans and the role of sport and culture in South African society. He has published widely in peer-reviewed journals, and his co-authored books include (with Ashwin Desai, Vishnu Padayachee and Krish Reddy) *Blacks in Whites: A Century of Cricket Struggles in KwaZulu Natal* (2002) and (with Ashwin Desai) *The South Africa Gandhi: Stretcher-Bearer of Empire* (2015). He was co-editor with Bruce Murray of *Empire and Cricket: The South African Experience 1884–1914* (2009).

Dr. Jonty Winch received a Master of Arts degree with distinction from De Montfort University's International Centre for Sports History and Culture and was then awarded his Ph.D. from the University of Stellenbosch. He has been involved in photography, journalism and education and has written six books on sporting history in southern Africa. They include *Cricket's Rich Heritage: A History of Rhodesian and Zimbabwean Cricket 1890–1982 (1983)*; *Cricket in Southern Africa: Two Hundred Years of Achievements and Records* (1997); and *England's Youngest Captain: the Life and Times of Monty Bowden and Two South African Journalists* (2003). He is also co-author of *Cricket & Conquest: The History of South African Cricket Retold 1795–1914* (2016) and has written articles for accredited international academic publications, winning the British Society of Sports History 'Best Article in *Sport in History*' in 2008.

LIST OF FIGURES

PART I

The Landscape

CHAPTER 1

Landscape, Players and Politics

Richard Parry, Jon Gemmell and Jonty Winch

This book examines aspects of South African cricket from the formation of Union in 1910 to the country's eventual isolation as a cricketing nation in 1971. It is a history of cricket and a history of how cricket was shaped by society and society by cricket. It explores the tangled and complex relationship between cricketers, politicians, and the economy during the period which started with South Africa at the beating heart of the imperial project and ended with the country as an international pariah.

Cricket, with a weight of ideological baggage unmatched by other sports, was influenced in many ways by the relations between land, labour and capital, town and country. South Africa's human landscape was divided by the state into English or Afrikaans-speaking whites, and blacks whether African, coloured or Indian, and by economics and culture on the basis of race, ethnicity, language, class, religion, and gender.

R. Parry
London, UK

J. Gemmell (✉)
Kennet School, Thatcham, UK

J. Winch
Reading, UK

© The Author(s) 2018   3
B. Murray et al. (eds.), *Cricket and Society in South
Africa, 1910–1971*, Palgrave Studies in Sport and Politics,
https://doi.org/10.1007/978-3-319-93608-6_1

These tensions, divisions and conflicts also influenced South Africa's relations within the Empire and the operation of the South African economy through an exploitative cheap labour policy sustained by a segregated regime which in its state-structured shape proved unsustainable by the end of the twentieth century. And all this occurred in a world at a time of unprecedented upheaval; the end of the construction of colonialism; the advent of economic imperialism after the South African War and the formation of Union; the struggle over labour; the involvement of the Empire in two world wars; decolonisation and finally the expulsion of South Africa from the imperial fraternity.

The various chapters explain and tease out some of the key strands in the evolving nature of South African cricket within the international landscape. The view through the cracks of history is often constrained by difficulties of evidence and establishing the decision-making processes which took place behind closed doors. Cricket not only reflected the evolution of the social order but was part of a strategy used to control that structure and maintain the global imperial network. All South African cricketers represented their own specific interest groups based on race, ethnicity, gender and class—whether Africans on the gold mines trying to forge a community; Indians trying to establish their identity as South Africans; Afrikaners rejecting one imperial game, cricket, for another, rugby; women fighting their ongoing battle for resources and recognition, or the final generation of white cricketing Springboks walking off the field in a futile protest aimed at saving their country's Test status, the last act before the shutters came down on South African participation in official international cricket.

Not surprisingly therefore, the historical experience of South Africa over the last hundred years has witnessed the tension between fragmentation and unity, as part of the struggle to weld a country from its disparate elements. This reflects on a smaller screen the global struggle over Empire as political 'colonial' control gave way to an economic and ideological framework.

South Africa was not unique among imperial cricket-playing countries in the extent to which cricket influenced the political and social order. But the South African dynamic was qualitatively different from the other parts of Empire where the racial questions of who could play for the country and who the country would play against did not arise. These questions lay at the heart of the South African social and political order. They still reverberate through the debate over the role of cricket in the collapse of apartheid, and the subsequent transformation process as well as the tensions in South Africa's current search to ensure that it fields a competitive international team which is representative of the whole country.

Cricket is and was a barometer of South African society as well as part of the complex and changing relationship between South Africa and Empire. This was shifting and ambivalent in nature, riven by economic and political tensions. From the late nineteenth century, white and black cricketers played their own segregated games, with the pervasive racism of the state and the white community always shaping the action. By the mid-twentieth century, the segregationist strategy had solidified, through the ostensible development of an ideology to justify its repression, into the apartheid regime. Who could play with or against whom, and where, were enshrined in law as well as practice.

This essential landscape had its key elements in place before the formation of Union in 1910 unified the previously separate British colonies—Cape, Natal, Transvaal and Orange Free State—into a self-governing dominion within the Empire. Cricket in earlier years had been a critical factor in the Cecil Rhodes imposed policy of segregation which concentrated economic and political power in white hands, and restricted representation at cricket to whites, whatever the nature of their ties to the country itself. Race was the key to qualification: white South Africans were 'citizens' of Empire, blacks were subjects, less to Empire than their white masters.

The opening section of this work explores the landscape in two main areas: first the evolution of South African sport and identity in its imperial context and second, the nature of the internal landscape and how it defined South African cricket.

Origins

During the latter part of the nineteenth century Cecil John Rhodes, by then Prime Minister of the Cape Colony and before that one of the first mining magnates who exploited the discoveries of diamonds in 1867 and gold in 1886, often expressed his desire that South Africa should be united under British leadership as part of the Empire. He did not wish to be left 'settled just on this small peninsula' but wanted the Cape Colony 'to be able to deal with the question of confederation as the dominant state of South Africa'.[1]

In order to achieve union, he sought to bring together the two dominant white 'races' (English and Dutch/Afrikaans speakers) at the expense of the Cape's grand 'liberal' tradition and the rights of the black population.[2] His aspirations to an Anglo-Afrikaner alliance were shared by the leader of the Cape Afrikaner Bond, J. H. 'Onze Jan' Hofmeyr. But while they agreed on an alliance for unity, Hofmeyr wanted a unified South Africa under its own flag and an independent republic beyond the ties of Empire. Whichever side won, black South Africans were to be the losers.

Rhodes and Hofmeyr both recognised the potential for sport to unify the region fully twenty years before this became a political reality. A 'South African' cricket team was selected for the first time in 1889 to play against Major Warton's English tourists. This team met Warton's on level terms and included representatives from the various self-governing colonies and independent republics in the subcontinent. Several months later the South African Rugby Football Board was formed, and in 1890 a meeting was held to establish the South African Cricket Association (SACA).

Cricket did not play the role in bringing together the two white 'races' which rugby, another imperial game, managed to do in the late nineteenth century. The problem was not the Afrikaner's lack of interest or ability in cricket. Stellenbosch, a side comprised almost entirely of players from the Dutch-speaking sector of the white population, was for a time the most feared team at the Cape. They produced several outstanding fast bowlers—notably Louis Neethling, E. L. Schröder, Pieter de Villiers, Johan du Plessis and Nicol Theunissen. The last named, renowned for his 'great knee-shaking, rib-roasting, finger-mangling bump', opened the South African bowling against Major Warton's side in 1888/89.[3]

The problem was what in the nineteenth century the Cape used to call 'race', that is the relationship between the Dutch/ Afrikaner and English, rather than class as they referred to white-black relations. William Milton, South Africa's leading cricket administrator and the Western Province Cricket Club—the self-styled MCC of South Africa which Milton controlled for many years—were reluctant to provide opportunities for the Dutch country district teams. Milton also became Rhodes's Private Secretary but his innate snobbishness and distaste for the Dutch meant that he did not share Rhodes's vision in this key area. The failure at this early stage to recognise the potential of the Afrikaner would prove detrimental to South African cricket for much of the twentieth century, The indifference shown by cricket's administrators towards teams outside the elite group of Cape Town's southern suburb clubs contrasted with the attitude of the progressive and democratic Western Province Rugby Football Union. Led by their young secretary, Carlo Douglas-de Fenzi, the Union actively encouraged the participation of the Afrikaans-dominated districts and introduced the successful Country Challenge Cup. Stellenbosch enjoyed marked rugby success and in the 1896 season not only won Western Province's premier competition—the Grand Challenge—but also secured the Junior Challenge for the third successive year.[4]

By the mid-1890s Afrikaner participation in cricket had declined at the Cape and elsewhere with the representative games essentially taking on an exclusively English-speaking white status. Interest flickered among Afrikaner communities in the different regions and in March 1892, for example, Charlie Fichardt and Vlooi du Toit attended a SACA meeting to set up the affiliation of the Orange Free State.

Yet during all of this, cricket was not just a white game. Black pupils were encouraged to play by the mission schools as proud harbingers of Empire, while the coloured and 'Malay' communities, who had not received a mission education, nonetheless had built a strong cricketing network in Cape Town and Kimberley by the 1880s. The quality of play was equally strong and their best players participated at a level directly comparable with white cricketers despite their limited resources. Cricket's popularity was in part due to the fact that it was emblematic of Empire and as such allowed for the aspirations of ambitious blacks who used cricket to build and advance their leadership status within their communities.

This was exemplified by the coloured 'Krom' Hendricks, a 'demon' fast bowler whom W. W. Read described as 'the Spofforth of South Africa'.[5] He was omitted on political grounds from the 1894 first South African tour to England. Hendricks was understandably eager to represent South Africa but, for a decade, Milton and his fellow white Cape cricket officials systematically excluded him from participation in all levels of representative cricket.[6] Through their treatment of Hendricks, the Cape administrators laid the foundations of segregated sport in South Africa. Established practice became enshrined in the law until more than seventy years later another player of colour from the Cape—Basil D'Oliveira—forced the sporting world to focus on what was happening in the country and South Africa was at last liberated in the 1990s.

The period in which Hendricks sought recognition for his cricket ability was one of immense political turmoil. A long struggle between the Kruger-led South African Republic and the foreign adventurers, miners and 'Randlords' over control of the mining industry followed the discovery of gold in 1886 on the Rand. In retrospect, there could only be one outcome. As Kruger lamented, 'it is not the vote they want, it is my country …' and that outcome was annexation or war. The Jameson Raid over New Year 1896—plotted by Rhodes, Jameson and John Hays Hammond, the American imperialist—was a dramatic attempt to usurp the Transvaal's autonomy, and effectively brought to a temporary end Rhodes's dream of uniting South Africa. It was a fiasco, as the bumbling Jameson was shadowed all the way by Kruger's forces and walked into an ambush. Meanwhile, the bellicose 'Randlord' Reform Committee in Johannesburg sat on their hands.

Hofmeyr and his followers at the Cape felt betrayed by Rhodes, who resigned and effectively disappeared from Cape politics. 'Afrikaners', said Robert I. Rotberg 'would never again trust Britons'.[7] It was questionable how much trust there had been in the first place but the Raid had created a watershed between the communities and provided Kruger's Republic with a moral and psychological triumph. 'The Jameson Raid', said the Boer leader, Jan Smuts, 'was the real declaration of War', adding, 'and that is so in spite of the four years of truce that followed … the aggressors consolidated their alliance … the defenders on the other hand silently and grimly prepared for the inevitable'.[8]

The second South African War was fought from 11 October 1899 to 31 May 1902. Cricket was played throughout the war and even included an ill-timed tour to England in 1901. It was financed by James Logan, and the manner in which the team was assembled is best exemplified by the fact that he selected his own son. In the aftermath of the War, the Transvaal mining magnate, Abe Bailey, took over responsibility for funding a game which had not yet managed to turn a profit in South Africa but would bring Rhodes's imperial dream to fruition in the cricketing context. As a result of Bailey's efforts and the systematic involvement of Lords Harris and Hawke and much of the English cricketing establishment with the South African gold mines, the Imperial Cricket Conference included South Africa as a founder member alongside England and Australia.[9] Symbolically, South Africa with its vast mineral resources was at the heart of Empire when the South Africa Act, which provided for Union, was enacted by the British Parliament in 1909.

A key to this was the development of a global generation of South African cricketers which for the first (and last time until the 1930s) proved competitive against England thanks to the all-round skills of Aubrey Faulkner and the performances of the googly bowlers who took an English invention and shaped it to South African ends.[10] 'Vogler, Faulkner, Schwarz and White', wrote Ian Peebles, were 'relatively and positively in fact, the greatest combination of pure spin ever to appear in a single team'.[11]

The captain of the side before and after Union and on tours to England and Australia was Percy Sherwell. In the opening chapter of this volume, Geoffrey Levett examines the issue of imperial and national identity through an analysis of Sherwell's career. The question Levett poses is that of 'race' in the sense of English and Afrikaner: what did it mean to be a white South African and a cricketer in the aftermath of the South African War? And why did Sherwell, who had the cricketing and personal credentials to be an authentic South African sporting hero, fail to achieve this status in the face of rugby and the achievements of Paul Roos, the South African rugby captain? The insights here are critical to key characteristics of Empire—its slipperiness, and its ability to claim those it wished to further its cause. But they also demonstrate the search by the majority Afrikaner population, still deeply traumatised by the war and the concentration camp deaths only a few years previously, for an authentic hero untainted by what they saw as a quintessential imperial legacy.

Union in 1910

Rhodes died in 1902 and did not live to see anything approaching his concept of a 'United States of South Africa'.[12] Nonetheless, the movement towards unification gathered pace following a severe depression in the middle of the decade, and a National Convention at Durban in October 1908 was followed by a gathering in Bloemfontein the following year. The leaders of the Afrikaner movements wisely decided that union rather than a federal form of government would be to their advantage. Crucially, no one either represented or stood up for the country's majority black population. English and Afrikaners agreed that only whites could become members of the House of Assembly with executive power being in the hands of the Governor-General and cabinet.

Despite the efforts of African leaders to persuade the British Government to honour the promises made in the course of a war in which thousands of Africans had died, the country was given inevitably to the white Afrikaans and English-speaking communities. The battle fought by Africans was waged primarily over the franchise: would the Cape's property-based system be exported into the rest of the subcontinent? The solution was to maintain the pre-war arrangements—racially exclusive voting rights to white males in all colonies except the Cape where qualifications which had undergone massive erosion from the mid-1890s allowed a small minority of 'civilised' black male residents to vote. These numbers dwindled year by year, as blacks struggled to meet requirements for qualification which involved salary, literacy and access to property, specifically land. The access that the remaining handful of blacks had to the ballot box under the 'colour blind' franchise in what was then the Cape Province was finally abolished on racial grounds in 1936.

In order to further placate the majority Afrikaners on which their Empire would soon depend, the British supported the former defeated Boer leader, General Louis Botha, as the best man to lead the Union government and promote a policy of reconciliation and co-operation between Briton and Boer. Enthusiasm for Union, however, failed to win over black South Africans who had gained nothing from the new dispensation. The South African Native National Congress, forerunner of the African National Congress (ANC), was created in 1912 to defend black rights and despite its lack of success so far continued a policy of engagement and persuasion rather than industrial or armed resistance.

Meanwhile, not all Afrikaners were bought off by the compromises of Empire. Two years later, in 1912, the National Party was formed in Bloemfontein by leading anti-imperialists, General J. B. M. Hertzog and the Fichardt brothers, Charlie and Everard. The original National Party attacked symbols such as the flag, anthem, currency and the monarchy as being alien to the Afrikaner cause, and they held little respect for the Commonwealth. In this regard, Charlie Fichardt's enthusiasm for cricket is interesting and it is perhaps unfortunate that it was not utilised to greater advantage in developing Afrikaner involvement in the sport. He was a South African player, as well as the Orange Free State captain, opening batsman and opening bowler in two Currie Cup tournaments and against the touring MCC sides in 1905/06 and 1909/10. His family had also hosted Emily Hobhouse during the South African War and he was a politician and businessman of considerable influence.

He was of German descent and fiercely committed to the Afrikaner cause, becoming known during the First World War for his 'sheer, open Germanism and hatred of all things British'.[13]

The First World War exposed these divisions within the Afrikaner ranks. Some under the influence of Lieutenant-General Manie Maritz supported the Germans while others under General Christiaan de Wet marched to Pretoria to demonstrate their discontent about the invasion of German South-West Africa. There were also Afrikaners who supported the subsequent conflict when a victory was achieved in less than six months at the cost of less than 300 South Africans killed in action.

There was a bitter debate within South Africa on entry into the war, but its white and black soldiers served with distinction in the East African campaign and on the Western Front, most famously at Delville Wood during the Battle of the Somme in 1916. In the first three weeks of July that year the South African Infantry Brigade lost 2536 men while 607 black troops in the South African Labour Corps were drowned when the *SS Mendi* sank in the English Channel in January 1917. It might be added that seven of the twelve Test cricketers who lost their lives while serving in the First World War had played for South Africa—Arthur Ochse, Reggie Schwarz, Gordon White, Eric 'Bill' Lundie, Claude Newberry, Reggie Hands and Frederick Cook.

Throughout this period, Jan Smuts was a dominant figure. Educated in the Cape and in the law at Cambridge, he had been one of the most resolute generals on the Afrikaner side in the South African War. In the First World War, he was invited to join the Imperial War Cabinet and he became the South African Prime Minister when Botha died in August 1919. Global racialism after the war—and of course events in Russia—was enflamed by the international recession. In South Africa, mine owners confronted by a fixed price for gold and escalating production costs endeavoured to use cheap African labour to challenge the 'job colour bar' or white miners' monopoly over skilled and semi-skilled employment on the mines. In 1922, white workers came out on the streets in an armed Rand Rebellion, chanting slogans like 'Workers of the World Unite and Fight for a White South Africa'.[14] African workers also came out in defence of their rights and the Government eventually called out the troops to suppress the rising. Smuts was 'severely criticised both for his initial apathy and his sudden ruthless quelling of the rebellion', and paid the political cost.[15] The same year, he suffered disappointment when Rhodesia voted against joining the Union and then in April 1923 the two opposition parties, Labour and Nationalists, agreed to work together, joining forces to form the Pact Government after the general election in 1924.

The cricket played in this period is recalled by Dale Slater's wide-ranging chapter which recounts the struggle over whether top-level cricket in South Africa would be played on matting or turf—a fundamental debate over the immediate landscape of cricket in its most concrete sense. The failure to introduce turf wickets—with its obvious benefits—for fifty years held up a mirror to the nature of empire and society in South Africa and Australia, and the development in South Africa of a narrow and defensive cricketing culture which reflected South African economic and political conditions. This had a huge impact on South Africa's international competitiveness, indicating the regional fragmentation which was not overcome until the late 1920s, and illuminating the fissures and stresses in South African society and its economy (Fig. 1.1).

Fig. 1.1 Two of South Africa's most famous cricketers at the time of Union in 1910 were Jimmy Sinclair (left) and Aubrey Faulkner

South Africa looked on with interest as their first opponents in the post-war period—the 1921 Australians—toured England prior to stopping off in South Africa on the way home. Warwick Armstrong's great team went through the English summer unbeaten until their thirty-fifth match when they were unexpectedly defeated by an England XI at Eastbourne. The game was won by a brilliant second innings of 153 by the South African, Aubrey Faulkner, which gave Archie McLaren's England XI (43 and 326) a surprise 28-run win over the Australians (174 and 167). Neville Cardus recalled having to leave the ground early in order to catch the train to London. He had reached the gate when Faulkner began his famous innings: 'I retraced my steps a little; I sat on a bench facing the pavilion. I did not go to London that day. Or the next. I stayed on at Eastbourne … I saw Aubrey Faulkner's last big innings'. He recalled 'the Australians would have given hairs from their heads to save themselves' and wrote with delight of the way Faulkner's googly tied up and ultimately dismissed the Australian captain.[16]

The scene was a flashback to a bygone era. Faulkner was living in England and no longer playing regularly when the Springboks lost at home against Australia 1-0 (1921/22) and England 2-1 (1922/23). An ageing South African team, brought up to play the game on matting, then travelled to England in 1924 and Faulkner hoped to give them encouragement when he wrote in the *Rand Daily Mail*: 'English sport is becoming decadent and that laziness of thought and deed seems a developed cult among the younger generation'.[17] It was a statement that he soon regretted making. The 1924 tour was a disaster for the South Africans and *The Cricketer* reflected on a political meeting at Durban on 16 June, the eve of the South African election, and also the second day of the Test match at Edgbaston.

> *Nationalist speaker*: What, I ask you, has England ever done for South Africa? Tell me that!
> *Voice from back of hall*: Bowled us out for thirty at Birmingham, anyway.[18]

Although the Smuts Government still had two years to run, the Prime Minister called an election in 1924. His South African Party was defeated and Hertzog formed the new government, which 'sought to establish parity for Afrikaners with English-speaking whites within South Africa and to make South Africa constitutionally independent from Britain … Segregation [or further repression of the African population] was to be elaborated and entrenched in the industrial arena'.[19] The hardening of the white government's attitude towards blacks fell on an already beleaguered African population and while the UK was aware of the worsening of conditions among a population they had a special responsibility to protect, this translated into apathy at the highest levels, concerned as they were only with the success of the economy.

On their next cricket tour to England in 1929, the South African management allegedly objected to the presence of the England qualified Indian-born batsman, K. S. Duleepsinhji, in the English team. 'Duleep', who was one of the outstanding players of his generation, played the first Test when the South African manager, apparently on instructions from South Africa, protested against his inclusion on the somewhat specious grounds that he was not eligible being an Indian. Ironically, the South African tourists of 1894 had in fact played against the last Indian to represent England, Duleepsinhji's uncle, Ranjitsinhji, without protest, and three players—George Glover, George Kempis and Dante Parkin—had recalled that 'a prettier bat all round the wicket it would be impossible to imagine'.[20] 'Nummy' Deane, the South African captain, wrote to Duleepsinhji denying any objections to his playing while research by Rex Roberts and Simon Wilde on Duleepsinhji suggests—with later echoes in the D'Oliveira affair—that the real objectors 'were situated not in South Africa but high places in the English game and English society'.[21] Whatever the origins of the protest, the point seemed clear that South Africans were able to push at an open door where the English establishment was concerned. In the case of 'Duleep', he averaged 58.52 in his twelve Tests but was never again selected to play against South Africa.

Hertzog Weakens Imperial Influence

After the Nationalists won the general election of 1929, Hertzog continued with his efforts to weaken the imperial influence on his country and in 1931 secured full sovereign independence for South Africa through the Statute of Westminster after the Wall Street crash and a deepening depression led to South Africa following Britain in abandoning the gold standard. In 1933, as the Depression bit deep, Smuts formed a coalition with Hertzog resulting the following year in a 'Fusion' government. The new structure was aided by sustained economic growth for South Africa due largely to a boom in gold mining. Gold dominated the economy, stimulating expansion in secondary industry and creating even greater demand for both black and white mine-workers. On the Witwatersrand, the white population increased from 233,000 in 1921 to 410,000 in 1936, and the black labour force in the mines and elsewhere on the Rand more than doubled from 304,000 to 620,000.[22]

During this period the Witwatersrand saw the development of an active and vibrant African cricket culture. The African petty-bourgeoisie formed a neglected and largely forgotten class-based cricketing community battling to play the game they loved in the face of shrinking African economic, political and social options. They became involved in cricket because of the opportunities this provided, often playing a crucial role in the leadership of a community that sought to maintain its own economic interests. At times it meant alliances with migrant workers, while they also formed a central element in the strategic development of the mining industry as well as the priorities of the municipal authorities. It is here that Richard Parry has produced a study of a hidden history of African cricket with his chapter focusing on the growth and popularity of African cricket and the complex class and entrepreneurial dynamics of cricketing relations and resistance to fragmentation within the black community which included Africans, Indians, coloureds and Malays. Amidst the overall increasingly repressive labour and social structure and political economy of the Witwatersrand, Africans like Piet Gwele, Sol Senaoane, Frank Roro and many others, were able to play cricket at a high level comparable to whites despite the myriad difficulties which they faced. This chapter rescues their achievements, on and off the cricket field, from obscurity. That they were able to play at all was surprising, but even more surprising was the way in which African sportsmen, particularly cricketers, exerted the leadership necessary to redefine their world, and develop a community which laid a platform for a brighter future.

In contrast, white cricket continued largely unaffected by political developments taking place. Their concern was to obtain turf wickets which would enable them to compete more effectively at international level. The early Tests on turf were played at Newlands and Kingsmead during the 1930/31 tour but, ironically, real pleasure was derived when 'Buster' Nupen led South Africa to victory on matting in the only Test that produced a result. He took 11 for 150 in the opening Test at the Wanderers, Johannesburg, an achievement that was no surprise as legendary opening batsman, Herbert Sutcliffe, had previously claimed Nupen's off-spinners 'turned at an alarming angle and I could not connect accurately'.[23]

Dale Slater and Richard Parry examine how South Africa succeeded in winning their first Test series in England in 1935, having failed so often before. The chapter looks at developments in South African cricketing culture, and the learning experience that white cricket underwent following defeats abroad, and particularly the humiliation by Bradman. It focuses on accumulation as a model for victory, and the significance of leadership by which Herbert Wade built on the platform established by Deane, and used the strengths of a young, fit and committed team. Above all, it describes the evolution of probably South Africa's best batsman before the 1950s—Bruce Mitchell—and his special moment in the Lord's sunshine. Of course, Mitchell's achievement needs to be located within wider social and political events at a time when the last building block of the system of racial segregation, which in the post-war period would form the basis for grand apartheid, was put in place with the passage of Hertzog's 'native' bills in 1936. Mitchell had a shadow—Frank Roro—a talented black Transvaal batsman whose career ran parallel in the same city at the same time but, however good any black cricketer might be, he would never win selection for white sides. White South Africans sought the service of the black population but not their presence.

Success for South Africa in Test cricket was relatively rare in contrast to the achievements of their rugby counterparts and this was clearly a major factor in rugby's status as the 'national game'. After defeat at the hands of the British in 1896, South Africa's rugby players did not lose another Test series until 1956. This run of success included three overseas 'grand slams'; defeating the All Blacks in New Zealand and beating them 4-0 in South Africa. The relative strengths of South African cricket and rugby at this time are encapsulated in the chapter in which Jonty Winch discusses Rhodes's attempt to maintain Empire in his own image and protect his legacy through the Rhodes Scholarships, limited unsurprisingly to students of white origin. Winch examines the impact of the scheme on Oxford sport and, in the case of rugby on the Home Unions, as well as its role in maintaining Empire through the consolidation of an ongoing imperial identity, and potentially delaying the impact of resistance to South Africa's racist regime.

A significant step forward in ensuring the future of South African cricket occurred in the 1938/39 season when Lord Nuffield announced at a dinner during the 'Timeless Test' that he would like to give £10,000 to SACA for the 'benefit and extension of South African cricket'.[24]

The committee which looked into the matter came up with the idea of a national schoolboy tournament involving all the provinces of South Africa and Rhodesia but limited to whites only. The result was the inauguration of a cricket week which was first played in January 1940 at Durban. With white schoolboys learning to cope in varying conditions at different centres, the Nuffield Cricket Week's record highest and lowest scores were set in the first three years of its existence. Rhodesia scored 399 for 9 against Orange Free State at Cape Town in 1941 and the following year at Durban, Western Province dismissed Border for 3.[25]

The Second World War once again highlighted the split between those who were prepared to serve Britain and those against. Historian, Frank Welsh, records that Smuts won the day through 'deploying the great moral authority that he had shown in previous crises'.[26] Based on the result of a relatively narrow margin of thirteen votes in the House of Assembly—80 to 67—South Africa declared war on Germany. Of the 343,000 men who volunteered for full-time service in the Union Defence Force during the Second World War, around 9500 were killed in action.

Two South African Test players made the supreme sacrifice, A. C. B. 'Chud' Langton and A. W. 'Doolie' Briscoe. Langton was killed in an accident in Nigeria at the age of 30 while serving with the South African Air Force and Captain Briscoe, who was awarded the Military Cross in Italian Somaliland, was killed in action at Kombolcha in Ethiopia.

APARTHEID AND CRICKET

In 1948, the *Herenigde* (Reunited) National Party under Dr. D. F. Malan defeated the United Party. Although the National Party received a minority of 37.70% of the votes, the weighting given to the rural seats in the 1910 constitution gave a parliamentary majority to the Nationalists in coalition with the Afrikaner Party. The National Party began to shape South Africa in the way they had promised. In aiming to break away from the British Crown, they hoped to gain total sovereignty and in 1949 adopted legislation which ensured that South African citizens were no longer British subjects. They began the process of dividing South Africans into four main racial groups, with the Population Registration Act of 1950 categorising people as white, coloured, Indian and African. Over time the legislative basis was established for the theoretical development of what was known as apartheid (separatism), a thorough-going system of white supremacy and racial segregation building on and extending ideologically, the racial historical platform.

A substantial Indian population was one good reason for the concerned parent country to emerge as a major opponent of South Africa's racial policies and place the matter on the agenda of the first meeting of the United Nations. South Africa's white cricket administrators had some contact with India over the years but this never resulted in contact on the cricket field. Goolam Vahed's chapter focuses on cricket in the Indian community in Natal, the origins of this community's involvement in the game, and the relations between the Indian community in Natal and India itself. He is concerned with the significance of cricket in the course of the South African and Indian governments clashing over the issue of apartheid, as well as the perceptions of South Africans in India and vice versa.

Amidst unfavourable political circumstances, the various racial boards of 'non-white' cricket formed the South African Cricket Board of Control (SACBOC) and adopted an ambitious approach in which they sought to play the game at the highest level. Requests were made to SACA that they be allowed to play against touring teams but these were denied. There was also good reason to believe that SACBOC players would strengthen South African cricket in the Test arena. A young white South African side had exceeded expectations by drawing the 1952/53 series 2-2 in Australia and, as expected, defeated New Zealand in the course of that tour and at home in 1953/54, but they were well beaten when they hosted the Australians in 1949/50 and 1957/58. They also failed to win any of the five series against England between 1947 and 1956/57. One sportswriter, Sy Mogapi, chose an ideal 'all-South African' team to play England at Trent Bridge in 1955, claiming he 'could not resist the urge'. It included six players of colour—Chong Meyer, Basil D'Oliveira (vice-captain), Tiny Abed, George Langa, Essop Jeewa and 'Mac' Anthony—and five white players.[27] The side of course never became a reality. The white Springboks lost that opening Test by an innings but they did recover from their poor start to win two of the remaining four Tests.

A mixed side was almost unimaginable. In June 1956, South Africa's Minister of the Interior, Dr. T.E. Donges, announced the country's first statement on Government policy on sport. It established the notion that whites and blacks should organise their sports separately (although inevitably unequally). It also ventured into the area of international selection, for mixed sport was formally prohibited within South Africa, and no mixed teams could compete abroad. Any international sides competing in South Africa would have to be all-white, though black sportsmen from overseas would be allowed to compete against South African blacks. In effect, this gave the Government the defining say in the composition of foreign national teams, with the D'Oliveira issue resting on this principle as far as they were concerned.

After SACBOC had arranged successful home and away series involving Kenya, they invited Frank Worrell's West Indies cricket team to tour South Africa in 1959. They were scheduled to play black teams in a programme that Jonty Winch's chapter notes did not meet with everyone's approval. The newly formed South African Sports Association raised an objection because the tour was arranged within the parameters of the prevailing racial structure and therefore lent credibility to the government's apartheid policy. There was, however, a strong counter-argument that a tour would project weaknesses in the apartheid structure, thereby creating serious difficulties and embarrassment for the South African Government. The subsequent debate included C. L. R. James taking an opposite viewpoint to that of Learie Constantine but, says Winch, irrespective of who was right, the cancellation of the tour had an immediate impact on the lives of South Africa's black players, some of whom left the country, while the West Indians became increasingly curious to find out more about Africa.

The early months of 1960 became increasingly eventful. Harold Macmillan, the British Prime Minister made his famous speech to the South African Parliament on 3 February in which he commented on 'the strength of the African national consciousness ... the wind of change is blowing throughout the continent'.[28] At Sharpeville on 21 March, a serious confrontation developed after a police station had been surrounded and shots were fired at demonstrators while many of them were running away, leaving 69 dead and 180 wounded. The Sharpeville massacre opened the world's eyes to the true nature of the apartheid regime and led to international condemnation. The government typically responded with further repression and on 7 April, the Unlawful Organisations Act declared the ANC and the Pan-Africanist Congress prohibited organisations, unable to function legally and where membership was a criminal act.

With world opinion strengthening against the South African Government, Geoff Chubb, the president of the SACA, predicted opposition to the 1960 England tour and warned the players that they were 'going to a country where certain sections of the population are not very favourably disposed towards South Africa'. He anticipated demonstrations, 'a lot of insulting remarks' and unfavourable press articles but pointed out in an optimistic attempt to maintain morale: 'We believe – and here we are supported by a lot of knowledgeable and highly-placed people in England – that this boycott will die a gradual death'. The rate of its falling away was, however, seen as being dependent upon how the players took 'the first impact'. Chubb prepared a standard brief for the touring side which required them to say, 'I am chosen to play cricket. I am not responsible for choosing the team or for arranging of tours against countries. I as a cricketer am only too willing to play at any time against any side'. It was made clear that all the players were 'completely barred from press interviews and the expression of any personal opinion upon the political situation here in South Africa'.[29]

The demonstrations against the cricketers in 1960 while visible were relatively ineffective and were overshadowed by the real crisis on the tour which was the 'throwing' controversy. Geoff Griffin, South Africa's twenty-one-year-old fast bowler, who had a permanently bent arm following a childhood accident, was no-balled eleven times for throwing in the second Test at Lord's. He did go on to achieve a Test hat-trick—the first by a South African and the first at Lord's—but there was further drama for him. The Test ended before the Queen's arrival and the South Africans were obliged to play an exhibition game. An uncompromising Syd Buller proceeded to no-ball Griffin out of the 'picnic' game and the tour. There was contempt for cricket's authorities and sympathy for the player. 'The exhibition', wrote Louis Duffus, 'was staged on the understanding that every player had to bowl. This at once denied adherence to the strict tenets of play'.[30]

The cricket tour was played out against fast-moving political events in South Africa. Macmillan's speech had forced English-speakers with pro-British feelings to reassess their position in South Africa and their feelings towards Dr. H. F. Verwoerd. There was clearly a change in attitude and it was to affect the referendum in October 1960 when 90.77% of registered whites cast their votes. There were 850,458 in favour of a republic and 775,878 against it.[31] A few months later, Verwoerd was made aware that there was opposition to his country staying in the Commonwealth. When South Africa became a Republic on 31 May 1961 its departure from the Commonwealth followed automatically.

The major political events that took place not only saw many English-speakers shift their allegiance from the United Party to the National Party, but also a greater confidence on the part of Afrikaners to accept parity between the two groups and then join the English in their traditional summer game. There are, of course, other reasons for this development which are dealt with in a chapter by Albert Grundlingh whose research in recent years has addressed the conditions which were necessary for the Afrikaner to play an important role in cricket at all levels. Grundlingh notes 'the trajectory of cricket among Afrikaners correlated closely with their ascendancy to power in 1948 and subsequent advancement especially during the 1960s'.[32] Also influential was the success of the national team in the latter part of the 1960s which encouraged the re-emergence of the Afrikaner as a cricketer but on a far more impressive scale than had previously occurred in the late nineteenth century.

EXCLUSION FROM THE ICC

Although the links were not completely severed the decision to leave the Commonwealth also meant that South Africa automatically lost its membership of the Imperial Cricket Conference. A worrying split in racial camps was feared by the cricketing establishment with England, Australia and New Zealand ranged against India, Pakistan and the West Indies. In the meantime, South Africa continued to play Tests but these were initially regarded as 'unofficial' with the New Zealand matches in 1961/62 staged over four days. However, the Australians in 1963/64 indicated that they regarded the Tests as official whatever the formal position and their Prime Minister, Robert Menzies reinforced this viewpoint. In a startling message of support for the apartheid regime, Menzies informed the South African captain that there were 'limits to even his patriotism … Victory for you Springboks might clear away all this nonsense about your Test matches being regarded as unofficial'.[33]

Across the Limpopo in Rhodesia, cricket matches were being arranged that involved West Indian, Pakistan and Indian Test players. Jonty Winch's chapter on African cricket in the territory notes that for several years world-famous players such as Everton Weekes, Wes Hall, Rohan Kanhai, Sonny Ramadhin, Hanif Mohammad, Subhash Gupte and Chandu Borde took part in matches in Rhodesia which was a cricketing 'province' of South Africa. The development was encouraged through the advent of the Federation and its promised 'partnership' ideal, but the 'multi-racial' concept did not extend to assisting local African clubs. This chapter focuses on a 'forgotten' period of cricket, one that owed much to cultural developments in Makokoba, a township at the heart of Bulawayo's—and, to an extent, Southern Rhodesia's—efforts to create an urban African identity in the aftermath of the Second World War. Africans looked to maximise their opportunities socially and financially through a cultural advance that embraced sport and progressed alongside a process of political mobilisation. Reflecting similar developments on the Rand, Africans who were administering football and cricket clubs would also hold positions in trade union and political movements.

There were four white Rhodesians in Trevor Goddard's 1963/64 Springbok team that surprised the Australians by drawing the series 1-1, with time alone saving the hosts from defeat. In 1965, the selection of Peter van der Merwe as captain was seen as a key factor in the team's progress as he had the necessary attacking vision to bring the best out of batsmen such as Eddie Barlow, Graeme Pollock and Colin Bland, and he 'welded them into a match-winning combination whose particular strength was their belief in themselves'.[34] The declining state of South Africa's image abroad, and concerns about the impact on investment brought South African businessmen and administrators together to promote the game, and the overall acceptance of South Africa on the world stage, through tours to England. Stanley Murphy, a wealthy farmer, sponsored the Fezelas, a team of promising players, in 1961 and Wilf Isaacs organised two tours in 1966 and 1969 on a similar basis. A schoolboy side that visited England in 1963 was captained by Barry Richards and included Mike Procter, Neil Rosendorff and Hylton Ackerman among their batsmen with Giles Ridley, who later captained Oxford University, the leading bowler. Another schoolboy side as well as the South African Universities toured in 1967.

South Africa won the 1965 series in England, thanks to a brilliant hundred by Graeme Pollock in the second Test at Trent Bridge where his elder brother, Peter, backed him up with ten wickets in the match. From this point on, South Africa went from strength to strength with series victories over Australia—3-1 in 1966/67 and 4-0 in 1969/70. It was the first time that the Australians had lost on South African soil. The two series drew attention to the depth of talent in South African cricket and stirred interest among Afrikaners for the game. Mike Procter took 41 wickets in just seven matches at 15.02 and Barry Richards, who scored

508 runs in four Tests at 72.57, emerged as two of the most exciting players in world cricket and spearheaded the new professional era for the South African game. But they were the last matches South Africa would play until readmission more than twenty years later.

The MCC was scheduled to tour in 1968/69. Bruce Murray examines the most significant series of events in South African cricket in the period covered by this volume which was the D'Oliveira Affair of 1968. John Vorster's National Party Government refused to allow Basil D'Oliveira, the South African-born coloured cricketer who played for England, to tour South Africa with the MCC team. That refusal led not only to the cancellation of the MCC tour but ultimately to South Africa's exclusion from all Test cricket for some 22 years. The notoriety of the D'Oliveira Affair derives not only from Vorster's ban, but also from the apparent complicity of the English selectors who initially decided to leave D'Oliveira out of the team to tour South Africa in 1968/69. A massive outcry in Britain claimed the MCC and its selectors had capitulated to pressure from the apartheid government. When Tom Cartwright withdrew from the team through injury, the selectors hastily drafted D'Oliveira into replace him. This, Vorster announced, was clearly a case of the MCC capitulating to anti-apartheid political pressure and he duly announced that he would not allow the team of the anti-apartheid movement into South Africa.

Unbeknown perhaps to most traditional male cricket followers, the sixties also saw the women's game follow a similar pattern to that of their male counterparts. Politics would affect cricket tours after South Africa's women cricketers had started playing Test cricket against a touring English team in 1960/61. In making use of much previously unpublished material, Raf Nicholson's chapter emphasises the importance of studying women's cricket in conjunction with the various bodies traditionally associated with men's cricket. She assesses the impact that the D'Oliveira Affair had on the women's game in South Africa. The English were initially prevented from playing the South Africans *en route* to Australia in December 1968. A replacement tour was quickly arranged against the Netherlands and in 1971/72 New Zealand visited South Africa, but ultimately the Springbok women would also face a long period of isolation.

Anti-apartheid forces were determined to end the all-white composition of South African sport. Peter Hain, a teenage activist who had been educated at Pretoria Boys' High School and Emanuel School, became chairman of the 'Stop the Seventy Tour' (STST) campaign. The protest movement seriously disrupted the Springbok rugby visit to Britain during 1969/70 and forced the cancellation of the 1970 South African cricket tour. 'More than 100,000 protestors', said Hain of the rugby tour, 'laid siege to the white South Africans during their 25 matches across Britain and Ireland, providing a perfect springboard from which to plan direct action to stop the cricket tour due to begin in May 1970'.[35]

ISOLATION

The subsequent isolation could not have come at a more inopportune time for South Africa's white cricket such was the pride in the Springbok performances. SACA felt trapped. In September 1970, Jack Cheetham told delegates that his Board could not make changes 'without a revision of the laws and customs of the land and which govern our sport in all ways ... And such change, gentlemen, has been vetoed by those in whose hands the decision ultimately lies'. Board member, Joe Pamensky was not satisfied. He thought the 'attitude of SACA was not positive' and that the governing body 'should not be made to suffer once again, should ignore political considerations, be more positive than in the past and do everything to promote cricket'.[36]

When the 1970 tour was cancelled, there were desperate efforts to save the tour to Australia planned for 1971/72. An approach was made to Vorster for permission to hold mixed trials. A request was also made to include two players of colour in the South African touring team but this was rejected by both Vorster and the president of SACBOC, Hassan Howa. The government was not prepared to make concessions even if it meant isolation for South African cricket while Howa opposed token 'non-whites' in the team In time, it became evident that a watershed had arrived where compromises were no longer possible. Belatedly, the white cricketers themselves woke up to their predicament, and the predicament of their sport.

On 3 April 1971, the day after the announcement of the government's rejection, a cricket match began between Transvaal and the Rest at Newlands, Cape Town, as part of the Republic Day Festival celebrations after ten years of Republicanism and isolation from the Commonwealth. Senior South African players planned to take a stand and decided to stage a 'walk-off' as a protest in support of merit selection. Patrick Ferriday explores the events surrounding and succeeding the 'walk-off', including a detailed account of the day itself and the following weeks as the media in South Africa and around the world dealt with the ramifications of the event and the government sought to quell what it saw as open revolt by cricketers from within. Interviews with major players in the action provide insights into the thoughts and views of South Africa's white cricketers at a time when the effects of this protest were felt throughout South Africa and around the world.

The actions of a talented group of white South African cricketers reflected an important change in attitude but it was all to no avail and the tour was cancelled. Vorster was critical, notes Bruce Murray, but 'apparently oblivious to the contradictions of his own position' when he stated of the Australians: 'It is time that democracies take note that minorities are trying to force their will on majorities'.[37] The period of isolation for men's cricket began, save for private ventures.

Despite these developments, there was still significant support for white South African sportsmen overseas. Former England cricket captain, Peter May, a pillar of the MCC establishment, spoke for many English professionals aware of the opportunities which South Africa had as a venue for winter employment, when he argued that South African cricketers should not be ostracised, and that 'sport and politics should not mix'. May was convinced, perhaps on ideological rather than evidential grounds, that old cricket friends in South Africa had 'done far more for the non-whites than their critics in England and elsewhere have ever done' ignoring the fact, for example, that Jackie McGlew—his opposing captain in Tests in 1955 and 1956/57—would soon afterwards associate himself with pro-apartheid politics by standing as a National Party candidate.[38]

The South African issue would stay in the headlines. The former Springbok, Owen Wynne, commented 'only now that they [white sportsmen] are being ousted from world sport do they, in the hope of again being accepted, turn to the non-whites and say "all right, we'll give you a chance"'.[39] The whites' change of heart came too late because they would be locked out of official competition for twenty-one years, a prisoner of a racial political system that germinated as a consequence of imperialism, flowered during the apartheid years and decomposed in the demise of racial rule in the early 1990s. Only then would South Africa join the wider cricketing fraternity and the wider family of humanity.

Notes

1. R. Rotberg, *The Founder: Cecil Rhodes and the Pursuit of Power* (Oxford: Oxford University Press, 1988), 164.
2. South African Dutch became recognised as a wholly separate language—Afrikaans—and owed much to S. J. du Toit's *De Afrikaanse Patriot*. See M. Tamarkin, *Cecil Rhodes and the Cape Afrikaners: The Imperial Colossus and the Colonial Parish Pump* (London: Routledge, 1996), 51–55.
3. A comment made by Charles Finlason who played for South Africa, *Daily Independent*, 1 March 1889. Neethling left Stellenbosch at the end of the year having taken 66 wickets for 117 runs (average 1.77) against the area's top sides.
4. See J. Winch, 'J.H. Hofmeyr and the Afrikaner Bond: A Challenge to William Milton's "Englishness" and the Advance of the "Coloured" Cricketer', *Historia, Journal of the Historical Association of South Africa* (Pretoria, May 2014), 18–36.
5. *Cape Times*, 11 January 1894.
6. See J. Winch, '"I Could a Tale Unfold": The Tragic Story of '"Old Caddy"' in B. Murray and G. Vahed (eds.), *Empire and Cricket: The South African Experience 1884–1914* (Pretoria: UNISA, 2009), 61–80.
7. Rotberg, *The Founder*, 550.
8. T. Pakenham, *The Boer War* (London: Weidenfeld and Nicolson, 1979), 18.
9. See B. Murray, 'Abe Bailey and the Foundation of the Imperial Cricket Conference' in Murray and Vahed (eds.), *Empire and Cricket*, 259–78.
10. See R. Parry and D. Slater, 'The Googly, Gold and the Empire: The Role of South African Cricket in the Imperial Project, 1904–1912' in Murray and Vahed (eds.), *Empire and Cricket*, 219–40.
11. J. Winch, *Cricket in Southern Africa: Two Hundred Years of Records and Achievements* (Rosettenville: Windsor, 1997), 56. Peebles, an English cricketer and journalist, might also have mentioned C. B. 'Buck' Llewellyn, a talented all-round player and the first 'coloured' man to represent South Africa in Test matches. Llewellyn was a slow to medium-pace, left-arm bowler who delivered both orthodox and wrist spin.
12. Rotberg, *The Founder*, 145.
13. *New Zealand Herald*, 5 February 1916. Fichardt was closely associated with Presidents Reitz and Steyn and the influential Carl Borckenhagen in setting up the Bloemfontein branch of the Afrikaner Bond. Thereafter, he founded the Orangia Unie in 1906 with General Hertzog and Abraham Fischer; helped establish and then chair Santam, the holding company for Sanlam, originally solely a life insurance company established in 1918, and served as Ladybrand's member in the Union House of Assembly.

14. E. Roux, *Time Longer Than Rope: A History of the Black Man's Struggle for Freedom in South Africa* (Madison: University of Wisconsin Press, 1964), 148.
15. C. Muller (ed.), *500 Years: A History of South Africa* (Pretoria: Academica, 1981), 410.
16. N. Cardus, *Autobiography* (London: Collins, 1947), 178.
17. *Rand Daily Mail*, 24 April 1924.
18. Winch, *Cricket in Southern Africa*, 74.
19. B. Murray, 'The Period 1924 to 1929' in T. Cameron (ed.), *An Illustrated History of South Africa* (Johannesburg: Jonathan Ball, 1986), 248.
20. *Cape Times*, 28 September, 1894.
21. R. Roberts and S. Wilde, *Duleepsinhji: Famous Cricketers Series No. 16* (Nottingham: Association of Cricket Statisticians and Historians, 1993).
22. Murray, 'The Period 1924 to 1929' in Cameron, *An Illustrated History of South Africa*, 257–58.
23. Winch, *Cricket in Southern Africa*, 84.
24. *Rand Daily Mail*, 4 March 1939.
25. Winch, *Cricket in Southern Africa*, 275–76.
26. F. Welsh, *A History of South Africa* (London: HarperCollins, 2000), 419.
27. B. D'Oliveira, *The D'Oliveira Affair* (London: Collins, 1969), 29
28. P. Coetzer, 'The Era of Apartheid, 1948–1961' in Cameron (ed.), *An Illustrated History of South Africa*, 286.
29. SACA minutes, 21 May 1960.
30. L. Duffus, *Cricketer Annual 1960–61*, 426.
31. Coetzer, 'The Era of Apartheid' in Cameron (ed.), *An Illustrated History of South Africa*, 287–88.
32. A. Grundlingh, *Potent Pastimes: Sport and Leisure Practices in Modern Afrikaner History* (Pretoria: Protea Book, 2013), 217.
33. L. Alfred, *Testing Times: The Story of the Men Who Made SA Cricket* (Cape Town: Spearhead, 2003), 178.
34. T. Bisseker, 'Biographies', in E. Swanton (ed.) *Barclays World of Cricket* (London: Collins, 1980), 222.
35. *Morning Star*, 7 December 2013.
36. SACA minutes, 27–28 September 1970.
37. B. Murray and C. Merrett, *Caught Behind: Race and Politics in Springbok Cricket* (Johannesburg: Wits University Press, 2004), 154.
38. P. May, *A Game Enjoyed: An Autobiography* (London: Stanley Paul, 1985), 134–35.
39. Quoted in J. Brickhill, *Race Against Race: South Africa's 'Multinational' Sport Fraud* (London: International Defence and Aid Fund, 1976), 49.

CHAPTER 2

Eclipse of the Summerbok: Percy Sherwell, Paul Roos and the Competition for a National Game for South Africa

Geoffrey Levett

INTRODUCTION

Percy Sherwell, captain of South Africa between 1906 and 1911, is an unfairly neglected figure in the history of cricket. Often overlooked in works on South African cricketing greats, he was renowned in his own time as a gritty batsman who led his team by example. As a wicketkeeper, he was deemed in the same class as the Australian Jack Blackham. He captained the team in every Test that he played, leading South Africa to their first victory and series victory against England at home in 1905/06; to a tight loss to England in 1907, as well as their first victory in Australia in the losing series of 1910/11.

'Summerboks' was a nickname given to the South African cricketers during their tour of 1907 to Britain, inspired by the 'Springbok' tag of the previous winter's rugby tourists (*Daily Mail*, 4 May 1907).

G. Levett (✉)
De Montfort University, Leicester, UK
e-mail: geoffreylevett@mac.com

© The Author(s) 2018   29
B. Murray et al. (eds.), *Cricket and Society in South
Africa, 1910–1971*, Palgrave Studies in Sport and Politics,
https://doi.org/10.1007/978-3-319-93608-6_2

Besides his cricketing exploits, Sherwell was also singles and doubles tennis champion of South Africa in 1904, played rugby union for Cornwall and was an international-class hockey player. Such achievements should be enough to make him a founding father of South African sport; indeed, E. W. Swanton called this golden age of South African cricket the 'Sherwell era'.[1] However, when looking at the historiography of South African sport and its relationship to national identity in the twentieth century, it is the figure of Paul Roos that casts a long shadow over subsequent generations of sportsmen. As a national figure, Sherwell is forgotten outside the writings of the cricket specialists. Roos, who captained the first South African rugby union team to tour the British Isles in 1906, has been held up as an exemplar of South African manliness, a man who is said to have become an 'icon' of South Africa, and indeed is credited with creating the 'Springbok legend'.[2]

One should be sceptical of Roos' ability to act as an icon for all South Africans, either in his own time—when there was a drive to political reconciliation between the two communities of European origin in the southern African British colonies—or in the modern, post-apartheid, multi-racial South Africa. Undoubtedly, the rugby union tour of 1906 saw a concerted political campaign to use sport as a means of effecting reconciliation between the two warring sides in the South African War.[3] And it remains true that as an embodiment of South African manhood Roos has renown beyond the aficionados of the sport he played. Yet in their own time, both Roos and Sherwell were exemplars of South African manliness. But while there was a political imperative for the Anglophone community to accept Roos as an exemplary figure, Sherwell had limited appeal to the Afrikaner community in his own time beyond those who played cricket. It is the purpose of this chapter to rehabilitate Sherwell's reputation as a cricketer and pay tribute to him as an outstanding sportsman, a task that is long overdue. But it also has a further purpose of examining how his leadership of the cricket team image was portrayed by the press in both the UK and its colonies in a way that developed him as an icon for the new South Africa that would come into being with Union in 1910. Further, it will show how Sherwell's failure to become established as a national figure in South Africa reflects the way in which Abe Bailey's attempt to develop cricket as a central part of South African national identity similarly failed as the nation's sporting culture fragmented in the years after the Great War.

THE REPRESENTATIVE OF 'AN UNKNOWN PEOPLE'

'An unknown people' is the phrase used by the historian John Lambert to describe the way in which South Africans of British origin, a group who were politically and culturally dominant in the subcontinent for much of the nineteenth and twentieth centuries, have been marginalised in South Africa's historiography.[4] He argues that since the mid-twentieth century, historians have tended to focus their attention upon Afrikaner and African nationalisms, as well as socio-economic studies of South African history as a whole, rather than examining the 'rich and diverse experience' of those South Africans whose English-speaking culture continues to form the arena in which the many diverse ethnic groups of the present-day nation come together to debate issues of identity and belonging.[5] This relative absence of British South Africans from the historical account of the development of the nation's culture is partly as a result of the lack of a founding myth for the group; the British were not tied to the soil in the same way that Africans or Boers were. As Alan Paton pointed out, English-speaking South Africans 'do not today have an identity', they 'never trekked ... never developed a new language ... were never defeated in war' and 'never had to pick [them] selves out of the dust'.[6] Their history was largely one of appropriation, exploitation and the integration of the colonies into a global British community, the 'British World', whose individuals had an imagined home in Europe even if they had never set foot outside of Africa.[7]

Such a 'hyphenated' form of belonging—to a real and an imagined home—felt by the British South Africans of Sherwell's generation was summed up by Percy Fitzpatrick's affirmation, 'I believe in the British Empire ... I believe in this my native land'.[8] In Fitzpatrick's phrase, one finds the sentimental expression of the political fact of the imperial relationship between colony and Mother Country. Settlers attempted to reconcile loyalty to their chosen land in South Africa with a strong attachment to their place of origin.[9] Such an experience was common to the British inhabitants of the other settler colonies of Australia, New Zealand and Canada. Yet other colonies had an easier story to tell of the development of a national identity where indigenous or rival European groups who challenged the British concept of colonial identity were either numerically small or politically weak in comparison with South Africa.

The situation in South Africa was further complicated by two factors that make the positing of a British South African identity a troublesome practice. One factor is shared with the other colonies of settlement in that Britishness, while being easy for outsiders to perceive, was itself an amalgam of distinct cultures that encompassed nationalities such as Scots, Welsh and Irish, regional identities like the Cornish, as well as different religious affiliations.[10] For Afrikaners, the English, or *die Engelse*, were a homogenous group whose internal cultural differences were trivial compared to those that separated them from people of Boer origin, above all that of language.[11] Yet the fact that British/Englishness was easily identified by non-Britons should not blind us to that fact that within the British community in South Africa there were differences; differences that in the context of cricket were most significantly expressed in the rivalry between the established colonies of the Cape with the rising power of the Transvaal. This tension between the Cape and the Rand was also expressed in the second complication in the formation of an English identity. As well as differences of geographical origin (which included settlers from other British colonies, as well as Europeans, Americans and Jews), the white English community saw tensions between those who saw themselves as established settlers at the Cape with their own brand of colonial nationalism, who compared themselves to those latecomers to the subcontinent who had been attracted by the lure of the mineral wealth discovered deep inland. And one should not overlook the subtle difference in outlook between the Western and Eastern Cape, as well as the more aggressively self-conscious Britishness of Natal. One should also factor in the element of class conflict that revealed itself in tensions between the Cape, the Rand and the other colonies.[12] This conflict manifested itself within the British South African community but also ran across ethnic boundaries with an élite Afrikaner politician such as Jan Smuts having as much common interest with the leading British colonial administrators, with whom he shared an educational background, as he did with the ordinary members of his political constituency, members from whom he was becoming increasingly alienated after the 1909 Act of Union.[13]

The colonial nationalist ideology of 'South Africanism', which Saul Dubow sees as emerging after the end of the South African War, was an attempt by unionist politicians, administrators and intellectuals to forge a common culture between Brit and Boer.[14] Sport played a significant role in this ideological push, with the South African rugby union tour to Great Britain in 1906 (as has already been noted) being billed as a tour of reconciliation.[15] However, while much of the focus of the historiography on South Africanism has been on the theme of bringing Brits and Boers together, I would argue that in fact it was as much a project to tie together British South Africans in a common culture in order to build up South Africa as a British imperial space.[16] Collective identity, as Vivian Bickford-Smith has noted, is 'constructed, situational, and conditional' in nature.[17] Actors in positions of power are able to use symbols, practices and role models to shape the public discourse around that collective identity.

Such a process is very easy to discern in the way in which Roos was developed as a symbol of Afrikaner manliness. His Springbok team was a great success on their tour to Britain in 1906, both on the playing field, where only two matches were lost, and with the general public, who flocked to the matches in great numbers. The tour was widely credited at the time with having achieved a reconciliation between the two sides divided by the South African War, with Roos himself stating on his return to South Africa that, 'the tour has united us. From Cape Agulhas to the Zambesi … South Africa was one and all differences had been forgotten'.[18] As captain of the team Roos was the model of the sporting South African man during the tour; his rugby career, and his career off the field, ensured that he became the prototype for a new kind of Afrikaner manliness. Before the South African War, Afrikaner masculinity centred on 'a rural system of production and a social system of kinship and patronage' that privileged the Afrikaner man over women, people of colour and uitlanders in the Boer Republics.[19] Helen Bradford argues persuasively that the war provoked an internal missionary drive by middle-class male Afrikaners to remake rural Boers into men in their own image as a means to 'fire the furnace of Afrikaner nationalism'.[20] As the state modernised and urbanised after the war Afrikaner masculinity came to be centred increasingly around the national institutions of rugby, church and school.[21]

Roos embodied all three institutions. He was the captain of the national rugby team. He was a committed Christian who preached to thousands of Wesleyans during the Springbok tour, being praised in the British and South African press for his spiritual leadership.[22] And during his absence in Europe, he was named on the committee of the South African Teachers' Union.[23] On returning to South Africa, Roos used his position as a teacher to champion rugby, and he was Rector of Stellenbosch Boys' High School for thirty years from 1910 to 1940, as a means of moral as well as of physical training for the next generation of white South Africans.[24] In combination with his acting as a role model as an educationalist, he also took an active role in politics, becoming a Member of Parliament for the National Party shortly before his death in 1948. While Roos himself was no extremist there is no doubt that in the years after the First World War Afrikaners 'co-opted rugby as part of their nationalist project' with the tour of 1906 becoming portrayed less as a vehicle of reconciliation and more as a founding event in the reinvigorated Afrikaner cultural identity.[25] Throughout the twentieth century, Roos symbolised the ideal Afrikaner sportsman, and he continues to do so in our own age, as shown by the publication of a commemorative book in 2006 celebrating the centenary of his famous tour (Fig. 2.1).[26]

Fig. 2.1 South Africa's cricket captain, Percy Sherwell is pictured with his English counterpart, Plum Warner before the historic first Test against England at the Wanderers in 1905/06. Sherwell led his side to their first Test victory and thereafter their first series win over England. Not long afterwards, Paul Roos captained the rugby Springboks on their memorable first overseas tour during 1906/07

Cricket on the other hand became identified as the English game and played a significant role in bonding South Africans of British origin together. The manner in which the South African cricket team was represented by the press during its tour of Britain in 1907 was part of an effort by Abe Bailey, the team's financial backer, to reassure the British public of the respectability of the new British colonies on the Rand in the wake of the War.[27] This chapter will develop that argument, showing how Percy Sherwell, as the leader of the team, was built up by the press as a representative of Englishness in South Africa around whom the British South African sporting public could rally, not just during the tour of 1907 but also in the home series against England and on the tour of Australia in 1910/11.[28] Sherwell's career forms a strong contrast to the trend in modern South African cricket whereby players take advantage of their ancestry to move away from the country of their birth to play county cricket in the hope of one day gaining selection for England. Such a move leaves them open to accusations of belonging neither to South Africa nor to England, with many English fans expressing ambivalence about a national team that over the last decade has often been made up of a significant number of 'imports'. Sherwell, by contrast, could happily incorporate an identity that was English yet also unequivocally South African. As such he emphasised that although British South Africans may continue to embody a hyphenated identity they have no less a claim to national identity in the post-apartheid state.

SHERWELL'S ORIGINS: 'A CLEAN-MADE, TYPICAL COLONIAL'[29]

Percy William Sherwell was born in Natal in 1880 at a village called Isipingo, the youngest of ten brothers.[30] His father, Thomas, was described as a 'Rand pioneer' and Percy was brought up and educated to follow in his father's footsteps as a mining man.[31] To this end, he was first sent to school at the Berea Academy in Natal, followed by St. Michael's College in Johannesburg, before rounding off his education in England at Bedford County School from the age of 15, followed by a spell at the Camborne School of Mines.[32] He returned to the Rand in 1902 to take up a managerial position in a gold mine.[33] It was while at Bedford, he said, that his cricket developed considerably. He became captain of the school as well as playing rugby. During his time at Camborne, he represented Cornwall at both cricket and rugby and took the opportunity of the long summer holiday to attend 'big matches' at Lord's and The Oval to pick up tips on technique from the best players.[34]

Sport was central to the educational curriculum of schools in Natal and Johannesburg in the early twentieth century, just as it was in the English public schools on which they modelled themselves.[35] In the colonial context, the playing of cricket by young boys was a means of inculcating in them, via the rituals of the game and the internalisation of the sport's moral code, a feeling of belonging to the supposed English race. Such a feeling of belonging was publicly displayed to other groups, whether Afrikaner or non-European, by the sectioning off of public land for the playing of sport, by setting up clubs with rules of access dependent on class and ethnicity and by the wearing of specific clothes and use of specialist equipment to play the game.[36] In this way, Sherwell's youth was typical of any number of middle-class boys scattered around the empire. His easy passage between a geographical home in his colony and the sentimental home of metropole was facilitated by his being schooled in the comportment of being an Englishman, of which the playing of sport was a key element. As John Tosh has pointed out, sport in the Edwardian period had become, 'a military code, to be exercised among men'. Sherwell's excellence at leadership on the cricket field would be used to make him an exemplary man in quasi-military terms during his career, something that held great significance in a region still attempting to recover from a brutal civil conflict.[37]

Having returned to South Africa to begin his career in Johannesburg in the mining industry Sherwell first came to notice as a cricketer as part of the Transvaal side that won the Currie Cup in 1902/03. While Frank Mitchell was the captain and best performing batsman in the series, Sherwell contributed an innings of 71 'with his usual vim' to secure their first win in the match against Griqualand West.[38] This was his Currie Cup and first-class debut and henceforth he would be a stalwart of the Transvaal team. His rise to international prominence, however, took place during the MCC tour to South Africa of 1905/06.

Sherwell was the captain of South Africa for the series, a fact that underlines how rapidly he had become a leading figure in South African cricket in spite of the golden generation of players then developing in the team. His force of character was well demonstrated in the famous victory in the first Test of the series at The Wanderers in January 1906. Sherwell came to the wicket to partner Dave Nourse with South Africa nine wickets down in their second innings and still requiring 45 runs to win the match. Nourse, who made 93 not out in the innings, later recalled that Sherwell's leadership qualities were in ample evidence despite the tenseness of the match situation, saying that if he felt any strain, 'he certainly concealed it well for he came in, as usual, laughing and full of confidence'.[39] As Pelham Warner was to testify, 'The odds would have been almost anything on MCC if the last man had been of the calibre of the usual eleventh man. But Sherwell is an extremely able bat, and from the first ball he received, which he hit for four, he appeared perfectly at his ease'.[40] Sherwell hit the winning runs in the game, prompting a pitch invasion by the crowd and scenes of hysterical celebration that the well-travelled Warner had never previously seen at a cricket match.[41] Sherwell modestly omitted any reference to his own contribution to the victory in his account of the game, which he described as, 'the most exciting match I have ever played in'.[42] An anonymous contributor in the same piece, however, testifies that on his coming to the wicket, Sherwell 'was the coolest man in the ground. He commenced his innings with characteristic imperturbability'.[43]

While Sherwell was not required to make such a significant contribution again during the series at its triumphant conclusion it was widely recognised that not only did South Africa possess an outstanding collection of players they also possessed an outstanding leader of men.[44] Warner's account of the tour, written on the hoof as he played the games and published immediately after his return to England, includes a portrait of the two captains together with Sherwell very much the idol of the crowd behind. Warner recognised that for the forthcoming tour of the South Africans to the UK in 1907, it would no longer be adequate for the home nation to field weakened teams: 'The Old Country shall have to take them very seriously and arrange a programme on the lines of the Australian tour'.[45] Coming as it did the year after the tremendously successful Springbok Rugby Union tour, the anticipation in both hemispheres was that the cricket tour would also excite the British public. The Chief Justice of Cape Town even went so far in his toast to the players at the conclusion of the fifth Test at Newlands, as to propose that the cricket tour could act as a tour of reconciliation along the lines of the rugby tour, stating that:

> The South African team has set a good example. It was a lesson even politicians might take to heart ... He was pleased to see that in regard to sport no question of racialism ever occurred. They worked harmoniously together; they were South Africans. No one asked whether the names were English or Dutch; they were all embraced in the term South Africans.[46]

Such optimism about the ability of cricket to forge a unified white South African identity, as shall be seen, was misplaced. The team was almost exclusively Anglo-South African, and Anglo-South African with a purpose.

THE MOTHER COUNTRY: SHERWELL AND THE 1907 TOUR

An analysis of the 1907 tour and its political significance for relations between Britain and the colonies of South Africa appeared in the publication, *Empire and Cricket: The South African Experience 1884–1914*, and thus it is not proposed here to cover the incidents in any great detail again.[47] However, in the context of the positioning of cricket as an English game it should be noted here that contrary to the rhetoric of the Chief Justice one of the key aims of the touring party was not just to demonstrate the cultural hegemony of Britain over the South African colonies—as argued previously—but also to ensure that Johannesburg was at the head of that process in terms of cricket. Abe Bailey, 'Randlord' and would-be successor to Cecil Rhodes, was the major financial backer of the tour. His influence ensured that the Transvaal was the major contributor to the South African team. It was with satisfaction that the Transvaal Cricket Union (of which Bailey was the President) noted that ten of the touring party to England in 1907 were from their province.[48] Such a situation caused some resentment among other provinces, especially in the Cape. On learning that one Johannesburg newspaper had stated that the team ought to be called 'All Transvaal' rather than 'All South Africa' a correspondent in Cape Town noted that 'Natal and Western Provinces have got the hump over the selections'. He also took satisfaction in the fact that 'ten of the team (were) Cape born and bred' before commenting of the Johannesburg press:

> Don't writings of this kind suggest that the Transvaal, who protest so extravagantly and vain-gloriously against the jealousies of other centres, actually try in these irritating ways, to create and foster ill-feeling?[49]

Such inter-provincial rivalry in the cricketing world is symptomatic of the way in which it was difficult to foster a British South African identity among the inhabitants of colonies whose British inhabitants, while appearing to have a homogenous culture to outsiders, actually had sharply divergent cultural identities.

In positioning the South African team as a natural part of the British world—its only Afrikaans member was J. J. Kotzé, who had acted as a British scout during the South African War—Sherwell as captain, acted as the figurehead.[50] In anticipation of the team's arrival in England *C. B. Fry's Magazine* ran a piece by the sportsman-journalist E. H. D. Sewell in which he played up their typically British virtues. In his profile of the players, he said, 'they have, as a body, more of the right type of confidence than any other team I have ever met'. He also singled out Sherwell as the leader of the team who personified the ideal cricketer, 'one of nine brothers, and the squarest-chinned, whitest man amongst hundreds of men in a white man's game'.[51] In the local press of London too, Sherwell's ability to act as a hyphenated representative of both British and South African manliness was commented on. Interviewed by the *Marylebone Times*, the paper's sports correspondent noted that, 'Mr Sherwell is a clean-made, typical Colonial, with keen blue eyes, and a frank and engaging expression. He is exactly one's conception of what the Briton beyond the seas should be'.[52]

Sherwell's position as the exemplar of cricketing leadership and grit was enhanced by his outstanding performance in the first Test against England at Lord's in July 1907. Forced to follow-on after falling some 288 runs behind after their first innings Sherwell was the pivotal figure in saving the match for his team. His 115, scored 'without giving the shadow of a chance', allowed them to bat out time for the draw.[53] *Cricket* further added to the status of the innings in reporting that it would be impossible to bestow higher praise upon it: 'Those who are fortunate enough to witness his play upon that occasion are unanimous in regarding it as one of the most brilliant ever seen in such circumstances. It is no exaggeration to say that that one innings alone would have proved sufficient to cause his name to live long after him'.[54] Gilbert Jessop, playing in the match for England, was impressed too, stating that, 'Sherwell played an innings which for soundness and forcing qualities was as good as any which I had seen in International matches'.[55]

For his excellent play in the match, Sherwell was rewarded with a 10-guinea cup by Sir Henry McCallum, the former Governor of Natal who was in London awaiting his next posting to Ceylon. In one of the more melodramatic (indeed, fatuous) comparisons between sport and war of the Edwardian period, the *Daily Mail* commented that 'he deserved a cup and in addition, the Victoria Cross'.[56] This story was picked up upon and embellished in a way that brought Sherwell into

the pantheon of English cricketing greats. In Australia, it was reported
that Sherwell's father had promised his son a sovereign for every run
he made in the first Test, just as F. S. Jackson's father had done when
the Yorkshireman was making his debut at Lord's for Harrow School.
'It is reported that at the house of Mr Sherwell, senior, in the presence
of a party of friends … Sherwell was handed a cheque for £123 by his
delighted father … he has seemingly good reason to remember the first
Test in England'.[57] The comparison between Sherwell and Jackson is
one that would have encouraged the sporting public to see the South
African as a worthy successor to the Englishman, who had captained
England to a 2-0 victory over the Australians a mere two years earlier in
1905.

'Just as British as You or I': Cricket in Southern Rhodesia and Australia

Coming back to Johannesburg after the tour of 1907 Sherwell returned
to his career in the mining industry, which saw him becoming increasingly connected with Southern Rhodesia. His work meant that he
would miss South Africa's home series against England in 1910 but he
did play some cricket that year. On this occasion, however, he joined
H. D. G. Leveson Gower's team on its tour to Southern Rhodesia, the
trip taking place shortly after the last Test. That he could switch easily from representing South Africa against a team from England to
then playing for Leveson Gower's side against a colonial team is typical of the way in which imperial Britons of the time had a transnational,
trans-colonial identity. Southern and Northern Rhodesia also had an
ambiguous identity at this time. The Union of South Africa was in the
process of being formed at the very same time in 1910 that Leveson
Gower was leading MCC through the colonies and there were voices
calling for the Rhodesian colonies to the north to be incorporated into
that Union. Indeed Leveson Gower used an article in *The State*, the leading Unionist periodical of the day, to argue for the explicit political value
of cricket as a unifying cultural force both in the southern African colonies and between those colonies and the Mother Country. He stated that
although the MCC had no interest financially in sending a team to South
Africa they take a very great interest in the welfare of its cricket, and
one of their chief objects—if not the chief object—was that the MCC

aimed to further cricket in every sense of the word, and by means of this national game, binding closer together the ties of friendship between the Mother Country and her colonies.[58]

While acknowledging the leading role in the development of South African cricket being played by the Transvaal, under the leadership of Bailey and Sherwell, he went on to advocate that other centres be strengthened in order that not all the best cricketers be concentrated on the Rand, arguing that, 'something is needed to give a fillip to cricketing centres outside the Rand: and because it is also felt that the visits of the MCC—though undoubtedly, I believe, doing good—are not benefiting to the fullest extent possible those centres where cricket stands most in need of encouragement'.[59] The tour to Southern Rhodesia was just such an act of encouragement, and the fact that Sherwell went as part of Leveson Gower's party is evidence of the way in which Transvaal cricket was acting as a hub for proselytising the game in the colonies to the north, in spite of misgiving among some on the Rand that the Rhodesians contributed very little of worth financially in return.

The importance of Sherwell as a figurehead of South African sport can be seen more significantly by the fact that for South Africa's first tour to Australia in 1910/11, he returned to skipper the side, as he had done in England a few years previously. The rhetoric surrounding the trip was of the brotherhood of the dominions of the Empire, emphasising the common British ancestry of both the Australians and the visitors. This was underlined by R. P. Fitzgerald, the manager of the trip, in his recollection of the tour:

> The first visit of a South African cricket team to Australia made history. Not history by way of cricket records, colossal scores, or other incidents in the game, but by opening up, as we hope, a series of inter-Colonial visits, not only of immense interest to all cricketers, but which will help to bring the people of the great dominions of the Empire into closer touch.[60]

This emphasis on Dominion cricket has a huge significance given the efforts of Abe Bailey, ever since the 1907 tour, to arrange a Triangular Tournament between South Africa, Australia and England.[61] The tour to Australia acted as a necessary precursor to the 1912 Tournament, demonstrating the capability of the South African team to rival the two more experienced Test nations. It would be significant in the light of the failed efforts of India and the West Indies, who had each sent representative touring teams to England in the 1900s, to gain the same level of recognition from the Mother Country. Their exclusion from the top table of the Imperial Cricket Conference in 1912 was evidence of the way in which cricket in the Edwardian period was increasingly becoming, to borrow Bill Schwartz's phrase, a 'White Man's World'.[62]

Fitzgerald was being rather ungenerous in his assessment of the cricketing side of the tour to Australia. The South Africans struggled in the Tests against a very strong Australian team, losing the series 4-1. As well as strong opponents they faced unfamiliar conditions. Unlike the tour to England, with whose conditions many of the South African players were familiar, Australia was a relatively unknown prospect for most of the team. The outstanding player on tour was Aubrey Faulkner, who scored heavily, including a century at Adelaide and a double century at Melbourne. Sherwell's form with the bat was not particularly impressive. He continued to impress, however, as a leader. Fitzgerald paid testimony to his qualities as both captain in the field and diplomat off it, 'responsible for the entire absence of any of those little unpleasantnesses and misunderstandings; that have marred so many cricket tours'.[63]

In interviews given to the Australian press, Sherwell continued the rhetoric of his side being a specifically British outfit that chimed with Bailey's push for the South Africans and Australians to be given a privileged place at the head of international cricket. Talking to the *Register* in Adelaide, Sherwell paid tribute to the resources that Bailey had put into developing cricket on the Rand, employing coaches from England to raise the standard of youth cricket and attracting cricketers from the other South African colonies to play in the Transvaal.[64] Before the match in Sydney he made the ideological purpose of developing cricket as a British game even clearer, stating:

> There's not a Dutchman in our party … we are an all-British team. Some people seem to think that there are Dutchmen amongst us because of one or two peculiar names. But Schwarz and Zulch and others are simply descendants of – I was going to say – centuries ago, and their representatives to-day are just as British as you or I. We all had a hand in the war – on the British side, of course – and Nourse is the 'record-breaking' soldier of the team. He went right through the campaign. Another false impression is abroad – that some of us were in the Boer trenches, but that is quite wrong.[65]

Such a statement is far from the rhetoric that surrounded the 'tour of reconciliation' that the Rugby Union team employed in 1906, or indeed that was used prior to the cricket team's departure for England in 1907. In this short interview Sherwell lays bare the way in which, by the time of the Triangular Tournament of 1912, cricket increasingly became a means of tying South Africa into the culture of the British world to the exclusion of other communities, of all ethnicities, in South Africa.

CONCLUSION

The final Test of the Australian tour in Sydney was Sherwell's last for South Africa, despite the fact that the Bailey-inspired Triangular Tournament was finally due to take place the following year in England. He cited business commitments as the reason for his having to miss the tour; being newly wed in the spring of 1912 may have also been a factor in his decision to remain in South Africa.[66] His absence was cited as one of the chief causes of the poor performance of the team. During a miserable summer, they lost five matches heavily to England and Australia with their sixth being drawn. Albert Vogler, who had also missed the tour due to a continuing feud with Abe Bailey dating back to the tour to Australia, was of the opinion that:

> The South African failure [was] largely due to the absence of Sherwell. One man cannot make a side, it is true; but the material was there, and it is astonishing what an influence the captain of the real 'lifting' type can exert.[67]

Sherwell continued to have an influence in cricket, however. First, as a club cricketer, after his last first-class season in 1913/14, and Test selector in Johannesburg, where he was manager of the City Deep Gold Mine from 1914 to 1929, and then, as a cricket administrator in Southern Rhodesia, where he was the managing director of the Premier Portland Cement Company, until his death in 1948.[68]

This biographical sketch shows that while Sherwell does not have the iconic status that Paul Roos now enjoys he nevertheless deserves wider renown both as a sportsman and as a representative of the South Africa of his time. And that means that we need to see him as a complex figure. It may be this complexity that led to his obscurity in the popular imagination. Roos' achievements as rugby player, teacher and Afrikaner politician fit in the conventional narrative of his century in South Africa, of the rise to cultural and political pre-eminence of middle class, Afrikaner men, a narrative which has been challenged radically by other classes, genders and ethnic groups over the last half-century. Sherwell, as a representative of the typical British South African, is less easily fitted into the conventional history of South Africa, and thus also less easy to challenge. His hyphenated identity acted as a passport to travel through the British Empire, from Natal to the Rand, from England to Australia, and finally from the Transvaal to Southern Rhodesia in a way that would not have been possible for Roos. The contrast between the reputations and careers of the two men in the years after their retirement from sport is symbolic of the way in which the uneasy settlement between the two white communities in South Africa was maintained by British South Africans ceding political authority in order to maintain their socio-cultural and economic hegemony. In the current complex environment where the relationship between Britishness and South African national identity continues to evolve, it is important to reflect on the achievements of Percy Sherwell, who was not simply a pioneer of South African sport. His is an important story in the development of the 'unknown' community of British South Africans in the twentieth century.

NOTES

1. E. Swanton, *A History of Cricket* (London: Allen & Unwin, 1962), 62.
2. D. Allen, '"Captain Diplomacy": Paul Roos and the Creation of South Africa's Rugby "Springboks"', *Sport in History*, 33, 4 (2013), 581.
3. D. Allen, 'Tours of Reconciliation: Rugby, War and Reconstruction in South Africa, 1891–1907', *Sport in History*, 27 (2007), 172–89.
4. J. Lambert, '"An Unknown People": Reconstructing British South African Identity', *The Journal of Imperial and Commonwealth History*, 37, 4 (2009), 599–617.
5. Ibid., 599.
6. A. Paton, *Save the Beloved Country* (New York: Scribner's, 1987), 124–25.
7. 'Mapping the British World', a seminal article by Carl Bridge and Kent Fedorowich, has inspired a whole strand of scholarship that debates the concept of a global British culture that developed as a result of the growth of the British Empire in the nineteenth century (C. Bridge and K. Fedorowich, 'Mapping the British World', *The Journal of Imperial and Commonwealth History*, 31, 2 (2003), 1–15).
8. P. Fitzpatrick quoted in S. Dubow, 'How British Was the British World? The Case of South Africa', *The Journal of Imperial and Commonwealth History*, 37, 1 (2009), 1–15.

9. S. Constantine, 'British Emigration to the Empire-Commonwealth Since 1880: From Overseas Settlement to Diaspora?', *The Journal of Imperial and Commonwealth History*, 31, 2 (2003), 17.

10. For accounts of sub-cultures within the British South African identity see, for example, J. Hyslop, 'Cape Town Highlanders, Transvaal Scottish: Military "Scottishness" and Social Power in Nineteenth and Twentieth Century South Africa', *South African Historical Journal*, 47 (2002), 96–114; D. McCracken, 'Irish Identity in Twentieth-Century South Africa' in *Ireland and South Africa in Modern Times* (Durban: Ireland and South African Project, 1996); J. MacKenzie and N. Dalziel, *The Scots in South Africa: Ethnicity, Gender and Race, 1772–1914* (Manchester: Manchester University Press, 2007).

11. The most famous example of this in a sporting context is related in an anecdote told about President Vorster in the 1960s. On being informed that in the Test match between South Africa and England 'die Engels' had lost three wickets, Vorster replied: 'Hulle Engelse of ons Engelse?'— 'Their English or our English?' See J.-P. Bodis, *Le Rugby Sud-Africain* (Paris: Karthala, 1995), 56.

12. Lambert, 'An Unknown People', 602.

13. Leonard Thompson, *A History of South Africa* (Yale: Yale University Press, 2001), 158.

14. S. Dubow, 'Colonial Nationalism, the Milner Kindergarten and the Rise of "South Africanism", 1902–10', *History Workshop Journal*, 43 (1997), 53–85.

15. Allen, 'Tours of Reconciliation'.

16. S. Dubow, 'South Africa and South Africans: Nationality, Belonging, Citizenship' in R. Roos, A. Kelk Mager, and B. Nasson (eds.), *The Cambridge History of South Africa: Volume 2, 1885–1994* (Cambridge: Cambridge University Press, 2011), 33.

17. V. Bickford-Smith, 'Writing About Englishness: South Africa's Forgotten Nationalism' in G. McPhee and P. Poddar (eds.), *Empire and After: Englishness in Post-Colonial Perspective* (New York: Berghahn, 2007), 58.

18. Quoted in E. Platnauer (ed.), *The Springbokken in Great Britain* (Johannesburg: George Wunderlich, 1907), 114.

19. R. Morrell, 'Of Boys and Men: Masculinity and Gender in Southern African Studies', *Journal of Southern African Studies*, 24, 4 (1998), 617.

20. H. Bradford, 'Gentlemen and Boers: Afrikaner Nationalism, Gender, and Colonial Warfare in the South African War' in G. Cuthbertson, A. Grundlingh, and M. Suttie (eds.), *Writing the Wider War: Rethinking Gender, Race and Identity in the South African War, 1899–1902* (Athens: Ohio University Press, 2002), 37.

21. Bradford, 'Gentlemen and Boers', 37.

22. *Rand Daily Mail*, 30 November 1906; *Methodist Recorder*, 27 December 1906.
23. *Rand Daily Mail*, 21 December 1906.
24. Allen, 'Captain Diplomacy', 580. The school was renamed Paul Roos Gymnasium in his honour in 1941.
25. R. Hyam and P. Henshaw, *The Lion and the Springbok: Britain and South Africa since the Boer War* (Cambridge: Cambridge University Press, 2003), 15.
26. P. van der Schyff, *Paul Roos, se Springbokken 1906–2006* (Stellenbosch: Paul Roos Gymnasium, 2007).
27. See G. Levett, 'Constructing Imperial Identity: The South African Cricket Tour of England in 1907' in B. Murray and G. Vahed (eds.), *Empire and Cricket: The South African Experience 1884–1914* (Pretoria: Unisa, 2009), 241–59.
28. For the purposes of consistency, I shall follow Vivian Bickford-Smith's example in employing the common South African usage of the time in treating 'English' and 'Englishness' as being synonymous with 'British' and 'Britishness'. Bickford-Smith, 'Writing about Englishness', 57.
29. *Marylebone Times*, 19 July 1907.
30. *Cricket: A Weekly Record of the Game*, 1 August 1907. Some sources place him as one of nine brothers.
31. *Bulawayo Chronicle*, 19 April 1948.
32. H. Grierson, *The Ramblings of a Rabbit* (London: Chapman and Hall, 1924), 13.
33. *The Daily News (Perth)*, 4 November 1910.
34. *Cricket: A Weekly Record of the Game*, 1 August 1907.
35. J. Mangan, *The Games Ethic: Athleticism in the Victorian and Edwardian Public School: The Emergence and Consolidation of an Educational Ideology* (London: Cass, 2000).
36. P. Thompson, 'Schools, Sport and Britishness: Young White Natal, 1902–1961', *South African Historical Journal*, 45 (2001), 223–48.
37. J. Tosh, *A Man's Place: Masculinity and the Middle-Class Home in Victorian England* (New Haven: Yale, 1999), 189.
38. W. Shalders, 'The Eighth Currie Cup Tournament' in M. Luckin (ed.), *The History of South African Cricket* (Johannesburg: W. E. Horton & Co., 1915), 247.
39. D. Nourse, quoted in T. Gutsche, *Old Gold: The History of the Wanderers Club* (Cape Town: Howard Timmins, 1966), 131.
40. P. Warner, *The M.C.C. in South Africa* (Cape Town: J. C. Juta and Co., 1906), 73.
41. Warner, *M.C.C. in South Africa*, 74.
42. P. Sherwell, 'The Fifth English Team in South Africa' in M. Luckin (ed.), *South African Cricket*, 547.

43. Sherwell, 'Fifth English Team', 549.
44. Sherwell's highest score in the series came in the final Test, 30 scored in an innings victory over England that ensured a 4-1 series victory.
45. Warner, *M.C.C. in South Africa*, 158.
46. Cape Town Chief Justice, quoted in Warner, *M.C.C. in South Africa*, 219.
47. Levett, 'Constructing Imperial Identity'.
48. *Transvaal Annual Cricket Report* (1906–07).
49. *The Owl*, 18 January 1907.
50. For Kotzé's incorporation into the British identity of the team see Levett, 'Constructing Imperial Identity', 248.
51. *C.B. Fry's Magazine*, 7 (1907), 416.
52. *Marylebone Times*, 19 July 1907.
53. *Wisden* (1907).
54. *Cricket: A Weekly Record of the Game*, 1 August 1907.
55. G. Jessop, *A Cricketer's Log* (London: Hodder and Stoughton, 1922), 208.
56. *Daily Mail*, 4 July 1907.
57. *The Daily News (Perth)*, 1 November 1907.
58. H. Leveson Gower, 'Cricket in South Africa', *The State*, 3, 4 (1910), 626.
59. Ibid., 633–34.
60. R. Fitzgerald, 'The First South African Team in Australia, 1910–11' in M. Luckin (ed.), *South African Cricket*, 771.
61. C. Merrett and J. Nauright, 'South Africa' in B. Stoddart and K. Sandiford (eds.), *The Imperial Game: Cricket, Culture and Society* (Manchester: Manchester University Press, 1998), 64. See also B. Murray, 'Abe Bailey' in Murray and Vahed (eds.), *Empire and Cricket*, 261–78; P. Ferriday, *Before the Lights Went Out: The 1912 Triangular Tournament* (Hove: Von Krumm Publishing, 2011).
62. B. Schwartz, *Memories of Empire Volume 1: The White Man's World* (Oxford: Oxford University Press, 2011).
63. R. Fitzgerald, 'First South African Team in Australia, 1910–11', 775.
64. *Register*, 27 October 1910.
65. *The Daily News (Perth)*, 30 November 1910.
66. Ferriday, *Before the Lights*, 135.
67. A. Vogler, quoted in Ferriday, *Before the Lights*, 289.
68. *Bulawayo Chronicle*, 19 April 1948.

CHAPTER 3

'Not the Same Thing as on Grass': Political Conservatism, Cultural Pessimism, Vested Interests and Technical Inhibition—Factors in South African Cricket's Commitment to Matting, 1876–1935

Dale Slater

AUSTRALIA AND SOUTH AFRICA: DIVERGENT CRICKET CULTURES

On 15 March 1877, a team representing Australia composed of players from Victoria and New South Wales engaged a team of English professionals under James Lillywhite in the first ever international Test match

Thanks to Peter Muzzell (UCBSA), Andrew McLean (Humewood Golf Club) and Craig Bruton (Grid Construction, Durban) for email exchanges on the viability of turf wickets in South Africa, and to Prof. Bruce Murray and Millicent Mhlambi for assisting me in the matter of access to SACA minutes. Thanks also to Robin Isherwood for his attention to detail, and to Jonty Winch for providing a number of press references.

D. Slater (✉)
Byfleet, UK
e-mail: daleslater@ntlworld.com

© The Author(s) 2018
B. Murray et al. (eds.), *Cricket and Society in South Africa, 1910–1971*, Palgrave Studies in Sport and Politics,
https://doi.org/10.1007/978-3-319-93608-6_3

49

at the Melbourne Cricket Ground (MCG). The four-day match was played on a turf wicket. Low second innings totals suggest its progressive deterioration, although Bannerman's hundred ended when he retired hurt on the second day, hit on the hand by a ball that rose unexpectedly, so perhaps the wicket was somewhat 'sporting' throughout. Still, if this match represented the first flowering of an Australian cricketing vernacular, of techniques developed to address the specific problems thrown up by the Australian playing environment, it was soon clear that where this differed from the model English technique such modifications would augment, not detract from, the basic English stock.

In Melbourne and Sydney, first-class cricket had been played since at least 1856 on turf wickets top-dressed with riverine clay taken from Merri Creek, a watercourse that flows into the Yarra River on its way towards North Melbourne. Augmented by a law dating from the dawn of Australian first-class cricket in 1851 that permitted the use of a new pitch if rain fell while a match was in progress, Merri Creek soil was found perfectly adequate in local conditions, even for long-form cricket. Further north in Sydney where the Victorian clay proved less suitable, players resorted to creative adaptation of the 1851 law: whereas matches in Melbourne were normally conducted on a single pitch, 'those in Sydney frequently utilised two or more pitches – sometimes a fresh one for each innings'.[1] This was clearly unsatisfactory and as cricket assumed increasing importance, a permanent resolution of the issue became mountingly urgent. In 1875, the New South Wales Cricket Association (NSWCA) assumed control of the Sydney Cricket Ground (SCG), as late as 1868 mere common land, part marsh and part sandhill, and still regarded as dangerous to play on. Edward ('Ned') Gregory, of the famous cricketing family, one of the eleven who had represented Australia in that first Test, was appointed curator. Backed by significant investment, Gregory began a programme of continuous improvement of SCG facilities, in particular its pitches. Using grounds at Manly and Canterbury for testing, Gregory experimented incessantly with new pitch construction techniques, new soils and bases. By 1882, sufficient progress had been made for the SCG to stage its own first Test match, but it was not until the late 1880s that a vital discovery was made at Bulli Point near Wollongong—fortuitously, since Gregory had family links to the area—of a black earth 'with excellent binding qualities', hard enough to provide a fast consistent surface, yet plastic enough to be largely impervious to rain.[2] Following extended trials (and the calamitous 1894

Australian collapse on a drying wicket after England had followed-on), Gregory reconstructed the SCG square with Bulli soil with such success that by the turn of the century the NSWCA was offering its members matching funding to do likewise, and Victoria soon followed suit.

Variations on these basic themes—investment, initiative, innovation— occurred all across Australia. At Adelaide in the late 1870s, H. Yorke Sparks and Jesse Hide, a Sussex player who had come with an England team and stayed on as the Oval's curator and professional, rebuilt a troublesome square with clay from Athelstone near the Torrens River, in accordance with advice from James Lillywhite and one Dr. Schomburg, a prominent local botanist.[3] In Perth around 1893, the WACA was built on reclaimed swampland and William Henry Wise, personal gardener to local politician Sir George Shenton, constructed turf wickets with soil from Waroona. At Brisbane's Gabba in 1895, soil from Goodna was used. Matting wickets were still used in schools and some district cricket—Bradman learned to play on matting, generally over concrete, in the Berrima District Association and first played on turf as late as October 1926; and the matting at Hobart's Bellerive Oval was not replaced until 1957—but for meaningful cricket, turf wickets were the standard.[4] In pursuit of a solution to the problem of turf, as in other facets, the cricketing culture of Australia displayed a rich and unremitting inventiveness, creative, resourceful, combative and energetic.

Yet in the previous southern spring (1876), matting wickets had been introduced at St George's Park in Port Elizabeth, the chief city of South Africa's Eastern Cape.[5] Formed in 1843, the Port Elizabeth Cricket Club (PECC) was then one of South Africa's foremost cricketing institutions, and this latest innovation placed them at its cutting edge. Their rivals still played on rolled bare earth, or grass strips in areas of higher rainfall. In 1879, the Western Province Cricket Club (WPCC) also moved to procure matting 'to be available for matches when the pitch, as the season advances, becomes unreliable'.[6] By the time South Africa entered international cricket in 1889, matting was ubiquitous for all first-class cricket. For a period of fifty years from 1876 to 1926—the same duration as between Australia's first Test match and Bradman's first-class debut—South Africa eschewed turf, playing all her cricket on matting.

The rationale for matting's introduction was the general belief that South African conditions, her soils and ecology, climate and weather, were unsuited to the development and retention of turf wickets, and that consequently cricket in South Africa required matting wickets if it were not to be played in a primitive state, especially in its longer forms.[7] Yet soon after South Africa's accession to international cricket, and certainly by the time of their first overseas tour in 1894, it became apparent that matting was exerting a deleterious effect upon the country's cricket, undermining its competitive advance and distorting the technical development of its players. Despite a growing body of evidence in support of this view, South African cricketing authorities continued to reject a change to turf, persisting with matting until 1926, by which time the country's decline threatened to prove terminal.

Yet the argument for South African singularity was fundamentally flawed, as the ensuing relatively painless establishment of turf wickets and outfields in the decade after 1926 was to demonstrate. The country in fact possessed in profusion all the ingredients necessary for the laying of turf wickets. Though Durban's turf pioneers, chiefly H. L. Crockett and Vic Robbins, imported Bulli from New South Wales to create their original turf wickets, this subsequently proved unnecessary. Crockett discovered a clay at Mount Edgecombe that 'displayed a striking similarity', all but identical except for its lower gravel content, and it subsequently transpired that there was in fact an abundance of suitable local soils, particularly in Natal.[8] North of a line on the map through De Aar, Cradock and East London and east of a line from De Aar to Kimberley, South Africa has copious deposits of melanic clays of the montmorillonite type, whose high smectite content makes them suitable for use in pitch construction, so much so that the country is today an exporter of Bullis.[9] Moreover, grass varieties that lend themselves to use on cricket pitches and outfields are also common in South Africa. Of the 967 grass types that grow in South Africa, only a handful are recommended for pitch or outfield construction, but these are widely distributed and grow naturally. Most groundsmen do not need to look beyond local varieties of Bermuda or couch grass, endemic throughout the country.[10] There is some question among botanists how many of these grasses are truly indigenous; varieties of pasture grass were introduced from abroad regularly throughout the nineteenth and early twentieth centuries, for colonial South Africa was inveterate at finding fault with the local flora.[11] Still, it is clear that no one who had engaged in pitch construction would have been short of the means to experiment. Contemporary pitch experts are thus unable to shed light on South Africa's fifty-year resistance to turf; if they did not lay turf, it was because they would not, it seems, not because they could not.[12] The contrast of the dynamic Australian approach with South Africa's cricketing culture—dour and characterised by caution and stasis, of which the recourse to matting was a trenchant example—could hardly be more pointed.

AUSTRALIA AND SOUTH AFRICA: WIDER CULTURAL DIFFERENCES

Cricketing culture was only one strand in a generally optimistic Australian cultural outlook. The relative homogeneity of its population facilitated the development of shared attitudes, purposes and symbols. Processes of self-definition (or redefinition) were uncontested and therefore relatively uncomplicated. Though interstate rivalries were real and sustained, differences were insubstantial compared with the bulk of common interests and, thus, with federation, were superseded by a common Australian nationalism. Also uncontested was colonial penetration and possession. Australia's indigenous population was small, sparse and rapidly marginalised in frontier wars that were limited in scale, low in intensity, and definitive in outcome. Challenges to colonial expansion thereafter were geographical not political, and consequent psychic damage sustained in the processes of conquest was contained, notwithstanding the harrowing genocides in Queensland and Tasmania.[13] While colonial South Africa huddled precariously at the extreme of an alien continent anxiously pondering its uncertain future, Australia achieved, in the words of W. K. Hancock, 'mastery of the continent' that 'followed from their triumphs in pastoral and agricultural technique'.[14] With mastery came a continental grasp of the opportunities that confronted them, helping to make Australia an early focus for surplus metropolitan capital, both human and financial, and bringing a correspondingly high degree of infrastructural development.

Where by the 1860s South Africa's total exports averaged £2,500,000 per annum, Australia's annual average was nearly eight times as large at £19,000,000, but the economic and social differences were qualitative as well as quantitative.[15] Feinstein demonstrates how and why Australia could surpass South Africa in so dramatic a fashion. Its export-led model of economic development was based upon 'small-scale, intensive, homestead farming', chiefly wool-farming, where the unit of production—not to be confused with actual area—remained small in scale, thereby freeing producers of over-reliance either on mass labour or on foreign capital, which was thus available for infrastructural development to connect producers more efficiently with points of export. The consequence of this mode of production was that 'The gains … were largely retained in the country, and spread out from staple producers until the economy as a whole attained high levels of physical and human capital, productivity, and living standards'.[16] But South Africa in contrast was shaped by diversity, not homogeneity, and a very different economic model catalysed its cultural enterprises. Though wool exports were equally central to its agricultural economy, the South African model was one of 'large owner-operated farms worked by a harshly exploited black labour force'.[17] In Feinstein's terms, this model, adopted in both mining and large-scale plantation-type production, required access to technology and mass labour to achieve economies of scale and was therefore dependent upon access to foreign capital. As a result, 'The distribution of income is highly skewed' as profits were repatriated and local demand stifled accordingly. Associated with this were correspondingly 'low standards of education, very limited advances in human capital, and authoritarian political systems'.[18]

Following Feinstein's schema, it becomes clear how two such different cultures arose. The key difference was the premium Australians placed upon the development of human capital in all its forms, this itself a function of egalitarian income distribution. Australia had no—or little—leisured class and no alternative sources of labour, and therefore, where in South Africa 'dirt on the hands' was regarded as 'a stain on the character', colonial Australians had little choice but to accept labour, manual or otherwise, as an unavoidable constraint of living, even a necessary means of economic and social fulfilment.[19] Australians thus formed a connection with the land they occupied that was mediated only by their own hand and from this secure material base rose a culture that was forward-looking, expansive and confident.

The contrast with South Africa was marked. The prolonged and violent processes of colonisation and dispossession, the deliberate destruction of independent African socio-economic life and their forced proletarianisation in the service of an emergent capitalist economy, had profound effects upon the cultural forms of settler life. While Australia achieved continental mastery, 'white South Africans graduated to uneasy possession of their own, less and less transigent internal colony'.[20] J. M. Coetzee examines the tradition of English letters of these 'dubious colonial children of a far-off motherland' and finds there a connected 'failure of the historical imagination', whose consequence was the 'occlusion of black labour', and a preoccupation with a South African landscape apprehended as inhospitable and resistant, 'intractable', 'trackless, refus[ing] to emerge into meaningfulness as a landscape of signs'.[21] In parallel, Paul B. Rich discerns a South African society so riven with division that it could develop 'no cohesive intellectual class able to formulate a set of national images and symbols that can command widespread consent'.[22] At an existential level, beneath the level of ideological narrative, colonial South Africa knew what it could not acknowledge: there was an implicit asymmetry between colonial and indigenous political claims. Neither white privilege nor the systematic exploitation of blacks was amenable to rational examination, based as they were on the partial logic of self-interest. Volatility compounded by its own suggestive ideological depictions, white colonial culture had compelling reasons for apprehension, or fatalism, the requirement for perpetual renovation and calibration of the apparatus of repression a task assuming a grim and Sisyphean cast. Occasionally, the ideological mask would slip, as in 1913 when J. M. B. Hertzog admitted, 'The European is severe, hard on the native because he is afraid of him'.[23]

Equally profound were the effects of black labour's 'occlusion'. The South African white-colonial view of labour was derived ultimately from the social mores of its early slave-holding society. Abolition rid the country of slavery's legal form but neither its social nor its economic content; given the scarcity of capital, the reproduction of labour was accompanied by a relentless struggle to reduce its costs. The creation, maintenance and exploitation of an inferior, servile class was therefore attended by the ongoing elaboration of an ideology of white industry and black indolence whose underlying aim was to justify a war on labour costs by constant reference to low levels of productivity. Pre-colonial resistance was thereby reinscribed as barbarous incapacity or sheer torpor and white lassitude in turn as the legitimate fruits of civilisation or, later, of evolutionary favour. Despite white denials, inevitably South Africa's servile class became its productive class as the division of labour reproduced the dominant ideological form. As John X. Merriman observed in 1907, drawing an explicit distinction with other 'white' colonies, in South Africa 'the Natives are the workers ... while a large class of Europeans are sinking'.[24]

Adopting a meniscoid relationship to African labour, South Africa's white minority thereby made themselves economically dependent on the disposition of its African masses.[25] A nativised form of the master–slave dialectic asserted itself at every political, social and economic turn. Acts or processes of production were invariably mediated by African labour, which frequently resorted to covert forms of resistance or subversion.[26] But since the agency of Africans had been ideologically abolished, the landscape that revealed itself to the white-colonial eye was one of emptiness and silence, unresponsive and dead.[27] The environment could not be engaged directly as Australians had done, for in South Africa colonial nature carried a double structure of alienation: locus of white South Africans' own alienation as colonisers, it was also, increasingly, the product of transformation by the alienated labour of others. Out of this landscape arose a culture that was stolid, sedentary and both defensive and predatory. Reductive of experience and plagued by unresolved questions of agency, white consciousness in South Africa subsumed a complex web of social, ethnic, racial and class divisions, and with it, the cultural pessimism of a people set down in an environment that, reflecting their own disdain, embodied an unremitting hostility.

The Eastern Cape: Cricket and White Culture

Nowhere were these factors more clearly at work than in the Eastern Cape, crucible of South Africa's colonial white culture, in the late nineteenth century. As Marks and Trapido point out, South Africa in the 1870s was hardly more than a 'geographical expression', whose regions were subject to the constant and contradictory strains of centralisation and fragmentation, their political and economic integration continuously tested by stress.[28] If the forms of Eastern Cape politics were dominated by its relationship to the established interests and relative wealth of the Western Cape, then its content was derived in large measure from the problem, as it was perceived, of the proximity of Xhosa clans disposed along their eastern flank.

As in Australia, wool was the chief agricultural export of the Eastern Cape, but the circumstances of its development led to very different outcomes. The hairy fat-tailed sheep traditionally kept by Khoisan farmers as a source of meat was replaced by merino sheep imported from Spain early on in the governorship of Lord Charles Somerset in order to exploit the export potential of its wool.[29] A government farm was established at Somerset East in the Cape Midlands in 1814 to provide a flow of breeding stock. Though dwarfed by the Australian wool clip, production nonetheless increased steadily from 20,000 lb in 1822 to nearly 26,000,000 lb by 1862 and over 37,000,000 lb by 1870.[30]

The Eastern Cape's reliance for capital upon the relatively meagre accumulations of the wheat and wine region of the Western Cape created a sort of sub-colonial relationship of dependence between the two, that fed an existing animus for, according to Ross, the east was populated mainly by those Afrikaners who 'were too poor to compete for better farms in the south west'. It was not until the 1840s, after the abolition of slavery and the compensation of slave-owners, that the Cape Town financiers began 'not so much advancing their own money as acting as agents for … British capital', thus easing to some degree the constriction of supply.[31] The general shortage of capital, exacerbated by the steady repatriation of profits, meant however that processes of economic stratification took on a sharply pronounced aspect, and neither the development of infrastructure nor the development of human capital was accorded the urgent priority they had acquired for Australian society.

Further, the ideologically determined division of labour that arose from the Eastern Cape's complex racial and socio-economic hierarchy meant that it was unable to replicate Australia's intensive small-scale production methods. Imported from the slave-holding south-west, the prevailing labour relations were regressive in more ways than one. In part a function of restricted access to capital, an onerous share of which was required to meet labour needs, their harsh tone was a principal factor in the low productivity. This in turn further inflated the overall labour requirements. Moreover, the ideological withholding of white labour was a supplementary overhead, meaning neither slavery nor its subsequent replacement by coerced African labour was cheap. Too, the supply of labour was subject to elaborate artificial restrictions rooted in traditional racial profiles. Axiomatic was the privileging of white labour, but these protocols of labour allocation—fine distinctions between '*hottentotwerk*' and '*kaffirwerk*', for instance, and the gendering of work—also represented an attempt on the part of colonial agriculturalists to appropriate, alongside their labour, the local and traditional knowledge, skills and experience of indigenous inhabitants. Finally, labour requirements were further inflated by primal environmental factors. The absence of predators in Australia limited any requirement for stock supervision. In South Africa, their profusion made supervision of stock a constant and general necessity, as well as restricting free movement and efficient foraging since each night herds were subject to the labour-intensive practices of herding and driving in order to be *kraaled* in safety.[32] Thus, by Beinart's reckoning, low productivity notwithstanding, overall 'More capital was probably invested into the pastoral farms of the Karoo and Eastern Cape than in the diamond fields of Kimberley'.[33] Mapped against Feinstein's schema, it is not difficult to see how a repressive authoritarian cultural strain developed and alongside it a sharply pronounced socio-economic hierarchy that formed the basis of South Africa's future racial ordering.

South African cricket spread in close alignment with the economic and political frontiers of colonial development and, as a time-consuming activity, was tied to the emergence of successive elites thrown up by local processes of stratification and capital accumulation. In the Cape Colony, cricket, the imperial sport, had long been the sport of the ruling class, meaning the institutions of the game were erected upon a narrow and exclusive social base, and where these articulated with wider cultural or political issues tended to express or reflect a contained and narrowly defined range of interests.

Port Elizabeth, the region's focal town and chief port, had grown moderately prosperous servicing the agricultural producers of its hinterland, chiefly her wool farmers. Seeking to remove obstacles to trade, Somerset had in 1826 granted Port Elizabeth the right to handle direct imports and exports and established a customs house there.[34] By 1854, on average 70% of Cape exports and 50% of her imports went through Algoa Bay instead of Cape Town. Thus, it was from here, the Eastern Cape's commercial centre, that frontier-based merchant capital set about its traditional task, of eradicating existing subsistence economies to create an army of suppliers with growing skills and efficiency, and consumers, with expanding wants and needs.[35] The shared interest in eradicating indigenous subsistence as a prelude to proletarianisation formed the basis of an alliance between agricultural and merchant capital which in Port Elizabeth soon brought to prominence a corresponding elite. Predominantly but not exclusively English-speaking, this new gentry was also much to the fore in civic and regional leadership. The establishment in 1843 of the PECC, a mere five years after the Melbourne Cricket Club, illustrates the progress of this alliance as bonds of scarcity were gradually loosened. That the club soon ceased to function illustrates the fitful nature of the Eastern Cape's economic and political development.

Nevertheless, Port Elizabeth's gradual commercial development also served as a lens to concentrate the separatist inclinations that had animated Eastern Cape politics since before the dawn of British control. By the 1870s, a number of internal and external factors had raised the political temperature of a region known for its febrile political atmosphere. Rising wool prices, peaking in 1875, alongside the development of a lucrative trade in ostrich products, had stimulated a general recovery from the sharp depression of the mid-sixties (a credit squeeze precipitated by the Standard Bank fiasco, itself a manifestation of separatist inclination, a colonial tail for once wagging the metropolitan dog).[36] Of greater long-term significance was the discovery of diamonds at Kimberley in 1867. Kimberley's proximity, near equidistant from both ports—485 miles from Port Elizabeth, 518 from Cape Town—intensified competition between the two Capes, as each sent out Kimberley-bound railways seeking to corner its trade.

The discovery of diamonds had wider ramifications. The prospect of future mineral wealth presented the Imperial government with a sudden opening to set at arm's length one of their expensive colonial burdens, and a plan was hatched for Southern African confederation. Minerals were to provide an engine of economic growth, their profitability underwritten by a surfeit of cheap black labour sourced from the remaining independent African polities lying along southern Africa's east coast, including those Xhosa clans beyond the Kei River. The subjugation of these polities and their incorporation into the existing British colonies were therefore a necessary precursor to the unfolding confederation plan. While the worthies of the Eastern Cape calculated the dividend in land, markets and labour that war beyond the Kei would bring, J. A. Froude, Carnarvon's agent, took to fanning the flames of separatism to drive home to Molteno's Cape administration the imputed benefits of confederation.

By 1875, then, separatism was a brimming vessel, its overspill running in many directions and stirring Port Elizabeth's gentry into action. As early as 1859, the newly resurrected PECC had leased St George's Park from Port Elizabeth Town Council, upon which they were well represented and in 1864, during the period 'of easy money and active speculation', had taken the opportunity to flatten and enclose it to facilitate the charging of spectators.[37] Under the stimulus of renewed prosperity and aiming to tweak Cape Town's tail, PECC announced plans for an inter-town cricket tournament. Mayor Henry Pearson, a future MLA and Colonial Secretary, presented a trophy on behalf of the Town Council and so, between 6 and 12 January 1876, the first Champion Bat tournament was contested there between the chief cricketing towns of the Cape Colony. It is significant that the trophy was intended to be named the Challenge Bat, acquiring its alternative name by error of the English supplier, for there can be little doubt that Port Elizabeth's plan was by this means to challenge Cape Town's presumptive leadership of Cape cricket. The plan failed miserably as the Port Elizabeth team was beaten successively by sides from Grahamstown, King William's Town and Cape Town, though King William's Town's overall triumph served notice of the relative strength of Eastern Cape cricket.

THE ADOPTION OF MATTING

If this failure spurred the introduction of matting, another factor was the absence of summer rainfall, the first intimation of the disastrous drought of 1876–79. According to Ivor Markman, the direct inspiration for matting's introduction was a press report of its use in South Australia where it was 'found to be far superior to the hard sunbaked soil which it covers'.[38] It would seem reasonable to suppose that the immediate motivation for its introduction was a desire to improve conditions in general and, as was then the pattern the world over, for batsmen in particular. The primitive pitches of the era were very much in the favour of bowlers, who required no particular skills beyond persistence to take wickets, chiefly by uneven bounce. Yet it is difficult to be certain precisely how effective it was in this respect, especially since uneven bounce remained one of the salient features of matting wickets. The figures over the span of five Champion Bat tournaments held between 1876 and 1891 are suggestive, but ambiguous.[39]

That matting's strongest and clearest effect was not necessarily the intended one, however, was soon apparent. At home, on the matting they knew and understood well, Port Elizabeth thrived, and their victory at St George's in the 1884/85 tournament marked a high point their cricket would never again reach. In the original tournament of 1876, the highest total achieved by a Port Elizabeth team was 89 against Cape Town, but by 1884/85, their *lowest* score in a completed innings was 165, this against the 'cracks' of Kimberley, and they twice topped 200. Kimberley, regarded as the 1884/85 pre-tournament favourites, found the alien conditions unmanageable: 'the change from hard and bumpy grounds to grass was too much for them; the only members to do anything with the bat were the Homeborn men; the young colonial batsmen, from whom great things were expected, all came to grief upon the turf-matting pitch'.[40] Roles were reversed in a subsequent friendly tournament in Kimberley in April 1887 where it was Port Elizabeth's turn to struggle as the pace and bounce of matting over bare earth saw them shot out for 37 and 70 and crushed by an innings and 37 runs.

These were early intimations of the way things were to develop subsequently across South Africa. Where Cape Town and Port Elizabeth retained their matting-over-turf, Kimberley's 'hard and bumpy' ground would be replicated at The Wanderers in Johannesburg and at Lord's in Durban, which had matting laid over soil obtained from crushed anthill. Matting wickets across South Africa had features in common, most palpably inconsistent but generally high bounce, and pronounced turn. But there were also important differences between matting laid over turf and matting laid over grass resulting from the former's harder compacted base. As future touring sides would find, it was not merely matting instead of turf that would disconcert them but also the fact that, effectively, South Africa had two different types of matting wicket, each requiring to be played by a different method. As Pelham Warner described it after touring with Lord Hawke's England team in 1898/99, the wickets in Johannesburg and Durban were extremely fast and bouncy but favoured a batsman who was prepared to brave unanticipated bounce by going forward, for he could 'make any amount of forcing strokes on both sides of the wicket'. Especially at The Wanderers where, alone of South African grounds, the outfield was level and true, though to cut was risky, 'Drives ... and push strokes can be made with great frequency, while the ball travels to the boundary at a great pace'. South African batsmen, not as well equipped technically as Warner or as generally committed to front foot play, instead developed a tendency to play the percentages by going back to allow themselves maximum time to judge the bounce. On the softer grass wickets at the coast however, even Warner agreed it was wise to stay on the back foot. Looking to go forward and drive at Port Elizabeth or Cape Town was fraught with danger. Though the matting here presented bowlers with the same advantages of variable bounce and 'considerable work' on the ball as on the hinterland pitches, the softer base beneath the matting made the ball grip and come off the pitch more slowly, with a sort of hesitation that seemed unnatural to a player used to turf. On these wickets, according to Warner, every forward shot was an essay in timing, for it was effectively a shot on the up. Even a half-volley 'does not seem the same thing as on grass, and forcing strokes are generally at a discount'.[41]

Thus, certain traditions in South African cricket ramified from these conditions. Spinners, especially left-arm or leg-spin, were found particularly effective on the coastal grounds, obtaining bounce and turn, and safe in the knowledge that they were unlikely to be driven. In the face of a well-set field, a batsman would have to risk playing to leg, against the turn, to score. Conversely, opportunities for fast bowlers were limited since often they bounced too much or cut off the pitch too much to be effective, while on inland strips they were expensive: pitching short they could be pulled or hooked, and pitching up, driven or forced. Following the path of least resistance therefore, South Africa's bowling resources over the fifty years of matting were funnelled towards the median: successive attacks relied primarily upon a procession of slow-medium to fast-medium bowlers, persistent rather than penetrative, reluctant to experiment and reliant on batsman error or the multiple hazards of matting for their wickets. In batting, the method was likewise attritional rather than aggressive, organised around watchful defence essential to counter late and pronounced movement, predominantly off the back foot because of the bounce, and favouring the leg-side for scoring. As H. L. Crockett, looking back in 1927 summed up the matter: since 'the ball gets a certain amount of grip', it

> will usually … go over the top … By reason of this high rise South African batsmen have developed the pull and hook shots to an extraordinary degree, and make them their most prolific scoring strokes … with perfect confidence, as they know if they miss a straight one they will not be bowled … The position of the body and feet may be all wrong, but what does it matter, the ball comes up nicely – at least thigh-high and very often waist-high – and he has only to swing his bat at it. On the other hand, the off-drive … on matting … is almost a lost art … owing to the sharp rise and turn of the ball from the mat…[42]

These were tendencies, of course, not absolutes, and there were exceptions. A Jimmy Sinclair could drive with the best of them, but taken all in all, the conservative culture of white South Africa as encapsulated in matting wickets had bred similarly cautious habits of cricket. In developing its own vernacular, South African cricket adapted itself to a limited and specific range of strokes and developed methods and techniques that were restricted and partial, even distorted, versions of the broader technical canons developed on turf. In the realm of cricket, as in the fields of politics and economic development, it seems, South Africa had effectively imposed upon itself an artificially low horizon, turning away from the challenges and opportunities offered by complexity in favour of virtuosity in a limited and more easily controlled sphere.

There was one earlier lesson to be drawn from Kimberley's travails in Port Elizabeth in December 1884. Though the Kimberley team in general struggled, those who were best able to cope, we are told, were the *home born* players, that is those who had learned to play on turf. They would presumably have been the most experienced players but also, their prior experience would likely have encompassed *the widest scope* of *variation* in conditions. Accustomed to confronting novel conditions, turf-bred players found it easier to adapt to new or unexpected problems such conditions threw up. Matting, on the other hand, was immune to the influences that work upon the states of a turf wicket. Virtually impervious both to wear and to weather, a matting wicket was no different in character on the fourth or fifth day of a match than it had been on the first. The toss was therefore all but meaningless, as in 1927/28 when Springbok captain Deane won all five tosses, and three times put England in: who batted last was not among his considerations. Thus, there was no such thing as a 'flat' matting wicket, or a worn one, or one made 'sticky' by rain. When it rained, matting played a little slower, flatter and easier for a brief period until the base had dried, but thereafter played exactly as before.

The practical significance of this asymmetry would not become fully apparent until the England tour of 1894 when, going from matting to turf in all its various gradations of character, weather and wear, South Africa's glaring technical deficits were badly exposed, and H. H. Castens' team judged 'scarcely above … a second-class county'.[43] Though there were exceptions—slow left-armer George Rowe who found the wet conditions to his liking, and Cyril Sewell, whose technique had been honed under the watchful eye of his father (J. J. Sewell), a former county player—the best performers were those with prior exposure to turf: Halliwell of course, and Castens himself, who had been schooled in England; 'Bonnor' Middleton, who had represented the British Army; and Mills and Hearne, former county players.[44] As Frank Mitchell observed of a later South African touring side, the comparative sameness of matting and its relatively narrow range of variation meant that South African players 'do not become accustomed to the frequent changes [English] players meet'.[45]

GOLD AND THE PATH TO TRANSVAAL HEGEMONY

By the time the last Champion Bat tournament took place in Cape Town in 1890/91, South Africa stood balanced on the brink of fundamental change. Gold discoveries in the South African Republic in 1886 had decisively changed the political mood, giving momentum to the centralisers and sending the forces of fragmentation into temporary eclipse. Though the advent of gold had tilted the political axis to the north, still, for the time being, the control of cricket remained a Cape affair and the WPCC 'the M.C.C. of the Cape Colony'.[46] In 1888/89 under the driving force of William Milton, the club had arranged and guaranteed a tour of South Africa by an England team managed by Major Warton. The tour was no small undertaking. Over 146 days and 15,975 miles, an English team, led by amateur C. Aubrey Smith but reliant on a backbone of experienced county professionals, criss-crossed the Cape and Natal, playing, *inter alia*, a Cape Colony XV, and ventured into the South African Republic to play two games at The Wanderers against Johannesburg and Transvaal.[47] Early difficulties with matting led to four defeats (against odds) in their first six matches, twice at Kimberley where the disobliging locals refused to paint the matting to reduce the glare as other regions had done.[48] Thereafter, the tourists were unbeaten in their remaining thirteen games including the two 'Tests'.

In the tour's aftermath, the South African Cricket Association (SACA) was formed in April 1890 to facilitate a newly instituted South Africa-wide tournament, the Currie Cup. It is frequently observed that SACA anticipated the Union of South Africa by twenty years. Without qualification though, the observation is more noise than light, for though SACA embodied the aspiration to unity, as an institution it bore unmistakeable marks of pre-Union origins. By this time, few discerning observers doubted that South Africa would sooner or later be united, or federated, if only because gold needed a port for shipping. The remaining question was: by whom and on whose terms. This political question had a cricketing analogue in the battle for control of SACA between the Western Province and Transvaal Cricket Unions. At its formation, SACA had seven members, four of whom—Western Province, Eastern Province, Border and Griqualand West—were regions of the Cape Colony. Nominally, each member had two votes. Thus, if Western Province could establish dominance over Cape Colony cricket, a Cape bloc could not be outvoted.

But if Cape hegemony were to be entrenched, this was the critical period. In 1890, the mining economy of the Witwatersrand languished in depression associated with the shift from outcrop to deep-level mining. Deep-level mining was dependent upon the solution of formidable technical, political and labour issues. It also required the commitment over the long term of huge reserves of capital, which in turn required a step-change in the relationship between mine-owners and metropolitan finance.[49] Solutions to these problems were at hand, but it would require time to assemble the necessary elements and set them in train. The depression of the early 'nineties' was thus a period of abeyance, during which the infant industry was preoccupied with its own prospects, engaged in determining its own reach and potential. Transvaal cricket was likewise poised alongside, already wealthy and powerful but not yet the juggernaut it was to become. In 1891, during the period when the Currie Cup was in format merely a Challenge match between holder and a single challenger, Western Province challenged Transvaal, the holders, to defend the Cup against a combined Cape Colony team.[50] Transvaal accepted, but under protest. Western Province, however, had done little to prepare the way for such an anti-Transvaal alliance, and the proposal was rejected by the remaining Cape regions, which saw no advantage in negating potential Transvaal hegemony only to reinforce that of their overbearing rival.

With this rejection went the last realistic chance of long-term Cape cricketing hegemony. Western Province won four of the five Currie Cups contested between 1892 and 1898; was the leading force in attracting English touring sides in 1891/92, 1895/96 and 1898/99; and in despatching South African sides to England in 1894 and 1901. Despite this, its longer-term fate was sealed. By 1894, the development of the MacArthur-Forrest process ensured high levels of gold retrieval even from pyritic deep-level ore and, critically, the organic, and structural, links had been put in place between Johannesburg's operators and City of London financiers. The future of the gold industry was thereby assured and, as word spread, a spectacular new 'Kaffir boom' followed. In the Cape, Rhodes supervened to unhitch the Cape economy from its hitherto mainly agricultural base, to hitch it instead to the locomotive of extractive mining. In the process, he sounded the death knell of incorporationism just as it had begun to make an electoral impact.[51]

Now that the economic fundamentals were settled, what remained to be managed in the Transvaal was the political risk, and here the Randlords were split. There were those, mainly of continental origin and connection but including the maverick J. B. Robinson, who favoured accommodation with Kruger's ZAR government if it could be accomplished on their terms, not his. Among Anglophiles, there was an Imperial faction egged on by Joseph Chamberlain, the British

Colonial Secretary, but for others, though there were distinct advantages to having such a powerful stakeholder at their side, there were costs too. Such a power would have interests of its own and be well placed to assert Imperial primacy or restrain the Randlords' freedom of action. According to Sir Thomas Fuller, Rhodes himself had declared a desire to 'eliminate the Imperial factor' by which he meant, not the factor itself, but the factor acting independently of colonial institutions.[52] In 1895, it was Rhodes who forced the issue, for reasons not entirely devoid from self-interest, employing the blunt instruments of Dr. Jameson and the British South Africa Police to 'free' Johannesburg from the Pretoria 'tyrants'. The Jameson Raid's failure thus clarified the political future by a cancellation of redundant terms. Whoever prevailed in the Transvaal would prevail in South Africa, for in the aftermath of the Raid, the Cape's ruling alliance split largely along language lines, the rift opening the sort of symbolic distance that, as Paul B. Rich observed, continued to resonate into the identity politics of the 1920s and beyond.

The Raid ended Cape hegemony in South African cricket as well as in politics.[53] Hitherto, the Cape Afrikaner gentry, in alliance with Rhodes, had played a strategically important role in persuading their Transvaal brethren by word and deed of the beneficent nature of British imperialism. The Raid broke this faith. Afrikaners across the Cape and Natal and in the Boer Republics now recoiled from cricket, as from most aspects of English culture tainted with the Imperial brush. The narrow base upon which the institutions of South African cricket had been constructed became narrower still as the game focused upon more explicitly English, and imperial, expressions. Momentum, and chaos in the Transvaal, kept Western Province at the cricketing forefront for the duration of the South African War: the tour to England in 1901 was almost entirely a J. D. Logan enterprise, and the team comprised, it seemed, of old boys of 'Bishops', of whom Logan's son was one.[54]

THE AUSTRALIAN MIRROR: DARLING'S TOUR, 1902

Rhodes, whose machinations had done much to widen the rift between the two territories, died in March 1902. Randlord and SACA Chairman Abe Bailey, who took his politics whole from Rhodes, declared himself ready to assume Rhodes's mantle, cueing a sardonic response by Sammy Marks.[55] A thrilling Ashes series in England that summer between two of the strongest elevens ever to grace a cricket field prompted Bailey, in partnership with The Wanderers Club, to dispatch Frank Mitchell to negotiate a whistle-stop visit to South Africa on their way home by Joe Darling's conquering Australians.[56] The South African War and the mining boom had increased South African contact with things Australian, but this was South Africa's first direct exposure to their cricket. Despite the heroics of Sinclair and Llewellyn, a hesitant South Africa, with nine debutants in three Tests (two of them new captains, in their only Test), was unable to stretch the Australians, whose depth of knowledge and commitment to the game was unrivalled. There was, according to L. J. Tancred, 'with the whole of the visiting team a "snap" that was lacking' in South Africa's cricket, an intensity they could not match.[57]

Nor were the matting wickets an issue for the Australians, many of whom had had prior experience of matting at lower levels of cricket before graduating to turf. Hustled straight off the boat to the altitude of Johannesburg for two Tests, thence to the coast at Durban and down to Cape Town for a third and final Test, neither matting over earth nor over grass upset their stride.[58] Trumper, who in the course hit his fourteenth three-figure score since his last previous duck, 'was as much at home on the matting as on any other type of wicket, and Clem Hill … seen to conspicuous advantage'.[59] Despite their short acquaintance with South African conditions, they were generous too with their advice. Noble, Darling, Armstrong, Trumper and Clem Hill, the keenest brains of Australian cricket, all warned that South Africa would remain 'second class' until they forsook matting for turf.[60] Trumper was most explicit, stating that 'So long as South Africa plays cricket with matting … she will not maintain the standard of a first-class cricketing country'.[61] This was the first direct challenge to the notion of South African singularity, by experts armed with incontrovertible first-hand knowledge of turf wickets established in directly comparable circumstances. Already looking to Australia for bloodstock for his newly established Colesberg stud farm, and motivated by the ease with which the visitors had brushed South Africa aside, Bailey sanctioned the import of a quantity of Bulli from New South Wales.

In 1903, F. J. Cook, a former Eastern Province stalwart who had more recently turned out for The Wanderers Club, proclaimed on a visit to England that 'a determined effort' was being made to introduce turf.[62] The Bulli consignment was trialled in experiments in Johannesburg and Durban 'with but indifferent results'.[63] Unlike Australia, South Africa had no structural equivalent of the curator, ambitious to drive the experiment to a successful conclusion. Before 1902, as we have seen, South Africa had had no exposure to Australian cricket and the attitudes that animated it. Their cricketing model was the English game and their cricket structured accordingly. In South Africa, as in England, amateurs controlled local cricketing committees and nominally, the maintenance of its grounds. In England, specialised groundsmen were tasked with their maintenance and development. In South Africa though, this task was delegated to imported English coaches who, as professionals, occupied a lower rung of the social scale, removing from the shoulders of the amateur committees the responsibility for overseeing manual labour, a lowly role incommensurate with their social standing. Not until the 1920s would South Africa begin to replace professionals (mostly hired on short-term contracts and therefore not given to long-term commitments) with dedicated groundsmen, current players or ex-players such as Robbins in Durban and J. J. Kotzé at Newlands, establishing the continuity necessary to sustain a migration to turf. Far from 'determined', the effort to establish turf wickets in 1903 appears to have been somewhat desultory, as South Africa retreated once more to its comfort zone. Soon discontinued, the experiment was forgotten, or remembered only as confirmation that the *status quo ante* was the natural state. Besides, it was about to be overtaken by events that would strengthen South Africa's conservative adherence to matting and to the English cricketing model, diminishing Bailey's dependence on the opinions of Australians.[64]

By the time Darling's side set sail for home, Frank Mitchell was already engaged on Bailey's behalf in negotiations for a South African tour of England in 1904. But a year previously, in 1901, Mitchell had toured the USA and Canada as part of a team led by B. J. T. Bosanquet. The tour was a light-hearted affair of Oxbridge amateurs. Taking time off to watch the America's Cup and the Harvard–Yale Athletics meeting, the players were accused by their hosts of treating it more as a 'jaunt' than a cricket tour.[65] Bosanquet was as yet scarcely known, a sometime Middlesex amateur who hit a long ball and bowled tearaway quick stuff, but among the cognoscenti, he was known lately to have turned his hand, with some effect, to a curious sort of wrist spin. Also in that team was a friend of Bosanquet, a well-connected young stock-jobber named Reggie Schwarz. Mitchell departed the tour early to take up his new position working for Bailey in Johannesburg, but not before he had persuaded Schwarz to consider doing likewise. So, by the end of 1902, Schwarz, newly arrived, was hustled straight into the Transvaal Currie

Cup team (to a well-rehearsed chorus of Western Province disapproval). By 1903, Bosanquet's googly was England's secret weapon as Warner's MCC regained the Ashes in Australia.

The inability of their batsmen to fathom the googly was only the start of a period of difficulties for the hitherto mighty Australians. The first Test in Sydney featured an episode of sustained barracking when Clem Hill was adjudged run out at a critical juncture in the match. For the watching MCC chairman Lord Harris, who had been personally caught up in the 'Sydney Riot' of 1879, and suffered a similar unseemly incident in India during his Governorship of Bombay (where his Military Secretary was Col Frank Rhodes), this was an incident too far.[66] One which played into his hands however for, having established in England the unquestioned authority of amateurs over the game and its professional players, Harris was intent on establishing amateur authority across the game worldwide. This meant enforcing a certain discipline over Australia, where power had been allowed to leak down from the vessel of the class of 'natural' authority. Harris's campaign against the Australians had consequences in South Africa too, for a significant plank in his platform was the idea that cricket displayed in manifest form the invisible relations binding the colonies to their metropolitan principal. 'Cricket', he maintained, 'has done more to consolidate the Empire than any other influence'.[67] Furthermore, Harris's influence in South Africa extended beyond the boundaries of the game to its political epicentre. In 1896, in the wake of the Jameson Raid, he had been appointed to the Board of Consolidated Gold Fields in place of Rhodes.[68] By the commencement of the South African War in 1899, he was Gold Fields' chairman.[69] By the war's end, also, the mining industry was in a dire state and required enormous draughts of new capital to restart. Thus, Harris's strong connection with Bailey was propelled by an intense synergy, a fourfold connection of cricket, the dominance of amateurism, adherence to Rhodes's—now Milner's—key political aims and a shared intense desire to see the South African mining industry prosper at any cost.

The propagation of an ethos of amateurism suited South Africa too, for it legitimised other forms of exclusion and privilege. Bailey's money and South African cricket's elitist values allowed them to portray themselves as true amateurs, alive to the game's wider purposes and immune to the unworthy considerations of profit that, in Harris's view, tainted Australia. More, cricket in South Africa had always demonstrated a marked propensity for sliding back and forth between social and political registers, between use value and exchange value. Now, in the throes of post-war reconstruction and the drive towards Union, cricket moved beyond these customary value forms, acquiring, to use a term from Benjamin, an 'exhibition value': as propaganda, to assure audiences home and abroad that the war had not severed the ties of Empire.[70] On the strength of South Africa's defeat of the MCC tourists in 1905/06 and the sensational impact of the googly bowlers in England in 1907, Bailey set to work to widen the cleavage opened by Harris between England and Australia. His chosen devices were the Imperial Cricket Conference (ICC) , founded on his initiative in 1909 to firm up South Africa's status as an equal in world cricket, and the Triangular Tournament, intended to supplant the Ashes as cricket's premier competition.[71] But if Australia was to be displaced as England's pre-eminent cricketing partner, South Africa had first to beat them, and it required no great genius to see that its best chance of doing so was to catch Australia cold against the googly bowlers on matting, as it had done to the MCC. Migration to turf was therefore out of the question. If South Africa was to supplant Australia, matting would need to stay.

Australia was quick to perceive the trap and set one of their own. Resisting Bailey's most lavish financial inducements to visit South Africa, they insisted it was South Africa's turn to come to them. On the matter of the Triangular Trophy, they filibustered, seeking to push it back to an indefinite date beyond 1909 when their next revenue-rich tour of England was due. In the face of a blunt ultimatum from the MCC, who by 1908 had accepted Bailey's draft proposal for the Triangular Tournament, they linked the two issues, insisting they would not agree to the Triangular Tournament until South Africa had visited Australia.[72] In response to Bailey's proposals, W. P. McElhone, Honorary Secretary of the Australian Board of Control, stated in plain terms that 'The feeling is growing stronger and stronger in this country that if South Africa so ardently desires the scalp of Australia she must come after it … Australia will be glad, perhaps, to welcome South Africa as a competitor for "The Ashes", but will suffer no slight in any arrangement that may be made to that end'.[73] However, Bailey's agenda had an internal aspect too. If the point of the Imperial Cricket Conference had been to fix in place the *status quo* of international cricket with South Africa in its top rank, a secondary aim was in like manner to fix Transvaal's position at the apex of the country's internal structure, as 'South Africa's MCC'.

Transvaal, the Googly and the Golden Age

Since the end of the South African War, a confluence of economic and political factors had geared together the interests of The Wanderers Club, the Transvaal Cricket Union (TCU) and South African cricket. In the aftermath of the war, Milnerism—arising from but not completely contained by the political programme of Sir Alfred Milner—sought to remould South Africa's elements to fit them for Union under the flag of Empire. The Transvaal's mineral wealth identified as the engine of future economic growth, the basic strategy of Milnerism was therefore to subordinate competing economic interests, particularly those of the 'discrete micro-economies' of Natal and the Western Cape, to those of the mining industry and its own supporting micro-economy of agriculture, finance and small-scale manufacturing.[74] Milner's chief concern was to end mining's labour shortages without increasing its production costs to encourage mine-owners to ramp up production. If the coercive labour policies Milner employed to this end, culminating in the import of Chinese labour, added yet another storey to the ramshackle structure of exploitative South African labour relations, this was a price worth paying, for his *quid pro quo* was a 10% tax on mining profits to build the capacity of the Reconstruction state. Though the Randlords agreed this grudgingly, they were not slow in discovering the upside of a state whose interests were so entwined with their own. It goes without saying, Milner being a self-proclaimed 'British Race Patriot', that his policy served Imperial interests too by increasing Britain's capacity for trade (a function, under the Gold Standard, of access to gold).

As in the economy, in cricket there was a similar elision of general with particular interests. The Wanderers Club had been formed in the run-up to the visit of Major Warton's English tour party, and was therefore dominated by the rump of life members and patrons, overwhelmingly Randlords and their associates, whose wealth had facilitated The Wanderers ground's urgent completion.[75] Voting power on the TCU was directly correlated with the number of teams a club fielded in local League competitions. The Wanderers Club, able by sheer financial muscle to subsidise employment and time off for any number of promising players, fielded many more teams than other clubs were able to. Afforded '20 or 25 per cent of the total voting power', it was well positioned to dominate the TCU executive body.[76]

Financial muscle was also the key to TCU domination of SACA. Though the TCU had only two votes in common with each of SACA's remaining nine member unions, SACA's constitution was procedurally weak and its processes liable to manipulation in a number of ways. Abe Bailey sometimes offered financial investment advice, but revenue was otherwise derived exclusively from the fixture list in the form of gates.[77] As there was only limited revenue pooling, the procedures for distribution tended to favour the powerful unions: in general, profit was shared in proportion to the amount of risk a centre was able to accept. Unions whose grounds hosted Tests—and The Wanderers as South Africa's premier venue attracted by far the largest crowds—did particularly well, retaining 75% of the net Test match gate.[78] Therefore, the rich unions got richer and the poor poorer, and the potential for the former to exert influence on the latter compounded.

The Currie Cup fixture list was one potent source of leverage. The tournament format varied between the 'Murray Bisset' system, where games were played on a home and away basis over the course of a season, and a 'Single Centre' system, where teams met at a chosen location and the entire tournament was played over the space of a single week. Poorer unions tended to favour the 'Murray Bisset' system, which guaranteed them home fixtures against drawcard teams, from which they retained 50% of the net gate. This made them vulnerable to the threat of the alternative format. Also, the TCU was especially adept at manipulating the fixture list. A favourite tactic was to grant (or withhold) friendly matches at the homes of the weaker unions. Especially during the period when Bailey was plotting to create an Imperial cricket authority, the powerful Transvaal cricket team, practically a Springbok side, would be dispatched at the end of each season to tour the lesser unions to create windfall profits for them, reinforcing Bailey's influence.

Bailey's financial web extended in all directions. The strength of successive Transvaal sides was built primarily by attracting promising players from other regions to well paid jobs on the Rand that would give them time for cricket. Moreover, since Transvaal influence extended into the processes of selection, a player's chances of recognition were greatly enhanced by such a move. The threat of losing their best players could concentrate wonderfully the minds of a disadvantaged administration averse to some aspect or other of Bailey's policies. This policy could be dangled as carrot as well as brandished as stick: Bailey sometimes paid for coaches for unions who could not afford them, or subsidised their leading players. For instance, having lured Albert Vogler from Natal to the Rand with a job at The Wanderers, Bailey then parachuted him into the Eastern Province side for the 1906/07 Currie Cup as a favour to the province of his—Bailey *and* Vogler's—birth. Then regarded as the world's best bowler, Vogler was able to use his familiarity with The Wanderers pitch to Eastern Province's advantage, with 41 wickets at 9.78 in five matches, including 16/38 against Griquas.

Then there was the question of representation. Until 1926, practically all SACA meetings were held in The Wanderers boardroom. Calls for the meetings to be rotated were resisted on the grounds that SACA's secretariat required a permanent base. Vast distances and slow modes of travel meant other unions had to be represented by Johannesburg-based agents, who had no intrinsic connection to their union. In theory, these agents voted only as instructed by the union they represented. In practice dependent for their livelihoods on the Rand, agents were exposed in a multiplicity of ways to Johannesburg's blandishments or admonitions. They were sometimes called upon to vote without instruction, as urgent or sensitive issues could arise at SACA meetings before member unions had been informed, or had met to formulate a local response. Besides, limited communications meant the connection between agent and union was always somewhat precarious and subject to disruption. It seems redundant to add that the SACA secretary too was an employee of The Wanderers Club, and the chairman generally a Transvaal man.

SACA's agenda was therefore shaped and its decisions constrained by the imperatives of Bailey and the TCU and, less directly, by those of The Wanderers Club. H. J. Lamb's 1915 lament that the Club 'with such a splendid cricket history has now no more say in the government of cricket than any minor club' hovered somewhere between hyperbole and misdirection.[79] Certainly, in the matter of matting versus turf, their opposition to turf was decisive. They controlled South Africa's premier Test venue, 'the Mecca of South African cricket' whose financial contribution was critical to SACA's functioning.[80]

Besides, if there was one ground that gave specific substance to South Africa's tenacity in clinging to matting, it was The Wanderers. Australia's Test grounds were all at sea level. Johannesburg, by contrast, stood at an altitude of 5751 ft (1753 m), giving it a complex subtropical highland climate. The ground was bare red earth, decomposed diorite, a substance so hard it was used to work granite and, in Frank Mitchell's phrase, entirely 'innocent of grass'.[81] It reflected fierce light and heat and removed the shine from a cricket ball in fifteen or twenty minutes. Play was sometimes stopped by thunder, hail or sandstorms, and Lord Hawke's 1895 England party was delayed outside Johannesburg by a locust swarm making the rail track too slick for traction.[82] Apart from summer heat, grass would need to survive severe winter frosts and occasional snows, most notably the heavy blizzards of 16–18 August 1909, which killed off the eucalyptus groves encircling the Old Wanderers.[83] Water was in short supply, and its provision subject to furious political controversy. The city was reliant on springs, wells and minor rivers that were prone to dry up in summer and, before the South African War, a monopoly on supply subject to the machinations of the Johannesburg Waterworks Company, controlled by Sivewright and Barnato, a duo not known for plain dealing. Soaring demand was a consequence of runaway population growth and intensive industrial use. To boost efficiency, the mines were freed to make their own arrangements, but the general populace had to wait until the 1930s before connection to the Vaal River definitively solved Johannesburg's water crisis.[84] Back in 1904, Wanderers and TCU secretary George Allsop plaintively noted of the ground 'I don't think we shall ever succeed in getting grass to grow on it'.[85]

Moreover, resistance to turf was about to be hugely reinforced as, on 4 January 1906, before a crowd in excess of 10,000, a last-wicket partnership of 48 runs between Sherwell and 'Dave' Nourse gave South Africa a win by one wicket over England, their first ever Test match victory. When Sherwell dispatched an Albert Relf full toss past square leg for the winning four, The Wanderers erupted with abruptly released tension. 'Men were shrieking hysterically, some even were crying, and hats and sticks were flying everywhere'.[86] Represented by the same eleven players in all five Tests, nine of them Transvaal players (though none were born there), South Africa won the series decisively, by four Tests to one.[87] The MCC, so recently successful in Australia, had signally failed to come to terms with South Africa's battery of googly bowlers, their depth in both disciplines and their mastery of matting.[88] Despite the jeremiads about matting, South Africa appeared after all to have established cricketing parity with the Ashes nations. By renovating the googly, a form that English cricket had already all but jettisoned, South Africa seemed to have contrived its own matting-based vernacular, and hoisted itself into the Golden Age.

Natal and the Threat of Secession

Despite their overpowering influence, Bailey and the Transvaal did not always have things their own way. With Western Province cricket in eclipse however, it was from Natal that the strongest challenge to Transvaal hegemony came. Undergoing profound economic transformation, and roused by the alarms of the 1906 Bambatha Rebellion, the colony of Natal had lately adopted a more vigorous approach to both internal and external relations, and its cricket union too had come to reflect this assertive mood. The 1906/07 Currie Cup was held in Johannesburg and Pretoria under the 'Single Centre' system to allow the Selection Committee for the England tour of 1907 access to all matches.[89] The Rand was then in the grip of sharp depression following the withdrawal from the mines of Chinese labour, and this badly affected gates, that yielded an average net take of less than £8.[90] Mainly on the strength of 'Dave' Nourse's superlative form Natal performed creditably, beaten only by Transvaal and finishing second in the table. Yet by the tournament's end, the Natal Cricket Union (NCU) faced a loss of £150, and so penurious was the Union that the loss had to be borne by the players.[91] Natal's anger was hardly assuaged by watching Durban-schooled Vogler, who had only ever played one Currie Cup match for the province before moving to the Transvaal, in record-breaking form in the EP ranks; nor by the announcement of the touring side that, with Cooley, Budgen and Carter missing out, featured only two Natal players—but included Vogler, Sherwell, White and Hathorn, all lured away from Natal to the Rand. As the team prepared for England, Bailey arranged for the large Transvaal contingent to travel to Cape Town via Natal and the Eastern Province where they played friendlies to generate funds and placate tempers.

Media reaction to the googly bowlers, who burst upon the unsuspecting English public as sensationally as the 1882 Australians had done, ensured that the tour of 1907 was financially successful, a first for South African cricket (and in a wet year too).[92] The tour has been discussed at length elsewhere.[93] It is enough to note here that South Africa's bowlers kept her in the series; the wet summer offered no foundation for her matting-bred batsmen. Midway through the tour, Faulkner was the highest South African in the first-class batting averages, at 32, while in the bowling averages, he was last of the googly quartet, at 13.[94]

Publicity surrounding the tourists ensured that 'Dave' Nourse's antecedents became a matter of common knowledge. Shortly after the tour, it was announced that he had been offered a contract to play as a professional in 1909 for Surrey CC for whom, of course, he was qualified by birth.[95] Natal's anxiety at facing the loss of yet another star player turned to downright rage when it subsequently transpired that Bailey had made Nourse a counter-offer to keep him in South Africa, but as a *Transvaal* player.[96] The NCU, long an outsider of South African cricket, now threatened secession from SACA, an occurrence that would have seriously undermined Bailey's position in negotiations for the Triangular Tournament and the formation of the ICC, as well as generating unwelcome political fallout in the run-up to Union.[97]

Thus, in 1908/09, a Transvaal team under SACA and TCU secretary Ivor Difford was dispatched once more to Natal and the Eastern Cape—another with secession in its heart—to head off such a development. Bailey's emissaries were Difford, Schwarz and Theodore Bell. Even as they briefed the Natal press, a deal was being hatched in the background whereby Natal dropped their threat to secede, and agreed to the winding up of the Pietermaritzburg-based NCU in favour of a new Natal Cricket Association (NCA) to administer the game from Durban. In return, Transvaal agreed to subsidise Nourse to stay in Natal and also, from 1909/10, to support a Test at Lord's in Durban. 'Umpire' (J. T. Henderson) in the *Natal Mercury* applauded

> the good which has accrued from our association with gentlemen who are heart and soul in the dear old game of cricket ... men who think a lot about cricket, and the very best means of elevating the standard of play, not only in Johannesburg, but throughout South Africa ... Does Johannesburg want to rule the roost? If the devotees of the game in the Golden City do, it is a noble desire ...

On the question of player poaching too the *Mercury* absolved Transvaal of all blame:

> Johannesburg is the richest city in the continent, and it contains some very rich men who are devoted to cricket, and who back up the game for all they are worth, with money, and that which is even more valuable— influence. We are inclined to think that Johannesburg attracts good men from other centres. If a successful man be so attracted, can he be blamed? But I do not really believe that Johannesburg attracts such men to enrich Johannesburg cricket, but for the good of South African cricket.[98]

As if to celebrate their accession to the ranks of Test match hosts, Natal thereafter set about extending their unbeaten run over several years to fourteen Currie Cup matches, culminating in successive Cup-winning triumphs in 1910/11 and 1912/13. If that were not enough, they succeeded in 1913/14 where South Africa could not, handing J. W. H. T. Douglas's powerful MCC team, Barnes and all, their only defeat. By the fourth Test of this series, Natal had six players in the Springbok side, unprecedented, and a decade previously, unthinkable.

Bounce, Footwork and the Renovation of Batting

Meanwhile, the wider cricketing world fretted over the question of the googly's longevity. On a visit to England in 1908, Reggie Schwarz proclaimed 'There is little doubt that "googlie" bowling will occupy a very important place in first-class cricket in the future', and indeed, South Africa at least was planning on the basis of such confidence.[99] But other commentators were not so sure, believing they had already detected in contemporary batting signs of a response. The *Morning Post* proclaimed:

> It is very doubtful if the efficacy of "googlie" bowling is destined to last long. Quickness of foot is the outstanding virtue of modern batting, and it is a virtue which tells against slow bowling. No amount of break, expected or unexpected, is of use if the ball is not allowed to touch the ground, or if the bowler has to drop them short to avoid being hit full pitch.[100]

The import of the *Morning Post*'s intervention was clear. The googly was dangerous only where it was allowed to paralyse footwork, and footwork would be the key to its overcoming.

W. G. Grace had previously inaugurated the Golden Age when he solved the problem of bounce. He accomplished this by converting the problem into one of length. Before Grace, bowlers bowled short, for catches, or fuller, to attack the stumps, and batsmen played off the back foot or the front according to predilection. Since there was little bounce—on the 'scythe-cut wickets' of the day a delivery was as likely to creep as lift—line was a greater concern than length, and footwork was accordingly attuned to such discriminations.[101] But with the legalisation of over-arm bowling in 1864, on pitches now good enough to sustain such bowling, a third, more complex, dimension entered the equation. As Ranjitsinhji put it, 'An under-arm bowler can make the ball twist – that is, curl off the ground – but he cannot make it break or bump; a round-arm can make the ball twist from leg and break somewhat from the off and also cause it to swing across the wicket; and over-arm can do all these things and also make the ball bump', adding 'The higher the arm is allowed to go, the greater the skill required in a batsman'.[102]

Grace's solution to this new level of complexity was elegantly simple. If the length was full, he would go forward, to intercept the ball as close as possible to its pitch, before the bounce could do its work. If not, he would go back to meet the ball as late as possible, at the top of its bounce. Uniting these two formerly separate modes by means of footwork backwards or forwards along a central axis, he 'turned the old one-stringed instrument into a many-chorded lyre'.[103] In doing so, he revealed another essential feature of the game's new form that highlighted the crucial importance of the pitch: that cricket, unlike other ball games, was now a game played, not *on* the ground, but *from the ground up*. Whereas rugby and football depended on the body being correctly positioned to enable the movements of the feet or hands, in cricket it worked the other way, the positioning of the feet being crucial to create a still base whence the eyes could supervise the action of the hands. Effectively, Grace had refitted footwork in accordance with the new dominance of the factor of length over that of line and thus 'founded the modern theory of batting by making forward- and back-play of equal importance, relying neither on one nor the other, but on both'.[104]

Grace, says C. L. R. James, developed a 'comprehensive style' and so 'the whole body of batsmen followed him … and a generation of orthodox batsmen came into existence'.[105] The revolution in batting, however, was to be completed by others building on this base. For Grace was no stylist and, though he could play to leg, for him cricket was still predominantly an off-side game. Fry describes the awkwardness of his leg-side play:

> What W. G. did was to throw his left leg across the wicket to the off ball and treat it as if it were a ball to leg bowled to him from the direction of mid-off or extra cover.[106]

It fell to the stylists Ranjitsinhji, Trumper and Fry to complete Grace's revolution by giving full rein to the versatile new footwork. In the first place, they gave it amplitude: Trumper would 'jump out', or go right back on his stumps, and Ranjitsinhji in back foot play too was seen to utilise the full depth of the crease. More, they augmented Grace's method by opening up the leg-side. Trumper developed the on-drive to the point of perfection; off either foot, he would hit a ball from outside off past mid-on's right hand. Ranjitsinhji effectively turned the batting axis through 90 degrees via the dexterity of his wristwork, exploiting the game's then prevalent off-side bias, and adding to the common stock of shots the press and the glance, and with Fry, who learned both from Ranjitsinhji at Sussex and from the South Africans on matting, he added too the hook and the pull. Most of these strokes were aimed at exploiting the relatively unpopulated leg-side field that had resulted from the game's long established off-side bias, particularly behind square where, since the redundancy of the back-stop, any fielder at all was a rarity.[107]

Upon this revolutionary chassis of integrated footwork, batting found its summation in the Golden Age. Though its greatest exponent was a professional (Hobbs), the mode of batting that had been developed was, in its preoccupation with style and the cult of personality, a perfect vehicle for the ideology of the amateur, providing as it did a gateway not only for self-expression but, beyond averages, analyses or talent for the game, also for social ascription.

Eclipse of the Googly

Predictably, it was Jack Hobbs, in 1909/10, who killed off the googly using the weapon of consummate footwork, as the *Morning Post* had foreseen. It was customary for England selectors to pick a 'bolter' or two for each South African tour on the principle that the peculiar difficulties of batting on matting wickets would tighten up their techniques, especially their defensive play. This was a stratagem that stretched back to Fry and Warner and ahead to Wyatt and Hammond. Coming from a Surrey season of 2114 runs at 40.65, the young Hobbs was in imperious form. While South Africa's batsmen propped doggedly on the back foot, Hobbs took on the googly bowlers trusting to speed of foot and sureness of eye, scoring all round the wicket. When he went back he went right back, watching the turn carefully, but mostly he went forward, meeting the pitch of the ball, negating both turn and bounce. With his opening partner Rhodes he instigated a policy of drop and run, taking short singles seemingly at will to disrupt the bowling; since he was so far forward, it often must have seemed simpler to keep on going. That South Africa took the series 3-2 was due to the weakness of the MCC attack. This was a mistake they would not repeat, bringing Barnes on their next visit, but for now they had only Buckenham and Thompson, both of a type who held few fears for South Africa, and the lob-bowler Simpson-Hayward. Blythe was a threat, but only at Newlands, and on the hard wickets of Durban and Johannesburg, Rhodes and Woolley were 'regarded as pie' by South Africa's batsmen.[108] Certainly, the MCC had no one to compare with Vogler, then at his very peak with 36 wickets in the series, or the all-round performance of Faulkner, with 29 wickets and 545 runs at 60.55. Nonetheless, Hobbs reeled off scores of 89, 35, 53, 70, 11, 93*, 1, 0, and 187, his first Test hundred. Despite his fourth Test failure, his game improved as the tour went on, his defence becoming near impregnable. His only dismissal in the last Test was 'hit wicket' as he went too far back. In a single series, Hobbs had already revealed the outlines of his future greatness, and his arrival saw the googly depart, at least as a specific mode of attack, as anything more than a leg-break bowler's variant. For South Africa there was a further, covert significance to Hobbs's exploits since, sitting in the stands observing closely was Syd Gregory, son of 'Ned' and mainstay of the current Australians, dispatched in advance of South Africa's forthcoming visit to Australia by anxious planners who, riled at Bailey's antics, were leaving nothing to chance. Gregory took home with him intelligence of the means by which Hobbs had tamed the googly bowlers, at their best and on their own wickets.

The googly had not changed cricket in any essential way, only emphasised its fundamentals. Prophets of doom notwithstanding, it could be countered by means of footwork. South Africa's short Golden Age was ended barely five years after it had begun, experiencing heavy defeats successively in Australia in 1910/11, in the Triangular Tournament in 1912, and at home against J. W. H. T. Douglas's potent MCC combination of 1913/14. The First Test of that series featured no less than seven new Springbok caps. Gone were Schwarz, Vogler, Faulkner and White, Sherwell and Sinclair, Hathorn and Shalders, 'Tip' Snooke, L. J. Tancred, Llewellyn, Frank Mitchell and Sid Pegler. Opposed by a fluent and settled MCC, the selectors could not fathom out their best side, averaging three debutants per Test. As the generation of the googly bowlers broke apart, South African cricket descended into a downward spiral, a long period of discontinuity that mirrored the social and political dislocations of the time. In thirteen of the next fourteen Tests South Africa would pick at least one new cap, and not until the 1931/32 tour of Australia, 35 Tests hence, would the same eleven appear in consecutive internationals. Barnes was rampant, but there was mayhem off the pitch too as political energies unleashed by the South African War and unsatisfied by the Act of Union began to crystallise around a new dynamic. The tour took place against a backdrop of burgeoning militancy culminating in massive strikes. Minister of Defence Smuts responded in equally militant fashion, calling out the Army to put down the strikes by lethal means and following up by the illegal deportation of the ring leaders. With war in Europe looming, matters of cricket were pushed to one side.

The Migration to Turf

The changeover to turf was finally initiated during South Africa's post-War return to international cricket, with the short tour by Australia in 1921. As ever, South Africa took the long and complicated way round. Though Bailey was no longer in control of South African cricket, the machinery of direction that he had assembled remained intact, its ideological edge sharpened if anything by post-war conditions. Anxieties about the long-term future of Empire and the consequent marginalisation of English-speakers were repressed under a façade of normalcy, lending an overtone of shrill exaggeration to customary expressions of loyalty. These doubts were exacerbated by the rise of two insurgent nationalisms, African and Afrikaner. For both these groups, the gains of wartime had been negligible, and both were subject to the constantly sharpening pressure of capital in a way that English-speaking whites were not. Both were thus forced to set about long-term political projects, but though the two movements shared a capacity for cross-class appeal, Africans were deprived of a political base from which to organise. So while Afrikaner nationalists worked with a sense of imminence, elaborating political programmes to enact notions of '*baasskap*', African leaders, exasperated by Imperial equivocation, at length began to look across the Black Atlantic for new models of liberation.

The grand coalition of African nationalism would not be completed until after the Second World War. For now, the leadership was outflanked by its own rank-and-file as unions, chiefly Kadalie's ICU, traversed in reverse the path of urban migrant workers, back to the rural communities in which the new proletariat remained rooted, where economic hardship had provoked rising militancy. Government pushback took predictably violent forms: Bulhoek, the Bondelswarts affair, the Masabela shootings, and the 1921 strike by 70,000 African mine-workers, all quelled with minatory force. In the face of such unrelenting repression, the victories of African nationalism were as yet occasional and symbolic as when, black, green and gold having been appropriated as the colours of liberation, the rugby Springboks abandoned their customary black shorts for white lest there be any misconstrual.

Natal, with its vast African populace, was once again in assertive mode. The incorporation of Zululand in 1897 had seen the rapid advance of its white agricultural sector, chiefly the sugar plantations worked by indentured Indian labour, but by the 1920s the costs to the indigenous population in land hunger, overcrowding, disease and malnutrition, and terminal poverty were becoming overt. As African desperation rose and the ICU made inroads from their Durban base, sugar and cotton planters combined with conservative elements of the African population to reinforce indirect control, using traditional loyalties and institutions as a bulwark against militancy.[109] These processes of 're-tribalisation' and partition by the consolidation of native reserves were based on the methods of mid-nineteenth century Natal administrator Theophilus Shepstone, but they also provided a practical template underwriting the ideology of segregation then being propounded, predominantly, as Shula Marks observes, by 'Natal men': 'M. S. Evans, C. T. Loram, E. H. Brookes … and G. Heaton Nicholls'.[110] This ideology was paternalistic and liberal in inspiration, ostensibly aimed at protecting Africans from exploitation, but its effect was to facilitate in intensified forms the continued extraction of surplus value, and it was eagerly seized upon by Nationalist segregationists, becoming, in the late twenties and thirties, the basis of a new political compact between English-speakers and the emerging Afrikaner middle-class. The rise of the Zululand planters was confirmed in Eshowe in January 1923, when F. T. Mann's MCC took on a Zululand team for whom the batting was opened by one H. Hulett. Other family names in the line-up familiar to observers of Natal cricket and politics were Bissett, Moor, Pearse and Henwood. Natal's new political configuration was in evidence at Kingsmead too as Zulus in tribal regalia gathered on the field before the start of play in the Third Test in Durban to dance and sing, just one year shy of the fiftieth anniversary of Isandlwana, Rorke's Drift and the military campaign of 1879 that had first opened Zululand up to penetration by capital.[111]

With the eclipse of the googly bowlers, the chief justification for maintaining matting wickets had been swept away, and newly energised Natal prepared to mount a challenge. There were modernisers in the Transvaal cricket administration, most notably Stanley Pitts, frustrated by the continued adherence to South African cricket's conservative orthodoxies but they were as yet too weak to challenge established interests. In Natal, conditions were somewhat different. Its original cricketing establishment had been swept away with the winding up of the NCU, and the administration had little of the baggage that weighed down the Transvaal organisation. Led by H. L. Crockett who had been elected Chairman in 1921, modernisers held sway in Natal's administration.

The key figure in the migration to turf, Crockett was a Durban-based, Surrey-born accountant with extensive links to the Natal hide-tanning industry, who having fought with the Imperial Yeomanry in the South African War, had emigrated to South Africa in 1902.[112] The hide-tanning industry had surged during the Great War as a result of demand for belts, boots, straps and saddles, and may have connected Crockett not only with Australian arboriculturalists, but also with the sugar planters of Zululand.[113] In the matter of turf, by Crockett's own account:

> Having always played on turf until I came to this country, it has been a dream of mine to see cricket played under similar conditions here, but, until 1921, the Natal Cricket Association had insufficient funds to spend on what has always been regarded as impracticable. That view was largely brought about by the fact that unsuccessful experiments had been made in Durban and Johannesburg.[114]

Crockett's reference was to the 'experiments' of 1903, whose indifferent outcome had formed the basis of received wisdom in South African cricket circles, but there were two other factors now pushing in the opposite direction. Around the time Crockett became chairman, it was announced that Lord's ground in Durban was to be requisitioned for South African Railways expansion, and a move to land at nearby Kingsmead was negotiated. This presented an ideal opportunity to upgrade and modernise facilities, the better to ensure the endurance of Durban's status as a Test venue. (St. George's Park in Port Elizabeth, for a spell South Africa's premier cricket ground and scene of two of the country's first four Tests, had been granted only one Test since, and would have to wait until after World War Two for the next.)

The second factor was the arrival of 'Horseshoe' Collins's 1921 Australians, managed by Sydney Smith, Jr. Smith was a Sydney merchant with long experience of cricket administration. In the course of the tour Crockett had several long conversations with Smith and Warwick Armstrong, who convinced him 'that what had been done in Australia, under almost precisely similar climatic conditions, could also be done here if the right "top-dressing" were found', a view given further encouragement by Percy Fender in 1922.[115] Thereafter there ensued a sustained correspondence between Crockett in Durban and Smith in Sydney in the course of which Smith provided 'detailed information as to the laying and preparation of wickets in Sydney'. On the basis of this progress, the NCA in 1922 'voted the necessary money for a proper experiment', despite opposition from some quarters in Durban who feared the possibility of losing Test match host status.[116] On Tuesday, 10 July 1923 the *Sydney Morning Herald*, recalling Smith's correspondence with Crockett, announced that 'last Saturday, a shipment of Bulli soil was consigned by the *Sophocles* to the Natal Cricket Association, Durban'.[117] Crockett and groundsman Vic Robbins set about laying turf wickets according to Smith's instructions, one dressed with Bulli soil and the other with Mount Edgecombe soil that, of local soils, 'bore the nearest resemblance to "Bulli"'. After an extended period of testing, Crockett concluded that he was 'entirely satisfied' with the outcome of the experiment, proclaiming that 'turf wickets out here are a practical proposition, and … we are entirely justified in laying turf wickets on all the principal grounds in Durban'.[118]

With this success behind him, Crockett began to test the SACA waters, applying for the position of manager on the 1924 tour of England. This was in any circumstances an important and prestigious position but more so now for, leaving aside the Triangular Tournament, South Africa had not toured Britain for a full series since 1907. Moreover, this was the year of the British Empire Exhibition, to take place at Wembley simultaneously with the tour. Generally such a prize would go to a Transvaal man, and indeed, in the end it did again, but only in a second ballot, The Wanderers' George Allsop winning by ten votes to eight after the initial vote was tied.[119] Crockett also scored a palpable if limited hit when, at Captain Taylor's suggestion, SACA agreed to send the Transvaal contingent plus raw young fast bowler Bisset of Griquas to Cape Town via Durban for a week's practice on the only turf wicket in South Africa.[120]

It was a good tour to miss. The unexpected collapse of 1924 proved 'most disheartening, and shook South African cricket to its roots – even to its administrative roots'.[121] In the tour's aftermath South African cricket was pronounced 'decadent', and a 'period of reconstruction' called for.[122] At the meeting of 12 January 1925, a motion was passed that 'a conference should be held at which all unions could be directly represented and air their grievances'.[123] The politics of the reconstruction were so convoluted as require their own chapter, and were further complicated by the fact that the S. B. Joel tour, which brought yet more issues, was going on in the midst of the turbulence. At a Special General Meeting held in The Wanderers Boardroom on 6 February 1925, recriminations flew as delegates let rip. C. V. Becker (Border) summed up the mood. There was, he said, 'A feeling ... that matters concerning the Association are not properly run; that there is a tendency to log-rolling, and also that the delegates have not carried out their functions in the best interests of South African cricket but more from a parochial point of view'. There is little doubt that members held successive Transvaal administrations chiefly responsible for SACA's failures, for Becker opened the meeting by stating that it had been called in Johannesburg because to do otherwise 'would have meant practically condemning behind their backs those who had been responsible for running the Cricket Association in the past'. Allan Reid, an Orange Free State delegate but long associated with Western Province, agreed: 'The rock bottom', he thundered, 'is that the Transvaal wish to control South African cricket'.[124] Nonetheless, Transvaal's interests could not be ignored. A plan concerted by Pitts and Crockett gained traction to streamline SACA's decision-making by amalgamation and disaffiliation of marginal centres, and the creation of a Board of Control to assume full control of affairs, its five members to be directly elected annually by representatives of all centres, but with permanent membership for the 'Big Three' of Transvaal, Natal and Western Province.

Quid pro quo for the smaller centres accepting the Big Three's permanent accession to power was financial reconstruction, with a greater degree of revenue pooling and redistribution than in the past. Intended to ensure the well-being of non-Test status centres, this was a change Natal supported against Transvaal opposition. The third major plank of reconstruction, the abrupt about-turn certified by the humiliation of 1924, was a rush for turf wickets, and recognition of Natal's 'pioneer work'.[125] Only The Wanderers of the Test grounds, still under the control of its own Randlord-dominated committee and wedded to the 'birthright' of days gone by, resisted.[126] But even in most quarters of the Transvaal, the change was recognised as desirable and inevitable for in 1927 Charles Neustetel, a former wicketkeeper who had played a handful of matches for Transvaal in the pre-Union days, had offered SACA £1000 to establish a Turf Wicket Fund on condition SACA matched this donation pound-for-pound. By 1927, turf had invaded even The Wanderers for though the Club itself continued to resist installation on the wickets where Wanderers teams played (including the main field), the Johannesburg Pirates, who leased two fields at the ground, had applied for and received funding from the Turf Wicket Fund to lay turf, upon one of which a Transvaal XI played an experimental one-day friendly. The Wanderers Club authorities were said to be awaiting 'proof of durability'.[127]

On 16 and 17 December 1926, the first Currie Cup game on turf took place at Kingsmead in Durban, Natal defeating Border by an innings and 122 runs. Just under a year later, on 3, 5 and 6 December 1927, the first match on turf against international opposition was played, as Natal took on R. T. Stanyforth's MCC side in a drawn game. Before that, the swing to turf had gained even greater momentum from events in England as the ICC announced the cricketing equivalent of the Balfour Declaration, that henceforth all countries who received tours from, or sent tours to, England would be entitled to equal representation at the ICC.[128] This meant New Zealand in Tests but, pointedly, it also meant India and the West Indies, and the possible ramifications of this decision would be driven home in 1928 when, with South Africa in the midst of devising policies of segregation, SACA received an invitation to tour India in 1929, which it expediently ignored.

After experiments in 1926/27 and 1927/28, during which time visiting English coaches reported themselves satisfied the wickets would 'easily last a four days' match', J. J. Kotzé and Frank Creese converted Newlands' entire square to turf using 'Natal Bulli' for the season of 1928/29, and in place of a Currie Cup tournament that year, a 'Turf Wicket Tournament' was held simultaneously in Durban and Cape Town, serving as a trial for the 1929 touring team. Though they lost the series, the team of 1929 already showed distinct signs of improvement over 1924.[129] A new era of international cricket began in South Africa on New Year's Day, 1931 when, having already won The Wanderers' Test by a mere 28 runs, South Africa amassed 513, with three centuries from the top four, but were unable, quite, to finish off England within the allotted four days. Draws in the three remaining (matting) Tests gave South Africa its first series win over England since Union. 1935 would see their first wins—Test and series—in England as Herby Wade's side scraped home at Lord's and drew the rest (Fig. 3.1).

By 1930, St George's Park, birthplace of South Africa's matting wickets, had laid turf too, leaving only The Wanderers with matting among South African Test grounds. But the advantages of turf over matting were starting to weigh. Transvaal had won five of six Currie Cups in the Twenties, one shared; in the Thirties, Natal would win two and share one other of five. Even so, it took an ultimatum from SACA in 1934 to force the hand of The Wanderers Club membership who, at a Special General Meeting on 7 August 1934, exhibited 'hostility and long

Fig. 3.1 England's Wally Hammond bowled by Cyril Vincent for 3, MCC versus Transvaal on matting at The Wanderers, December 1930

argument' before accepting there was no alternative.[130] In March 1935, Transvaal belatedly entered the world of turf, piling up 609 against the Orange Free State.

There remained only the matter of Australia. In 1935/36, Victor Richardson's side handed South Africa their habitual hiding, but for the first time all five Tests were played on turf. Previously, in 1931/32 South Africa had been visitors themselves, losing 5-0 against a potent Australian side, and Louis Duffus noted how often South African batsmen still went back to balls of a length that brought Australians forward. However, in later years Duffus would speak of 'the change to turf [that] ushered in a new age, an age of confident batsmen who went forward to the pitch of the ball without fear of the pronounced spin to which their prede-cessors had been accustomed'.[131] To speed the integration of turf and technique, the newly-established Nuffield Tournament for schoolboys, a project set in motion by J. P. W. Howden, a close associate of Crockett in Durban, was explicitly declared a turf wicket tournament that could not be hosted by any province unable to provide turf wickets. Coming generations of players would at last be able to go forward 'without fear', if only in the narrowest technical sense. Finally, South African cricket could complete the revolution Grace had initiated.

Yet fear still ruled, for SACA continued to march in political lockstep with successive segregationist governments into the apartheid era, con-demning black cricketers and their Asian and Coloured compatriots to decades more in dismal conditions. Their only contact with turf would be as labourers. In the period of rapid economic expansion that followed the Second World War, the 'Old' Wanderers was expropriated for Railways' use, the fate that had once befallen Lord's in Durban, and for a decade Ellis Park was shared between rugby and cricket. In 1955 work on the 'New' Wanderers was commenced and by September the new ground was ready to receive grass. In accordance with the old Australian recipe, South African grounds were planted rather than turfed, and Charles Fortune witnessed the process:

> For this a labour squad of about a hundred Africans was used. It was a remarkable sight, for many of the workers were native women, with a tiny babe wrapped into the small of the back with a close-drawn shawl. All day they sang or chattered as in a line abreast they worked across the terrain … Such is the speed with which things grow in a Transvaal spring that … just two months from planting, the grass was ready for its first mowing.[132]

NOTES

1. A. Miller (ed.) and R. Webster (compiler), *First-Class Cricket in Australia, Volume 1, 1850–51 to 1941–42* (Victoria: Ray Webster, 1991), preface. In his excellent biographical work on the Gregory family, S. Wark refers to a match in 1881 between New South Wales and Victoria where, by agreement of the captains Murdoch and Cooper, each innings was played on a different pitch, but according to Miller this match was not at all unique. Miller also records a curious match in Adelaide in November 1877, the first ever first-class game on South Australian soil. After Tasmania had managed only 72 in reply to South Australia's first innings 182, the captains requested a new wicket for the second day's play even though the original wicket 'had played well until late in the afternoon'. Unfortunately, 'the change was anything but an improvement' and Tasmania were bowled out for 97 to lose by an innings and 13 runs (Miller and Webster, *First-Class Cricket in Australia*, 38).

2. S. Wark, *Book on the Gregorys*, thevictortrumpercricketboard.yuku.com, accessed 19 December 2014.

3. J. Pollard, *Australian Cricket: The Game and the Players* (London: Angus and Robertson, 1988), 11–12. According to Pollard, Schomburg advised the planting of couch grass as 'English clover and rye grasses would not withstand mid-summer heat'.

4. Pollard, *Australian Cricket*, 190; Sir D. Bradman, *The Bradman Albums: Selections from Sir Don Bradman's Official Collection, volume 1, 1925–1934* (London: Queen Anne Press, 1988), 12–18; www.espncricinfo.com/australia/content/ground/56407.html, accessed 1 May 2015. The Bellerive Oval was not at the time in use for first-class cricket, which was played until 1987 at the Queens Domain.

5. J. Noble, writing in 1915, claims to have played on matting in Kimberley as early as 1874, but the game he describes was a knockabout on a narrow scrap of matting laid along a cart-track. There were no boundaries, fielders were often waylaid by root or scrub or rut, and play was subject to frequent interruptions to allow carts loaded with 'maiden blue' to pass. See J. Noble, 'Early Days of Kimberley Cricket', M. Luckin (ed.), *The History of South African Cricket: Including the Full Scores of All Important Matches Since 1876* (Johannesburg: Hortor, 1915), 35.

6. W. Mars, 'The History of Cricket in the Western Province' in Luckin (ed.), *History of South African Cricket*, 139.

7. Though the argument for South African exceptionalism seems on first inspection to be based upon uncontroversial observations of then-prevailing environmental conditions, it was informed by a larger argument of impeccably conservative credentials: that both the natural

world, and the social world insofar as it reflected natural states of being, were structured according to ineluctable hierarchies wherein each thing was allotted its own 'natural' place. Grass grew simply and easily in the pastures of Europe, seemingly irrespective of human agency; not so here. Viewed in this light the argument reveals its kinship with another argument deployed to legitimise slavery and labour co-optation in numerous colonial settings: the notion that 'Europeans' were naturally unfitted to manual labour in tropical or sub-tropical environments but were providentially equipped rather to manage and direct the labour of indigenous non-Europeans better able to withstand such conditions.

8. *The Cricketer*, vol. 5, 17 May 1924, 74.
9. M. Fey, *Soils of South Africa* (Cambridge: Cambridge University Press, 2010), 44.
10. N. Tainton and J. Klug, *The Cricket Pitch and Its Outfield* (Pietermaritzburg: University of Natal Press, 2002), 7–13, 62.
11. See, for instance, W. Beinart, 'Fire, Vegetation Change, and Pastures, 1860–1880' in *The Rise of Conservation in South Africa: Settlers, Livestock, and the Environment 1770–1950* (Oxford and New York: Oxford University Press, 2003), 99–127.
12. Private correspondence with Peter Muzzell, UCBSA pitch consultant 30 July 2014; Andrew McLean, Humewood Golf Club, 24 July 2014.
13. According to De Kiewiet, one unnamed Australian governor referred to Australia's Frontier War as part of the 'natural progress of the aboriginal race towards extinction': C. de Kiewiet, *A History of South Africa: Social and Economic* (Oxford: Oxford University Press, 1942), 179.
14. W. Hancock, *Australia* (London: Ernest Benn, 1930), 4.
15. C. Feinstein, *An Economic History of South Africa: Conquest, Discrimination and Development* (Cambridge: Cambridge University Press, 2005), 3.
16. Ibid., 91–93.
17. R. Ross, 'The Origins of Capitalist Agriculture in the Cape Colony' in Beinart, Delius, and Trapido (eds.), *Putting A Plough to the Ground*, 58.
18. Feinstein, *An Economic History*, 91–93.
19. L. Curtis, *With Milner in South Africa* (Oxford: Basil Blackwell, 1951), 226.
20. J. M. Coetzee, *White Writing: On the Culture of Letters in South Africa* (New Haven and London: Yale University Press, 1988), 11.
21. Ibid., 5, 9, 11, 43.
22. P. Rich, *Hope and Despair: English-Speaking Intellectuals and South African Politics 1896–1976* (London: British Academic Press, 1993), 5, 200–1.
23. C. Tatz, *Shadow and Substance in South Africa: A Study in Land and Franchise Policies Affecting Africans 1910–1960* (Pietermaritzburg: University of Natal Press, 1962), 31.

24. J. X. Merriman to Professor G. Smith, 26 October 1907 in P. Lewsen (ed.), *Selections from the Correspondence of John X. Merriman 1905–24* (Cape Town: The Van Riebeeck Society, 1969), 54.
25. 'The very presence of black men in large numbers,' wrote Lionel Curtis in 1901, 'makes the white minority indolent and incompetent ... It would be a blessed thing for [white South Africans] if the [black man] like the Red Indian tended to die out before us, for he acts like decay among teeth' (Curtis, *With Milner*, 226).
26. Examples of this are legion, but William Beinart provides a compelling example in his account of the campaign to eradicate Prickly Pear. See chapter 8, *The Rise of Conservation in South Africa*. For an account of an entire industry started in unsuitable conditions predicated almost entirely upon the advantage of black labour, see M. Schnurr, 'The Boom and Bust of Zululand Cotton, 1910–1933', *Journal of Southern African Studies*, 37, 1 (2011), 119–34.
27. Coetzee, *White Writing*, 36–62.
28. S. Marks and S. Trapido (eds.), *The Politics of Race, Class and Nationalism in Twentieth Century South Africa* (London and New York: Longman, 1987), 3.
29. A. Kendal Millar, *Plantagenet in South Africa: Lord Charles Somerset* (Cape Town, London and New York: Oxford University Press, 1965), 88, 102. See also '*A Proper Degree of Terror: John Graham and the Cape's Eastern Frontier*' (Johannesburg: Ravan Press, 1986), 40–41, where Ben Maclennan asserts that Spanish merinos were imported from Holland as early as 1789, and that their introduction to the eastern Frontier was largely the work of a predecessor of Somerset as Governor, Sir John Cradock.
30. Feinstein, *An Economic History*, 28; E. J. Inngs, 'Mfengu Beach Labour and Port Elizabeth Harbour Development', Contree, *Journal for South African Urban and Regional History*, 21 (1987).
31. Ross, 'The Origins of Capitalist Agriculture in the Cape Colony', 70.
32. W. Beinart, *The Rise of Conservation in South Africa: Settlers, Livestock and the Environment 1770–1950* (Oxford and New York: Oxford University Press, 2003), 45.
33. Ibid., xviii–xix.
34. T. Keegan, *Colonial South Africa and the Origins of the Racial Order* (London: Leicester University Press, 1996), 71.
35. 'The development of commerce and commercial capital brings about everywhere an orientation of production towards exchange values ... Commerce therefore has everywhere more or less of a dissolving influence on the existing organisation of production, which, in all its different forms, is primarily oriented towards use value'. Karl Marx, 'Forms of

Property and Modes of Production' in T. B. Bottomore and Maximilien Rubel, *Karl Marx: Selected Writings in Sociology and Social Philosophy* (Harmondsworth: Penguin Books, 1973), 124.

36. The *Standard Bank of South Africa, Limited* was founded in London by John Paterson in 1862, one of the first companies started up under the Limited Liability clauses of Britain's new *Companies Act*. Paterson was an Aberdeen-born teacher, founder of the Grey Institute (later Grey High School), reborn as a Port Elizabeth merchant and Member of the Legislative Assembly (MLA). Reflecting his own separatist sympathies, Paterson established the bank's international headquarters in Port Elizabeth with 'local' offices in Cape Town and London. The *Eastern Province Herald* [*23 Dec 1862*] was quick to applaud this reversal of general practice—unsurprisingly, since Paterson was in secret its proprietor—that would bring the area 'into closer and direct contact with monied men of the old world, who will soon find that the South African Colonies offer a fine field for legitimate trading … and the profitable employment of surplus capital'. By 1865, however, after a run of double-digit dividends followed by well-publicised London share offerings, the old world monied men began to smell a rat. Sent to investigate, Lewis (later Sir) Michell found the fox already fled: local directors had sold their holdings and siphoned off large amounts of capital into other speculative enterprises. It was discovered that the Port Elizabeth office had been running:

> a system of unlimited credit. Private persons ran accounts with their tradesmen for all the necessaries of life, and payment, which was at rare intervals, took the delusive form of promissory notes, frequently renewed.
>
> Retail dealers, in their turn, gave six months' acceptance to the merchants and the latter fell back on their home supporters. Everybody took and gave credit, bad debts were common, and prices therefore ruled high. (Amphlett, 24)

Among the merchants who had taken advantage of unlimited credit facilities, it transpired, was Paterson's own firm. In 1866 the bank was forced to restructure, £73,000 in bad debts written off, and Paterson bankrupted. The price of money was forced up and the taps of credit abruptly shut off. Amphlett dubbed 1866 'the year of convulsion' as 'the whole fabric of credit was shaken to its foundations': G. Amphlett, *History of the Standard Bank of South Africa Ltd 1862–1913* (Glasgow: Robert Maclehose and Co., 1914), 26. The ensuing depression lasted into the 1870s.

37. Ibid., 3; I. Markman, www.stgeorgespark.nmmu.ac.za/contents/grounds, accessed 18 July 2014.

38. Unattributed press article reproduced by Ivor Markman, www.stgeorg-espark.nmmu.ac.za/contents/grounds, accessed 18 July 2014.
39. There was a marked improvement in scoring over the fourteen-year history of the Champion Bat tournaments, but this was neither even nor unbroken. Two of the five tournaments, in 1876 and 1884, were held at St George's Park, the latter on matting. In 1876, 82.7% of innings ended in fewer than 10 runs at an average runs per wicket (RPW) of 7.06. There were no scores above 50, and only 4 (2.16%) of 30 or more. By 1884 (on matting), the RPW had risen from 7.06 to 13.10, an 86% increase, and the percentage of single-figure scores fallen from 82.7 to 61.08%. Scores between 10 and 29 rose from 15.14 to 27.59%, of 30 and above to 7.88%, and above 50 to 3.45%. However, the King William's Town tournament of 1880, played without matting, exhibited a far larger relative increase over 1876's RPW (10.97, an increase of 55%), than was subsequently achieved between 1880 and 1884 (13.10, an increase of only 19%). This suggests that there were other factors at work apart from matting, for instance the progressive introduction of professional coaches after 1882 when Port Elizabeth blazed a trail by hiring H. H. Webster of Yorkshire. Yet against this, the Grahamstown tournament of 1887 that reverted to wickets without matting, exhibited a dramatic decline in RPW (10.27, a decrease of 22%) and a distribution of score that closely mirrored that of the last previous 'primitive wicket' tournament in King William's Town, with seven innings in ten ending in single-figure scores (70%), and only 4 scores above 30 (1.82%).
40. J. Noble, 'Early Days of Kimberley Cricket' in Luckin (ed.), *History of South African Cricket*, 37–38.
41. P. Warner and H. Hutchinson (ed.), *The 'Country Life' Library of Sport: Cricket* (London: Country Life, 1903), 397–400.
42. H. Crockett, 'Turf Wickets in South Africa' in Luckin (ed.), *South African Cricket 1919–27* (Johannesburg: The Author, 1927), 37.
43. *The Cricketer*, 3 May 1924, vol. 5, no. 1, 3.
44. Mills, who came to Kimberley as a professional, played two games for Surrey in 1888, having previously been on the staff of Surrey Club and Ground alongside Frank Shacklock and the young 'Bills', Brockwell and Lockwood.
45. 'Second Slip', 'A Review' in *The Cricketer Spring Annual, The Cricketer*, vol. 10, 1929, 8.
46. Luckin, *History of South African Cricket*, 365.
47. 13,003 miles by steamer, 754 by coach and 2218 by rail: 15,975 in all. The trip from start to finish lasted 146 days, of which 41 were spent on board ship and 25 in coach, cart or train: W. Bettesworth and F. Ashley-Cooper, *Chats on the Cricket Field* (London: Merritt and Hatcher, 1910), 225.

48. J. Winch, 'The Role of the Press' in Murray and Vahed (eds.), *Empire and Cricket: The South African Experience 1884–1914* (Pretoria: University of South Africa, 2009), 53.
49. C. van Onselen, *Studies in the Social and Economic History of the Witwatersrand 1886–1914, vol. 1: New Babylon* (Harlow and New York: Longman, 1982), 11.
50. G. Allsop, 'Reminiscences of Cricket' in Luckin (ed.), *History of South African Cricket*, 127–28.
51. R. Parry, 'In A Sense Citizens, but Not Altogether Citizens: Rhodes, Race and the Ideology of Segregation at the Cape in the Late Nineteenth Century', *Canadian Journal of African Studies*, 17, 3 (1983).
52. Sir T. Fuller, KCMG, *The Right Honourable Cecil John Rhodes: A Monograph and Reminiscence* (London: Longman, 1910), 29.
53. Merriman to J. Currey, 9 May 1896 in Phyllis Lewsen, *Selections from the Correspondence of John X. Merriman*, 226.
54. There were five Bishops' Old Boys in the side. Eight of the fourteen-strong party were from Western Province, not including Tancred and Sinclair, both Cape-born but resident in the Transvaal.
55. R. Mendelsohn, *Sammy Marks: 'The Uncrowned King of the Transvaal'* (Cape Town: David Philip, 1991), 238. "When he heard, after Rhodes's death, that Abe Bailey vainly believed that the mantle of the Great Cecil had descended upon him, he told the Cape millionaire, who had taken over both Rhodes's Muizenberg house and his parliamentary constituency that 'I have dealt in old clothes myself and you can take it from me they never fit'."
56. *Cricket*, vol. 21, 1902, 346; *Cricket*, vol. 27, 1908, 33; H. Lamb, 'The Wanderers Club' in Luckin (ed.), *History of South African Cricket*, 357.
57. L. Tancred, 'The Australians in South Africa, 1902' in Luckin (ed.), *History of South African Cricket*, 632.
58. Attempting to inject a note of realism after the drawn first Test, the *Natal Mercury* wrote of the Australians that they had been 'three weeks on the water, and then three nights on a train. They played on a strange wicket, in strange weather, and against men they held cheaply from the first' (Cited in *Cricket*, vol. 21, 1902, 457).
59. *The Cricketer*, vol. 5, 1924, 4.
60. *The Cricketer*, vol. 2, 2 September 1922, 18.
61. *The Cricketer*, vol. 8, 1927, 389.
62. *Cricket*, vol. 22, 1903, 225.
63. *The Cricketer*, vol. 8, 1927, 390.
64. *The Cricketer*, vol. 5, 17 May 1924, 73–74; vol. 8, 1927, 390.
65. *Cricket*, vol. 20, 1901, 445.

66. *Cricket*, vol. 25, 1905, 447.
67. *Cricket*, vol. 25, 1906, 449.
68. The Consolidated Gold Fields of South Africa, Limited, *The Gold Fields 1887–1937*, 63.
69. Ibid., 73.
70. W. Benjamin, 'The Work of Art in the Age of Mechanical Reproduction' in Hannah Arendt (ed.), *Walter Benjamin: Illuminations* (London: Fontana, 1973), 226–27.
71. For an account of Abe Bailey's role in the genesis of the ICC, see B. Murray, 'Abe Bailey and the Foundation of the Imperial Cricket Conference' in Murray and Vahed (eds.), *Empire and Cricket*, chapter 14.
72. *Cricket*, vol. 27, 1908, 264.
73. *Cricket*, vol. 27, 1908, 90.
74. Marks and Trapido, *The Politics of Race, Class and Nationalism*, 3.
75. Gutsche, *Old Gold*, 19–29.
76. Luckin, *History of South African Cricket*, 816.
77. In 1906, for instance, on Bailey's advice, the Board of the TCU spent £887-10s on 100 Premium Preference Shares, 'upon which they afterwards received a dividend ... of 6s 3d per share, equal to £31-5s': *Cricket*, vol. 25, 1906, 431.
78. The TCU's share of net receipts from the four tour games played at the Wanderers during the tour of 1905/06 amounted to £4 440-2-3. SACA's share (15% of tour matches and 25% of Tests) was £606-5-9.
79. Luckin, *History of South African Cricket*, 357.
80. Warner, *The MCC in South Africa*, 55.
81. *The Cricketer*, vol. 8, 1927, 200.
82. C. B. Fry, *Life Worth Living* (London: Eyre and Spottiswoode, 1939), 109.
83. www.snowreport.co.za/history-of-snow-in-south-africa-1853-2014, accessed 15 January 2016.
84. Water was central to the ore-milling process: 1520 litres of water were needed to mill one ton of gold-bearing gravel, and between 1889 and 1898 the number of mills rose from 316,163 to 7.3 million. J. Tempelhoff, 'On Laburn's "Mystery" Query—A Prehistory of the Vaal River as Water Source of the Witwatersrand (1887–99)', *Historia*, 45, 1, May 2000, 88–117.
85. *Cricket*, vol. 23, 1904, 401.
86. Warner, *The MCC in South Africa*, 74.
87. Three were born in the Northern or Western Cape, three in the Eastern Cape, three in Natal, and Schwarz and Nourse in Kent and Surrey respectively.
88. Though according to Sherwell, only Schwarz and Faulkner bowled the googly as yet.

89. Luckin, *History of South African Cricket*, 273.
90. According to the *Times of Natal*, the receipts net of expenses for 30 gates (that is, ten three-day matches) were only £235 [Cited in *Cricket*, vol. 26, 1907, 74]. In the end both the TCU and SACA agreed to donate their 20% share towards the 1907 tour guarantee [*Cricket*, vol. 26, 1907, 27].
91. *Cricket*, vol. 26, 1907, 74.
92. South Africa's profit over the three Tests was £2,558-1-6, the lion's share of which would be returned to TCU coffers as the greatest contributor to the guarantee [*Cricket*, vol. 26, 1907, 458].
93. For the 1907 tour, see G. Levett, 'Constructing Imperial Identity: The 1907 South African Cricket Tour of England' in Murray and Vahed, *Empire and Cricket*, chapter 13. For more on Bosanquet, Schwarz, and the development of the googly, see R. Parry and D. Slater, 'The Googly, Gold and the Empire: The Role of South African Cricket in the Imperial Project, 1904–1912' in Murray and Vahed (eds.), *Empire and Cricket*, chapter 12.
94. *The American Cricketer*, vol. 30, 1907, 234.
95. *Cricket*, vol. 27, 1908, 88.
96. *Cricket*, vol. 27, 1908, 154.
97. *Cricket*, vol. 27, 1908, 458.
98. *Natal Mercury*, cited in *Cricket*, vol. 27, 1908, 115–16.
99. *Cricket*, vol. 27, 1908, 137.
100. *Cricket*, vol. 27, 1908, 163.
101. *The Cricketer*, vol. 3, 1922–1923, 20.
102. Prince Ranjitsinhji, *The Jubilee Book of Cricket* (London: William Blackwood and Sons, 1897), 459–60.
103. Ibid., 460.
104. Ibid.
105. A. Grimshaw (ed.), *C. L. R. James: Cricket* (London: Allison and Busby, 1986), 247.
106. C. B. Fry, cited in David Kynaston, *W. G.'s Birthday Party* (London: Chatto and Windus, 1990), 18.
107. In *The Jubilee Book of Cricket*, Ranjitsinhji provides 'Plans' of field settings recommended for different types of bowlers in varying conditions. Disregarding the field for the lob-bowler, only three of fourteen fields recommend any fielder behind square on the leg-side, and in each of these three cases, only as an alternative to other more favoured placements (Ranjitsinhji, *The Jubilee Book of Cricket*, 114–27).
108. *The Cricketer*, vol. 8, 1927, 521.
109. S. Marks, 'Natal, the Zulu Royal Family and the Ideology of Segregation' in W. Beinart and S. Dubow (eds.), *Segregation and Apartheid in Twentieth Century South Africa* (London: Routledge, 1995; Taylor and Francis e-book edition, 2003).

110. Ibid.
111. *WOOP ... WOW ... ZUNG ... ZOO!!! (1928)*, Pathe film clip, www.britishpathe.com, accessed 5 June 2015.
112. *Cricket*, vol. 5, 17 May 1924, 73–74.
113. The most important tanning agent in South African hide preparation was a tannin derived from the *Acacia Mearnsii*, or the Australian Black Wattle. This tree had first been imported to South Africa in 1864 and planted extensively at Camperdown in Natal by John Vanderplank for timber, telegraph poles and pit props. Subsequent uses were of the bark for paper, dyes and tanning. There were strong links between wattle production and sugar planting as the two grew best in similar soils and climatic conditions, and together shared Natal's northern coast 'mist belt'. It was soon discovered that planting sugar in fields where black wattle was formerly grown greatly expanded yields, the slow decay of wattle litter increasing the soil's nitrogen content. Wattle plantations therefore provided the perfect form of diversification for Zululand's sugar barons, since over a cycle of twenty or thirty years they could be rotated into high-yield sugar crops (G. Darby, 'Characteristics of Some Wattle Soils', *Proceedings of the South African Sugar Technologists' Association*, March 1965).
114. *Cricket*, vol. 5, 17 May 1924, 73–74.
115. Ibid., 74.
116. Ibid.
117. *Sydney Morning Herald*, 10 July 1923, 12.
118. *Cricket*, vol. 5, 17 May 1924, 74.
119. Minutes of SACA Meeting, 8 February 1924 and 19 February 1924.
120. Minutes of SACA Tour sub-committee, 10 March 1924.
121. Luckin, *South African Cricket 1919–1927*, 17.
122. Ibid., 18.
123. Minutes of SACA meeting 12 January 1925.
124. Minutes of SACA meeting 6 February 1925.
125. SACA Annual Report for the Year ended 31 July 1928, 4.
126. S. Pardon, 'Notes by the Editor', *Wisden Cricketers' Almanack* (London: John Wisden and Co., 1913), accessed 24 March 2015. In response to Frank Mitchell's post-Triangular Tournament call for South Africa to develop other bowling skills than the googly, Pardon wrote: 'This does not seem wise or reasonable. The "googlie" failed in Australia, but though it has not had the devastating effect on cricket that certain extremists predicted it is still a power on the matting wickets at Johannesburg, Durban and Cape Town. To ask South African bowlers to give it up is like telling them to part with their birthright'.
127. *The Cricketer*, vol. 8, 1927, 80.

128. *The Cricketer*, vol. 7, 1926, 106, 388.
129. *The Cricketer*, vol. 8, 1927, 390; www.espncricinfo.com/ci/content/story/60245.html, accessed 20 April 2015.
130. Gutsche, *Old Gold*, 172.
131. Louis Duffus (compiler), *South African Cricket 1927–1947: Volume III* (Johannesburg: SACA, 1947), 11.
132. Charles Fortune, *The MCC Tour of South Africa 1956–57* (London: George G. Harrap and Co., 1957), 65.

PART II

The Players

African Cricket on the Rand: Piet Gwele, Frank Roro and the Shaping of a Community

Richard Parry

African Cricketers and the Making of an 'Elite'

The adoption of cricket among African and other black communities, on the mission stations and the Kimberley Diamond Fields in the 1880s and 1890s, played a significant role in enabling black players and administrators to define themselves within the evolving South African political economy. While playing cricket implied a badge of commitment to imperial values, black cricket survived the extended death throes of the Cape liberal dream (where culture not race defined human potential) and continued to play a disproportionate part in the long struggle over race, class and the impact of segregation in South Africa. This chapter suggests that African elites on the Witwatersrand between the 1920s and 1940s used cricket and the opportunities which sport as a whole provided as a channel through which to exert political and economic leadership in the

R. Parry (✉)
London, UK

© The Author(s) 2018
B. Murray et al. (eds.), *Cricket and Society in South Africa, 1910–1971*, Palgrave Studies in Sport and Politics,
https://doi.org/10.1007/978-3-319-93608-6_4

face of ever tightening colour bars focused on employment, restrictions on movement, land ownership and vestigial voting rights.

The history of black cricket in South Africa is also part of the broader national struggle to maintain a unity of black identity among Africans, Indians, coloureds and Malays struggling to find ways of resisting the racist system which, throughout the period from the beginning of Union, sought to control society along racial lines. The ring-fencing of cricket between whites and the rest was effectively established in 1894, with the de-selection of the 'coloured' player, 'Krom' Hendricks, from the South African team for the first UK cricket tour. Once it was clear that only whites counted as South Africans, the question then became whether blacks could resist the state's divide and rule strategy based on both race and class. In cricket, this translated into whether blacks could maintain the inclusive structures underpinning the non-racial values of the 'Barnato Board' created at the turn of the century. 'Barnato' cricket survived until the late 1920s, when the game split into separate ethnic structures, but by the mid-1930s, the Inter-Race Cricket Board in the Transvaal was already taking the first step back towards a unified non-racial cricketing framework.

African elites played the game not only because they loved it, but also because it fulfilled a role in reinforcing their class position in the complex and dangerous realities of domination from above and challenges from below. But black cricket was not simply a weapon in the class struggle; it was a game played by a talented community whose exploits, both as cricketers and as leaders, deserve recognition. This chapter is intended to shine a light on their cricketing and other achievements hitherto ignored within the South African racist discourse.

African players and administrators such as Frank Roro, Piet Gwele, Hamilton Masiza, Sol Senaoane, Titus Majola, H. B. Piliso, John Mpiliso, D. M. Denelane and Dan Twala shaped their world in their own economic and political interests and those of the wider community. They were part of an elite (the *amaRespectables*) separated from the vast majority of migrant African workers by their mission education and permanent urban residence.[1] They were drawn predominantly from around two thousand *malabanas* (mine clerks/interpreters) and *indunas* (head men), differentiated economically and culturally from two hundred thousand migrant workers slaving deep underground on short-term contracts under highly restrictive conditions. Both permanent elites and migrant workers shared ethnic, linguistic and political roots, as well as the coercive experience of a racist denial of political and economic rights. In structural terms, the elites were a classic petty bourgeoisie, responsible for administering and controlling the labour force on behalf of management on the one hand, while resembling the working class in performing manual or menial labour.

At the same time, the industrial colour bars formed an iron ceiling between black and white mine employees blocking any chance of black advancement. The colour bars were the theatre for skirmishes between both whites and Africans, and African elites and unskilled workers. African elites were caught on the horns of a strategic dilemma—how far to maintain their own position of relative class privilege through separation from the migrant labour force or ally themselves with them.

What this community lacked in size, it made up for in its significance in the mining moral economy. Caught in the middle of complex economic forces, the *malabana* class exploited the moral economy within which they operated and invented and networked their way to increased opportunities in the nooks and crannies of the system. The mining industry and the Municipality on the Rand encouraged sports participation as a mechanism for social and labour control among the black population. Cricket was encouraged as a means to differentiate the elites from migrant workers, reducing the ever-present white fear of a black industrial alliance.

From the participants' perspectives, cricket opened employment doors and increased job security within large mines. But the reasons they played lay partly in the economic and social opportunities opened up by the operation of the game. Control over cricket meant control over a significant community with disposable income, and a social network. Cricket had its own economy with money changing hands for subscriptions, ticket sales and gate money, refreshments and food, equipment and clothing, printing and trophies. Cricket teams needed transport, grounds and practice facilities, some but not all of which were sponsored. But perhaps even more significantly, cricket allowed for access into an underground economy characterised by the availability of alcohol, banned in principle on the Rand beyond minimally alcoholic compound rations.

Cricket matches provided significant opportunities for illegal beer sales and *skokiaan* drinking, *dagga* dealing and betting operations. Thanks to their duration, leisurely unfolding afternoons at the cricket lent themselves to extensive social engagement across the Rand and gave

African entrepreneurs access to a market of relatively affluent consumers, conscious of their social and class positions, and eager to enhance their status and attractiveness through fashionable clothes, culture and style. Most importantly, for a preponderantly male population, cricket provided an opportunity to meet women, who expressed their class aspirations outside the less genteel environments of *shebeens* and mine compounds.

African cricketers performed to a high standard, clearly comparable to white cricket in the period. To do so, they had to overcome huge odds to perform in a game uniquely dependent on physical conditions. The state of pitches, outfields and equipment would have horrified their white counterparts, had they even been aware that Africans too played the game.

African cricket was always played in the shadow of the white game which unfolded on verdant grounds diligently prepared by black workers for whites' enjoyment. Cricket was only a small if visible example of how the advantages and opportunities open to whites were directly and indirectly underwritten by a black workforce.

But it was not just cricket that a small group of African leaders used to build their community. The absence of opportunities for political engagement beyond the restricted possibilities provided by the Transvaal Native Mine Clerks Association, the Industrial and Commercial Workers Union or (until the late 1940s) the relatively moribund ANC encouraged Africans in this period to control and administer a bewildering amount of sporting activity on the Rand. A small group of a couple of dozen leaders, lacking political and economic opportunities for building a community and exercising power, stepped into the cultural vacuum and organised and controlled the participation of thousands in a network of football, rugby, tennis and athletics competitions, in addition to cricket itself.

In summary, this chapter suggests that African cricket on the Rand provided a mechanism for Africans to define themselves ideologically, exert leadership, develop institutions and create and leverage political, social and particularly economic opportunities otherwise denied to them. It was part of a broader strategy encompassing experiences, networks and opportunities in town, on the mines and in the rural areas. African workers, even if classed as 'elites' in the mining hierarchy, needed as Ralph Callebert has noted in the case of Durban dock workers, to exploit all economic possibilities, and livelihood strategies straddled wage labour and informal trade as well as the rural and the urban.[2]

CRICKET, MINE CULTURE AND THE MORAL ECONOMY

After the South African War (1899–1902), fought primarily to control the mining industry, the chase was on for the slender veins of gold spreading downwards from the exhausted outcrops, deep into the bowels of the Witwatersrand. But the cost structure of the industry was determined by the fixed price of gold, and the cost of accessing it kilometres below the surface. Consequently, in the decade after the war, following a failed experiment with Chinese labour, gold mining was reconstructed on the basis of a huge black migrant labour force allowing most of the costs of social reproduction to fall on the increasingly impoverished rural areas, thus minimising wages. These workers were housed in overcrowded and insanitary prison-like compounds to maximise labour control.[3] In addition, the system required a phalanx of underground 'boss boys' responsible for production; an elite group permanent African overseers (*indunas*), who appointed their own black 'police boys' and an educated cohort of clerks and personnel assistants (*malabanas*), responsible for the administration, establishment and maintenance of order; and a white semi-skilled work force with job protection (thanks to a colour bar on blasting certificates) and monopoly access to the political process.

The hazardous working and insanitary living conditions endured by migrant workers caused appalling annual labour death rates, at times amounting to around 10% of the annual labour force. The African 'permanent' labour force played a key role in recruitment, social control and management of labour unrest. They were responsible for regulating the informal trading economy, preventing drinking and other 'undesirable' behaviour. The moral economy of the mining industry ran deep, both inside and outside the compounds, and for underground migrant workers, the intensity of their experience made survival a source of pride, and resistance a badge of honour. And for the elites, their survival and their ability to wield power, sometimes against but often in conjunction with the needs of migrant workers, meant that they were able to substantially remake the world they found themselves in their own terms. White managers, despite their pretensions of control, expressed their power more in ignorance, or in turning a blind eye, than in knowledge.

Consequently, *indunas* and other permanent workers exercised relatively untrammelled power, presiding over *imiteto*, both formal and unwritten rules which governed daily interaction and regulated the three main foci of mine culture—drugs (*dagga*), alcohol and sex.

Black mine officials ensured, for example, that *dagga* and knife searches were conducted at specific and predictable times (often standard practice in prisons).[4] The building of an alliance between permanent workers and migrants was a mutually beneficial means to exploit the myriad of economic opportunities which conditions on the mines provided for petty trade, and other illicit activities. These served a specific purpose in the overall scheme of the mining economy, as the mines were in constant competition for relatively scarce labour throughout this period, and workers selected the mines they wanted to work on, considering potential quality of life, as well as their very real understanding of benefits and risks. While the *indunas* and *mabalanas* were exploiting the opportunities which such power brought, African migrant workers, as Dunbar Moodie has suggested, were equally able to subvert the formal structure of the institution of the compound for their own ends.[5]

Cricket was an unlikely, even outlandish, element in this extreme and dangerous world, but its significance for the elite was partly in its ideological distancing from the work processes themselves. It provided an entry point into the overall mine structure for educated Africans and a cultural outlet for African elites who supervised what was effectively a prison system including dangerous hard labour. And more significantly, cricket created an economy of its own including preparation and maintenance of grounds and matting, travel and transport, membership fees, subscriptions, the sale of tickets, prizes and trophies, and of cricket clothing and equipment. It was no co-incidence that tailors and clothes salesmen were involved in cricket, and that, for example, Herby Taylor's sports outfitters sponsored trophies for black cricket leagues. Cricket represented a long and leisurely afternoon out, where the social event blended seamlessly with the game itself unlike the 90 focused and hectic minutes taken up by football. It provided a sanctioned space which could encompass illegal activities, including illicit sales of alcohol, as well as betting and other activities on the margins, which made cricket of considerable economic significance to those involved in it.[6]

The mines were a key element in the equation, but their needs were relatively specific—a constant source of cheap labour. Workers on the other hand required alcohol which played a key role in attracting as well as maintaining the labour force. By 1926, the average beer quota per worker on the mines amounted to 8.5 quarts per month. Contrary to management expectations, this weak and inadequate ration did little more than whet appetites, and a huge area of the informal economy revolved around enhancing the alcohol content of beer supplied, through the addition of golden syrup or brown sugar, as well as illicit brewing of the stronger *skokiaan*. Social as opposed to workplace control was of secondary importance, which allowed the African elite to use the structural conditions to exercise considerable informal power. Women living in the elite 'married' quarters within the compounds, or located outside the mines, were responsible for brewing, selling cooked meat and vegetables, tailoring and other such activities. The Johannesburg Municipality, on the other hand, responsible to citizens rather than mine owners, sought to find mechanisms to control the burgeoning African population of the Rand, as well as the flows of African workers which ascended into the city from the mine shafts and compounds at weekends. More particularly, the Municipality increasingly sought to impose a municipal alcohol monopoly following the lucrative 'Durban System' which ultimately formed the platform for municipal financing throughout the subcontinent.[7]

Alcohol was always a central part of cricket culture, and cricket matches provided a huge opportunity for the illicit sale and consumption of alcohol. Perhaps alcohol consumption was relatively restricted for those who took part, but the behaviour of African cricket crowds was often well lubricated by alcohol, as spectators, like sports fans the world over, were provided with a rare opportunity to let off steam in the open air. The fact that the Reverend Xaba, captain of Natal in the 1934/35 Native Recruiting Corporation (NRC) African provincial tournament, felt encouraged to write to the Transvaal captain noting that the tournament had been uniquely free of misbehaviour and drunkenness gives an indication of the role alcohol generally played in African cricket, as it has done in cricket since time immemorial.[8]

The experience of individuals suggests that it would be a mistake to see a fundamental separation between miner and city dweller, migrant and elite worker, and informal trader and wage slave. African 'permanent' workers were able to build and develop close economic and political linkages with migrant workers, and with elites outside the mines in both town and country, building where appropriate on the rural traditions where many had their roots. Individual Africans with luck and the right connections could play a variety of roles in the political economy as they sought to develop and exploit opportunities available to them, to improve their own positions and directly or indirectly benefit the wider community.

The early career of Jason Jingoes illustrates this potential fluidity between town and country, elite surface and underground worker, enforcer and entrepreneur, labour leader and soldier. Jingoes was born in Basutoland (Lesotho) at the turn of the century, had a mission school education and started his working career thanks to his rural connections as a police groom in Ficksburg. He then became a police trap (inevitably high risk and short term) enforcing the alcohol prohibition on Africans, a domestic worker, an underground worker, a clerk on the Rand mines, a travelling salesman selling suits and trousers, a soldier in the South African Labour Corps in France, a government clerk in the Orange Free State and by the late 1920s an organiser for the radical ICU.[9] This flexibility and fluidity of opportunity may have been rare, but political and economic oppression clearly required positive and creative strategic responses.

CRICKET, SEGREGATION AND THE 'BARNATO BOARD'

The story of African cricket on the Rand celebrates the achievements of the fine players active in the period, and the astonishing energy and creativity of African players and administrators who developed highly complex social networks based on leagues as numerous and sophisticated as the white cricket establishment in a situation of extreme economic and physical precariousness. These officials not only played the game themselves in any spare time available but also acted as selectors, fixture secretaries, rule makers, groundsmen, treasurers, technical coaches and managers as well as mentors to players, all in an environment where even travelling to games could be a daunting challenge and a lack of the right endorsements on a pass could mean a significant fine, dismissal or imprisonment. The African elite sought to use all means at their disposal to strengthen the position of Africans on the Rand as the jaws of the segregationist state with its array of land and residence prohibitions, pass laws, labour colour bars and liquor prohibitions tightened around them. While economic survival was of course a critical driver, and cricket clearly offered economic as well as social advantages to the enthusiasts who promoted the game, they sought to leverage all opportunities which arose, where necessary mediating between the Rand establishment and the fractured interests of urban and mine workers, and petty traders. It allowed them to build community pride, aspiration and achievement as well as excitement and enjoyment, and from the most inauspicious circumstances.

The growth of communities along 'ethnic' lines, dividing Muslim and Christian coloureds, and Indians, from each other, and from Africans, was a response to 250 years of slavery, war, colonialism and resistance. But black cricket was notable for the extent to which 'ethnic' exclusivity was resisted until the practicalities of segregation and its differential impact on the communities themselves made this impractical and segregationist ideology seeped into the discourse across society in the 1920s and 1930s. This was partly a reflection of the solidarity shared by all disadvantaged groups in the face of a repression which if uneven in impact, nonetheless bore down on all. Cricket in South Africa was therefore resistant to communalism, unlike in India where, as Ramachandra Guha describes, cricket and communalism went hand in hand.[10]

And even when exclusivity won out as an organising principle for representative cricket competitions in the late 1920s and 1930s, (in part because of the growth of Garveyism and African self-help initiatives and ethnic competition for scarce resources, as well as the tightening influx restrictions over the African population), it would soon be overtaken by a rejuvenated political imperative for unity in the face of oppression in the 1940s and 1950s. The debate between inclusivity as an organising principle for resistance to the South African state, and the desire for communities to manage the practicalities of the situation as best they could, was played out on the sports field through this period.

Cricket among African communities on mission stations in the Eastern Cape was transplanted into Kimberley during the 'diamond age' in the 1870s and 1880s. The black cricketing community, both African and coloured, played a key leadership role within the community both on and off the field and continued to influence black cricketing developments, even after the discovery of gold on the Rand changed the face both of South Africa and of Empire itself. Not only were black cricketers around the early 1890s strong enough to hold their own against representative teams of whites, but the league organisation and structure, in Kimberley and the Cape Colony as a whole, was at least as well organised and as important in the social life of the community as the white game. And in April 1891, both the white and black Kimberley cricket teams won the Currie Cup and its equivalent for black teams, the Glover Cup, respectively.[11] The Glover family (George Glover played for South Africa on the 1894 tour) were supporters of black cricket in the 1890s and as well as donating a trophy, arranged games between the successful white and black teams. Control of cricket was an important business opportunity. Glovers' Athletic Rooms emerged as a hub of the cricketing community, both white and black. And profits could be made not only at the bar and through the sale of refreshments. George Glover (the 'father of the tournament') faced accusations relating to 'missing' gate receipts of £80 following the 1891 black cricket tournament in Kimberley.

As a result, the Griqualand West Coloured Cricket Board (GWCCB) was set up in 1892 to take control over black cricket away from the Glovers, and by the mid-1890s, there were eight black clubs of which six were predominantly coloured while two—the Duke of Wellington and Eccentrics—were primarily African. This was not without ethnic tensions and clashes over control, and three predominantly coloured clubs withdrew from the league when Joseph Moss, an African court interpreter, was elected as Vice-President of the Board in 1895.[12]

In 1897, the mining industry took its first steps in the encouragement of black cricket through the presentation by Sir David Harris, Chairman of De Beers, of the Barnato Memorial Trophy, to the GWCCB. The wish of the donor was that the trophy 'should become a symbol in fostering and developing the game among all sections of the non-European communities through the land'.[13] It became a symbol of non-racism in representative cricket despite being rather bizarrely named after the flamboyant and eccentric mining magnate, Barney Barnato, who had just died in suspicious circumstances and had not been notably interested in either cricket or the welfare of the black population. The trophy could be seen in part as a philanthropic gesture, cashing in on the success of Kimberley cricket, and in part an attempt to help secure a settled labour force in Kimberley, as educated black workers streamed north to the Rand goldmines. As a gesture, it was much more cynically aimed at the Mother Country, where the reputation of the mining industry had taken a series of jolts, not least from the antics of Leander Starr Jameson and his infamous 'Raid' in 1896, as the phoney war in the Transvaal moved incrementally but inevitably towards the real thing.

The first SACCB Barnato tournament was held in 1897 between three Cape teams—Western Province (Cape Town), Griqualand West (Kimberley) and Port Elizabeth including 'Malay', 'Christian' and African players. It was won by Western Province who would go on to triumph in all but one of first ten tournaments played before 1946. In the meantime, in the more racially exclusionist Transvaal, signs appeared of exclusive ethnic Boards when an Indian Cricket Board was set up in 1896, and an African Cricket Board in 1898, but the outbreak of war in 1899 derailed any further activity and both failed to play an active role after the war.[14]

The SACCB, reflecting a leadership actively politically committed to gaining their rights from a victorious Empire, had a specifically non-racial constitution and did not 'recognise any distinction among the various sporting peoples of Africa, whether by creed, nationality or otherwise'. The popularity and strength of black non-racial cricket immediately after the South African War was illustrated by four successful provincial tournaments between 1904 when Transvaal competed for the first time, and 1913.

At the same time, according to Piet Gwele, a key figure in cricket in Johannesburg for almost half a century, all black communities were playing together at local level by 1913 in the City and Suburban Cricket Union. At the representative level, the 'Barnato' model had brought all black cricketers together in a national tournament.[15] However, following the intervention of the Great War, this 'non-racial' approach progressively came under threat in the 1920s, as the political leadership began to lose its way. The move away from 'Barnato', however, reflected local tensions as well as national political preoccupations, when a 'Malay'–Christian coloured split at club level in Cape Town led in 1926 to the coloureds breaking away to form the South African Independent Coloured Cricket Board.

OWNING LEISURE TIME ON THE RAND

The global conflagration of 1914–18, fought by South Africans of all races under the banner of Empire, meant that cricket at representative level was not resurrected among Africans until the early 1920s.[16] When it was, the segregationist constructions of the South African state had gathered pace, while the labour struggle had intensified. The discriminatory South African Union constitution of 1910 maintained the pre-war status quo of voting rights restricted to whites in all regions while reducing opportunities for Africans in the only province with a 'non-racial' property franchise—the Cape.[17] Then between 1913 and 1936, the Government put in place a series of formal colour bars depriving Africans of access to land, jobs, votes and freedom of movement.

The 1920s on the Rand were also characterised by labour unrest, both black and white, in the peculiar South African version of the struggle between labour and capital where white labour encouraged workers to 'unite and fight for a white South Africa'. The 1922 white General Strike was defeated by bombs and South African troops, but white workers won the peace. The entrenchment of a job colour bar in the mining industry meant access to all skilled and most semi-skilled occupations were restricted on racial grounds to white labour. This nailed down even more firmly a clear reliance for industrial profitability on cheap black labour in indentured conditions.

The intense post-war political activity among Africans culminated in a brief moment where the perceived possibility of a cross-class alliance gave African elites an opportunity, through the Transvaal Native Mine Clerks Association, to negotiate wage increases and accommodation for *indunas* and clerks but the door was quickly slammed shut.[18] By the mid-1920s, Prime Minister Hertzog's Native Policy was aimed at what Sir Abe Bailey MP, the man who did most to put white South African cricket on the map as a founder member of the Imperial Cricket Conference, approvingly called 'keeping the native in his place'.[19] Bishop Talbot of Pretoria more aptly described the policy of segregation as 'passing a harrow over the cricket pitch before the match has begun'.[20]

From the African point of view, the question was how best to ride the storm. One option was the direct action and strong rhetoric of Clements Kadalie and his Industrial and Commercial Workers Union ('ICU, white man'). As Kadalie put it, 'there is no native problem, but a European problem of weakness, greed and robbery'.[21] The ICU was a curious amalgam of personality cult, trade union and Garveyite movement, supported by some South African Communists and elements of the international labour movement, and by many African rural and urban workers. Kadalie's cry of rage lacked a practical platform for change and was undermined by internal dissension, including regionalism and accusations of corruption, and put down by the machinery of the state.[22] But it managed to create local structures which enabled Africans, particularly in rural areas, to use the support of the ICU to challenge the white theft of African resources.[23] Both Garveyism and trade unionism had the potential to build cross-class alliances, in opposition to the state, as Afrikaner nationalism was beginning to do in the 1920s and 1930s, and the ANC would do after 1945.

The African National Congress, less convinced by the self-help approach of the ICU, focused on retaining access to the political process through the Cape franchise (a battle lost by 1936 when the non-racial property-based franchise was abolished). ANC leaders argued that the Garveyite rhetoric of 'Africa for the Africans' was a gift to a white regime looking for excuses to isolate Africans entirely from the political process. In practice, this focus on maintaining a political toehold accounted for much of the apparent passivity of the ANC leadership in this period and meant that African elites on the Rand sought to improve their position within the social order rather than transforming it.

Cricket and cultural development in the 1920s linked elite African opinion with a mining industry anxious to retain a small but influential black labour aristocracy, and a Johannesburg municipality concerned to maintain social control. More fundamentally, the Municipality aspired to introduce 'the Durban system' and finance municipal operations for both black and white from the institution of a municipal beer monopoly through beer halls outside the mines. As suggested above, alcohol was central to the operation of the mining and municipal economies, as production of beer (and sale in the towns) was a mainstay of the informal rural economy. Alcohol, as a ubiquitous component of *shebeen*, music and sports culture, encompassed the mutual interests of mainly female rural and urban beer brewers. Once again, the cultural links between town and country were important. Beinart and Bundy in their study of the bitter East London strikes of 1929–30 have shown how attempts by various municipalities across the country to introduce Durban-style controls were a major flashpoint and were a principal factor in forcing elite black politicians to take rural and proletarian interests seriously.[24]

As the African population was increasingly squeezed, a minority of whites felt that repression and deprivation was an inadequate and precarious solution to what was defined by the state as the 'native problem', and that facilities for what they saw as African 'improvement' were necessary to ensure the longer-term stability of the system. One concrete result was the setting up of the Bantu Men's Social Centre (BMSC) in 1924, by institutions committed to the stabilisation of the African middle class including the Joint Council of Europeans and Natives and the South African Institute of Race Relations to provide facilities for education and entertainment among middle-class Africans. This was followed in 1931 by the inauguration of the Bantu Sports Club (BSC) substantially underwritten by the Chamber of Mines to encourage the wider interest of Africans in sport. Aimed unashamedly at '*amaRespectables*', the BSC included a park with trees, fishpond and gardens, a club veranda for socials and concerts, as well as a refreshment room, football and cricket grounds, three tennis courts and a gym. Membership cost five shillings a year.[25]

Dan Twala, the General Secretary of the BMSC, argued in 1929 that 'no sane person who has wished for the development of South Africa could possibly canvass for such a retrograde step as the segregation of whites and blacks. There is more to be gained by our race in a South Africa built on rocks of mutual co-operation than the sands of segregation'.[26] However, whether the result of paternalist endeavours and/or calculated policy to reinforce the status quo, these initiatives were segregationist solutions, developing separate institutions segregating African elites by both race and class. Not surprisingly, these efforts by white paternalists in league with mining industry and municipality were not met with universal approval. Many Africans were deeply sceptical of white efforts to achieve what Ray Phillips of the American Mission Society described as 'moralising the leisure time of natives'.[27]

The ambiguities and limitations of these initiatives are illustrated by the appearance of the South African Davis Cup captain—George Dodd—playing doubles tennis at the BMSC in 1926. This was a coup for Sol Senaoane, who was appointed Membership Secretary of the BMSC in the same year. Senaoane was born in the Northern Cape in 1894, educated at Bensonvale Mission School and, like Jason Jingoes, became an 'assistant' commercial traveller. He handled the sales and customer sides of the operation, with a white commercial traveller 'overseeing' the selling of fashionable suits and clothes to African customers, mainly on the mines for the City's tailoring industry.

The itinerant tailoring trade was one of most successful methods of integrating African permanent and migrant workers into the economy, representing their initiation into credit at exorbitant interest rates. Previously, a key feature of the South African economy had been the virtually total exclusion of Africans from the availability of credit beyond that controlled by employers in the 'company store'. Itinerant jobs of this kind were also highly valued by the African petty bourgeoisie as they provided a freedom of movement, circumventing pass law restrictions, and significant economic freedom, including opportunities for the smuggling of stock and supplies for the informal trade.

No doubt, building on his mining connections, and perhaps his cricketing talents, Sol Senaoane then joined City Deep Mine as *amalabana*
(clerk) in 1916. He joined the TNMCA representing mine clerks and
became Acting Chairman in the crucial year of 1922. As a political moderate, Senaoane was to make a huge leadership contribution to the development of sport, and particularly cricket, on the Rand.

Dodd partnered another prominent white player to play doubles
against the black champion J. Smith who was partnered by Senaoane and
the whites astonishingly in the view of the press, lost by three sets to one,
providing a huge boost for the African sporting population. It was rare
for Africans to get the opportunity to take on whites at their own games
particularly stars of the stature of Dodd, and even rarer to get one over on
them. Apart from bragging rights, it provided a marker as to how good
African sportsmen were, and perhaps indicated how much whites struggled with less than pristine playing conditions and facilities. The alienation
of Africans from the white South African system is clearly demonstrated by
the fact that black South Africans at least until the 1990s always supported
the opposition against white South African teams (as evidenced from the
first England cricket tour in 1888/89),[28] and understandably also supported black athletes against whites wherever possible.[29] This made this
occasion particularly sweet and did much to encourage interest in tennis,
and sport generally, among potential black players.

There was general press denunciation of Dodd's actions in risking white prestige (and the fear of being shown up was clearly no small
factor in white resistance to sporting contact and reinforcer of sports
segregation). Distance was necessary to preserve the myth of white superiority. The outcry encouraged the (white) South African Lawn Tennis
Union to launch an enquiry into the match. Dodd responded that as the
son of a missionary he was interested in African sporting advancement.
The editorial in the Chamber of Mines-owned, *Umteteli Wa Bantu*,
aimed at black permanent workers who made up the 'sporting classes',
reflected the views of its mining masters that '… in sport as in social
affairs both black and white should be rigidly separated'. This was apparently 'in the interests of both black and white'. But the (African) editor
was in favour of 'meeting occasionally in public contest without it being
the thin end of the wedge'.[30]

Cricket in South Africa was inevitably determined by its environment.
Segregation presented fundamental challenges to Africans who organised
and took part in sport. Their heroic efforts particularly in cricket given

the resource-intensive nature of the game and its demands for space, equipment, time and technique, always framed in a climate of economic deprivation and formal harassment through application of the Pass Laws, controlling movement and residence, form the main theme of the rest of this chapter. The reality was expressed by one African correspondent who resignedly noted: 'It is discouraging … to follow that the decrease of the number of our good players of sport is credit to the [police] pick-up vans … it would be a good idea if the powers that be … impress on each member to pay his tax before he is overtaken'.[31]

PIET GWELE AND THE EVOLUTION OF AFRICAN CRICKET ON THE RAND

African cricket on the Rand began when prospectors and workers streamed north soon after the discovery of gold, direct from the mission stations or from the lively African cricket scene around Kimberley's diamond mines. Leagues were developed on the initiative of mission-educated African elites, and with the support of the various gold mines which used the game as a means of attracting skilled and educated black workers, particularly from the Eastern Cape. While documentation on the early years of African cricket on the Rand is almost non-existent, black teams consisting of Africans, coloureds and 'Malays', played together in regional teams for the Barnato Trophy up till at least the First World War. At a local level, however, the mining industry sponsored African rather than black cricket, and African teams affiliated to the Witwatersrand Native Cricket Union were competing for the Native Recruitment Cup (NRC) in the second decade of the twentieth century.[32]

Orientals (Crown Mines) won the Cup in 1915, and following the war break which lasted until 1920, won again in 1923 and 1926. Stonebreakers shared a healthy rivalry with Orientals winning in 1921, 1924 and 1925.[33] They had been named after the abandoned stone-crusher dump that had been levelled to form the Wemmer ground. Building the ground was one of the many achievements of Sol Senaoane who, while Municipal Recreation Officer, also spearheaded the Stonebreakers' bowling attack until the late 1930s.

Stonebreakers were captained by 'Oom' Piet Gwele, the father of African cricket on the Rand. Piet Gwele had followed a much-travelled route. Born in the Eastern Cape in 1891, and mission school educated, he initially settled in Kimberley, and by 1911 was working as a clerk on the Rand mines. He was co-founder of the Transvaal Bantu Cricket Board, captained Transvaal Africans on their tour to Port Elizabeth in 1926, and in the 1930s again skippered the Transvaal teams in the inter-provincial African tournament for which the Chamber of Mines donated a new trophy.[34] Gwele was an all-rounder, and a renowned fielder and taker of miraculous catches on outfields where grass was a rarity. He retained his athleticism until well into his 40s when finally, having exercised his leadership qualities on the field for many years, he moved into an active role as an administrator.

In the endless search for more and cheaper labour, recruitment was king, and the Native Recruitment Corporation was tasked with ensuring its supply within South Africa's borders. It was headed for much of the period by the formidable Henry Taberer (himself an Oxford and Essex fast bowler and captain of South Africa in his only Test against Australia in 1902/03). It was no surprise, therefore, that the NRC also sponsored the new Native Recruitment Cup played for by provincial African cricket teams, once the earlier 'Barnato' competition, which had included cricketers of all ethnic groups, had folded.

African cricket really took off with the opening of the Bantu Sports Club (BSC) in 1931. The BSC was located on twelve acres donated by Howard Pim and John Hardy, both active in both the Joint Council and the Institute for Race Relations. The grounds provided a venue for cricket outside the control of the Johannesburg Municipality, in a more sociable environment for spectators as well as players, and significantly increased opportunities for the African petty-bourgeois elite to increase their involvement in cricket. The General Secretary of the BSC, Dan Twala, was himself an excellent cricketer as well as footballer.[35] The BSC was inaugurated by a cricket match (even though in April it might have begun with a game of football) suggesting cricket's predominant significance for the African elite. Watched by a reported (though probably overestimated) crowd of 15,000 spectators, the match pitted a white team against the BSC Select XI. The African side made 155/7 while the whites, who hung on for a last-ditch draw, finished on 118/9. Top-scorer for the Africans was Lockington Moedi Seti, a product of Lovedale and a pioneer of early African cricket, who made 40. Seti, who played for Van Ryn Deep, was a left-handed forcing player, specialising in attractive late cuts and leg pulls which 'thrilled the spectators'.[36]

With the euphoria of a moral victory against the whites, and a new ground, Rand cricket had a strong platform for take-off.

In the following year (1932), the South African Bantu Cricket Board (SABCB) was founded as an Africans-only body. Its formation was the decisive element in the final breakup of the non-racial Barnato Board (formally the South African Coloured Cricket Board) which had lasted for more than 30 years. The SABCB was set up following the Orpen Cup tournament competed for by Africans from East London, King William's Town and Kimberley in 1931. Hamilton Masiza, who had been secretary of the Barnato Board, became the first Secretary of the SABCB, and H. B. Piliso, Clerk and Headman of Crown Mines, was elected President, reflecting the importance of Transvaal African cricket (Fig. 4.1).

Fig. 4.1 Frank Roro (left) was captain of the South African Bantu Cricket Board national team and named by the United Cricket Board of South Africa as one of the ten 'Cricketers of the Century' in 1999. 'Oom' Piet Gwele was the 'father' of African cricket on the Rand, and after a thirty-year playing career as an all-rounder and legendary fielder, he became a key administrator at provincial and national levels

Frank Roro and the Golden Age of Transvaal African Cricket

The decision by Africans to go it alone, took place partly because African cricketers felt that they were getting a rough deal under Barnato, and along with the opening of the BSC, was to be a key element in the blossoming of African cricket on the Rand. A further element was the arrival on the Rand of Frank Roro. Roro appears to have been recruited primarily as a result of his cricketing talents, along with a number of other promising players who were able to find mine contracts, where they effectively operated as semi-professional cricketers.

Philip Vundla, for example, was a Crown Mines clerk (working with H. B. Piliso) who got his job thanks to his skill as a fast bowler.[37] Like his fellow educated Africans, Vundla demonstrated how African leaders (and cricketers) played a variety of political roles and resisted being pigeon-holed. In 1943, Vundla was dismissed from his mine clerk's job for attacking the industry in his evidence to the Witwatersrand Mine Native Wages Commission, in which he detailed the physical abuse of black underground workers and spelt out the difficulty blacks had in complaining against underground assaults by white mineworkers. White mineworkers, he explained, as the privileged minority always surfaced first and laid a charge against the worker they had attacked. Few whites were prepared to accept the African's later claims of assault. So the complaint system, pointed to by the white owners in response to liberal criticisms, was essentially nullified. In the same year, Phillip Vundla became leader of the African Mine Workers Union, and became a key figure in the 1946 African mineworkers' strike. Mine clerks provided most of the strike leadership and unsurprisingly a major demand related to their class concerns with the restrictions of the job colour bar. Nonetheless, the strong worker support focused the strike on the key issues of wages. But while strongly supported by workers, the strike was ultimately unsuccessful and broken by violent and vicious police action.[38] Vundla then became a regional leader of the ANC, playing a key role in the protests against the demolition of Sophiatown in the early 1950s.[39]

Half a generation younger than Piet Gwele, Frank Roro was born in Kimberley in 1908 and was educated at the United Mission School, under the guidance of Hamilton Masiza, principal and cricket enthusiast. Masiza's contacts quickly helped Roro find a clerical position on the Mines. Between his arrival on the mines in the early 1930s, and the early 1950s he became the greatest African batsman that South Africa has so far produced. His total exclusion from the advantages of the white game means his achievements cannot be compared directly to those of his white contemporaries. He clearly stood head and shoulders above other black cricketers, although the magnitude of his career cannot be precisely established owing to incomplete record-keeping, patchy newspaper coverage and non-availability of documentation. In 1954, Reddy and Bansda, in nominating him as the first of their black cricketers of the year, estimated that he had recorded 20 centuries in inter-provincial tournaments, and over 100 centuries in league cricket at an average of above 100.[40]

Available newspaper reports indicate that while he was the benchmark for all other African batsmen to follow, his career statistics were probably not quite as astonishing as Reddy and Bansda suggested. The poor quality of outfields and pitches made up of mat on gravel, which were prone to uneven bounce, meant that an innings generally did not last long enough to allow for huge scores, though Roro did hit a triple-hundred and several double-hundreds.[41]

But it does not diminish his status to suggest that these career figures may be overstated. Nor was it his fault that records were sketchy. And Frank Roro was also a stylist, and not just a run-maker. He was remembered (in words that might have belonged to Cardus) 'for the quietude of his manner, the perfection of his technique and the poise and poetry of his stroke making'.[42] Above all, he was an entertainer who could not resist smashing a quick full-length delivery straight back over the sight screen for six to win a game.[43] Roro's reputation as a crowd pleaser was a major impetus in encouraging popular interest in the game.

The SABCB arranged an inter-provincial tournament for Africans to be held on the Rand at the end of 1932, but the depression put paid to attendances from the other centres.[44] Instead, the Transvaal Bantu Cricket Union took on the City and Suburban Coloured Cricket Union on January 1 and 2, and received a serious wake-up call, losing by an innings and 113 runs. This was a performance consisting of two batting collapses and forgettable, apart from the six by Titus Majola smashed over the neighbouring Acme Iron Foundry. Post-game comments suggested that poor selection had not done African cricket any favours.[45]

Further games were held at Bantu Sports Club (BSC) against Young India (another loss, with Dan Twala the only batsman in double figures) and against a touring Pretoria team. Perhaps over-optimistically, the white BSC officials attempted to pursue a social control agenda beyond the African cricketing and tennis playing elites and 500 *Amalaitas* and stick fighters were invited to the BSC to be introduced to boxing. The result was summed up by a headline writer as 'Much Blood Shed at Boxing Display by Amalaita Boys' but the 'profuse bloodletting did not shake the organisers' belief that the participants now felt at home in the club grounds and that 'with the introduction of appropriate rules' boxing should become one of Bantu South Africa's national sports.[46] Nelson Mandela, of course, famously boxed at the BSC in the 1940s and early 1950s.

This attempt to move beyond the gentility of cricket towards specific social control of the urban proletariat was tried on a number of occasions. The main aim, explained Bullard the BMSC boxing trainer, was to encourage Africans to use their 'god given fists instead of devil given knives'.[47]

The BSC continued to host games against the top Indian sides and in 1933, had their revenge against Young India with Conference Setlogelo taking 8/16 in a Young India total of 22 and then making an unbeaten 73 in 'hectic' fashion. The 'Indian' game was the curtain-raiser to the first national tournament for Africans described in the European press as the 'native Currie Cup' which was finally held at the end of 1933 in Johannesburg. Border, Eastern Province, Griqualand West, Western Province, and Transvaal, whose teams were all heavily rooted in the Cape missionary-based cricket tradition, competed. Several centuries were scored, including two by S. Fongqo and S. Ndlwana in Western Province's total of 368/6 declared against Griqualand West.

Transvaal won all three of their matches to take the trophy, defeating Border by an innings (Transvaal 213: Border 96 and 14).[48] The Transvaal captain and fast bowler, Titus Majola, destroyed the Border batting taking 6/6 in the second innings. Border made 243 against Eastern Province on the following day but ended at the foot of the table with Western Province in second place, followed by Eastern Province, and Griquas.

The closing social function at the BSC brought together most of the leading figures in African sport. H. B. Piliso, as Acting President of the SABCB, presented the Chamber of Mines trophy (the Native Recruitment Cup) to Titus Majola. H. C. Wellbeloved, Chamber of Mines Chief Native Advisor, made a welcoming speech on behalf of the industry, emphasising the importance of African community across tribal barriers and the impact of the depression. He was followed by music supplied by the Merry Blackbirds whose line-up included the ubiquitous cricket-playing BSC Manager, theatrical impresario, and Johannesburg football supremo, Dan Twala.[49]

Port Elizabeth was the venue for the next tournament in December 1934, and the games were held at the New Brighton Oval, which was claimed to be the best sporting facility for Africans outside Johannesburg. Piet Gwele was brought back as skipper at the age of 43, replacing Titus Majola, and M. Xinime (who was to be elected on to the SA Bantu Rugby Board set up in the following year) was appointed manager.[50] After a two-day trip on the train, the team stayed at the Municipal Compound and were entertained by the African Community in New Brighton. But conditions at the ground were reported to be far less accommodating at least for batsmen. Two pitches were available and made up of pure fresh anthill with a liberal sprinkling of stones under the mat. The Press considered that the goddess of luck alone apparently prevented any serious injuries, and the pitches were deceptive and very fast. Only Roro's excellent eye and solid defensive technique could successfully counter their vagaries, and experienced and accurate bowlers like John Mpiliso reaped a rich harvest of wickets.[51]

Transvaal's batting on the road to the final did not necessarily justify the Press criticism of the wicket, and it was Frank Roro who towered above his contemporaries. In their first game against the hosts, they made 305, beating Eastern Province who were all out for 150 and 109, by an innings and 46 runs. Frank Roro in his role as an occasional off-spinner took 4/5 to wrap up the second innings in front of 400 spectators. Then facing Natal in their first appearance in the competition, Transvaal scored 309/6 declared with Roro contributing a superb 134, and Piet Gwele, 47 not out.[52] Despite coaching from the legendary cricketer, Herby Taylor, who was coming to the end of his illustrious career as one of South Africa's greatest players, and as a result of the selection of a number of locally based Fort Hare students to save costs, Natal's inexperience showed and they went down by an innings and 104 runs.[53]

The final against Border was 'nerve wracking and suspense filled' and did more to justify the criticism of the pitch. Roro again batted majestically scoring an undefeated 95 to single-handedly drag Transvaal's first innings total up to 127. Border rued the fact that he had been dropped on 19 and were then routed by the unplayable Mpiliso who took 7/13 in Border's first innings total of 54. Border improved second-time around, but Transvaal made the best of their first innings lead, and eventually prevailed by 32 runs.[54]

The Mayor of Port Elizabeth hosted a reception at the end of the tournament, and once again, the now President of the SABCB, H. B. Piliso proudly presented the trophy to Transvaal's captain, Piet Gwele. J. P. McNamee the Location Superintendent of New Brighton outlined the history of the New Brighton Oval and praised the high standard of the cricket. A diligent newspaper reporter then listed the names of all 60 ladies present and described the dresses they wore, in an attempt to market the newspaper among women readers.[55] The Reverend J. Xaba, captain of Natal, later wrote to Piet Gwele, congratulating him on the '...fine sporting spirit and good conduct', feeling it noteworthy that '... the tournament was unique by the absence of misbehaviour and drunkenness'.[56]

CRICKETERS, MINES AND MUNICIPALITY

From the high point of successive inter-provincial trophies, Transvaal cricket was subjected to two significant challenges. First, the Transvaal African league cricket fixture list was curtailed to fit in more football fixtures and cricket's role as the summer sporting counterbalance to the far more popular football (12,000 attended soccer matches at the BSC in the mid-1930s) was under threat as football began to colonise the summer months.[57] But cricket did continue into April, with a regional competition (the Flag Cup) won by West Rand (Roro 47) despite 70s from East Rand's Mpiliso and Seti, and a touring team from Cape Town defeated a combined Orientals and Stonebreakers team including Gwele and Senaoane.[58]

The second major challenge lay in the efforts by the Municipality to resist the mining industry's hegemony over African sport. The struggle had begun in football where the mining league was disbanded in 1929 and replaced by a Municipal league (the Johannesburg Bantu Football Association). Control was exercised by the Johannesburg Municipal Native Affairs Department (NAD) through Manager, W. D. Ballenden, and Sol Senaoane, who was now NAD Native Sports Organiser and Secretary of the League. The objective of the Johannesburg Municipal NAD was to 'control all branches of native sport in the city' using access to facilities and equipment as weapons in the war.[59] Resistance to white municipal control in football led to a breakaway by Zulu mine clerks who relaunched the mine association competition, which had existed in the early 1920s, and renamed it the Johannesburg African Football Association in 1933.[60]

By August 1935, the same scenario was being acted out on the cricket field. As the Transvaal African player Tatius Sondo commented, the Transvaal Union was in crisis facing jealousies and disputes over fixtures from the previous season. The catalyst was the election of municipal officials—specifically Sol Senaoane—to the Transvaal Bantu Cricket Union. Cricket looked like following the unhappy situation created by the municipalisation of football with rival leagues reflecting the mines and municipality respectively. During the NRC league period, the NAD had previously failed to induce cricket clubs not connected with the Mines to form a separate municipal league, using access to the Municipal Stonebreakers/Wemmer Ground and the offer of cricket equipment. As Sondo put it, '… sport in general and cricket on the Rand is bound up with the mining companies which never stamped their views on the Union nor contended for that control which seems to be an obsession with some Municipal employees'.[61]

The TBCU, however, with Piet Gwele taking over as Chairman, brokered a truce and reformed the cricket league system which included both mine teams and others into senior and junior divisions.[62] Sol Senaoane played the key role on the fixtures sub-committee and with Sondo and Gwele starred in the league games for Stonebreakers in the last few months of the year. Senaoane's bowling was devastating against Simmer and Jack, the 1934/35 champions, thanks in part to Tatius Sondo's three brilliant one-handed catches in the slips, and Gwele scored 62*, 24, 100 and 70 in consecutive innings.[63]

Following an extended series of trial matches, Gwele (as skipper) was selected for the next inter-provincial tournament in East London, along with Frank Roro (who made 99 in the trial), Roro's brother Harley who had been playing on the East Rand with Van Ryn Deep, and Tatius Sondo. Transvaal went into the tournament with high hopes as they also possessed a pair of fearsome fast bowlers in Titus Majola and Edson Masiza.

In the first game against Griquas, Roro was cheered to the rafters as he walked out to bat in front of a 'huge' crowd, but the fans were to be disappointed as he was bowled in the first over for a duck. It quickly became apparent that the ground was not batting-friendly, and that Transvaal's classical cricketing approach with out of tune. The grass was very long, and sloggers were needed to take the aerial route. In fact, the outfield was so bad that Griquas, the fielding side, successfully appealed against the conditions. And the 'bumping' pitch 'taxed the energies of the location nurse, Miss Mapikele, who worked night and day in massaging and repairing injuries'.[64] Transvaal's batting was the main let down, Frank Roro was unable to reprise his heroics from the previous tournament, and Transvaal could not retain its Chamber of Mines crown, despite winning three out of five games, with Edson Masiza's 70 against Border being the only substantial individual score. Transvaal did not even make the final, in which Border beat Western Province.[65]

THE INTER-RACE BOARD—A BLUEPRINT FOR THE FUTURE?

By the early 1930s, African cricket at both representative and local level played exclusively against other Africans in local league and provincial representative levels though occasional ad hoc games were played against Indian and coloured teams. But in the mid-thirties, the African cricketing leadership was working towards an inter-community tournament on the Rand in partnership with the other communities, particularly Indian cricketers led by the Reverend Bernard Sigamoney. Like several of the Transvaal African cricketers, Sigamoney was active across a range of political and sporting activities.[66] As an Indian and a Christian Sigamoney's perspective was inclusionist. As a long-term trade unionist particularly in Durban in the garment making industry, Sigamoney was closely associated with the class of 'penny capitalists' who were trading in suits, shoes, illicit beer and other necessities in the mine compounds themselves.

The involvement of the African mine elite, who had much to gain from the informal economics of the compounds, were quick to work with Bernard Sigamoney who inaugurated the Transvaal Inter-Race Cricket Board in early 1936 along with leaders from the other cricketing communities. He also donated a trophy. This initiative had the objective of 'bringing together all portions of the nation through the medium of this sport' with any race eligible for membership. And the Board saw this as a first step towards the more radical objective of the development of a non-racial cricketing environment, going beyond Barnato which had been limited to black cricket only. Racial differences, Sigamoney believed, should be cast aside: 'For in sport there should be no differences of race, colour, and creed. A South African team is not complete until the membership is open to all races in the country. It is with this in mind that the Board is being created'.[67]

To modern eyes, there was a fundamental contradiction between the non-racial ideal and the exclusionist approach (accurately reflected by the name of the Board) which pitted teams from the various ethnically defined communities against each other. But this was the first step towards common engagement. The Patron of the Inter-Race Board was J. H. Hofmeyr, the liberal cricket-loving Cabinet Minister; Sigamoney was elected President, and Vice-Presidents represented the African, coloured and Indian communities. The tireless Sol Senaoane was elected Treasurer. The organisers were concerned to be inclusive in bringing together all communities, and in a particularly radical move encouraged European participation. Understanding the difficulties in achieving this in practice, the Board decided that in the absence of the affiliation by a European Union, they would accept applications from a European club, college, school or university. A white North-Eastern Transvaal team agreed to take part in the first tournament, though nothing is known as to how this came about. In addition to the Transvaal Africans, the Witwatersrand Union (Indians), the City and Suburban Coloureds ('Malays'), and the Transvaal Coloured Union (coloureds) were also affiliated.[68]

For the first tournament—and conscious of their failure in the recent East London tournament—the TBCU decided to use the opportunity to blood younger players. The African team included Majola and Senaoane, but were beaten by both the Indians, and the City and Suburban team, who were the ultimate winners. The white North-Eastern Transvaal team seems to have played a single game, losing to the City and Suburban team, and does not appear to have taken any further part in the competition. Inter-race tournaments were held annually from the mid-1930s. This model was also used in football where the various ethnic groups played in the annual William Godfrey Challenge Cup.

The 1936/37 Chamber of Mines tournament was held in Cape Town, and once again Transvaal disappointed. Highly eccentric selection meant Roro did not go. Border sailed to victory on basis of its fast bowlers, M. T. Chiepe who was concluding his degree at Fort Hare, and J. Kempi. The absence of Roro laid bare Transvaal's batting weakness as Border beat them by an innings and 45 runs when Transvaal were dismissed for a dismal 46 and 22 (Kempi 8/11).

This result did nothing to encourage African cricket, and the subsequent cancellation of the 1937/38 tournament meant that interest was centred on the 1938 tour of the Rand by the outstanding Fort Hare based Border side under the leadership of Chiepe. Border played against the various Rand regions, with West Rand scoring 408 (Roro 131), and Border replying with 158 and, and following on, 137/7, when stumps were drawn. The tour culminated in a 'Test' between Border and Transvaal, played at the coloured ground at Jeppe Reef. In a low-scoring and very tense game, Transvaal made 167 (Roro 'a brilliant 34', Eric Fihla 24, Eddie Majola 23) and 68 which proved enough to win against Border's 118 and 70. John Mpiliso's outstanding figures of 15-4-19-3 and 11-1-26-5 carried the day despite Chiepe contributing 10 wickets and 32 runs for Border.[69]

Mpiliso was spotted bowling on waste ground at a paraffin tin at 6 am on the morning of the 'Test', and his accuracy and consistency showed that practice paid off.[70] The sports editor suggested in *Bantu World* that he would make an excellent full-time coach for the TBCB. Ever conscious, as all Africans had to be, of the spider's web of racist legislation awaiting the unwary, the Editor noted that a TBCB employed coach would be unaffected by the Native Laws Amendment Act which forbade the presence of Africans unemployed in the urban areas.

By 1938, Sol Senaoane had taken over as President of the TBCB, as well as playing his key role as Treasurer of the Transvaal Inter-Race Board. Piet Gwele and C. M. Kieviet were vice-presidents. He told the annual general meeting that the Border tour had been the salvation of Bantu cricket on the Rand (he had himself played in the 'Test') and Rand cricket now encompassed 53 teams in the East Rand and 28 teams on the West Rand.[71] Cricket had avoided the divisive split in football between mines and municipality thanks to the efforts of Gwele and Senaoane who, while employed by the Municipality, maintained his close ties with the mining industry.

Sol Senaoane's 'CV' was startling. In 1938, he was the Recreational Director in the Municipal NAD, and beyond cricket his list of responsibilities included serving as secretary of the SA Bantu Football Association, the William Godfrey Inter-Race [Football] Cup, the Transvaal Bemba Football Association, the Wits Bantu Cycling Association and the Transvaal Bantu Tennis Association, and he served at the same time on the executive committee of the BMSC and was organiser of the South African Athletic Championships. He was also a qualified referee, book-keeper, typist, painter and harness-maker.[72]

Talented administrators such as Senaoane were used by the white authorities in their efforts to shape African leisure time, but the degree of control by the African petty bourgeoisie over African sport was fundamental. And it is at least partly true that sports and games were successful in channelling the African elite away from the attractions of urban back-yard culture and were a factor in maintaining the moderate positions espoused by the ANC in the period. But, this tells only half the story, and it is unfair to use hindsight to criticise African sports leaders for apparent lack of revolutionary zeal. Some cricketers such as Phillip Vundla were clearly in the vanguard of the mineworkers' struggle. For others, given the political and economic circumstances they had to deal with, they were able to act positively in creating an African urban culture, and a social structure based on cricket that enlivened and enhanced the existence of thousands of Africans whose daily experiences beyond the boundary were both oppressive and abusive, even if they did not approach the hellish conditions suffered by the majority of unskilled underground workers.

Senaoane and his colleagues were able to build a political base and exercise significant community leadership at a time when real political opportunities for Africans were fewer than ever. In the 1930s the South African Communist Party was in some disarray following the failure of its anti-Pass Law campaign, thus losing much of its popular following. This was largely the result of state harassment, but the Party had lost significant African support as it had focused on combating fascism among white workers, rather than supporting the interests of African workers. The ANC on the other hand, foundered when faced with the political and economic challenges of the decade. Its efforts to reconcile traditional elites with the aspirant commercial classes were not very successful, and it was not until the Second World War that African resistance to increasing rural landlessness and urban unemployment and overcrowding, and the widening wages gap began to fundamentally change the political landscape.[73]

The esteem in which Sol Senaoane was held was suggested by the fact that on his tragically early death in 1941, a procession of more than a thousand people marched from his home in Sophiatown to the African Methodist Church and the Reverend Sigamoney and D. M. Denelane were among those who spoke to commemorate his achievements.[74] His memory remained alive with the naming of one of the new townships after him in 1957.

Transvaal now dominated the country's African cricket having wrested control from the game's heartland in the Eastern Cape. Off the field, the SABCB had a Transvaal president (H. B. Piliso) and secretary/treasurer (D. M. Denelane). J. H. Hofmeyr was patron of this organisation as well as the Transvaal Inter-Race Board.[75]

On the field, the Border tour had revitalised cricket on the Rand, with younger players such as Eric Fihla and R. Sibenya reducing Transvaal's batting reliance on Frank Roro. But Roro was still a huge presence belying his small stature. Playing for Orientals against West Rand in October 1938, Roro (228) and Fihla (99) added 202 together out of 440 in less than a day, featuring Roro's magnificent driving all around the ground.[76] With Piet Gwele, now Induna at Rand Leases and showing batting form and Grace-like longevity despite his forty seven years, and other excellent performances from C. Mandlana (129* with 12 sixes and 7 fours), W. Mzondeki, and M. Voss Mtshekisa, the team that headed for Durban to contest the first Chamber of Mines tournament for two years 'looked robust, and gave the impression they meant business'.[77]

Frank Roro was at the start of a long captaincy career, and with almost all key players available and Sol Senaoane as Manager, expectations were high. Orange Free State and the North-Eastern Cape were represented for the first time, joining Transvaal, Border, Natal, Eastern Province and Griquas. Some matches were played on outlying fields at the white sporting citadel at Kingsmead, giving many cricketers the experience and challenge of playing on turf wickets for the first time.

The support of the Durban white community was important. Mayor Johnson, employer of Sid Pashe, Natal's vice-captain, opened proceedings, and business shared the budget costs of around £100 with the Durban Council. Not surprisingly cricket was seen as an ultra-elite activity among Durban's African population, and the few African spectators dressed formally in blazers and ties, but there was minimal interest in the event from the working-class Zulu population of the City.[78] On the field, the experienced and well prepared Transvaal team lived up to expectations this time and massacred the opposition in all three of their games, beating Natal by 217 runs, Eastern Province by an innings and 42 runs, and finally demolishing a hapless North-Eastern Cape side by an innings and 230 runs. The overall batting statistics reflected Transvaal's dominance in that they averaged 21 per wicket in contrast to their opponents' sorry 6 runs per wicket, but no individual scores are available.[79]

Roro was at the height of his powers. His Orientals (Crown Mines) team once again won the NRC tournament in April 1939, as well as the Sugar Cup and the Flag Cup, while the 'B' side won the Pilup and Senaoane Cups.[80] Orientals had recruited Frank's brother Harley, as well as Sydney Hashe who announced himself with 200 out of 504/6 declared against Orientals 'B'.

The Johannesburg African elites had more than just cricket to look forward to. In the same month, the Bantu Dramatic and Operatic Society staged an opera 'Moshoeshoe' about the African leader whose kingdom was never conquered and remained outside the Union of South Africa; the Wilberforce Choir, conducted by C. Yabanisa was broadcast on the SABC, and the Darktown Strutters and Jazz Maniacs performed at a Concert and Dance in aid of the BMSC.[81]

No NRC tournament event was then held until late 1940, and the state of the Transvaal game was criticised in the Press particularly concerned at the failure to complete matches. With fixtures played home and away across two weekends, teams that faced large scores accumulated on the first Sunday of the fixture at their home ground were not turning up for the second Sunday at the away ground. The Press also attacked the 'awful practice' of players acting as umpires and took the selectors to task for 'preferring their pals'.[82]

Despite this, Transvaal once again won the Chamber of Mines trophy hosted by Port Elizabeth in 1940/41 without losing a game, beating both Border and Eastern Province by an innings. Individual scores were again not fully recorded but P. Mama hit a hundred in the first game against the Orange Free State and Harley Roro had a consistent tournament. Frank Roro was described as a 'born captain' by C. M. Kieviet, not always the most flattering of critics.[83]

Aftermath

The 1940/41 tournament was the last to be staged for Africans until after the Second World War, when the world and the Rand had changed dramatically. In Johannesburg, the African urban population almost doubled between 1939 and 1952, and the expansion of the African working class, partly the result of a brief suspension of influx control in 1942–1943 ushered in an era of direct resistance, beginning with the Alexandra Bus boycotts of the early 1940s. The housing crisis and massive overcrowding resulted in a complex struggle between squatters and municipality over the next few years, and the ANC slowly began to build on the political opportunities afforded by grassroots action. In 1944, the ANC Youth League was set up, which began the political career of a new generation of Africans led by Nelson Mandela, Walter Sisulu and Oliver Tambo, which was to change the face of African politics.[84]

On the cricket field, a non-racial South African Cricket Board of Control (SACBOC) including the South African Bantu, Malay, Coloured and Indian Cricket Boards, was inaugurated in 1951, and drew on the example of the local Inter-Race tournaments which had begun in the 1930s. The first tournament was held in Johannesburg in December 1951 and Frank Roro, now 43, captained the South African Bantu side. They beat the South African Indians on the first innings. Frank Roro fittingly scored the only century of the week (116 out of 258), and 66 out of 124 in the second match against the South African Coloureds, for whom Basil Waterwich's 12 wickets proved decisive.[85] Black cricket was on the move again in the national context, but it would be forty more years before the dawn of a democratic society allowed for real non-racial cricket.

The 1930s, in comparison with the more radical 1920s, are often looked upon as an era of political quietude where depression and repression allowed Africans little opportunity to shape their social and economic environment. But this chapter, in sketching the roles played by African leaders in developing a vibrant cricket culture demonstrates that African elites were able to build their own world, shaping their personal destinies through sporting leadership. They reinforced their class position, effectively as mine employed semi-professional cricketers in a South Africa where all cricket was supposedly strictly amateur, and as entrepreneurs arranging tournaments, catering, ticketing and provided significant economic opportunities around the availability of alcohol. Not least they developed their power in the community, as cricket acted as catalyst for social interaction. Watching cricket, unlike football, was popular among women as well as men and the BMSC ground operated, what in Kimberley cricket at the turn of the century, was known as the 'marriage market'. While the mining industry supported cricket as a device to retain a permanent workforce to recruit, supervise and control the huge migrant workforce on which mine profitability depended, and the Johannesburg Municipality sought increased social control, talented Africans were able to manipulate such institutional support for their ends and achieve a measure of leadership and control otherwise denied to them.

Finally, the whole question of the extent to which black cricket sought to nuance the question of exclusivity and inclusivity, of who plays with and against whom, in the face of state oppression to entrench segregation, was the key to an understanding of the political dynamics of the period. Black leaders showed imagination and a steadfast adherence to the ultimate goal of non-racism in sport. This had been encouraged by David Harris's grant of the Barnato Trophy to be played for by all black cricketers, a formulation that was taken a stage further by the non-racial constitution of the SACCB in 1902. By the end of the 1920s, community tensions meant that it was no longer possible to hold the Barnato ideal together, but the principle was never lost and within four years an inter-race Board was set up on the Rand with the intention of achieving non-racial sport even if that needed to start with communities playing against each other again.

In summary, this chapter seeks to recognise the importance of African cricket on the Rand in building and maintaining an elite community reflecting petty bourgeoisie interests, against the forces of a racist and oppressive state, and its efforts to keep alive the ideals of non-racial sport. Beyond this, it celebrates the skills and abilities of the Gweles, Setis, Majolas, Mpilisos, Senaoanes, Roros, Fihlas and thousands of other players whose natural ability, enthusiasm and hard work allowed them to succeed in the face of often appalling social and political conditions. And finally, it applauds the achievements of an African leadership which, while it did not transform their world, changed the lives for the better of the many who took part in it, and contributed to the goal of non-racial sport in a non-racial society. Who knows how good Frank Roro could have been given the same opportunities routinely available to white South Africans? Sadly, he did not live to see himself named as one of South Africa's ten cricketers of the millenium in 1999.[86]

NOTES

1. For the ideological significance of secondary education see Helen Bradford, *A Taste of Freedom: The ICU in Rural South Africa, 1924–1930* (New Haven: Yale University Press, 1988), 65.
2. R. Callebert, 'Working Class Action and the Informal Trade on the Durban Docks, 1930s–1950s', *Journal of Southern African Studies*, 38, 4 (Abingdon: Routledge, 2012), 849.

3. Approximately 80 African workers were housed in space measuring 42 feet by 30 feet. T. Dunbar Moodie, *Going for Gold: Men, Mines and Migration* (Berkeley: University of California Press, 1994), 73.

4. T. Dunbar Moodie, 'Mine Culture and Miners' Identity on the South African Gold Mines' in B. Bozzoli (ed.), *Town and Countryside in the Transvaal* (Johannesburg: Ravan Press, 1983), 183–87.

5. Moodie, *Going for Gold*, 21.

6. Thanks to Dale Slater for discussions around this issue as well as for his detailed comments including those on the relationship between cricket, class and the economy.

7. For alcohol, the compounds and the city see Julie Baker, 'Prohibition and Illicit Liquor on the Witwatersrand, 1902–1932' in J. Crush and C. Ambler (eds.), *Liquor and Labour in Southern Africa* (Athens, OH: University of Ohio Press, 1992), 139–61.

8. *Umteteli Wa Bantu*, 22 February 1935.

9. S. Jingoes (compiled by J. Perry and C. Perry), *A Chief Is Chief by the People* (London: Oxford University Press, 1975), 56–126; C. van Onselen, *The Seed Is Mine* (New York: Hill and Wang, 1996), 148–51.

10. R. Guha, *A Corner of a Foreign Field: The Indian History of a British Sport* (London: Picador, 2002).

11. A. Odendaal, *The Story of an African Game* (Cape Town: David Philip, 2003), 31–39; R. Parry, 'Black Cricketers, White Politicians and the Origins of Segregation at the Cape to 1894' in B. Murray and G. Vahed (eds.), *Empire and Cricket: The South African Experience 1884–1914* (Pretoria: Unisa, 2009), 23–37.

12. B. Willan, 'An African in Kimberley: Sol T Plaatje, 1894–1898' in S. Marks and R. Rathbone, *Industrialisation and Social Change in South Africa, 1870 to 1930* (Harlow: Longman, 1982), 251–52.

13. S. Reddy and D. Bansda (eds.), *South African Cricket Annual 1953–54* (Cape Town, 1954), 83.

14. B. Murray and C. Merrett, *Caught Behind: Race and Politics in South African Cricket* (Johannesburg: Wits University Press and University of Kwa-Zulu-Natal Press, 2004), 11.

15. A. Desai, V. Padayachee, K. Reddy, and G. Vahed, *Blacks in Whites: A Century of Cricket Struggles in KwaZulu-Natal* (Pietermaritzburg: University of Kwa-Zulu-Natal Press, 2002), 44.

16. See, for example, Jingoes, *A Chief Is Chief*, 72–99.

17. The African leaders who were included in the 1909 Delegation to protest the proposed Union constitution in London were often directly involved in cricket administration. Dr. Walter Benson Rubusana, for example, President of the South African Native Congress (soon to become the ANC), was also President of the East London and Border Cricket Union, the strongest in the sub-continent (Odendaal, *African Game*, 83).

18. Both H. B. Piliso and Sol Senoaone who played a key role in the sporting developments of the 1920s and 1930s were Acting Chairmen of the TNMCA in the early 1920s. Alan Cobley, '"Why Not All Go Up Higher?" The Transvaal Native Mine Clerks' Association, 1920–1925', *South African Historical Journal*, 62, 1 (2010), 143–61.

19. *Umteteli Wa Bantu*, 3 April 1926.

20. Ibid., 6 March 1926.

21. T. Lodge, *Black Politics in South Africa since 1945* (London: Longman, 1983), 6.

22. J. and R. Simons, *Class and Colour in South Africa*, 1850–1950 (Bellville: Mayibuye Books, 1983), 353–85.

23. Jingoes, *A Chief Is Chief*, 99–126.

24. W. Beinart and C. Bundy, 'The Union, the Nation and the Talking Crow' in Beinart and Bundy (eds.), *Hidden Struggles in Rural South Africa* (London: James Currey, 1987).

25. *Bantu World*, 18 September 1937.

26. *Umteteli Wa Bantu*, 5 October 1929.

27. P. Alegi, *Laduma! Soccer, Politics and Society in South Africa* (Pietermaritzburg: University of Kwa-Zulu-Natal Press, 2004), 42.

28. The switch in the white supremacist area of rugby, when Mandela wore Francois Pienaar's number 6 shirt at the World Cup in 1995, was a moment of high drama overturning a century of cultural practice. Clint Eastwood's film, *Invictus*, emphasises the importance of this change but inevitably fails to grasp the real historical magnitude of this step.

29. For example, *Bantu World* noted that Harry Smith, the black world middle-weight champion, beat Willie Unwin, a white South African: 'Non-European boxing fans throughout the country will receive the news with great joy' (*Bantu World*, 10 October 1932).

30. *Umteteli Wa Bantu*, 16 October 1926.

31. *Bantu World*, 10 July 1937.

32. *Umteteli Wa Bantu*, 17 April 1926.

33. Ibid., 17 April 1926 lists the winners and victory margins.

34. Ibid., 25 December 1926.

35. Dan Twala was one of the founders of the Johannesburg African Football Association and the South African Soccer Federation. His uncle was R. W. Msimang, one of the founders of the SANNC (later the ANC) in 1912. T. Couzens, 'An Introduction to the History of Football in South Africa', in Bozzoli, *Town and Countryside*, 199.

36. *Umteteli Wa Bantu*, 30 November 1935.

37. Alegi, *Laduma!* 41.

38. Moodie, *Going for Gold*, 212–14.

39. T. Lodge, 'The Destruction of Sophiatown' in Bozzoli, *Town and Countryside*, 345.

40. Reddy and Bansda, *Almanack*, 57.
41. See chapter on Frank Roro in, A. Bacher and D. Williams, *South Africa's Greatest Batsmen* (Johannesburg: Zebra Press, 2015).
42. Bansda and Reddy, *Almanack*, 57.
43. *Umteteli Wa Bantu*, Orientals versus Rand Leases, 21 March 1936.
44. *Bantu World*, 31 December 1932.
45. Ibid., 7 January 1933.
46. Ibid., 28 January 1933.
47. Ibid., 10 April 1937.
48. *Rand Daily Mail*, 1, 2 January 1934.
49. *Bantu World*, 6 January 1934.
50. *Umteteli Wa Bantu*, 30 March 1935.
51. Ibid., 16 March 1935.
52. Ibid., 5 January 1935.
53. Desai et al., *Blacks in Whites*, 140–41.
54. *Umteteli Wa Bantu*, 5 January 1935.
55. Ibid., 12 January 1935.
56. Ibid., 22 February 1935.
57. Ibid., 9 March 1935.
58. Ibid., 16 April 1935.
59. Ibid., 31 August 1935.
60. Alegi, *Laduma!* 43–44.
61. *Umteteli Wa Bantu*, 31 August 1935.
62. The senior league included Randfontein Estates. Simmer and Jack, Orientals, Rand Leases, West Rand Bantu, City Deep, Mendies (a reference to the sinking of the *SS Mendis* when more than six hundred African troops lost their lives during one of the worst disasters of the Great War), Ottomans, Willows, Stonebreakers, Independents, Orlando Brotherly, Gaikas and Deeps.
63. *Umteteli Wa Bantu*, 30 November 1935.
64. *Bantu World*, 1 February 1936 and 28 March 1936.
65. *Umteteli Wa Bantu*, 11 and 18 January 1936.
66. Reverend Sigamoney had a rich and colourful life. Like many of the African leaders who were his contemporaries he resisted stereotyping as his interests in workers, cricket, religion and later commerce indicated. He was born in Durban in 1888 and represented Natal Indians in the Barnato Trophy in 1913. He helped form the Indian Workers Commercial Union in 1917; was briefly a boxing promoter, and went to England to study for the priesthood in 1923. On his return he moved to Johannesburg and became President of the South African Indian Cricket Union in 1942. See Desai et al., *Blacks in Whites*, 59–61.
67. *Bantu World*, 8 February 1936.
68. *Umteteli Wa Bantu*, 1 February 1936.

69. *Bantu World*, 22 January 1938.
70. Ibid., 5 February 1938.
71. Ibid., 8 October 1938.
72. Ibid., 8 January 1938.
73. Lodge, *Black Politics*, 9–12.
74. *Bantu World*, 5 September 1942.
75. Ibid., 10 December 1938.
76. Ibid., 29 October 1938.
77. Ibid., 5, 12 November and 31 December 1938.
78. Desai et al., *Blacks in Whites*, 145–47.
79. *Bantu World*, 7 January 1939.
80. Ibid., 15 April 1939.
81. Ibid.
82. Ibid., 14 and 28 December 1940.
83. *Bantu World*, 25 January 1941.
84. Lodge, *Black Politics*, 11–28.
85. Odendaal, *African Game*, 151–55.
86. The ten cricketers of the Millennium were selected by a representative South African panel including Krish Reddy, Coetie Neethling and Zim Mbatani. The ten selected were Basil D'Oliveira, Frank Roro, Dudley Nourse, Hugh Tayfield, Aubrey Faulkner, Eric Peterson, Graeme Pollock, Barry Richards and Mike Proctor.

CHAPTER 5

Rhodes, Cricket and the Scholarship Legacy: A Southern African Perspective, 1903–1971

Jonty Winch

INTRODUCTION

Cecil John Rhodes spent nine terms at Oxford University that were spread over eight years, during which time he did not neglect his interests as one of Kimberley's leading diamond diggers. He was able to enjoy two invigorating but sharply contrasting societies in the knowledge that in South Africa he could rely on the acumen of his business partner, Charles Rudd, whilst his time at Oxford compensated for missing out on a public school education. In the course of perhaps the most detailed survey of Rhodes's life, Robert I. Rotberg states that Rhodes used Oxford to 'make contact with the cream of the English ruling class', men who could help him achieve his goals. He rarely attended lectures, socialised rather than worked, yet gained much despite achieving no more than a pass degree. 'Rhodes paused and consolidated at Oxford', said Rotberg, 'He brooded, constructed, and dreamt, and dreamt some more. Without this moratorium [he] might never have honed his own

J. Winch (✉)
Reading, UK

© The Author(s) 2018
B. Murray et al. (eds.), *Cricket and Society in South Africa, 1910–1971*, Palgrave Studies in Sport and Politics,
https://doi.org/10.1007/978-3-319-93608-6_5

sense of purpose or realised the immensity of his own inner conviction and strength'.[1]

The Oxford experience was invaluable in the establishment of his scholarship scheme. Young men identified as future leaders of the English-speaking world would from 1903 interact within the university's residential system to help prepare them for a world where Britain and her empire set and maintained standards. This chapter will focus on one aspect of the qualities that Rhodes deemed necessary in the selection of the ideal student. It will seek to examine the part played by southern African Rhodes Scholars in the imperial games—cricket in particular—as it serves as a window on aspects of the workings of a scheme designed to carry out Rhodes's ideals and protect his legacy. Ability in sport was seen as relevant to the selection and training of the Scholars, not least because the games reflected imperial ideology in the development of ethical behaviour and the formation of sound social attitudes. The investigation will also endeavour to explore the extent to which sport's role in the scheme was dependent on empire, and will take into account the decisions and values of trustees, selection committees and the attitudes of the University, as well as political, economic and social developments that unfolded during the twentieth century.

The period under consideration is framed between two major developments in southern African sport. It was in March 1895 that Rhodes, then prime minister of the Cape and in the process of setting up his scholarship scheme, mentioned to a young Pelham Warner over breakfast at Oriel College, Oxford, that he had opposed the selection of a player of colour—'Krom' Hendricks—for the previous year's first South African cricket side to tour England. Warner's acceptance of 'how far [Rhodes] was looking ahead' represented a general lack of concern over the Cape Government's racial policies at that time. The subsequent exclusion of 'non-whites' from South African sports teams—and effectively from the allocated Rhodes Scholarships—did not attract criticism during the first half of the twentieth century.[2] It was not until Basil D'Oliveira was prevented from touring South Africa with the MCC in 1968/69 that Springbok cricket and rugby teams were penalised. The reaction then was to oppose tours by South African teams, with Oxford University at the forefront of the aggressive anti-apartheid protests.

It took until 1971 for South Africa's first black Rhodes Scholarship candidates to be shortlisted. In 1978, Loyiso Nongxa, later Vice-Chancellor and Principal of the University of the Witwatersrand, was

South Africa's first African Rhodes Scholar. He was a mathematician of note and a sportsman who had played rugby for the University of Fort Hare 'Baa-Baas'.

THE RHODES SCHOLARSHIP, GAMES AND OXFORD UNIVERSITY

In 1891, Cecil John Rhodes declared, 'I find I am human and should like to be living after my death'.[3] At that time he possessed a growing fortune and in the years which followed he gave thought to living on through his scholarship scheme which would be used to promote imperial unity and interest. The prestigious scholarship programme at Oxford was to be administered by the Rhodes Trust and, it has been said, 'designed to provide immortality for Rhodes'.[4] The idea of 'national or imperial scholarships' is thought to have originated with a journalist, John Astley Cooper, and taken further by an Australian expatriate working in England, Thomas Hudson Beare, prior to Rhodes being in a position to put it into practice (Fig. 5.1).[5]

According to the Zimbabwean historian R. J. Challiss, the scholarships originated 'in the founder's belief that Anglo-Saxons were "the finest race in the world" and ... that the world could only benefit from unity under their sway', but the plan went beyond empire.[6] The importance Rhodes attached to Anglo-American partnership meant an initial

Fig. 5.1 Cecil John Rhodes played cricket at thirteen for Goodman's high school (*Left*). Oxford University cricketers from the former Rhodesia at Lord's in 1971 (left to right): Mike Burton, Barry May, Peter Jones and Christopher Ridley. Burton, May, Jones and Ridley's brother, Giles, were Rhodes Scholars who captained Oxford at cricket (*Right*)

thirty-two scholarships for the USA, whilst a further five for the Germans came in the belief that '... an understanding between the three great powers will render war impossible'.[7] There were twenty for the Empire, of which the five allocated to South Africa, included certain secondary schools in the Cape: the Diocesan College (Bishops); St Andrew's College, Grahamstown; Boys' High School, Stellenbosch (now Paul Roos Gymnasium), and the South African College School (SACS).[8]

Rhodes advocated support for the all-rounder, reflecting the 'special admiration he had conceived second-hand of the British public school'. His criteria drew from concepts of manliness 'associated with the rigours of the games field and the cadet corps, and the hardness, even brutality, of much of school life'.[9] In his Will, he noted as guidance that the proportion of four-tenths should be attached to 'literary and scholastic attainments', and two-tenths to 'fondness for, and success in, manly outdoor sports, such as cricket, football and the like'. He then suggested two-tenths to 'qualities of manhood', and a similar share to 'moral force of character' through which he expected the ideal candidate to have demonstrated 'instincts to lead' and to 'esteem the performance of public duties as his highest aim'.

The nineteenth-century games cult coincided with the extension of British influence overseas. Public schools were the driving force in disseminating a unique educational ideal around the globe, one which recognised the value of character-training through team games. Qualities advanced by playing sport—such as courage, resourcefulness and perseverance—were considered invaluable in governing and defending an empire. The ideal was taken further by those from public school and ancient university who served as headmasters and teachers in South African schools. They helped establish an educational system based on the 'Tom Brown formula' that was comparable with the English model. In so doing, cricket and rugby were seen to thrive in southern Africa as part of British imperial ideology; a development that was not lost on Rhodes when he embarked on his ambitious scholarship scheme that he hoped would play a part in uniting the English-speaking peoples of the world.

When the scheme came into operation in 1903, the opportunity to play in the Oxbridge contests proved to be a great attraction to young sportsmen from southern Africa. They were able to demonstrate their sporting skills and in doing so strengthen the games at Oxford University. 'Over the full spread of years', wrote E. W. Swanton, the well-known cricket correspondent of the *Telegraph*, 'no nurseries of talent can compare with The Parks and Fenner's'. He calculated the universities had produced '120-odd Test cricketer Blues', and that 'thirty have been captains of England, thirteen of other Test countries'.[10] Tony Lewis in *Double Century: The Story of MCC and Cricket* dwelt on 'leadership being in plentiful supply ... bred in the public schools and refined at Oxford or Cambridge'.[11]

'The last thing' Rhodes wanted was 'a bookworm'—no Greek and Latin 'swots'. Under the usual modern system of competitive examinations, he asked: 'Do we ... get the best man for the world's fight?' 'I think not', he answered.[12]

Rhodes did not specifically refer to colour when he directed his trustees to establish 'colonial scholarships' for 'male students'. The scheme included the provision that 'no student shall be qualified or disqualified ... on account of his race or religious opinions'. At the time this would have been seen to relate to the English-Dutch division, although Challiss does note that Christopher Ngukoyena Lobengula, son of the late Ndebele king, was considered for one of Rhodesia's Rhodes Scholarships in 1908.[13] It did not happen as Lobengula chose to settle in the Cape Colony and southern African selection committees were under no pressure to appoint persons of colour until the 1970s.[14]

The ability or desire to adhere to Rhodes's criteria became increasingly difficult in the changing world of the twentieth century. 'The issue which most perplexed trustees and selectors', said Philip Ziegler, '... was that of "brains against brawn".' From the outset, there were those who challenged the importance attached to sport, notably George Parkin, former principal of Upper Canada College and the first Secretary of the Trust, who interpreted 'success in manly outdoor sports such as cricket, football and the like' as 'thinking not of runs or goals or cups for championships but of the moral qualities inspired by team games'. These he saw as 'the training in fair play, the absence of all trickery, the chivalrous yielding of advantage to an opponent and acceptance of defeat with cheerfulness'. Ziegler was critical, arguing 'it would be hard to conceive any set of characteristics more remote from Rhodes's own practices in politics or business'.[15]

OXFORD UNIVERSITY AND THE EARLY CRICKET YEARS

There is a reference to cricket being played at Oxford University as early as 1729. The famous Dr. Samuel Johnson, best known for his *Dictionary of the English Language*, was a student and later stated that he played cricket there at that time. The founding of the Oxford University CC occurred at the beginning of the nineteenth century, and in 1827 a game was played against Cambridge in the first-ever 'University Match', arguably the oldest first-class fixture in the world. One of the early stars was George Cotterill, later headmaster and 'father of cricket' at St Andrew's College, Grahamstown, who represented Cambridge from 1858–60.[16] Some years afterwards, two future South African cricket captains played the game at Oxford. Herbert H. Castens, who was from Port Elizabeth and attended Rugby School, became involved at inter-college level, whilst Henry Taberer, a product of St Andrew's College, Grahamstown, represented the University in 1891 and 1892 but did not gain a 'Blue', which is awarded to those selected for the annual intervarsity. The *South African Review* remarked that 'favouritism of the grossest kind robbed [Taberer] forever of the great, trebly great, honour of a triple blue', adding: 'Mr Palairet, the Oxford captain, had a brother's interest nearer his heart than the honour of his university'. The report concluded 'of course Oxford lost the match' because of the omission of Taberer, 'a better bowler than there was in either the Oxford or Cambridge team'.[17]

The early South Africans were capable players but generally not deemed to be of the standard required to earn a 'Blue'. Worthington Hoskin, the first Rhodes Scholar from St Andrew's, Grahamstown, was good enough to play first-class cricket for Oxford and later Gloucestershire but missed out on the intervarsity match when he broke his ankle. There were others who played Test cricket for South Africa but were unable to gain 'Blues'. They include Norman Reid and the three Hands brothers—all Rhodes Scholars but restricted to playing inter-college cricket.[18] Plum Lewis, the first SACS student to receive a Rhodes Scholarship, represented Balliol at cricket from 1903 to 1907 and captained the College First XI in 1905. Although a 'Blue' eluded him, he went on to score 151 for Western Province against J. W. H. T. Douglas's touring MCC team in 1913/14 and was selected for South Africa.

Turf wickets, short seasons and the frequently unpleasant English weather were factors that counted against the success of cricketers who were used to playing on matting in a warm climate. Oxford teams in the early years came from the public schools that made much of the prestige attached to their products winning 'Blues'. Success on the English schoolboy circuit gave players a head start when it came to selection for university teams, whilst those from foreign outposts often had relatively few opportunities to convince captains that they deserved to play in the

University eleven. Rhodes Scholars nevertheless competed for places in the teams and George Chesterton, an Oxford 'Blue', believed that Rhodes 'through his will, and not quite in the manner he had intended, had introduced a revolution to the Oxford world'.[19] By 1909—the year that the Imperial Cricket Conference was formed—there were four Rhodes Scholars in the Oxford eleven: three Australians and a South African, Ronald Lagden.

The election of Lagden as a Rhodes Scholar was interesting because he was educated at Marlborough College and therefore familiar with playing conditions. The son of Sir Godfrey Lagden, the former Resident Commissioner of Basutoland, he was listed as an 'extra South African Rhodes Scholar' in 1908. He excelled at sport, becoming the first Oxford student to win 'Blues' in four sports (cricket, hockey, rugby and racquets), and was also an England rugby international.

The first South African-educated player to obtain a 'Blue' was Basil Melle, a Rhodes Scholar from SACS. He was, said Geoffrey Bolton in his *History of the O.U.C.C.*, 'a freshman of real ability' who captured 55 wickets at 15.90 during the 1913 season; figures that could have been better but he was 'very dependent on his short-leg fieldsman and at this time the technique of close-in fielding was only beginning to develop'. David Frith saw Melle as playing a role in the origins of body-line bowling through his 'inswingers with three short-legs'.[20] And at Lord's in 1913, Cambridge had 'no bowler who could rank with Melle'. Displaying 'untiring accuracy', he returned figures of 6/70 and 2/46 but could not prevent an Oxford defeat by four wickets.

Melle helped Oxford gain a convincing 194-run victory in 1914 but, not long afterwards, when he had bowled a mere six overs with the new ball in a match at Trent Bridge he was handed a telegram. He had been called up by the Oxford University detachment of the King's Colonial Corps and left the field immediately. Captain Melle's best cricket years were to be lost to the War which had been declared two days earlier. Six players who took part in the 1914 match between the universities at Lord's were killed in action and 'at least four of the others suffered such disability that they could never again play cricket with full enjoyment'.[21] No intervarsity cricket fixtures were arranged during the period of fighting in the course of which some 2700 Oxonians lost their lives, including Reginald Hands and Ronald Lagden. When peace was finally secured and the spoils divided, Britain's Foreign Secretary, Arthur Balfour, observed the map of the world had 'yet more red on it'.[22]

Cricket resumed, with Oxford teams fielding the occasional South Africans. In 1919, Gerald V. Pearse, a Natal Rhodes Scholar, took 4 for 66 in Cambridge University's first innings to assist Oxford in their 45-run win. Two years later came V. H. 'Boet' Neser—the recipient of a Military Cross; a Transvaal Rhodes Scholar; double 'Blue'; a 'First' in law; future international rugby referee and South African cricket captain[23]—who played alongside Douglas R. Jardine of 'bodyline' fame. Also in the team for just one match against Hampshire in 1921 was a SACS Rhodes Scholar and Test player in the making, Jacobus Duminy, who wrote of his English experience: 'The first occasion on which I met any non-white who was not a farm-labourer, or a dock-worker or a semi-skilled artisan was when I went to Oxford at the age of twenty-three'.[24] Greatly respected as an academic, Duminy went on to become Vice-Chancellor of the University of Cape Town. Said a former colleague: 'Cecil Rhodes would have been well pleased with his Scholar'.[25]

Not all Rhodes Scholars returned to South Africa, some serving elsewhere in the empire such as the Oxbridge-dominated Sudan Political Service. Others pursued their own careers. Guy 'Bill' Blaikie, the most successful of the country's cricketers at Oxford during the 1920s, was 'head-hunted' by a chemical company and settled in Canada. In 1924, he had topped the University's batting averages, scoring 507 runs at 42.25. According to *Wisden*, he 'astonished the critics by the vigour of his left-handed hitting' when he hammered 120 against the MCC at Lord's and then 'hit away with amazing brilliancy' in the intervarsity.[26]

There were no South Africans in the Oxford University team for the next five years and the fact cannot be overlooked that the country's leading schools seemed to be producing relatively few cricketers of the quality of their English counterparts. South Africa's overall contribution to Oxford cricket in the first thirty years of the century was modest despite a flow of able players through the Rhodes Scholarship scheme. A few promising cricketers such as the St Andrew's, Grahamstown, Rhodes Scholar, Harland Rees, who batted so well for the South African Schools XI against the touring MCC in 1927/28, chose not to sacrifice the time necessary to play the game and instead focused on rugby.[27]

At this stage, it is relevant to compare the cricket achievements by South Africans at Oxford with those of their rugby counterparts during the same period.

St Andrew's and Bishops Reveal Rugby Prowess

The advent of the Rhodes Scholarship scheme coincided with a period when Oxford and Cambridge 'produced some of the most famous players in the history of British rugby' such as Kenneth G. MacLeod, Adrian Stoop, V. H. 'Lump' Cartwright, Henry Vassall, John Raphael and Ronnie Poulton.[28] 'It is difficult', wrote James Corsan in *Poulton and England*, 'to overstate the position of Oxbridge within the Edwardian rugby scene' adding, 'in terms of lifetime achievement, a "Blue" was regarded as next after an international cap'.[29]

It was in this era of advancement that South Africans had considerable influence on the game at Oxford. Prowess in rugby was part of the make-up of young men elected Rhodes Scholars by two of the South African schools, St Andrew's College, Grahamstown, and the Diocesan College (Bishops), Cape Town. The Canadian, George Parkin who served as Secretary of the Trust from 1902 to 1920, complained that at St Andrew's College, Grahamstown, 'the boys practically controlled the election, which was "decided almost entirely by the result of play on the [rugby] football ground!"'[30] The method of pupils voting was originally suggested by Rhodes and said to contribute towards the South Africans placing greater emphasis on sporting prowess than other countries.

Parkin thought the Canadians were 'a fine set of fellows', but made the bizarre claim that South African Rhodes Scholars 'were inadequate not so much because most of them were picked from the restricted field offered by the four schools as because "the stimulating air of the high veldt and plateau country tends to nervous exhaustion"'. He also believed their 'reliance on black people meant they were ill-prepared for Oxford' and further argued that 'parents with clever boys' had told him at St Andrew's, Grahamstown, that 'they had given up all hope of competition with the sporting interest'.[31] All but one of the pre-War Rhodes Scholars from St Andrew's gained rugby 'Blues'. Yet from this group emerged a judge, a professor, a vice-principal of the *alma mater*, a couple of barristers, a mine manager and Lennox Broster OBE, 'a very eminent surgeon in Harley Street'.[32]

A St Andrew's rugby product, Rupert 'Mop' Williamson, who was described as 'definitely the "find" of the 1907/08 season as far as England were concerned', partnered the black player, James 'Darkie' Peters, at halfback on the international stage.[33] Yet Parkin questioned the contribution of South Africans to college life and claimed they 'found the problems of adjustment harder than did most colonials'.[34] He ignored the extent to which rugby consumed the time and interest of young players. Seven of the first eight Rhodes Scholars from St Andrew's earned rugby 'Blues' with six playing for the Barbarians and Williamson for England. Bishops had a similarly impressive record with six out of their first ten Scholars winning 'Blues'; three playing for the Barbarians, and Reginald Hands (England) and Stephen Steyn (Scotland) achieving international honours.[35] There were also southern African 'Blues' from other schools and some who were not Rhodes Scholars. Before the War, 19 southern Africans—15 being Rhodes Scholars—won 34 Oxford rugby 'Blues'.

The Scholarship years were a grand adventure for the boys, many arriving straight from school as Rhodes intended. Oxford did not lose to Cambridge between 1906 and 1911, with just one draw in 1908. The intervarsity became a great occasion and by 1911 there were 16,000 in attendance at the matches held at Queen's. Rising gates eventually forced a switch to Twickenham in 1921, with games attracting 30,000 in 1923 and 40,000 in 1925. The South African influence continued either side of the First World War, one report stating the only time that Cambridge had a run of four successive victories (1925–28) was when Oxford had fewer overseas players than in any other period.[36] The 'dark blues' regained the ascendancy in 1929 when Thomas Gubb, with five other South Africans to assist him, led Oxford to victory.[37] Said Matthew Robson, one of just four players from England in that year's team, 'it was quite an achievement for an Englishman to get into the Oxford side – the few places left after the South Africans had picked themselves were normally filled by Scots, Welsh, Irish and New Zealanders'.[38]

The emphasis that the St Andrew's, Grahamstown, and Bishops' selection committees placed on sport had a notable impact on the balance of Oxford teams. But, once again, the academic standard of the former was cause for concern when the new secretary of the Trust adjudged it 'undistinguished by comparison with other schools'.[39]

OWEN-SMITH ELECTRIFYING AS SOUTH AFRICANS 'LOOM LARGE' IN 1930s

After the dark years of the late 1920s, cricket did improve at Oxford during the early part of the next decade. Peter Davies wrote in his short history of the University's cricket club that two South Africans, Alan Melville and 'Tuppy' Owen-Smith, and the Indian, Nawab of Pataudi, 'would play a significant role in elevating Oxford cricket to a different level in this period'. They were seen as the first of many distinguished 'imports' with the 1931 season being the best for many years.[40] Melville, who had attended Michaelhouse, took over the captaincy in his second year, 'the first time since 1863 that the honour had fallen to one so junior' and in Owen-Smith, a Bishops' Rhodes Scholar, he had one of *Wisden's* 'Five Cricketers of the Year' in 1930. Owen-Smith was a player who 'had an electrifying effect on any side for which he played; he was a very hard-hitting batsman, an accurate bowler who was always doing something with the ball, and as a fieldsman he was impeccable'.[41]

In 1931, it was the Nawab of Pataudi who enjoyed the most remarkable of seasons, surpassing previous batting records when he amassed over 1300 runs, with six hundreds and an average of 93.35. As many as 30,000 spectators paid to watch the intervarsity at Lord's during which the Nawab made a record score of 238 not out.[42] He added 174 in an hour and a half with Owen-Smith (78)—whose footwork befitted a boxing 'Blue'—and Oxford won their most important cricket encounter by eight wickets. Bolton described the occasion as a glorious victory through which 'Oxford could take down their harps from the trees by the waters of Babylon'.[43]

The following year, the *Cricketer* noted that Eton, Harrow and Rugby no longer monopolised the two university sides as they had done for many years: 'There was only one Etonian, [Arthur] Hazlerigg, playing, and no one from either Harrow or Rugby ... South Africa loomed large on the Oxford side ...'.[44] Pieter van der Bijl, a Bishops' Rhodes Scholar, joined skipper Melville and Owen-Smith in the 1932 team. Van der Bijl, who would later represent South Africa in the Test arena, had initially battled to secure his place in the Oxford eleven. That season, however, he scored a fine 73 against the Indian tourists and won a coveted 'Blue' in a match that was evenly poised when play ended.

Melville, tall and elegant in his stroke play, attracted the attention of both Douglas Jardine who would lead the 'Bodyline' tour in 1932/33, and the South African Cricket Association. But, said Luke Alfred, a leading South African cricket journalist, Melville's father encouraged him to refuse 'both overtures' and bide his time with Sussex.[45]

The intervarsities in 1932 and 1933 were drawn with Owen-Smith and Melville key performers for Oxford. The number of people who turned up to watch the students play grew significantly between the Wars. They warmed to the efforts of the young South Africans in helping revive the fortunes of Oxford cricket. And, back home in South Africa, there were rewards for those who had encouraged turf wickets. The Springboks toured England in 1935 without the Oxford men but enjoyed considerable success. Victory at Lord's by 157 runs enabled them to win their first Test series in England.

There were no further Oxford 'Blues' for South African cricketers in the 1930s but Rhodes Scholars created an impression in rugby. Owen-Smith stood out and Swanton described him as 'the most remarkable all-rounder of my time ... inimitable, a genius – and he did everything with a grin'.[46] He went on to captain England to a triumphant 1937 rugby season, which included their first-ever win at Murrayfield, a victory that gave them the Triple Crown. The qualities that Rhodes admired were there in abundance: '... although he was not heavily built, he was won-derfully tough, and could take any amount of punishment ... His value in morale alone was invaluable'.[47] Teammate, Vivian Jenkins, recalled playing cricket with him at Oxford, when he kept wicket and Owen-Smith fielded 'at cover point and would throw in at me like a bullet'. They were also opposing full backs at Twickenham, Jenkins for Wales and Owen-Smith for England:

> It was 0-0 at half-time and we had been trying to outdo each other all half. As the referee blew to start the second half, I happened to catch his eye across the pitch from about thirty yards away. He threw his lemon at me exactly as he would have done from cover point and I caught the thing like a wicketkeeper, then off we went to play like hell for the second half.[48]

On qualifying as a doctor, Owen-Smith returned to the Cape. He was offered the captaincy of the South African cricket side in 1938 but was unable to take up the opportunity as he had just embarked on a business venture.

The leaders that Rhodes expected appeared both on and off the sports-field. Natal Rhodes Scholar and England international, H. D. 'Trilby' Freakes, captained Oxford in 1938 and played rugby along-side some interesting fellow Scholars in the course of his three years at the University.[49] In 1936, there was Gideon Roos, son of the legend-ary Springbok rugby captain, Paul Roos, and later Director-General of the South African Broadcasting Corporation.[50] Then, in 1938, the side included (Sir) Richard 'Dick' Luyt, who played first-class cricket for the University and became Governor-General of Guyana, and Hilgard Muller who was South Africa's last High Commissioner and first Ambassador in London, and later Minister of Foreign Affairs. The year after Freakes left, Michael Davies was selected as Wilf Wooller's partner at centre in the Welsh team, and after the War became a cabinet minister in the government of Tanganyika.

'By 1939', said Ziegler, Rhodes Scholars 'were established as a major force'. The number of overseas students at Oxford 'veered between 525 and 600 of which a third were Rhodes Scholars who made a notable contribution to the colleges to which they were assigned'. Between the Wars, 24 South Africans—19 being Rhodes Scholars—had earned 38 rugby 'Blues'. Sport was thriving and encouragement during this period was received from staff members of the University; an Oxford don of some standing was starting a campaign urging the Trust 'to abandon the intellectual qualification and to select good Rugger toughs, as they are the people the Empire really wants'.[51]

Chesterton recalled certain dons 'would seek out players, even finding funds to help where necessary, although always demanding academic attainments as well'. He noted 'great Oxford figures' helped in this way; men such as Philip Landon (a famous name at Trinity College); William 'Sonners' Stallybrass (the Principal of Brasenose who became the University's Vice-Chancellor) and Sir John Masterman (who toured Canada with the MCC and later became Vice-Chancellor, but is best known as chairman of the Twenty Committee which during the Second World War ran the Double-Cross System).[52]

Sir Herbert Stanley, who had served as High Commissioner in South Africa and was Governor of Southern Rhodesia from 1935, called for 'more brainy Rhodes Scholars' but the *Morning Post* dismissed the plea, stating 'it is expected of our territories that they should despatch something upstanding and freckled. We have enough brainy, spectacled youth at home'.[53] The situation in this regard would change after the Second World War. There would also be political change in South Africa where the liberal Jan Hofmeyr, nephew of 'Onze Jan', had been acting prime minister for much of the War. A SACS Rhodes Scholar at the age of sixteen, he was a keen cricketer and, when Principal of the University of the Witwatersrand during 1919–24, would play in the annual staff versus student matches.

LARGE CROWDS AS OXFORD BECOMES A CRICKET FORCE

In October 1942, the editors of *Life* magazine printed an open letter to the 'People of Britain' in which they made it clear that the Americans would not be fighting in order that Britain might hold on to its empire. It was an attitude that offended the British but a wartime alliance was of great importance. 'Without American money', said historian Niall Ferguson, 'the British war effort would have collapsed'. Whilst the British political elite found it 'extraordinarily hard to accept that the empire had to go as a price of victory ... the foundations of empire had been economic, and those foundations had simply been eaten up by the cost of the war'. Britain owed billions to its creditors, most notably the USA.[54]

The aftermath was marked by hardship and uncertainty, and Tony Pawson, later a cricket scribe with the *Observer*, recalled 'going up to Oxford as a twenty-five-year-old student with considerable experience of life and death but rather rusty on book learning'.[55] In rebuilding the country, determined efforts were made to accommodate inevitable changes during the period of transition. When the University arranged concessions for men returning from the navy, army and air force, Chesterton noted 'such a multitude poured into Oxford'. As a result, 'special arrangements had to be made to work off the backlog'. Examinations—'schools' as they were known—took place in June and December: 'for cricketers this offered a joyous choice!'[56]

Swanton recorded the immediate post-war years as 'halcyon ones for university cricket, with Oxford at first the stronger side of the two'.[57] For five successive years, the 'dark blues' won more matches than they lost in each season. Furthermore, only one intervarsity was lost and that a major surprise. The run of success began in 1946 when the New Zealander, Martin Donnelly—'the greatest left-hand bat of the day'—hammered 142 to set up victory over Cambridge.[58] Donnelly, who 'planned to do only as much work as was necessary to scrape a pass', was already at Oxford when he applied for a Rhodes Scholarship. He was turned down by the New Zealand selection committee, but the Trust did not wish a double international with a distinguished War record to slip by unrewarded and provided Donnelly with a grant.[59]

New Zealand—and Australian—selection committees differed in attitude with certain of their South African counterparts insofar as emphasis on sport was concerned. This was brought home by a report in the

Cape Times in 1946 which stated that only 9.3% of South Africa's Rhodes Scholars took firsts (as opposed to New Zealand's 34.2% and Australia's 32.9%) and 5.2% failed to get any degree (compared to no failures for New Zealand and 0.7% for Australia).[60]

It would take several years before relatively weak academic performances were addressed and priorities changed. In the meantime, Cambridge followed on at the 1947 intervarsity and had to fight hard for a draw after Oxford posted 457. It was not a case of Cambridge being weak. 'There were players such as Trevor Bailey and Douglas Insole', wrote Michael Melford, '... and Bailey was employing all his defensive ability, later to become so well known, to save the match, when it rained'.[61] The quality of the cricket played at the universities was praised in the media and the intervarsities were festive occasions. Swanton commented: 'The gates in those days will be hard to credit by the undergraduates of today – 15,000 on the first day of each of the 1947 and 1948 matches, and a record 17,000 in 1949'.[62]

'South Africans were warmly received in England', said Bishops' Rhodes Scholar, Clive van Ryneveld, 'because English people were appreciative of the support South Africa had given England during the War'.[63] A fine all-rounder, Van Ryneveld played for a strong Oxford cricket side that took on all-comers during the 1948 season and remained undefeated, except for the match against the 'Invincibles', the most famous of all Australian teams. In the intervarsity, Van Ryneveld 'took charge' with his 'leg breaks and googlies' to record second-innings figures of 7 for 57 in thirty-four overs.[64] Abdul Hafeez Kardar picked up a further two wickets and victory came by an innings, after which Swanton concluded that Oxford 'have shown themselves a better side than most of the counties'.[65]

Players from the empire had a great influence on the University's cricket at this time. Several writers reflected on an occasion at Lord's when the team had gone against Pawson's nomination of his successor and elected Clive van Ryneveld as their leader for the 1949 season. Chesterton noted it was contrary to custom that the secretary was not elected as captain and he put it down to 'the strong Commonwealth element [that] carried the day'.[66]

Another powerful Oxford side was fielded in 1949 with victories over New Zealand and the joint county champions, Yorkshire and Middlesex. The touring Kiwis played 36 matches and lost just one encounter when the Cape Province Rhodes Scholar, Murray Hofmeyr, batted through the

Oxford innings to record an unbeaten 95 in a low-scoring match. But for Sir Pelham Warner the greatest delight was the defeat of Yorkshire, an achievement that prompted a telegram to Van Ryneveld which read: 'Congratulations. The last time Oxford beat Yorkshire was in 1895 when I was up'.[67]

Cambridge won the 1949 intervarsity at Lord's. It was a tense affair in which Hofmeyr 'played a dogged and courageous innings and carried his bat'—the first player from Oxford University to have done so in an intervarsity for sixty-eight years. He scored an unbeaten 64 (out of 169) and 54 in the unexpected defeat. There was nevertheless much to be pleased about as *Wisden* stressed in their praise for Van Ryneveld's 'spirited captaincy' which had enabled Oxford 'to enjoy one of their best seasons for many years'.[68]

The Rhodes Scholar influence continued as Hofmeyr was in splendid form in 1950, a season in which he scored 1063 runs at 55.94. The Lord's intervarsity was drawn but South Africans were again prominent. Van Ryneveld claimed 5 for 78 in Cambridge's first innings of 200 and Hofmeyr recorded 75 out of Oxford's reply of 169. An unexpected victory followed in 1951 when Cambridge assembled one of their most talented sides in history—David Sheppard, Peter May, Raman Subba Row, John Warr and Robin Marlar. Opening batsmen and England rugby internationals, skipper Hofmeyr and Brian Boobbyer, batted well for Oxford but it was Indian spinner, Ramesh Divecha, who bowled with great skill to record an analysis of 7 for 62 in 43.2 overs to ensure a dramatic 21-run victory.

The immediate post-war period was one of the most successful in Oxford's cricket history. It owed much to Rhodes Scholars—'Jika' Travers (Australia), Basil Robinson (Canada) and the South Africans—as well as influential Asian players. Efforts had been made for some time to internationalise the Trust and move it away from the traditional view of empire, but it was not until 1946 that Rhodes Scholarships were allotted to the sub-continent. That was the year India placed South Africa's racial policies on the agenda for the first meeting of the United Nations. And with India gaining independence in 1947, an already divided empire was by then beginning to disintegrate 'with astonishing – and in some cases, excessive – speed'.[69] Clive van Ryneveld was surprised to hear 'that Smuts had lost the 1948 general election and [had] misgivings about what it meant'. He recalled an occasion when he and Abdul Hafeez

Kardar—who became Pakistan's first captain and a father figure in their cricket history—were travelling to a match together:

> I said to him that if he went back to India by ship round the Cape I would be very happy to show him Cape Town. Hafeez responded: 'But I wouldn't be very welcome there, would I?' I assured him I would give him a great welcome and we left it at that. There was no likelihood of his coming round the Cape. I think Indians were more conscious of our racial policies than others in England because of the Indians in Natal and arguments at the United Nations.[70]

Ziegler points to the death in 1955 of Leo Amery, a prominent imperialist and Rhodes Trustee for 36 years—22 as chairman—as 'the last link between the Trust and the ideology of Empire'.[71] Circumstances were changing rapidly in the last years of an era in which white, male South African sportsmen were conspicuous in taking advantage of a generous scholarship in order to gain a prestigious 'Blue' and Oxford degree. Newly emerging independent nations meant the end of an ideal through which games-players from public school and ancient university were valued in the administration of distant outposts. The cricketing Rhodes Scholar became a rare breed amongst South Africans, and John Arenhold, who went on to play cricket and rugby for Ceylon, was in 1954 the last South African Rhodes Scholar to win a cricket 'Blue' until Malcolm Brown, a fellow Bishops product, in 1988.[72]

There was, of course, another reason for the disappearance of South Africans from the game at The Parks. Oxford's colleges were striving to attract the intellectual at the expense of the talented all-rounder. As a consequence, selection committees for Rhodes Scholarships increasingly favoured academic achievement over other criteria, with prowess in games no longer carrying the weight it did in the first half of the century.

An eventual decline in the standard of Oxbridge cricket might also be attributed to a decision to end compulsory military service in 1961, which resulted in undergraduates generally being less experienced, whilst cricket authorities moved to end the distinction between 'amateurs' and 'professionals'. The last Gentlemen versus Players match was held in 1962, a decision that had an important influence on English cricket and ultimately the international game. It provoked criticism of university cricket where, said Davies, 'the notion that students at two "elitist" universities should continue to pit their wits against county and international players was an anachronism – or so it seemed to the anti-Oxbridge camp …'.[73]

South African universities in the meantime were providing quality teaching and students were increasingly discovering courses tailored to their own requirements. Those who were showing outstanding talent at the cricket (Nuffield) and rugby (Craven) weeks were approached by universities offering generous bursaries. An annual intervarsity tournament produced cricket of a high standard as it featured numerous players with first-class experience and a South African Universities team made a successful tour of Britain in 1967 during which Oxford University was defeated by an innings and 13 runs.

THE UNIVERSITIES GALVANISE RUGBY IN THE POST-WAR ERA

South African rugby was a focus for national pride as the Springboks had emerged as world leaders in the game. Unbeaten in a series since 1896, they had defeated the All Blacks 2-1 in New Zealand in 1937 and 4-0 at home in 1949. They also achieved their third successive northern hemisphere 'grand slam' in 1951/52.[74] A further demonstration of their strength in depth came through continued opportunities for South African students to play for Oxford University and, in some cases, international rugby. Rhodes Scholars were at the forefront of the University's rugby when it was at its strongest and did much to galvanise the English game in the post-war period.

Few epitomised the spirit of the period quite as much as 'Ossie' Newton-Thompson, a Rhodes Scholar and cricket and rugby 'Blue'. He had served in the forces during the previous four years; an experience which involved 'flying Spitfires, winning the DFC and reaching the rank of Wing Commander'.[75] He captained and coached Oxford in 1946, the side arriving at Twickenham having won all their 11 games, with a record 53 tries to three and a points difference of 260-22. The intervarsity was won 15-5 with seven of the team—four Rhodes Scholars—playing for England (Newton-Thompson, David Swarbrick, Martin Donnelly, Jika Travers and Syd Newman) or Scotland (George Cawkwell and Gully Wilson).[76]

Cambridge won in 1947 because they landed two splendid penalty kicks and Oxford missed five. Clive van Ryneveld described as 'a midfield player of outstanding natural ability' was a nineteen-year-old 'freshman' in this match and would, the following season play international rugby. He was one of a number of southern Africans playing for the home countries during the late forties and early fifties.[77] Rugby historian, Tony Collins, said 'the game saw itself as part of an imperial British network through which players, like businessmen and members of the professional classes, could move without restriction'. He put it down to 'the shared sense of Britishness of the "home" unions and the white dominions of the empire'.[78]

It was how Rhodes would have wanted it, although Van Ryneveld is not sure how he qualified for England other than he was playing his rugby there and 'nobody asked any questions'. He was of 'Dutch, German and French origin' and benefited from sporting genes in the family—his father was a rugby Springbok and his uncle, Jimmy Blanckenberg, played in eighteen Tests for the South African cricket team.[79] It was unexpected that after an outstanding first season playing for England, Van Ryneveld should inform the England selectors that he was unavailable for a second year because of examinations. He admitted later: 'That was a poor decision'.[80]

The Van Ryneveld brothers, Clive and Tony, were joined by fellow Rhodes Scholars, Murray Hofmeyr and Nelles Vintcent, in the 1948 Oxford team that triumphed 14-8. Vintcent captained Oxford in 1949, with *Country Life* taking the opportunity to write of 'gentle grumbles at there being five South Africans in [that] year's Oxford fifteen', but accepting they were 'very fine players and greatly contributed to their team's victory in a very hard-fought match'.[81] Oxford won again in 1950 but resentment crept into the ranks. Dudley Wood, later the Rugby Football Union secretary, recalled participating in the 'freshmen's' trials at Oxford in 1951: 'It was very strange because at that time varsity rugby was very much dominated by South Africans. I packed down with so many of them that often they would speak to each other in Afrikaans and I felt totally left out of it'.[82]

Oxford enjoyed their fourth successive win in 1951, which put them seven games ahead of Cambridge in the series, 'a statistical high water mark in the whole history of this fixture'.[83] Over the next two years the South African contingent continued to grow. The 1953 Oxford team included two Rhodesians and five South Africans. Wood was one of only four Englishmen in the side which the press referred to repeatedly as 'Springboxford'.[84] Ross A. McWhirter and Sir Andrew Noble in their *Centenary History of Oxford University Rugby Football Club 1869–1969*, thought sportswriters were 'following a subtle change in social mood, perhaps a dawning recognition of the smaller part being played by the British Isles in world affairs'.[85]

Springbok, Paul Johnstone, was named Oxford captain in 1954 and compatriot, Roy Allaway, the following year. Southern Africans continued to play a part in the intervarsity matches with four appearing in 1956 and two in 1957 and 1958. There were three Rhodesians (two Rhodes Scholars) and just five South Africans (three Rhodes Scholars) in Oxford sides between 1960 and 1967. Two of the Scholars were Ian Jones, who played for Wales, and Tom Bedford, the Springbok loose-forward who first coined the phrase that Natal was 'the last outpost of the British Empire'. After Bedford's last year in 1967, there was no South African 'Blue' until another Natal Rhodes Scholar, provincial centre Tim Seymour, was selected in 1971.

A total of 37 southern Africans—22 Rhodes Scholars—won 68 rugby 'Blues' between 1945 and 1971.

Rhodesia's Rhodes Scholars Assume Control of Oxford University Cricket

For some years, those who administered the Rhodes Trust believed that the number of scholarships available to Rhodesians was disproportionate to the field of eligible candidates. They were therefore in favour of Rhodes Scholars being drawn mainly from boys educated outside the country but, said *The Times*, schools there desired 'to retain the scholarship entirely as a stimulus for local institutions'. One of the most controversial of all Rhodes Scholar selections was that of Kingsley Fairbridge, who spent some time at St Andrew's Grahamstown, but was mostly self-taught, and did not pass the Oxford Responsions until his fourth attempt.[86] Yet, Fairbridge, through the establishment of his child emigration scheme which took poor children and orphans from England to farm schools in the empire, became one of the most famous of all Scholars and 'the paradigm of success in the meaning of Rhodes's will'.[87]

Sir Carleton Allen, warden of Rhodes House from 1931 to 1952, wrote later of the quality of the Rhodesian Rhodes Scholars: 'It always surprises me that so small a community can keep up such a decent average'.[88] In time, they also proved to be good sportsmen. In the 1950s and early 1960s, there was a steady supply of Rhodesian cricket and rugby 'Blues', with David Pithey the best known. He played in the last Gentlemen versus Players match at Lord's in 1962, but his finest performance was for the University against Richie Benaud's 1961 Australians. He took 7 for 47 off twenty-seven overs in what *Wisden* described as a 'devastating spell'. Pithey's off-spinners were said to have 'perplexed the Australians' and on the conclusion of his university studies, he was selected for South Africa's cricket tour to Australia and New Zealand during 1963/64.[89]

Pithey's success foreshadowed an extraordinary period for Oxford cricket when five Rhodesians captained the university in the course of six consecutive seasons. The achievement was given prominent publicity in the Rhodesian press, not least because it came against the backdrop of British sanctions following Ian Smith's Unilateral Declaration of Independence in 1965. Despite the political differences, Rhodesia retained much of its 'Britishness' and the 'Tom Brown formula' prevailed in white schools where cricket was the major sport for two out of three terms.

The Rhodesian captains—all Rhodes Scholars—emerged as highly promising players from the rebel country's impressive schoolboy structure which involved selection for the annual Nuffield Week staged annually in one of southern Africa's cricket centres. Giles Ridley (Milton), who led Oxford in 1967, had represented the South African Schools XI as a left-arm spinner and at Oxford took 121 wickets over four seasons at a commendable bowling average of 23.87. Mike Burton (Umtali), who was a 'very useful off-spinner' according to the *Cricketer*, had been chosen for the South African Schools XI before gaining experience at first-class level through representing Eastern Province.[90] The other captains—Fred Goldstein (Falcon), Barry May (Prince Edward) and Peter Jones (Milton)—had also been brought up in the competitive Rhodesian schoolboy environment with Goldstein and Jones playing in the Nuffield Week. A sixth Rhodesian to win a 'Blue' during this period—Peter Wilson (Milton)—had been selected for the South African Schools XI and would later play hockey for the then Springboks. Also from Milton—named after Rhodesia's former Administrator and South African cricket captain—was Ridley's brother, Christopher, who represented Oxford in 1971.

Oxford did not lose an intervarsity from 1959 to 1971 although the majority of the matches did not produce a result. The draws were not necessarily dour affairs and in 1967, Ridley became only the second Oxford captain ever to declare twice against Cambridge—Colin Cowdrey was the other in 1954—and bowled superbly in a vain effort to claim another victory.[91]

Goldstein, who captained the University in 1968 and 1969, amassed 409 runs (average 58.42) in his four intervarsities and was described as 'one of the best of Oxford's post-war batsmen'.[92] A devastating striker of the ball, he 'launched the [1968 University Match] with a magnificent innings of 155 in the first three and a half hours'—'a hundred coming in boundaries, mostly fierce pulls and on-drives, in addition to three sixes'.[93] In 1969, a Cambridge declaration that left Oxford 249 runs to make in three-and-a-half hours was considered 'sporting, realistic and challenging' simply because of the presence of Goldstein at the top of their opponents' order. When he went for 69 the match was over as a contest; 'Oxford did not have the fire-power to clinch the issue, nor could Cambridge find anyone to administer the *coup de grâce*'.[94]

After completing his studies, Goldstein returned to South Africa and represented Western Province. In 1971, he joined leading cricketers in a Newlands protest against the intrusion of apartheid in cricket, which led to a 'walk-off' shortly after the start of a match between Transvaal and a Rest of South Africa XI.[95]

Conclusion

Segregated cricket in South Africa had continued without effective protest until 1968 when a 'coloured' player from the Cape was selected to represent the MCC on tour to the country of his birth. More than seventy years after Rhodes had blocked the selection of Hendricks for a South African touring side—as the English would have expected the cricketer to throw boomerangs during the lunch interval—another prime minister, John Vorster, refused to accept Basil D'Oliveira.[96] In the latter controversy, the MCC were accused of giving into elements of the anti-apartheid movement. Vorster's decision provoked a bitter reaction that led to protests aimed at preventing the Springbok cricketers from touring England in 1970.[97]

Oxford University was prominent in this campaign, being an institute that was 'as likely to produce progressive free-thinkers as champions of the established order'.[98] In 1969, two South African tours were targeted as dress rehearsals for the 'Stop The Seventy Tour' campaign. The first, a visit by a Wilfred Isaacs' South African cricket side, was disrupted through a focused attack in which protestors dug a 45-yard trench across The Parks square. Demonstrators then followed up by staging a sit-in on the wicket.[99] A few months later, the threat of student protests forced

Oxford University's match against the Springbok rugby players to be transferred to Twickenham. According to Peter Hain, who led the protest movement, the 're-arranging by the rugby authorities' of the tour's opening fixture was the 'strongest single contributory factor' in enabling the protest campaign to gather momentum.[100]

South Africans were being viewed differently some twenty years on from the immediate post-war period. The retreat from empire forced closer scrutiny of the country's racial policies, with opposition mounting on several fronts. The scholarship scheme produced a range of talent and viewpoints, and its products were not necessarily on the same side in the 'world's fight' in which Rhodes had wished his men to become engaged. When Newton-Thompson and Van Ryneveld returned home, they became Members of Parliament, both serving parties that opposed the government.[101] Others worked behind the scenes, Brian Boobbyer singling out his opening partner, Murray Hofmeyr, as 'a brilliant sportsman who later played a big part in creating a new South Africa'. Yet there were also Rhodes Scholars on the other side—that of the ruling National Party Government—including the Minister of Foreign Affairs, Hilgard Muller, and future Minister of Sport, Piet Koornhof.

The end of empire was not as damaging to the scholarship scheme as might have been expected. Challiss saw the basis of the awards being 'flexible enough for adaptation to change in the modern world'.[102] Ziegler added that 'to take the empire out of the Rhodes Scholars [had] not deprived them of validity' as there was still 'an English-speaking world; to whose cohesion and harmony Rhodes attached so much importance'.[103] There were, as previously outlined, fewer cricketers of ability emerging amongst Rhodes Scholars, but the game was not lost to the University. The student players continued to participate in the first-class game although the plan could no longer exist, as Lewis reluctantly admitted, whereby young amateurs 'should pass through Oxford or Cambridge and go on to captain their counties'.[104]

Administrators of the scholarship scheme perceived the need to reinterpret Rhodes's desire for 'success in, manly outdoor sports, such as cricket ...' Sir Carleton Allen conceded that it was 'an old and difficult subject' and 'in the early years of the [Rhodes] Scholarships there was a tendency to over emphasise athletic prowess at the expense, in some instances, of academic proficiency'. Yet, he could not help but think a trend had set in whereby the University moved to the other extreme. This upset him because he had occasion to admire the manner in which

Rhodes Scholars combined their studies with sport: 'they seemed to be an example to many English graduates who were much less successful in balancing their activities'. He pointed out that the careers of Rhodes Scholars show 'there is no necessary antinomy between the physical and the intellectual, for it is remarkable how many who have won high success in games at Oxford have had distinguished careers in later life'.[105]

Obviously, there were outstanding sportsmen amongst the Rhodes Scholars from other parts of the empire but South Africans were conspicuous because of the emphasis some of their selection committees placed on sport. Another long-serving warden of Rhodes House, Sir Edgar Williams, shared Allen's opinion that selectors went 'too far in favouring academic achievement over other qualifications'. At one stage, he criticised committees that picked a candidate who was academically first-rate and then searched the testimonials to find the man 'once opened a window' as 'clear evidence of his interest in the outdoors'. But, sensing a change in attitude on the part of the colleges, Williams—who had been Field Marshal Montgomery's Chief of Intelligence during the War and was treasurer of the University's Cricket Club—felt it necessary to reword the criteria concerning games for the benefit of the selection committees. He wrote in a memorandum in 1961: 'Physical vigour is an essential qualification for a Rhodes Scholar but athletic prowess is less important than the moral qualities developed in sports'.[106]

It appeared as if Williams had conceded considerable ground but the colleges were effectively dictating academic standards to Rhodes Scholar selection committees by the 1960s. Whilst the trustees claimed to be 'looking not for mere bookworms, but for future leaders', the Oxford Colleges 'seemed to be interested only in academic potential'. It was a process that Lord Blake, a later chairman of the Rhodes Trust, called 'deplorable'. In time, said Ziegler, there was 'growing tension between the narrow professionalism increasingly valued by Oxford tutors and the requirements specified in the founder's Will'.[107] In this regard, the scholarships were not meeting Rhodes's objectives but in a changing world the all-rounder as he knew it had disappeared.

Taking the cricketers' position, Davies thought that whilst the policy of emphasising academic distinction 'was not applied 100%, the net effect was fairly drastic'. The development, he said, resulted in 'a decline in the number of sportsmen arriving from the empire and notably South Africa'.[108] There again, the problem as Davies saw it was purely from an Oxford perspective and did not take into account the new age of professional cricket which took over from the scholarships in allowing South Africans and other players from the former outposts of empire to play in the United Kingdom. Leading cricketers were able to take advantage of a change of rule that occurred in English cricket in 1968 to allow each county to employ overseas players. Promising young professionals from southern Africa would go on to make a greater impact on English cricket than the Scholars had done. Similarly, where the scholarship scheme had offered South African rugby players opportunities to represent the 'Home' unions during the first half of the twentieth century, professionalism created such openings during the latter years.

There is reason to argue that Rhodes would not have considered prowess at sport as being of decisive importance in his scheme. He was ultimately concerned with other issues such as 'the performance of public duties'. In this regard, says Ziegler, the scheme met Rhodes's objectives in that an 'extraordinarily high proportion' of Scholars accepted the role of public service as one 'which they were morally bound to pursue' and in some way contributed 'to the betterment of the lot of one's fellow men'.[109] That Rhodes Scholars should in time comprise men and women of all races intrigued Rotberg in that he saw the scheme's success thereafter as being 'in defiance of the design of their founder ... an ironic tribute to the final workings of his uncommon genius'.[110]

The extent to which sport played a part in moulding the characters of men during the period under investigation cannot be easily measured, save to state that southern Africans were prominent and often leaders in the years when games 'were the wheel around which moral values turned'.[111] It is nevertheless possible statistically to examine the impact that southern African Rhodes Scholars had on Oxford sport. Between 1904 and 1971, 26 southern African cricketers—18 Rhodes Scholars, won 56 'Blues'. Seven captains amongst that number led Oxford over nine seasons, and more southern African Rhodes Scholars achieved cricket 'Blues' than Australia and New Zealand combined. The rugby statistics are even more revealing in placing southern Africa's record in perspective, as an impressive 79 players—11 captains and 55 Rhodes Scholars—gained 140 'Blues' in 58 intervarsities. Adding to their laurels, 36 southern Africans—30 Rhodes Scholars—played for the Barbarians and 13 became international players for the 'Home' Unions.

NOTES

1. R. Rotberg, *The Founder: Cecil Rhodes and the Pursuit of Power* (Oxford: Oxford University Press, 1988), 107.
2. P. Warner, *Lord's 1787–1945* (London: Harrap, 1946), 60; *Long Innings: The Autobiography of Sir Pelham Warner* (London: Harrap, 1951), 36–37. Warner would later play an important role in promoting the selection of blacks for colonial and West Indies teams.
3. Rotberg, *The Founder*, 663.
4. R. Brown, *The Secret Society: Cecil John Rhodes's Plan for a New World Order* (Cape Town: Penguin, 2015), 248.
5. P. Ziegler, *Legacy: Cecil Rhodes, the Rhodes Trust and Rhodes Scholarships* (New Haven: Yale University Press, 2008), 16.
6. R. Challiss, 'The Rhodes Trust' in I. P. MacLaren (ed.), *Some Renowned Rhodesian Senior Schools 1892–1979* (Bulawayo: Books of Zimbabwe, 1981), 336.
7. Rotberg, *The Founder*, 663.
8. Three to Canada/Newfoundland; six to Australia; five to South Africa (one for Natal and four to designated schools), three for Rhodesia and one each to New Zealand, Jamaica and Bermuda.
9. J. Honey, *Tom Brown in South Africa* (Grahamstown: Rhodes University, 1972), 16–17.
10. D. Rayvern Allen (ed.), *E.W. Swanton, A Celebration of His Life and Work* (London: Cohen, 2000), 339.
11. T. Lewis, *Double Century: The Story of MCC and Cricket* (London: Hodder and Stoughton, 1987), 170.
12. Rotberg, *The Founder*, 666–67, 669.
13. R. Challiss, *Vicarious Rhodesians: Problems Affecting the Selection of Rhodesian Scholars 1904–1923* (Salisbury, Rhodesia: The Central African Historical Association, Local Series 33, 1977), 22.
14. R. Gokal was in 1967 the first Rhodes Scholar of colour from southern Africa—he came from a well-known Rhodesian sporting family.
15. Ziegler, *Legacy*, 33–34.
16. R. Currey, *St Andrew's College, Grahamstown, 1855–1955* (Oxford: Basil Blackwell, 1955), 28. Cotterill's best performance occurred in 1859 when he scored 17 and 55 and took 5 for 23 and 3 for 47 in a 28-run win over Oxford.
17. *South African Review*, 11 August 1893.
18. They were the sons of (later Sir) H. Hands who, controversially, gave 'Krom' Hendricks the chance to play against the Western Province Cricket Club at Newlands.
19. G. Chesterton and H. Doggart, *Oxford and Cambridge Cricket* (London: Collins, 1989), 135.

20. D. Frith, *Bodyline Autopsy: The Story of the Most Controversial Test Series in Cricket's History* (London: Aurum Press, 2003), 15.
21. G. Bolton, *History of the OUCC* (Oxford: Holywell Press, 1962), 219.
22. N. Ferguson, *Empire: How Britain Made the Modern World* (London: Penguin Books, 2003), 315.
23. He captained the South Africans in 'unofficial' Tests against S. B. Joel's touring team in 1924/25.
24. J. Duminy, 'The Call for Reappraisal', 13 October 1961, University of South Africa.
25. Professor S. Bush, *Honoris Causa* (Pietermaritzburg: University of Natal Press, 1968), 90.
26. S. Pardon (ed.), *Wisden Cricketers' Almanack* (London: John Wisden & Co., 1925), 66, 426.
27. R. Byron scored 101, Rees 60 and Owen-Smith 55 for the Combined South African Schools XI against the MCC in 1927/28. The schoolboys posted 291 (A. P. Freeman 6 for 53) in a drawn encounter, with Rees singled out as a fine prospect by Herbert Sutcliffe. See *Daily Telegraph*, 8 August 2002.
28. D. Frost, *The Bowring Story of the Varsity Match* (London: Macdonald Queen Anne Press, 1988), 39.
29. J. Corsan, *Poulton and England: The Life and Times of an Edwardian Rugby Hero* (Leicester: Matador, 2009), 143–44.
30. Ziegler, *Legacy*, 34.
31. Ibid., 77–78.
32. R. McWhirter and Sir A. Noble, *Centenary History of Oxford University Rugby Football Club 1869–1969* (Oxford: OURFC, 1969), biographies, section 2, 213.
33. J. Griffiths, The *Book of English International Rugby 1871–1982* (London: Willow Books, 1982), 116.
34. Ziegler, *Legacy*, 78.
35. Four South Africans who won Oxford Blues and played international rugby—M. Dickson, R. Hands, R. Lagden, and S. Steyn—were killed in action during the First World War.
36. J. Greenwood, *A Cap for Boots: An Autobiography* (London: Hutchinson Benham, 1977), 101.
37. Gubb toured Argentina with the British side in 1929.
38. McWhirter and Noble, *Centenary History*, 141.
39. Report by C. Allen, Secretary for the Trust, 1936–37 in Ziegler, *Legacy*, 34.
40. P. Davies, *From Magdalen to Merger: A Short History of Oxford University Cricket Club* (Buxton: Church in the Market Place Publications, 2004), 59.

41. Bolton, *History of the OUCC*, 271–72.
42. Davies, *From Magdalen to Merger*, 63.
43. Bolton, *History of the OUCC*, 273.
44. *The Cricketer*, vol. XIII, no. 10, 1932, 18.
45. L. Alfred, *Testing Times: The Story of Men Who Made SA Cricket* (Cape Town: New Africa Books, 2003), 19.
46. E. Swanton, *As I Said at the Time: A Lifetime of Cricket* (London: Unwin Paperbacks, 1986), 86.
47. H. Marshall, *Oxford v Cambridge: The Story of the University Match* (London: Clerke & Cockeran, 1951), 197, 202.
48. Frost, *The Bowring Story*, 72; *Lions Versus Barbarians Programme*, 10 September 1977, 6.
49. Freakes, who had played cricket for Eastern Province, succeeded Owen-Smith as England's full back.
50. The son of P. Roos's eldest sister, J. H. Pienaar (Stellenbosch Boys' High School), won 'Blues' in 1933-34-35.
51. Ziegler, *Legacy*, 110, 151.
52. Chesterton and Doggart, *Oxford and Cambridge Cricket*, 192.
53. *Rand Daily Mail*, 5 February 1936.
54. Ferguson, *Empire*, 352–54.
55. Davies, *From Magdalen to Merger*, 70.
56. Chesterton and Doggart, *Oxford and Cambridge Cricket*, 191.
57. Swanton, *As I Said at the Time*, 319.
58. G. Bolton and A. Gibson, 'Oxford University' in E. Swanton and J. Woodcock (eds.), *Barclays World of Cricket, The Game from A to Z* (London: Collins Publishers, 1980), 442.
59. Ziegler, *Legacy*, 240.
60. *Cape Times*, 21 September 1946.
61. M. Melford, 'University Match' in Swanton and Woodcock (eds.), *Barclays World of Cricket*, 445.
62. Swanton, *As I Said at the Time*, 320.
63. C. van Ryneveld to author, 12 October 2012.
64. Bolton, *History of OUCC*, 311.
65. Swanton, *As I Said at the Time*, 320.
66. Chesterton and Doggart, *Oxford and Cambridge Cricket*, 193; *The Cricketer*, July 1980, 39.
67. C. van Ryneveld, *20th Century All-Rounder* (Cape Town: Pretext, 2011), 54.
68. *Wisden: Cricketers' Almanack* (Sporting Handbooks, 1950).
69. Ferguson, *Empire*, 356.
70. Van Ryneveld to author, 12 October 2012.
71. Ziegler, *Legacy*, 199.

72. Brown did not actually get on to the field as rain prevented a ball from being bowled—the first time this had occurred in 144 matches.
73. Davies, *From Magdalen to Merger*, 83.
74. In 1912/13 and 1951/52 the Springboks defeated England, France, Ireland, Scotland and Wales, but in 1931/32 there was no fixture arranged against the French.
75. Frost, *The Bowring Story*, 86.
76. Newman, a Transvaal Rhodes Scholar, was captured at Tobruk and spent three years as prisoner-of-war.
77. The international players from southern Africa during 1945–55 include: Noel Estcourt, Murray Hofmeyr, Robert Kennedy, Nick Labuschagne, Syd Newman, Ossie Newton Thompson, Harry Small, Clive van Ryneveld, 'Tug' Wilson (all England) and Kim Elgie, Chick Henderson and Patrick MacLachlan (all Scotland). Of these, Hofmeyr, Newman, Newton-Thompson, Small, van Ryneveld and MacLachlan were Rhodes Scholars.
78. T. Collins, *A Social History of English Rugby Union* (London: Routledge, 2009), 165.
79. H. Schulze, *South Africa's Cricketing Lawyers* (Halfway House: Interdoc Consultants, 1999), 151–57.
80. Van Ryneveld, *20th Century All-Rounder*, 61.
81. Old Diocesans, Cape Town, captained Oxford at cricket (C. van Ryneveld) and rugby (N. Vincent) in 1949.
82. Frost, *The Bowring Story*, 104.
83. McWhirter and Noble, *Centenary History*, 141.
84. Frost, *The Bowring Story*, 104; McWhirter and Noble, *Centenary History*, 182.
85. McWhirter and Noble, *Centenary History*, 182.
86. The minimum requirement for the admission of students who had not written entrance examinations.
87. Ziegler, *Legacy*, 155: the scheme involved taking poor children of London to the wide, open spaces of empire.
88. Ziegler, *Legacy*, 144.
89. *Wisden Cricketers' Almanack* (London: Sporting Handbooks, 1962), 288.
90. *The Cricketer*, vol. 50, no. 6, 1969, 24.
91. In his four intervarsities, Ridley bowled 199.2 overs, with 87 maidens, to return figures of 20 for 345 (average 17.25).
92. Bolton and Gibson, 'Oxford University', 443.
93. Melford, 'University Match', 445.
94. *The Cricketer*, vol. 50, no. 8, 1969, 28.

95. See the chapter by P. Ferriday, 'Newlands "Walk-off": Politics and Players' *current volume*.

96. It was a subtle reference to the Aborigine players who had toured England in 1868 and were regarded as curiosities.

97. See the chapter by B. Murray, 'The D'Oliveira Affair: The End of an Era' *current volume*.

98. Ziegler, *Legacy*, 57.

99. Chesterton and Doggart, *Oxford and Cambridge Cricket*, 231; P. Wynne-Thomas, *The Complete History of Cricket Tours at Home and Abroad* (London: Hamlyn, 1989), 332. Isaacs' team included V. van der Bijl, son of the former Oxford Blue, P. van der Bijl.

100. P. Hain, 'Direct Action and the Springbok Tours' in R. Benewick and T. Smith (eds.), *Direct Action and Democratic Politics* (London: Allen and Unwin, 1972), 193.

101. They were initially MPs for the United Party but Van Ryneveld later joined the Progressive Party.

102. Challiss, 'The Rhodes Trust', 336.

103. Ziegler, *Legacy*, 189.

104. Lewis, *Double Century*, 342.

105. Sir C. Allen, 'Records and Statistics' in Lord Elton (ed.), *First Fifty Years of the Rhodes Trust and the Rhodes Scholarships 1903–1953* (Oxford: Basil Blackwell, 1956), 257–58.

106. Ziegler, *Legacy*, 240.

107. Ibid., 243–44.

108. Davies, *From Magdalen to Merger*, 75–76.

109. Ziegler, *Legacy*, 332–33.

110. Rotberg, *The Founder*, 691.

111. J. Mangan, *The Games Ethic and Imperialism* (Harmondsworth: Viking, 1985), 18.

CHAPTER 6

India in the Imagination of South African Indian Cricket, 1910–1971

Goolam Vahed

Introduction

This chapter focuses on the establishment of cricket within the diasporic Indian population in South Africa, with a particular focus on the province of Natal. Indians began settling in Natal from 1860 when the first indentured workers arrived in the colony. They were soon followed by free migrants. As Indians established a presence in Natal, they set up sporting, religious, cultural, educational and political organisations which were race-based because of the politics of exclusion adopted by successive white minority regimes. Indians in South Africa, partly as a result of the presence of Mohandas K. Gandhi, who lived in the country from 1893 to 1914, and subsequently because of their reliance on India for political succour, maintained close ties with the Motherland. This was most obvious in the political realm but was also evident in areas such as cultural and sporting contact, tourism and marriage. Several cricketing tours were undertaken to and from South Africa; however, India's

G. Vahed (✉)
University of KwaZulu-Natal, Durban, South Africa
e-mail: VAHEDG@ukzn.ac.za

© The Author(s) 2018
B. Murray et al. (eds.), *Cricket and Society in South Africa, 1910–1971*, Palgrave Studies in Sport and Politics,
https://doi.org/10.1007/978-3-319-93608-6_6

taking up the cause of Indian South Africans at the United Nations from 1946 led to a termination of such contact. The decision by the South African Government in 1953 to ban future marriages between Indian South Africans and prospective partners in India reflected more than anything the changing relationship between Indians in South Africa and their attachment to India. From this point, there was no attempt to maintain sporting contact with India. Politically, of course, the Indian Government continued to take up the issue of apartheid at the UN and provided material and moral support to the African National Congress (ANC). Indians in South Africa, while not able to maintain much contact with India, followed Indian and Pakistani cricket passionately. Local South African ethnic newspapers such as *The Graphic* and *The Leader* reported on Test matches and included 'exclusive' photographs of the teams, while older people testified that they listened to cricket commentary on BBC Radio and Radio India.

BACKGROUND

The bulk of South Africa's Indians arrived in two streams. Between 1860 and 1911, 152,641 indentured workers were drawn to Natal to work, mainly on the colony's sugar plantations.[1] They were followed by traders from Gujarat state on the west coast of India who began arriving in substantial numbers from the mid-1870s. They were termed 'passengers' because they came on their own accord and at their own expense. These traders included a few wealthy merchants with transnational connections, small shopkeepers and a large number of workers who laboured in relatives' stores.[2] The British introduced cricket to most of their colonies, and the game was well established by the time Indians began arriving in Natal. Due to the racial hierarchy in place, cricket was mainly played by and developed for white settlers but educated black Africans at mission schools took it up, as did the newly arriving Indian migrants although they did not receive state support.[3]

As background, this chapter examines the settlement of Indians in Natal and the establishment of sport amongst them in the period to 1914, which coincided with the departure of Mohandas K. Gandhi from South Africa and the outbreak of World War One. This is followed by a discussion of cricket amongst Indians in South Africa in the post-Gandhian period, with a particular focus on sporting relationship with India.

RACE, POLITICS AND CRICKET, 1880s–1914

Around 60% of indentured migrants remained in Natal after their contracts had expired. By 1894, there were 46,000 Indians and 45,000 whites in the Colony.[4] White settlers wanted to establish a white-dominated colony, and after achieving self-government from Britain in 1893, they used their political power to pass laws aimed at forcing Indians to re-indenture or return to India after completing their initial indentures. The Indian Immigration Law of 1895 compelled Indian adults to pay an annual tax of £3; Act 8 of 1896 imposed franchise restrictions; and the Immigration Restriction Act of 1897 gave the state power to control new Indian entry, while the 1897 Dealer's License Act was used to segregate Indian traders.[5]

Mohandas K. Gandhi, who had been brought to South Africa by an Indian trader to assist in a private legal matter and remained in the country until 1914, helped traders to establish the Natal Indian Congress (NIC) in 1894, which spearheaded Indian resistance to state repression. Gandhi sought parity with whites on the basis of Imperial citizenship in terms of Queen Victoria's 1858 proclamation. He argued that the 'few' rights that Indians enjoyed were due to their being British subjects; otherwise, they would have been on the same footing as Africans. Gandhi served the British as a stretcher bearer during the South African War of 1899–1902 and again during the Zulu Bhambatha Rebellion of 1906. Gandhi saw these as opportunities to demonstrate his loyalty to Empire. In doing so, he hoped to give impetus to his pleas and petitions for Indians, as British subjects, to gain limited integration into white South African society. Despite being rebuffed time and again, during his South African years Gandhi never gave up on his belief that protection could be found under the paternal embrace of Empire.[6]

This strategy failed because white settlers saw race as the most effective political and ideological means of ensuring a cheap labour supply and separated Natal's population into discrete racial groups and ruled them accordingly. From 1906 to 1913, Gandhi implemented his newly developed strategy of *satyagraha* (non-violent resistance) which culminated in a national strike from October to December 1913. This spontaneous outburst against terrible working conditions and the poll tax saw all classes of Indians unite for the first time during Gandhi's stay in South Africa. The Indian Relief Act of 1914 made some concessions to Indians but left most of their grievances unresolved at the time that Gandhi left for India at the end of July 1914.[7]

ATTACHMENT TO EMPIRE

These early decades of the twentieth century witnessed the emergence of an Indian professional class of mainly teachers and clerks, who were educated at English-language mission schools. Their numbers were small; the 1904 Census showed that only 5211 of 100,918 Indians in Natal were literate in English. These schools emphasised Indians' multiple loyalties. The St Aidan's School song, compiled by students in 1905, reflected this multiplicity of identities as it stressed loyalty to India, to the school, to Africa, and the Empire.

> Sons of Hind! rally round, join hands!
> Join hands in strong endeavour!
> In distant clime, 'mid Africa's sands.
> Our College claims us forever.
> India's Sons where'er they be
> Ne'er forget their loyalty
> Parted by the ocean-wave,
> India, still for thee we crave.
> Parted, yet united, we
> Own the bonds of loyalty
> Homeland, though to thee we turn,
> Here to find a home we learn.[8]

Indian elites in India and across the Empire imbibed the nineteenth-century Imperial message that sport disciplined citizens and taught social values such as respect for authority and fortitude. As Ashis Nandy points out, during the nineteenth century, 'various post-Utilitarian theories of progress began to be applied to the new colonies of Britain. The emerging culture of cricket came in handy to those using these theories to hierarchise the cultures, faiths and societies which were, one by one, coming under colonial domination'.[9] Hobsbawm makes the point that the 'extraordinary speed' with which all forms of organised sport conquered bourgeois society between 1870 and the early 1900s suggests that it filled a social need for considerably more than open-air exercise. Paradoxically, in Britain at least, an industrial proletariat and a new bourgeoisie or middle class emerged as self-conscious groups at about the same time, defining themselves, against each other, by ways and styles of collective living and action. Sport, a middle-class creation transformed into two obviously class-identified wings, was one of the major ways of doing so'.[10] Sport was crucial in the formation of the governing class and was introduced to public schools.

The educated and trading elite in Natal stressed the benefits of sport, such as entrenching a healthy value system and teaching social values like allegiance to fellow players, respect for rules and authority, and fortitude. Writing in the newspaper that Gandhi had founded, *Indian Opinion*, Joseph Royeppen, son of indentured migrants who was educated in England, expounded on the 'greater purpose' of sport:

> Here is the meaning and the interpretation of the famous saying, 'the battles of England have been won on the playing fields of Eton'. As yet there are little signs of our battles being won upon our playing fields of South Africa, and the reason is not far to seek; for, so long as young men will follow sports without eye or ear to their final value for us in this our adopted land of one continued struggle for honourable existence, but merely for the passing excitement and intoxication of the thing, our playing fields must continue to be, not the school and the training ground to higher calls of life and duty, but scenes of our sure damage and loss.[11]

Cricket was one of the key cultural institutions by means of which the British socialised their population and those in their colonies. As Mangan explains, 'where youth was concerned, transmission was frequently a moral enterprise. Games of cricket on the pitches of Trinity College, Ceylon, Upper Canada College, Ontario, and Mayo College, Ajmere, and elsewhere, had a profound purpose: the inculcation of "manliness"'.[12] The game was especially popular among Indian elites. Bombay was the centre of Indian cricket from the 1870s, and from the 1890s, annual matches were played between the Parsees and the English. They were joined by Hindus in 1907 and Muslims in 1912 in a Quadrangular tournament.[13] Cricket was probably familiar to many Indian trading-class migrants to Natal.

Organised Sport in Natal

By 1886, newspaper reports indicate that football and to a lesser extent cricket were played in Durban. Cricket took longer to establish than football and was given impetus when the English toured South Africa in 1892. Three clubs were formed in September 1892, Bluebells, Union Jacks and Western Stars. In October 1894, the Durban Indian Cricket

Union (DICU) was formed with nine teams as members.[14] Sport suffered during the South African War (1899–1902) but the DICU was reconstituted as the Durban District Indian Cricket Union (DDICU) in 1901. New clubs included the Standard Cricket Club which was formed by educated Christians, while Hindus formed the Pirates of India, Muslims formed the Ottomans, and Mayville and Greyville represented residential areas. From Durban, the game spread throughout the colony, with Pietermaritzburg, Stanger and the Northern Natal centres of Ladysmith and Newcastle becoming important centres of sport. The formation of the Natal Indian Cricket Union (NICU) in 1902 reflected the expansion of the game. Cricket was largely controlled and played by traders and members of the educated elite such as R. B. Chetty, Parsee Rustomjee and G. H. Miankhan. These were 'community' leaders who held positions in multiple social, religious, educational, economic and political organisations.[15]

Cricket was played along race lines in most parts of South Africa. The first meaningful attempt to cross racial boundaries was made in 1913. In January 1913, the DDICU affiliated to the South African Coloured Cricket Board (SACCB), which had been formed by Griqualand West, Eastern Province and Western Province in 1902 and which hosted a national provincial tournament in Kimberley in 1913. The DDICU represented 'Natal' in Kimberley in 1913. Western Province, Eastern Province, Natal and Griqualand West participated in the tournament, which was won by Western Province. Natal's players impressed off the field. *Tsala Ea Batho*, a Kimberley newspaper, reported that the tournament 'brought from Natal the finest type of British Indians, natives of Natal who ever graced any company with their presence. Sociable, refined, gentlemanly, scholarly, they seemed to combine these qualities in a manner which captivated all who came in contact with them, and could scarcely have had a more enthusiastic reception than was accorded these modest sons of tea and sugar planters'.[16]

Natal lost all its matches by huge margins. DDICU secretary, N. Sullaphen optimistically wrote in his 1913 Annual Report that, with improved facilities and coaching, 'I sincerely hope, we will have a better and more successful time next year and that the day may yet dawn to show, if you persevere, that you are not unworthy followers in the footsteps of "Ranji"', with reference to Prince Ranjitsinhji, the Indian batsman who played for England from 1896 after coming to study at Cambridge'.[17] Together with the Englishman, W. G. Grace and Australian, Victor Trumper, Ranji was part of the golden age of cricket, 'men who changed the game and defined an era'.[18] Indian flirtation with non-racialism was short-lived. The DDICU affiliated to the SACCB in January 1914 but the next tournament was cancelled because of the First World War and did not resume afterwards.

Cricket was not immune to broader developments. Fixtures were suspended from October to December 1913 because of a strike by Indians in support of Gandhi's passive resistance campaign, and during the First World War, which Indian elites used as an opportunity to prove their loyalty to Empire, in the hope that British Imperial goodwill would result in their grievances being addressed in the post-war period. A meeting of Natal's Indians on 27 August 1914 resolved that the 'consideration of grievances had given way to the performance of duty to the Empire' and 'declared its loyalty to the King-Emperor, and readiness to serve the Crown and co-operate with the government in defence of the country'. The meeting ended with three cheers for the King-Emperor and the singing of the South Africa national anthem. Several hundred Indians served in East Africa as ambulance corps bearers but to no avail; racist policies intensified in the years after the War.[19]

CHRISTOPHER'S CONTINGENT, 1921–22

Though Gandhi left South Africa in 1914, South African Indians' political links with India intensified in the following decades. Anti-Indian legislation after the World War led to the revival of political activity on the part of South African Indians. At a conference in August 1919, delegates emphasised the link with India and stressed that failure to act would be tantamount to letting down the 'Indian nation … The destinies of India and ourselves are one, and we cannot afford to dissociate ourselves from our Motherland'. In 1919, Swami Bawani Dayal represented South African Indians at the annual meeting of the Indian National Congress (INC) at Amritsar. In 1922, he persuaded the INC to agree that South Africa could send ten delegates to their annual meetings.[20]

Indians in the British colonies and dominions had some cricketing heavyweights batting for them. The Indian prince, Kumar Shri Ranjitsinhji (1872–1933), who played for England, is considered one of the greatest batsmen of his age and of any time, not only because of his runs (averaging over 56 in first-class cricket) but also 'because he brought new strokes to the game. His keen eye, unorthodoxy and speed of reaction meant that he introduced the late cut and leg glance, as well as the art of back-foot defence'. Ranji, as he was known, played for Cambridge, Sussex and England. The great cricket writer, Sir Neville Cardus, wrote that 'when Ranji passed out of cricket a wonder and a glory departed from the game forever'.[21]

During the First World War, Ranji returned to India and was the Indian delegate to the League of Nations in 1920, 1922 and 1923. Though he had played cricket for England, Ranji was an Indian national representative. According to Sen, he 'understood that he represented a colonised nation … [but] also that he had a second affiliation, which was the British Empire'. He therefore critiqued the Empire 'while being careful never to disavow it'. He functioned as a 'double agent': an Imperial insider who had left the colony, ideologically speaking and then infiltrated back in.[22] Ranji forcefully raised the issue of the prohibition on the right of Indians to migrate freely to South Africa, Australia and Canada, and the disenfranchisement of Indians already in those countries. This was a view that he raised at the League, and it was one that he had raised as early as 1909 in a speech at a banquet in Cambridge: 'The British Empire ought to treat all British subjects alike. The doors to Indian people have unfortunately been shut in Australia, and in Canada and South Africa. I cannot but regret it, and I think that the Home Government ought to try and make some scheme by which Indians could give their labour and trade in *our* colonies'.[23] In subsequent years, he would argue that white racism threatened the unity of the Empire. As Sen points out, 'he used the language of sport to criticise the Empire. It was the Empire that had not played with a straight bat and betrayed its own British character … He was sincere in his conviction … "Equality" was a legitimate Indian demand, and he associated its denial with the racial injustice of the Empire'.[24]

The white rulers of the British Empire's dominions, such as Canada, Australia, New Zealand and especially South Africa, were in no mood to compromise on the race question. At the Imperial Conference in London in 1921, where New Zealand, Australia and Canada were prepared to consider granting the franchise to their Indian citizens, Smuts 'alone stood out against the policy of granting equal rights to Indian immigrant communities across the Empire'.[25] No wonder that the African American W. E. B. Du Bois described Smuts in 1925 as 'the world's greatest protagonist of the white race ... He expressed bluntly, and yet not without finesse, what a powerful host of white folk believe but do not plainly say in Melbourne, New Orleans, San Francisco, Hong Kong, Berlin and London'.[26]

The intervention of this cricketing great turned politician did not help Indians in the colonies and dominions who faced ever tightening racial policies. Even in the midst of their political troubles, many in the colonies continued to look to India for emotional and political succour. The highlight for many South African Indians during these decades was a tour to India from November 1921 to March 1922 for a series of cricket and football matches. Shortly after Gandhi's departure from South Africa in 1914, he sent messages that students from different colleges in India were keen to meet South Africans to find out more about the country.[27] The war put these plans on hold but after it there was correspondence with and encouragement from the likes of the Reverend C. F. Andrews, who had visited South Africa in 1914, as well as S. R. Bhagwat, general secretary of the Indian Olympic Association, who promised 'every assistance to your team during its tour in India'.[28] The purpose of the tour was sport matches and acquainting local Indians with the cultural richness of the 'Motherland'.

This pioneering group of sportsmen set sail for India on the steamship *Karagola* in November 1921 and returned some three and half months later in early March 1922. They visited Bombay, Ahmedabad, Calcutta, Chinchura, Benares, Allahabad, Agra, Delhi, Madras and Poona. The team carried a letter dated 29 November 1921 from the Mayor of Durban, Fleming Johnston, testifying that they were 'well-known residents of Natal, respected not only by their fellow-Indians in the field of sport, but also by the European community'. The tourists were not fully representative as several of the best players could not get leave for the four months long tour.[29]

The group played fourteen football games in various cities in India and two cricket matches in Calcutta, against the Presidency College XI on 14 January 1922 and Mohun Bagan the following day. Against College, 'the South Africans impressed the spectators as fine cricketers'. In a game curtailed by rain, South Africa scored 108 for 4 and College replied with 74 for 5. S. M. Timol took 2 for 9 and S. Sham 2 for 19. Maharaj scored 31 and Subban 33 not out. Against Bagan, South Africa scored 100 for 6 before making a 'sporting declaration'. Bagan replied with 229 for two, with M. Das scoring 102 not out. Maharaj scored 51 and Subban 22 for South Africa. *Statesman* described Maharaj's batting as 'very sound, especially on the leg, and he contributed 51 which included eight boundaries'.[30] At a post-tour welcome reception, Albert Christopher told the gathering that they had 'shown to the Motherland that her sons away from home are doing everything to uphold its honour and ancient traditions'.[31]

Soodyall tried to get the team to participate regularly in the Quadrangular tournament in India so that South African Indians could 'see more of our beloved Motherland and learn more of Englishmen'. During their 1922 tour, he said that, he found the English 'to be very impartial in their kindness and courtesy. I personally feel that there are some very loyal and patriotic Englishmen in India who really feel for India, … are the real gems of the English race … who are ready to shoulder the burdens of India. Anti-Indians of the "Sahib" class are a very negligible quantity'. Soodyall urged South African Indians to learn from Englishmen 'more of the real game of cricket, how to field, keep wicket, bowl and learn the arts and rudiments of the game, as experts do before they become famous batsmen. Englishmen have become famous throughout the world on account of their fine sporting qualities … We want Indian Hobbs and Meads, and we are going to have them'.[32]

Soodyall failed to join the Quadrangular but the link with India remained strong. At a NICU meeting on 14 November 1925, Sarojini Naidu was elected patron, S. L. Singh president, and R. Manicum (Maritzburg) and A. Sookdeo (Durban) vice-presidents. Sarojini Naidu was an acclaimed Indian poetess and politician, who visited South and East Africa in February and March 1924. Her election as patron is remarkable given the virtual absence of women in Indian public spaces, and it reflects the continuing attachment of local Indians to India. Naidu was the first high profile Indian to visit South Africa after the departure of Gandhi. Her visit highlighted local Indians' reliance on India for political redress. Naidu stood out because she emphasised that Indians in South Africa were national citizens who owed their allegiance to their adopted home and should aim for broad black unity. By emphasising 'South Africanness', she put paid to the idea of Imperial citizenship, but Indians continued to hanker for the paternal embrace of India.[33]

In the face of increasing discrimination, the South African Indian Congress (SAIC) proposed that the Union Government hold a round-table conference with the Imperial and Indian Governments. The resulting Cape Town Agreement of 1927 implemented a system of voluntary repatriation. The South African Government agreed to 'uplift' the social and economic position of Indians who remained in the country, and an Agent General was appointed to facilitate relations with the Union Government.[34] The Agent served as a reminder of the link to India and ensured that the struggle of Indians would be fought in isolation from that of Africans and coloureds as successive Agent Generals insisted that this separation be maintained in order to receive support from India.

BAREFOOTED TOURISTS, 1934

Aside from the several Indian political delegations that visited South Africa in the late 1920s and early 1930s, there was a return sporting visit in 1934 when an Indian football team arrived on the SS *Karanja* on 30 May. The Indian team, which played barefoot, won most of its 14 matches which were played throughout South Africa. Crowds of up to 10,000 attended the matches.[35] The All India soccer team's visit was followed by that of the Baroda Girl Guides who arrived on the SS *Tairea* on 16 July 1934. This group of 22 girls came on an educational tour in the care of Pandit Anandpriyai, his wife and Swami Adyanda. The school in Baroda had been set up in 1925 with four girls and had over 300 members when the Guides toured. They visited Kenya, Rhodesia (Zimbabwe and Zambia) and major centres in Natal, Transvaal and the Cape.[36]

On the domestic front, cricket, like politics and society more generally, continued to be played along racially segregated lines. While Indians did not participate in the Quadrangular tournament in India, the game did undergo important changes at domestic level. Until 1940, the main focus was on inter-district cricket within each province while other 'race' groups played inter-provincial cricket; coloureds competed for the Sir David Harris Trophy; Africans for the NRC Trophy; and Malays for the Barnato Trophy. This was in contrast to soccer where Indian provincial teams participated for the Sam China Trophy from the turn of the twentieth century. The 1930s and 1940s saw cricket in Natal developing outside the main centres of Durban, Pietermaritzburg and Ladysmith. An Inter-District Union was formed by teams on the South Coast in 1937. Soon, Lower Tugela, North Coast and Port Shepstone also established cricket unions. There was progression from inter-district to provincial cricket competition as Transvaal, Eastern Province and Western Province had already formed provincial unions.

It was Natal officials, M. S. Badat, S. L. Singh, E. I. Haffejee, who were all involved in soccer administration and politics, and A. Sookdeo of Natal, and Transvaal officials, Willie Ernest, Bob Pavadai and the Reverend Sigamoney who formed the South African Indian Cricket Union (SAICU) in Johannesburg on 23 March 1940. The Reverend Sigamoney was involved in forming an inter-race board in the Transvaal in 1936 and the failure to follow on from there in terms of achieving interracial provincial competitions reflects the broader reality that black South Africans were not yet ready for unity. For example, Cissie Gool had tried to form a Non-European Unity Front in 1938, and while local Indian political leaders were on good terms with her personally, they were advised by the Indian Agent General that the forging of Non-European Unity would be the death knell for the support of India for Indian South Africans.[37]

The patron of SAICU was Albert Christopher, and its president was S. L. Singh, secretary, M. S. Badat, treasurer, A. Sookdeo and vice-presidents, J. Reddy, Sigamoney and E. I. Haffejee. The first of the biennial tournaments was held in Durban during Easter 1941. In all, nine tournaments were held between 1941 and 1958; three times in Durban (1941, 1945, and 1951) and Johannesburg (1942, 1947, and 1955); twice in Port Elizabeth (1949 and 1958); and once in Cape Town (1953). Natal won the Christopher Trophy in 1941, 1942, 1945, and 1951 and Transvaal in 1947, 1949, 1953, and 1955; Natal and Transvaal appropriately shared the trophy in 1958, the last time the tournament was played. Broader social and political changes made race-based and inter-race tournaments an anachronism. From 1951, inter-race tournaments had been initiated in response to the demand for contact across the colour line. This was not enough by the end of the 1950s. Most cricketers and administrators called for non-racial structures.[38]

While white South Africans largely avoided sporting contact with Indian, African and coloured sportsmen and women, they were forced to compete against a well-known player of colour in England. Kumar Shri Duleepsinhji, nephew of the more famous Ranjitsinhji, followed in his uncle's footsteps and was one of the outstanding batsmen of his generation. Duleep was born in India in 1905 and impressed as a schoolboy prodigy at Cheltenham where he went to study. He attended Cambridge University where he represented the first team and subsequently played county cricket for Sussex. In 1929, according to the 1930 edition of the cricket 'bible' *Wisden*:

He was again in brilliant form, seven times exceeding the hundred, with 246 and 202 as his best scores, and, with an aggregate of 2,028 in thirty-six innings, once more coming out at the top of the batting with an average of over 56. His most startling performance was in the match against Kent at Hastings in August when he followed 115 in the first innings with 246 in the second. Only on four previous occasions in first-class cricket had a player in one match made a score of 100 in one innings and over 200 in another. He took part in the first Test match against the South Africans at Birmingham but failed and, unwisely as many people thought, the Selection Committee did not pick him again. To the surprise of nearly everybody he was not chosen for the Gentlemen at Lord's.[39]

There were rumours that the South Africans influenced the decision to drop Duleepsinhji after only one Test. Alan Ross, biographer of Ranjitsinhji who was the uncle of Duleep, wrote that Duleep 'played in the first Test but objected to by the South Africans, agreed to stand down for the rest of the series'.[40] In the following season, when the Australians toured England in 1930, Duleepsinhji made scores of 173, 48, 35, 10, 54, 50, and 46 in seven innings but was excluded from the English side that toured South Africa that winter. South African cricket writer Louis Duffus wrote in the aftermath of the controversy surrounding the selection of a coloured South African, Basil D' Oliveira, for England, 'England knew the law when a much greater cricketer, K. S. Duleepsinhji, could have been chosen for his country. He was not selected and nothing was said about it'.[41]

Within South Africa, there was a match between a South African Indian XI and a (white) Transvaal Cricket Union XI at The Wanderers on New Year's Day, 1944, to raise funds for the Bengal Famine Relief Fund. In a match preview, the *Rand Daily Mail* predicted that the game would 'attract a large attendance of non-Europeans, while the knowledge that Indians are good cricketers and fine sportsmen will ensure a big attendance of Europeans who will be anxious to see the "foreigners" in action'. The Indian High Commissioner (formerly the office of Agent General), Sir Shafa'at Ahmed Khan, spoke positively about the power of sport: 'Sport has never known distinctions of race or creed', he said. 'Courage and skill in games have established their own separate republics, where youthful prowess and enthusiasm meet on a footing of equality'. The Indian XI was captained by Essop

Saloojee, a Krugersdorp Old Boys' player, and included M. I. Yusuf, who had scored a record unbeaten 412 in a Bulawayo League match in 1936/37, still the highest score recorded in southern Africa; 'Mac' Anthony, an opening bowler who had recently taken all ten wickets in an innings in a league match; Goolam Mahomed, the leading Natal all-rounder who was also vice-captain of the side; accomplished batsman, Davidson Chellan; the imperious 'Shorty' Docrat and one of the best wicketkeeper-batsmen in the country, 'Goofy' Timol. Dr. Goolam Gool, who had played cricket overseas, was unable to take part in the match. His withdrawal was a blow because he was one of the few Indian cricketers in South Africa to have had experience in playing on a turf wicket. However, pre-match fears proved unfounded because the wicket offered little assistance to the bowlers. The Transvaal Cricket Union XI, which included three Springboks—Syd Curnow, Len Brown and Xenophon Balaskas—and some fine provincial players, scored 284/7. The South African Indians replied with 159 for 3. Dawood Hassen, a left-hander who had suffered three stitches in a finger after taking a scorching catch earlier in the day, scored 71 (Fig. 6.1).[42]

Fig. 6.1 An early twentieth-century photo of Greyville Cricket Club in Durban. Seated in the centre is Mahatma Gandhi

While the match was successful in terms of fund-raising, this exercise in race relations was really going against the overall trend in the country which was towards segregation.

THE GHETTO ACT, APARTHEID AND THE UNITED NATIONS

During this period, in fact until 1961, Indians were indeed seen as 'foreigners' by successive white minority governments that aimed to segregate them in both Natal and the Transvaal. The Smuts Government passed the Asiatic Trading and Occupation of Land Restriction (or 'Pegging') Act in 1943, which prevented for three years the further acquisition of land by Indians in the two provinces. In 1946, the provisions of this Act became permanent and the Act came to be known amongst Indians as the Ghetto Act. Indian politics was dominated by moderates until the 1940s. The emergence of trade union leaders and professionals such as Dr. Monty Naicker and H. A. Naidoo led to their ousting from the NIC leadership in 1945 and a passive resistance campaign against segregation from 1946 to 1948. India responded by withdrawing its High Commissioner in 1946 and taking up the cause of Indians at the United Nations.[43]

Following the Ghetto Act, on 26 June 1946 the Indian Government asked United Nations Organisation (UN) Secretary-General, Trygve Lie to place the treatment of Indians in South Africa on the agenda of the UN General Assembly during that body's first meeting from October to December 1946. The South African question was raised annually by India without effective action being taken because of the support that South Africa received from its traditional Western friends such as the USA and Britain. India and Pakistan also raised the South African question at successive conferences of the British Commonwealth, which came into being with the London Declaration of 18 April 1949.[44]

The National Party (NP) Government that came to power in South Africa in 1948 was determined to relegate 'non-Europeans' to second-class status. Its apartheid policy aimed to 'maintain and protect the purity of the white race' through territorial segregation, confining Africans to rural areas, labour control and separate political representation. Indians were regarded as 'temporary sojourners' who should be repatriated to India.[45] This was incorporated into the NP's election manifesto:

The National Party holds the view that the Indians are a foreign and outlandish element which is inassimilable. They can never become part of the country and must, therefore be treated as an immigrant community. The party accepts as a basis of its policy the repatriation of as many Indians as possible ... No Indian immigrant will be allowed to enter the country. In view of the seriousness of the problem, South Africa must be willing to make great financial sacrifices for the achievement of the aim. So long as there are still Indians in the country a definite policy of separation will be applied.[46]

The South African Government's ignoring of successive UN resolutions led the *India News Chronicle* to observe on 25 September 1949:

Malan's government was emboldened to defy with impunity the decisions of the UN ... [apartheid] constitutes nothing less than the most blatant and open defiance of the authority, and an utter disregard of the prestige of the UN ... India must not allow itself to become a pawn in the imperialist strategy of America and Britain. Commonwealth connections and dollar aid mean nothing if they stand for the perpetuation of racialism and colonialism, for the utilisation of the newly-won status of Asian countries for the maintenance and extension of imperialist interest and domination. In dealing with the question of racial discrimination in South Africa, the UN is called upon to answer the question: peace or war? And India, the question: national independence or subservience to Anglo-American policy?

Nehru won a moral victory in 1952 when India succeeded in placing apartheid on the agenda of the General Assembly. A UN commission of inquiry into apartheid, chaired by Dr. Herman Cruz of Chile, reported to the General Assembly in 1955 that South Africa was 'the only government in the world which believes it can carry such a fabulous experiment [apartheid] successfully'.[47] The Indian High Commission in South Africa was closed in 1954.

THE PROPOSED 1953 TOUR

Cultural, sporting and economic links between South Africa's Indians and India receded from the 1940s although there were sporadic attempts to organise cricket tours. In December 1951, Rashid Varachia visited India and Pakistan to negotiate a 'goodwill' tour of South Africa. Anthony S. de Mello, president of the Indian Cricket Board, was warm to the idea provided that the Indian Government approved it. However, the Indian Government rejected the idea.[48] The president of SAICU, Hoosen Parker visited India and Pakistan during 1952 in another attempt to negotiate a cricket tour. He too failed, as Pakistan was given Test status in 1952, and both countries saw little benefit in playing against Indian South Africans. India toured England in 1952, and India and Pakistan played against each other during October to December 1952. The SAICU AGM minutes of 1956 note that Parker stated that India and Pakistan 'had wider fields to conquer'.[49]

Football officials who travelled to India in 1952 on a similar mission had more luck, and the South African Indian Football Association (SAIFA) scheduled a tour to India by its team in May 1953. The team had been selected and had assembled in Durban to depart on the *Karanja* on 3 May when the Minister of Interior, Dr. T. E. Donges, refused them passports. Football officials appealed to the Administrator of Natal, D. G. Shepstone, to intervene on their behalf but to no avail as the Minister declined to issue passports to the players even though SAIFA stated that the tour was apolitical. *The Graphic*, a weekly Indian ethnic newspaper, described the cancellation as 'one of the greatest disappointments in the history of Indian soccer ... For many of the players it was the first and perhaps only opportunity in their lives to see the motherland of their forefathers. Their dream is now shattered'. SAIFA's statement on the cancellation emphasised that 'the entire sporting community of South Africa of all races, we are sure, will be seriously grieved with the Minister's decision'.[50] The South African government was afraid that the cricketers would use the tour to publicise the political grievances of Indians in South Africa.

The political context explains this decision.

INTERNATIONAL AND DOMESTIC PRESSURE

In 1955, India secured the exclusion of South Africa from the Asian-African Conference in Bandung. Under Nehru's leadership, the South African issue was kept high on India's agenda although the first Security Council action was Resolution 134 which was adopted on 1 April 1960 and which criticised the South African Government's handling of the Sharpeville protests on 21 March. The Council called upon the government to abandon its policies of apartheid and racial discrimination. Another reflection of South Africa's increasing isolation is that after the country became a republic in 1961, it was forced to withdraw from the Commonwealth due to opposition from newly independent African states as well as India and Pakistan.[51]

Aside from the fact that India was pressuring South Africa in international forums such as the UN, on the domestic front Indian political bodies, spearheaded by dynamic leaders such as Dr. Yusuf Dadoo in the Transvaal and Dr. Monty Naicker in Natal, had joined forces with the ANC, the Congress of Democrats (COD) and the Coloured People's Congress (CPC) to embark on sustained non-racial resistance to apartheid. Around 8000 people were arrested during the Defiance Campaign of 1952 while ongoing mobilisation would lead to the Congress of the People and the adoption of the Freedom Charter in 1955. The state responded by banning or arresting many activists, with the Treason Trial that lasted from 1956 to 1961 defining the decade.[52]

Black sports followed opposition politics in striving for non-racialism. Following the cancellation of the 1953 tour, no other attempt was made to organise a tour to India. Instead, the game expanded to include matches across the colour line, reflecting political developments. In 1950 the Indian, Coloured, and African cricket associations formally constituted the South African Cricket Board of Control (SACBOC), with Malays joining in 1952. Tournaments were held in 1951, 1953, 1955, and 1958, with Indians and coloureds each winning twice. A high point during this period was the tour during November and December 1956 by a Kenyan Asian team that played against a non-racial SACBOC team comprising of Indians, Africans and coloureds. This, Oborne points out, was 'the first non-racial South African cricketing team ... It was a triumphant tour which put non-racial South African cricket on the international map for the first time'.[53] The significance of this tour, Odendaal points out, was that it resulted in 'the racial divisions [being] breached to such an extent that it was regarded as ridiculous that they should not all play together'.[54] The relaxing of race boundaries and excitement of cross-race cricket teams increased calls for the scrapping of the racial format of cricket. At a meeting in Johannesburg on 9 April 1960, SACBOC was restructured along non-racial lines.[55] Whites continued to play separately.

The success of the Kenyan tour led to new efforts to organise international cricket but SACBOC's attempts to organise tours by teams from India, Pakistan and the West Indies failed. In 1959, Rashid Varachia of the Transvaal negotiated for a West Indian team to visit South Africa. With preparations at an advanced stage, the South African Sports Association (SASA), an organisation formed by black South Africans in

October 1958 to organise an international campaign to boycott South African sport, opposed the tour on the grounds that it would allow the apartheid government to argue that its policy was justified since Blacks could play against Blacks.[56]

P. Subroyan, a former president of the Indian Cricket Board, Member of Parliament in India and president of the All-India Council of Sports, told reporters that he would be 'sorry' if the tour went ahead because 'the grave matter of the colour-bar is involved ... Under the humiliating conditions, I am surprised Mr. Worrell [of the West Indies] is going on with the proposed tour'.[57] This view was shared by *Indian Opinion* whose editorial on 19 June 1959 stated that in order to secure the tour, black South Africans would have to 'be humiliated to get a little bread in the form of recognition, or will they stand on their dignity and refuse to play Verwoerd's game? The question does not leave the self-respecting non-European with much of a choice. He just cannot kow-tow to Verwoerd'. The tour was cancelled as a result of the pressure placed on the organisers and the West Indies players.

Black cricket was isolated, and white cricket followed a decade later as a consequence of the D'Oliveira Affair of 1968, and the subsequent cancellation of the MCC tour of South Africa in 1968/69, the South African tour of England in 1970 and the South African tour of Australia in 1971/72.[58]

CONCLUSION

For many decades after their arrival in South Africa, Indian South Africans maintained close links with the Motherland. This was most obvious in the political realm but was also evident in other areas, especially cultural and sporting contacts, tourism and marriage. The decision by the South African Government in 1953 to prevent a South African Indian sports team from touring India and, at the same time, banning future marriages between Indian South Africans and prospective partners in India reflected the breakdown in relations between India and South Africa, and the attachment to Indian South Africans to India. South Africa was home for Indians living in the country even though the South African Government aspired to repatriate them. Indians were finally accepted as South Africans in 1961, and a separate Department of Indian Affairs was created to fit in with the separate development ideology of apartheid.[59] The South African Government was determined to cut the links of its Indian population with India as a means to reduce their reliance on the land of their birth and ensure that India did not embarrass the government by constantly raising the issue of apartheid in international forums. From the late 1950s, there was no attempt to maintain sporting contact with India. Though the Indian Government took up the issue of apartheid at the UN and provided material and moral support to the ANC, there was a general reduction in transnational contact.

Indians in South Africa, however, followed Indian and Pakistani cricket passionately. White cricket, on the other hand, took little interest in Indian cricket; this chapter concludes with a recollection by journalist and cricket writer, Mihir Bose, which shows just how little was known about Indian cricket. Bose was writing of his visit to South Africa on the occasion of that country's cricket unification when Indian great, Sunil Gavaskar was amongst those invited:

> I had played a small part in helping Gavaskar and the Indian journalists get to Johannesburg. When [Ali] Bacher [who was the effective head of South African cricket] drew up the list of those to be invited he had no problems with cricketers from England, Australia or even Garry Sobers. While South Africa had never played the West Indies, West Indian cricketers were known and Bacher knew Sobers. But he knew nobody from India and turned to me for help. My visit to South Africa made me aware of how little white South Africans knew of Indian cricket. India may have been a Test-playing country since 1932, but white South Africa had not only never played them, but never taken any interest in their cricket. Growing up in India in the 1960s, I had, like many cricket-mad Indians, followed South African cricket. But for white South Africa Indian cricket just did not exist. Indeed, soon after I got to South Africa it amused me to ask white South African cricket followers which cricketer had the second highest first-class batting average, after Don Bradman's 95. When I said it was Vijay Merchant, the look on their faces told me everything. Apartheid had also cut any surviving historic links between South African Indians and India. I was therefore not surprised to receive a call in my London home from Bacher asking for the names of Indians to invite to the black-tie event.[60]

NOTES

1. A. Desai and G. Vahed, *Inside Indian Indenture. A South African Story, 1860–1914* (Cape Town: HSRC Press, 2010), 35.
2. G. Vahed and S. Bhana, *Crossing Space and Time in the Indian Ocean: Early Indian Traders in Natal. A Biographical Study* (Pretoria: Unisa Press, 2015), 31–40.

3. G. Vahed, 'The Control of African Leisure Time in Durban During the 1930s', *Journal of Natal and Zulu History*, 18 (1998), 67–123.
4. G. Vahed, 'The Making of Indian Identity in Durban, 1914–1949' (Unpublished D. Phil thesis, Indiana University, Bloomington, 1995), 42.
5. M. Swanson, 'The Asiatic Menace: Creating Segregation in Durban, 1870–1900', *International Journal of African Historical Studies*, 16, 3 (1983), 401–21.
6. See A. Desai and G. Vahed, *The South African Gandhi. Stretcher-Bearer of Empire* (Stanford: Stanford University Press, 2015), for a discussion of Gandhi's deep-seated attachment to Empire during his South African years.
7. Desai and Vahed, *The South African Gandhi*, 253.
8. G. Vahed and V. Padayachee, 'Empire, Race and Indian Cricket in Natal, 1880–1914' in B. Murray and G. Vahed (eds.), *Empire & Cricket. The South African Experience 1884–1914* (Pretoria: Unisa Press, 2009), 81–100.
9. A. Nandy, *The Tao of Cricket. On Games of Destiny and the Destiny of Games* (Oxford: Oxford University Press, 2001), 5.
10. E. Hobsbawm, *The Age of Empire 1875–1914* (London: Penguin, 1987), 183.
11. *Indian Opinion*, 5 October 1912; Vahed, 'The Making of Indian Identity', 147.
12. J. Mangan, *The Game Ethic and Imperialism. Aspects of the Diffusion of an Ideal* (London: Frank Cass, 1985), 17–18.
13. M. Bose, *A History of Indian Cricket* (London: Andre Deutsch, 1990), 32–33.
14. *Natal Mercury*, 10 October 1894.
15. Vahed and Padayachee, 'Empire, Race and Indian Cricket', 89.
16. *Tsala Ea Batho*, 12 April 1913.
17. Vahed and Padayachee, 'Empire, Race and Indian Cricket', 95.
18. Bose, *A History of Indian Cricket*, 39.
19. G. Vahed, '"Give Till It Hurts": Durban's Indians and the First World War', *Journal of Natal and Zulu History*, 19 (1999–2001), 41–61.
20. Vahed, 'The Making of Indian Identity', 60–62.
21. M. Williamson, 'Ranji,' Cricinfo at http://www.espncricinfo.com/ci/content/player/19331.html. Accessed 25 June 2015.
22. Satadru Sen, *Migrant Races: Empire, Identity and K.S. Ranjitsinhji* (Manchester: Manchester University Press, 2005), 146.
23. Sen, *Migrant Races*, 149.
24. Satadru Sen, *Disciplined Natives: Race, Freedom and Confinement in Colonial India* (Delhi: Primus Books, 2013), 92–93.
25. M. Lake and H. Reynolds, *Drawing the Global Colour Line: White Men's Countries and the Quest for Racial Equality* (Melbourne: Melbourne University Publishing, 2008), 302.

26. Lake and Reynolds, *Drawing the Global Colour*, 330.
27. *Indian Opinion*, 3 March 1915.
28. *Latest*, 26 November 1921.
29. *Statesman*, 15 January 1922.
30. *Latest*, 26 March 1921.
31. Ibid., 15 April 1922.
32. Ibid., 13 December 1924.
33. G. Vahed, 'Race, Empire, and Citizenship: Sarojini Naidu's 1924 Visit to South Africa', *South African Historical Journal*, 64, 2 (2012), 319–42.
34. Vahed, 'The Making of Indian Identity', 64–69.
35. *Indian Opinion*, 15 June 1934.
36. *Natal Witness*, 19 July 1934.
37. A. Desai, V. Padayachee, K. Reddy, and G. Vahed, *Blacks in Whites: A Century of Cricket Struggles in KwaZulu-Natal* (Pietermaritzburg: University of Natal Press, 2002), 98–122.
38. Ibid., 110–22.
39. *Wisden Cricketers' Almanack*, 'Cricketer of the Year 1930: Kumar Shri Duleepsinhji,' at http://www.espncricinfo.com/wisdenalmanack/content/story/154691.html. Accessed 24 June 2015.
40. A. Ross, *Ranji. Prince of Cricketers* (London: William Collins Sons, 1983), 67.
41. A. Odendaal, *The Story of an African Game: Black Cricketers and the Unmasking of One of South Africa's Greatest Myths, 1850–2003* (Cape Town: David Philip, 2003), 332.
42. *Rand Daily Mail*, 2 January 1944.
43. Desai and Vahed, *Inside Indian Indenture*, 122–52.
44. B. Pachai, *The International Aspects of the South African Indian Question 1860–1971* (Cape Town: Struik, 1971), 247.
45. R. Elphick and T. Davenport, *Christianity in South Africa. A Political, Social, and Cultural History* (Los Angeles: University of California Press, 1997), 203.
46. S. Mukherji, *Indian Minority in South Africa* (New Delhi: People's Publishing House, 1959), 161.
47. Ibid., *Indian Minority in South Africa*, 160.
48. Desai et al., *Blacks in Whites*, 216.
49. Ibid.
50. *The Graphic*, 2 May and 9 May 1953.
51. A. Desai and G. Vahed, *Monty Naicker. Between Reason and Treason* (Scottsville: Shuter and Shooter, 2010), 228–30.
52. G. Vahed, '"Gagged and Trussed rather Securely by the Law": The 1952 Defiance Campaign in Natal', *Journal of Natal and Zulu History*, 31, 2 (2013), 68–89.

53. P. Oborne, *Basil D'Oliveira: Cricket and Conspiracy: The Untold Story* (London: Little, Brown, 2004), viii.
54. A. Odendaal, *Cricket in Isolation. The Politics of Race and Cricket in South Africa* (Cape Town: C. Blackshaw and Sons, 1977), 337.
55. Desai et al., *Blacks in Whites*, 206.
56. M. Allie, *More Than a Game: A History of the Western Province Cricket Board 1959–1991* (Cape Town: Cape Argus, 2001), 20.
57. *Indian Opinion*, 15 May 1959; Desai et al., *Blacks in Whites*, 221.
58. See the chapter by Bruce Murray, 'The D'Oliveira Affair of 1968: The End of an Era'.
59. G. Vahed and T. Waetjen, 'Passages of Ink: Decoding the Natal Indentured Records into the Digital Age', *Kronos*, 40, 3 (2014), 62–66.
60. M. Bose, *The Spirit of the Game: How Sport Made the Modern World* (London: Constable, 2012), 436–37.

CHAPTER 7

Diffusion and Depiction: How Afrikaners Came to Play Cricket in Twentieth-Century South Africa

Albert Grundlingh

A cursory survey pertaining to the literature on cricket in South Africa will reveal that for very good reasons, given the country's volatile history, much has been made of the impact of segregation and apartheid on the game.[1] While perfectly understandable, this perhaps had the effect of preventing a more even spread of attention covering other dimensions. A surprising omission in this respect, when one takes into account the crucial role of Afrikanerdom in shaping the contours of twentieth-century South African history, is that the changing Afrikaner interest in the game has not been subjected to a sustained analysis.[2]

This chapter attempts to address this shortcoming by focusing on the trajectory of Afrikaner involvement in cricket, trying to account for the initial reticence to embrace the game as enthusiastically as they did with rugby. Afrikaner interest though grew apace during the 1960s, and the conditions which facilitated such a turnabout are explored.

A. Grundlingh (✉)
University of Stellenbosch, Stellenbosch, South Africa
e-mail: amgrund@sun.ac.za

© The Author(s) 2018
B. Murray et al. (eds.), *Cricket and Society in South Africa, 1910–1971*, Palgrave Studies in Sport and Politics,
https://doi.org/10.1007/978-3-319-93608-6_7

191

Equally, the intricacies of the way in which prominent cricketers from an Afrikaans background have been portrayed and represented in terms of identity politics are outlined.

AMBIVALENCE

Cricket has long been regarded as the quintessential English game, synonymous with the British upper classes and dispersed throughout the British Empire as part of the cultural glue that helped to bond the 'mother' country with the colonies, and wherever the game was played, it was to be closely associated with the imperial heritage and ethos. For all the physical skills and mental challenges the game demanded, it also carried with it the overtones of ritualised behaviour, at times an exaggerated sense of what was considered gentlemanly conduct and was often thinly disguised elitist snobbery.[3] As cricket could be time-consuming, its upper-class status was at least in part linked to the availability of free time, a commodity in plentiful supply to those who were not compelled to work long hours. This, as well as the leisurely pace of the game, caused one sceptic to dub it as a form of 'organised loafing'.[4]

In the South African context, cricket was imported in the nineteenth century by British soldiers, imperial administrative functionaries, missionaries and immigrants who were all in their own way part of the imperial project and instrumental in the diffusion of the game.[5] The animosities and associations spawned by South Africa's turbulent past meant that the very disseminators of the game were also often deemed to be adversaries of or at least at loggerheads with the local Afrikaner population which had developed divergent political and cultural orientations. Throughout the nineteenth and well into the twentieth century, Afrikaner attitudes towards British cultural forms and their carriers were carefully weighted, ambiguous and at times openly dismissive. Cricket was bound to suffer the same fate.

English speakers for their part did not view Afrikaners as natural recruits to the game. Writing shortly after the devastating Anglo-Boer War of 1899–1902, John Buchan forcefully vented such views. 'It is worth considering the Boer at sport,' he wrote, 'for there he is at his worst. Without a tradition of fair play, soured and harassed by want and disaster, his sport became a matter of commerce (shooting game for profit)'. Afrikaners to him 'were simply not a sporting race'.[6] Such essentialist views are of course more revealing of the imperial mindset than Afrikaner prowess at sport.

Cricket had some appeal among Afrikaners in the nineteenth-century Cape Colony, but while the game penetrated the interior, especially in the wake of the discovery of diamonds and gold, it held no real attraction to the Boers of the republics. Those Afrikaners who played the game in the republics, such as Pieter de Villiers and G. P. Kotzé, were mainly migrants from the Cape. The game nevertheless featured in the politics of the day in what must count as one of the first attempts in South African history to use sport as a so-called nation-building tool. Cricketing officials planning a tour by a South African team to England in 1894 argued that besides English speakers, cricketers of 'Dutch descent' should also be included in the side in order to ensure that it was a team representative of the country, albeit whites only. Furthermore, during the volatile politics in the Transvaal preceding the Anglo-Boer War with *Uitlanders* agitating for full citizenship and racking up the tension with the Boer government of President Paul Kruger, it was emphasised in the local English press that the tour should 'assume its true importance as a national affair' and they called upon Kruger to contribute towards the funding of the tour. Such a gesture, it was claimed, 'would show the *Uitlanders* that he sympathises with their old national game ... a game which will do more to merge Boer and *Uitlanders* into good Transvalers than any elaborate measure that can be devised by the Volksraad. Boers and *Uitlanders* must not only work together but play together ...'.[7] There is no evidence that Kruger responded to this.

During the Anglo-Boer War, the British employed their prisoner-of-war and concentration camps to transmit British culture to the Boers, and in Ceylon in 1901, a celebrated game between the Boer POWs and a Colombo Colts XI, the Ceylonese champions, was staged.[8] This event has bulked large in the writing of the history of South African cricket, mainly because it was regarded as unique to find such an event taking place during wartime, but especially because of its white-brown dimension. While intriguing, it certainly was not evidence of a widespread Boer fondness of cricket. Overall, the bitter animosities generated by the Anglo-Boer War fuelled general Afrikaner resentment and antipathy towards British cultural practices and leisure pursuits.

This differed somewhat from the situation before the war in the Cape Colony where to some extent British influences had over a considerable period seeped into the cultural outlook of Cape Afrikaners. At Stellenbosch, there was a fairly strong cricket team and

N. H. C. Theunissen, an Afrikaner theology student from Stellenbosch University, represented South Africa in 1889. Although chosen for the first Test in Port Elizabeth, his university professor showed complete disdain for such secular frivolities as cricket and refused to give him time off to play.[9] A few others followed Theunissen, most prominently J. J. Kotzé, nicknamed 'Boerjong,' a farmer from the Western Province who was described as a 'Boer who preferred cricket to war'.[10] As a fast bowler, he 'hated being punished by the batsman' but was considered a poor batsman and a clumsy fielder.[11] He played in England while the war was still in progress and visited England again for the Test series of 1907. During the tour, sections of the British press invoked the stereotypical imagery of rural village cricket where the farmer, blacksmith and squire all harmoniously indulge themselves in a game during a long summer day. Kotzé was seen to fit this scenario perfectly; given his rural background, he was described as taking life 'calmly and deliberately,' despite his fearsome qualities as a bowler. Kotzé also became a symbol of wider import: his presence in the team was taken as evidence that Afrikaners had taken to the British cultural ways and was a tribute to successful anglicisation.[12] Sporting identity could clearly be manipulated to serve the discourse of the day.

Rugby, equally, though with a different slant, served a similar purpose. The first and highly successful Springbok rugby tour of the UK in 1906, under the captaincy of Paul Roos, was acclaimed as a major venture in nation-building, with Afrikaners being accepted on par with their British counterparts. Initially, cricket was assigned a noticeably modified role by the game's leaders, who represented this particular sport as 'the Empire's game,' played primarily by those of British stock on their own terms where someone like Boerjong Kotzé could only appear in the guise of a successfully assimilated Englishman. The primary symbolic political object of tours between South Africa and England was to help integrate post-war South Africa into the British Empire and to reassure the 'mother country' that South Africa was now safely British. In 1909, on South African initiative, the Imperial Cricket Conference was founded, which firmly and officially tied the game even closer to the imperial project. 'Subsequently,' it has been argued, 'the Boers did not feel either welcome or inclined to participate in the game, which remained very much an expression of Anglo-Saxon separateness and superiority in the eyes of Afrikaner farming people' (Fig. 7.1).[13]

Fig. 7.1 South African opening bowler, J. J. 'Boerjong' Kotzé (left), was the best known of the Afrikaner cricketers in the early years of the twentieth century, while cricket appealed to the higher sensibilities of South Africa's Deputy Prime Minister, J. H. Hofmeyr. Formerly Vice-Chancellor of the University of the Witwatersrand. Hofmeyr is pictured batting for the Staff XI

For the greater part of the first half of the twentieth century, cricket among Afrikaners remained largely in the doldrums, although there were occasional Afrikaners who featured in first-class cricket between the wars.[14] For those who bought into cricket's symbolism, it was a deplorable situation, as a potential opportunity of establishing closer bonds between the two white groups through sport was being wasted. It occupied the mind of at least one dignitary, J. H. Hofmeyr, Administrator of the Transvaal who in the late twenties, besides being a protégé of Premier Jan Smuts, was also a cricket fanatic. Cricket appealed to Hofmeyr's higher sensibilities; 'It satisfied his moral sense, for here was a human activity, governed by the rule of law, competitive in nature, yet devoid of rapacity or fear or cruelty, and pleasurable to enjoy'. Infused with such enthusiasm, he was convinced of the power of cricket to draw men together. Accordingly, he was instrumental in arranging school cricketing tours which had one of its aims to promote the game at certain Afrikaans schools.[15] However, greater white unity and a common interest in cricket were a distant chimera only destined to manifest themselves as reality several decades later. As late as 1951, there was among certain members of the Afrikaner elite an almost complete ignorance of the game. Therefore, the first post-1948 Afrikaner National Party premier, D. F. Malan, a rotund, bespectacled, former minister of religion to whom sport was decidedly otherworldly, told Dudley Nourse, the astonished captain of the South African cricket team which consisted of English speakers only, on the eve of their departure on a tour of England in 1951 that he hoped they had enjoyed their stay in South Africa.[16]

While the anti-cricket ideology of many Afrikaners can be understood at one level, it does, however, raise the question of why cricket was rejected, but at the same time Afrikaners readily took to rugby which was also a British upper-class import. This apparent paradox calls for some elucidation. While avoiding the trap of arguing that certain ethnic groups are genetically programmed for specific sports, it can be pointed out that rough-and-tumble contact sport like wrestling has since the days of the Boer republics been a popular pastime for young Afrikaners which could have acted as a bridging platform for making the transition to a physical game like rugby.[17] The nature of cricket can also have a bearing on the matter.

Writing on immigrant sporting acculturation in Australia, academic authors have pointed out that 'undoubtedly it is more difficult for immigrants to acquire complex cricket skills than it is to learn simpler football skills, especially if one is not brought up on the intricacies of cricket'.[18] Similar comments have been made by another observer pertaining to Afrikaners; 'Cricket is a game that takes a long time to learn, it is not like rugby or soccer which you can learn quite quickly … You have to start playing very young. Afrikaners schools did not promote it …'.[19] These arguments may have their own validity, but cannot claim to provide a comprehensive explanation.

Cricket must also be positioned in the wider socio-economic context. The first few decades of the twentieth century were difficult ones for some Afrikaners as successive droughts and increasing commercialised farming forced many off the land and into the cities.[20] It was a debilitating trek for many and the luxury of playing a relatively expensive game like cricket and belonging to an English club where most of the cricket was being played was not a realistic proposition for Afrikaners who had more pressing financial needs and less leisure time. Likewise, in the countryside, the lack of facilities and competitive structures inhibited the spread of the game. In comparative perspective, it was a situation which closely and illuminatingly resembled similar circumstances in New Zealand where the Maori section of the population experienced the same kind of barriers which prevented a large-scale entry into the game and which made it easier for them to turn to rugby as a sport of choice.[21]

In addition, one should consider the symbolic dynamics of a game like rugby. As we have seen earlier, it can be argued that the combative nature of the game appealed to the evolving self-image of nationalist Afrikaners during a period of accelerated growth of nationalism in the 1930s and 1940s. Having said that, the situation was not static. Although rugby's position as the premier Afrikaner sporting code was not to be seriously challenged, in the ensuing decades as the political and economic landscape changed, Afrikaner interest in sport was set to broaden.

EMBRACING THE GAME

Concomitant with the historic National Party victory of 1948 was an incremental Afrikaner rapprochement with British cultural manifestations. While Afrikaner cultural interests still occupied pride of place, the acquisition of power meant that sufficient confidence prevailed for the opening up of spaces to explore areas of leisure pursuit which up till then had at best only elicited lukewarm responses. Furthermore, power also meant the assertion of Afrikanerhood in areas where it was previously absent.

Hence, in language reminiscent of current black demands that sporting teams should reflect the composition of the 'nation,' it was argued in 1956 in Afrikaner circles that 'until the Afrikaner takes his place on our cricket fields, no Springbok team can be said to be truly representative of our country's cricketing ability'. Yet this quest was not formulated in terms of present-day transformational charters, but a different route was suggested. Emerging Afrikaner interest had to be channelled into the 'establishment of Afrikaans clubs, or rather clubs where the atmosphere is Afrikaans so that the newcomer will readily feel at home and will be able to concentrate all his endeavours on the mastery of the game itself'.[22] The need for such an Afrikaans cricketing environment stemmed from antipathy towards what was regarded as snobbish English-speaking clubs where Afrikaners were often deemed to be marginalised.[23] What was ideally required was an opportunity for 'Piet van der Merwe and Jan Burger to learn the game' in an enabling context.[24] Given such stepping stones, the assumption was that eventually Afrikaner cricketers would be able to hold their own at national level.

Although some predominantly Afrikaner clubs were formed, in a broader context Afrikaner interest in the game benefited from socio-economic and attendant cultural changes which permeated white society during the 1960s. With an average growth rate of 6% during most of the decade, South Africa experienced a period of unprecedented prosperity. In tandem with this, there was a trend among Afrikaners to move away from unskilled or semi-skilled relatively poorly paid labour to skilled and better remunerated positions with stable career prospects in the burgeoning nationalist bureaucracy and other associated enterprises. In addition, the business world saw greater collaboration between English companies and rapidly emerging Afrikaner concerns along with a general realignment of the ownership of the urban economy. While Afrikaners still lagged behind English speakers in terms of total income (45% against 55%), overall they made significant strides in the 1960s. These developments brought in its trail a set of gradually unfolding cultural correlates, reflected, for example, in the greater acquisition of material goods such as expensive cars, architecturally designed houses and also as a new marker of status, overseas tours.[25]

Along with lifestyle changes facilitated by increased wealth, recreational patterns showed greater differentiation and there was a deliberate attempt to master new kinds of sport. Golf was one sporting code which increasingly attracted Afrikaner players, and at the same time, Afrikaner interest in cricket showed a steady upward curve. Between 1955 and 1970, the number of white cricketers, many of them from Afrikaans homes, more than doubled.[26] This was underpinned by the emergence of a slowly convergent and more homogenous Afrikaans- and English-speaking youth culture. 'White children increasingly began to share the same middle-class interests,' it has been observed, 'pop music, shopping mall fashions and games, including cricket'.[27] What is more, there was a significant growth in the number of educational institutions during this period. The number of white school teachers, many of them Afrikaners, grew by 34.6% between 1960 and 1972.[28] Such an expansion of the educational field held in turn the potential for exploring variegated ways of self-expression by overseeing the introduction of new sporting codes at school level.

In 1975, it was possible to report that during 'the last ten years the Afrikaner's involvement in the game has increased rapidly. Afrikaans schools where the word cricket has sometimes hardly been heard started organising and playing the game'.[29] Greater financial resources available to schools in the wake of the 1960s also aided the process as more schools were able to afford expensive equipment and the upkeep of the grounds.[30]

While the game in general gained more popular appeal, it was left mainly to more established and elitist schools with a traditionally strong sporting ethos to come into their own and catapult a number of Afrikaans players onto the provincial and national scene. The name of Grey College in Bloemfontein stands out in this regard. Grey, a leading school in the Free State, was established in 1855 and attracted the sons of elite Afrikaners in the province. It was a bilingual school with a fair amount of cross-cultural fertilisation between English and Afrikaans speakers.[31] For Afrikaners with a talent for ball games, it was an ideal environment to be exposed to sports other than rugby. Gradually from the 1950s, the game started to attract Afrikaans speakers. With dedicated teachers who especially from the 1960s had a particular interest in cricket, and somewhat later the introduction of professional coaches, the foundation was laid for the emergence of new talent. Corrie van Zyl, a national player, explained the connection bluntly, 'I started playing cricket because of Grey'.[32]

Others elevated the connection to an even higher level. Two gifted Afrikaans players, Kepler Wessels and Hansie Cronjé, both destined to become South African captains, were illustrious sons of Grey College who bestowed on the school a special aura in the South African cricketing world and helped to foster a closer identification of Afrikaners with the game.[33] Almost equally so, Allan Donald, though not from Grey College, was despite his surname an Afrikaans speaker from lower-middle-class Bloemfontein whose exploits as a lightning-fast bowler in the 1990s bequeathed him legendary status.[34] In the decades from the 1970s onwards, Afrikaans speakers started to be chosen more frequently for the provincial Free State Nuffield team, the tournament which showcased South African schoolboy cricket. Besides, some Grey College cricketers not only performed well during the tournament but also impressed with their leadership skills, so that increasingly they were appointed as captains of the South African Schools Nuffield team.[35] Grey's success spilled over into senior cricket and in 1995 the entire Free State senior provincial team was Afrikaans speaking.[36] The province also became a force to be reckoned with. In the late 1980s, a previously lacklustre Free State team was transformed by an increasing number of Afrikaans-speaking Old Greys. 'The fresh young men, brains washed clean, bodies hardened in the Grey ethos, started to turn Free State around,' it was claimed.[37]

Grey College might have nurtured a special relationship between Afrikaners and cricket, but there were similar, if less-concerted, developments in other places. Gradually players from several Afrikaans schools elsewhere in the country started making an impact in senior cricket; for example, Nantie Hayward from Eastern Province, Albie Morkel and Andre Nel from the East Rand, Francois Herbst from Gauteng, Arno Jacobs from North West Province, Tertius Bosch and Fanie de Villiers from Pretoria all came into prominence from the 1990s onwards.[38]

Indicators of an increased Afrikaner presence and skill in the higher echelons of the game had already become evident in the early 1970s as the social yeast of the 1960s started to foment in the form of a new generation of Afrikaners. In the Nuffield tournament of 1972, Afrikaans speakers constituted about 20% of the total number of players—a marked increase from earlier tournaments where the percentage of Afrikaans speakers was negligible. 'Afrikaner boys,' it was reported at the time, 'are currently busy making a name for themselves …. The teams of Griquas and Northern Transvaal are now being captained by Afrikaners while the strength of a few other teams is in their Afrikaans players'.[39] Afrikaners also started to make their presence felt in other areas of the game. In the early 1980s, Willie Basson of the then Northern Transvaal was the first Afrikaans speaker to be named administrator of the year for his role in making the province—described as the 'ugly stepchild of the Currie Cup scene: the unwanted Cinderella'—a more competitive force.[40]

In assessing the reasons for the growth of cricket among Afrikaners, it is useful to factor in that besides the socio-economic and cultural developments of the 1960s, political developments were propitious for greater integration of Afrikaans and white English speakers. South Africa's departure from the Commonwealth in 1961 and the establishment of a republic, although initially rued, had over time the effect of forging closer identification with Afrikaners as English speakers gradually came to terms with the irretrievable loss of former imperial ties. Coupled with this realisation and also fearful of the winds of change which had started to blow in Africa, English speakers started to shift their allegiance away from the struggling United Party towards the National Party.[41] Afrikaners for their part welcomed the move as it signalled a newfound parity between the two groups and opened the possibility for greater white cohesion. With these developments, playing a British game no longer had the same kind of perceived negative association it might have had earlier. In 1970, a sport analyst was able to write: '[T]he game is no longer an English game and therefore an alien institution: it is a South African game and now that the political connection with England has been severed, the Afrikaner can play cricket with a quiet conscience'.[42]

What happened on the field was also of considerable importance. In 1966/67, South Africa won an epic series against Australia which sparked a general sense of sport euphoria and triumphalism. It was a most ebullient team, brimful with confidence and talent and singularly expressive in its cricketing ways.[43] Its prowess captured the imagination, and its enthusiastic pursuit of victory was contagious. That's why an Afrikaner reporter reflected in 1975: 'Like everybody else, we like winning. We are proud of the successes of our national teams. So when the Springboks emerged as a world power in cricket in the early years of the previous decade, the Afrikaners were very much behind them. That was where support of the game really started'.[44] Cricket books were published in Afrikaans and in one such book, Peter van der Merwe, an Anglo-Afrikaner and the victorious captain against the Australians, prefaced the book by saying that 'there has never before been such an interest in cricket among Afrikaans speakers as is the case currently. As a player it has been clear to me from the numerous telegrams I have received from [Afrikaans] enthusiasts over the whole of the country'.[45] Other players concurred. Ali Bacher, Springbok captain in 1970 and destined to become a prominent cricket administrator, recalled: 'What was very significant to me was that, for the first time, thousands of Afrikaners came to watch cricket and show their support. This continued throughout the Test series when Afrikaans folk became very committed cricket fans. I believe they were attracted by our success'.[46] In a similar vein, Peter Pollock, a fast bowler and one of the heroes of the 1960s, predicted that the Afrikaner's enthusiasm for cricket would come into good stead in the future, explaining that 'such is his temperament and personality that in years to come he will become an even more faithful patron than his less volatile English counterpart'.[47]

The Afrikaans press reported widely on the cricketing feats of the national team. At a symbolic level, it appeared that Afrikaans speakers had laid equal claim to these victories as part of the achievements of a new white republican nation. Along with economic prosperity, political dominance and the initial illusion that apartheid provided the answer to South Africa's racial issues, Afrikaners now had the confidence to regard themselves on par with English speakers and this realisation extended to the cricket field where successes in the sporting arena ensured wider traction, providing the opportunity of showcasing and appropriating sporting talents to demonstrate the fruits of National Party rule. In addition, with the looming prospect of international isolation as anti-apartheid forces gathered strength abroad, sporting prowess was a way to keep South Africa prominently before the eyes of those who might be considered potential allies.[48]

Looking at the diffusion and non-diffusion of cricket in a global context, American sociologists, Jason Kaufman and Orlando Patterson, have isolated a number of factors which under certain conditions can facilitate or retard the adoption of the game where there was a significant British presence. Probably because of a lack of detailed research on southern Africa, the area is dismissed in a rather cursory fashion. Nevertheless, they came to the conclusion that of the multiple factors that can play a role, 'it is social stratification that lies most fundamentally at the heart of the matter. The extent to which an elite cultural practice like cricket was shared with, or shielded from, the general population was a direct result of the elites' own sense of their place atop the social hierarchy'.[49] Equally pertinent here is the finding of Boria Majumdar and Sean Brown that cricket in twentieth-century India became part of the nationalist project and accomplishment in the game was a cultural response to outdo the British elite, while the absence of cricket in America can be ascribed to the fact that the USA achieved independence a century and a half earlier than India, which meant that the need to use a specific sport as a cultural form of self-assertion did not arise.[50]

These observations can be tweaked as far as South Africa is concerned. Cricket was not really part of the Afrikaner nationalist armoury, and Afrikaners generally only showed an interest in the game once the movement had peaked in the 1960s. Its earlier absence was at least in part a result of antagonism between English speakers and Afrikaners and also because, as we have seen, rugby has already been harnessed to serve nationalistic causes. However, as English-speaking businessmen started to mix with their newly arrived Afrikaner counterparts and politically English speakers edged closer to the Afrikaner government, tensions between whites in general gradually began to dissipate. These societal shifts contributed to a cultural space potentially opening up for cricket to broaden its base. Such a structural approach to the issue had the salutary effect that essentialisms about the acquisition of a sporting culture could at least be moderated if not totally discarded. The sport historian André Odendaal has argued the trajectory of an Afrikaner entry into the game succinctly: 'Afrikaners did not get their place in the sun in cricket because they practised hard for fifty years and eventually acquired a cricket "culture". It was political power, increasing wealth and greater social opportunities and confidence that broadened the base and paved the way ...'.[51]

While Afrikaners started to assert themselves more forcefully in several spheres of society, it did not imply that all underlying English/Afrikaner animosities evaporated overnight or that Afrikaners rapidly started playing at the top level. In the 1960s, Afrikaners were still invisible in the national team. It was the 'Englishness' of the game that caused Prime Minister B. J. Vorster to quip when told what the English batting score between England and South Africa was: 'Their English or our English?'[52] On the field, Afrikaners were at times riled by ethnic jibes from English speakers; some might have been good-natured, others not. Albert Morkel who played in the Transvaal Premier League during the 1970s recounts how he was treated by some fellow team members; 'I used to play for Old Johannians [the club associated with the elite South African private school St John's College] with players like Don Mackay-Coghill. He always used to joke that I wasn't part of the team. They only brought me along so that I could make the braai after the game. We were called everything during those days, rock-spiders, hairy-backs, you name it'.[53] Kepler Wessels, known for his intensity, was outspoken on the kind of treatment he received during his first few years of provincial cricket. He recalled that many players 'thought I was a stupid Dutchman from the Free State. They can say what they like now but that's how it was. There is no doubt that Afrikaans-speaking guys were not regarded that highly'.[54] These were not isolated incidents, and several such observations found their way into the press.[55] In time though, as players mingled to a greater extent and along with broader shifts in South African society as the country lurched towards full democracy, petty white ethnic rivalries receded in the face of larger issues. Afrikaner representation at the highest level grew steadily, and it was calculated that out of the 86 white players to represent South Africa between 1991 and 2012, a total of 30 (35%) were from an Afrikaans background.[56]

NOTES

1. For a bibliographical overview see South African Sports Documentation and Information Centre, *South African Cricket, 1889–1989* (Human Science Research Council, 1989).

2. However, for a brief but suggestive account see A. Odendaal, 'Turning History on Its Head: Some Perspectives on Afrikaners and the Game of Cricket' in C. Day (ed.), *Cricket—Developing Winners* (Illovo: United Cricket Board, 2011), 29–34.

3. The literature on symbolism of the game is extensive. See, for example, R. Holt, *Sport and the British: A Modern History* (Oxford: Clarendon Press, 1990), 204–209; B. Stoddart and K. Sandiford (eds.), *The Imperial Game: Cricket, Culture and Society* (Manchester: Manchester University Press, 1998), 58–59 and *passim*, J. Mangan (ed.), *The Cultural Bond: Sport, Empire, Society* (London: Frank Cass, 1992), 1–10.

4. J. Simons, 'The "Englishness" of English Cricket', *Journal of Popular Culture* 29, 4 (Spring 1996), 45.

5. J. Nauright and C. Merrett, 'South Africa' in Stoddart and Sandiford, *Imperial Game*, 55.

6. Holt, *Sport and the British*, 227.

7. J. Winch, 'Sir William Milton: A Leading Figure in Public School Games, Colonial Politics and Imperial Expansion, 1877–1914' (Unpublished D.Phil thesis, Stellenbosch University, 2012), 122–23.

8. W. Schulze, 'Boer Prisoners of War in Ceylon' in B. Murray and G. Vahed (eds.), *Empire and Cricket: The South African Experience, 1884–1914* (Pretoria: Unisa Press, 2009), 179–96; D. Allen, 'Bats and Bayonets: Cricket and the Anglo-Boer War, 1899–1902', *Sport in History*, 25, 1 (April 2005), 34–35.

9. G. Stander, 'Die Geskiedenis van Matie-Krieket' (Unpublished M.A. thesis, Stellenbosch University, 2000), 108.

10. Merrett and Nauright, 'South Africa' in Stoddart and Sandiford (eds.), *Imperial Game*, 58. See also Schulze, 'Boer Prisoners of War in Ceylon', 185.

11. C. Martin-Jenkins, *The Complete Who's Who of Test Cricketers* (London: Obis Publishing, 1980), 263.

12. G. Levett, 'Constructing Imperial Identity: The 1907 South African Cricket Tour of England' in Murray and Vahed (eds.), *Empire and Cricket*, 248.

13. Holt, *Sport and the British*, 227.

14. Merrett and Nauright, 'South Africa' in Stoddart and Sandiford (eds.), *Imperial Game*, 59. Jacobus Duminy played in three Tests for South Africa in the late 1920s.

15. A. Paton, *Hofmeyr* (Oxford: Oxford University Press, 1964), 140–41.
16. D. Woods, 'African Sunrise' in *Wisden* (London: Wisden and Co., 1993). See also E. Robins, *This Man Malan* (Cape Town: SA Scientific Publishing, 1953), 56.
17. D. Allen, 'Beating Them at Their Own Game: Rugby, the Anglo-Boer War and Afrikaner Nationalism, 1899–1948', *International Journal of the History of Sport*, 20, 3 (September 2003), 50.
18. P. Mosely, R. Cashman, J. O'Hara, and H. Weatherburn (eds.), *Sporting Immigrants: Sport and Ethnicity in Australia* (Sydney: Walla Press, 1997), 182.
19. R. Archer and A. Bouillon, *The South African Game* (London: Zed Press, 1982), 87.
20. H. Giliomee, *The Afrikaners: Biography of a People* (Cape Town: Tafelberg, 2003), 315–54.
21. Compare G. Ryan, 'Few and Far Between: Maori and Pacific Contributions to New Zealand Cricket', *Sport in History*, 10, 1 (January 2007), 88.
22. *South African Cricket Review*, December 1956, 'Need for Afrikaans Cricket Clubs'.
23. Archer and Bouillon, *The South African Game*, 87.
24. *South African Cricket Review*, December 1956, 'Need for Afrikaans Cricket Clubs'.
25. A. Grundlingh, '"Are We Afrikaners Becoming Too Rich?" Cornucopia and Change in Afrikanerdom in the 1960s', *Journal of Historical Sociology*, 21, 2/3 (June–September, 2008), 144, 148–51.
26. Archer and Bouillon, *The South African Game*, 87.
27. Odendaal, 'Turning on Its Head', 30.
28. Grundlingh, 'Cornucopia and Change', 145.
29. *South African Cricketer* (February 1975), 'Krieket, Lekker Krieket'.
30. *The Independent*, 11 December 1993.
31. *Grey College Centenary Publication* (Cape Town: Juta, 1955), *passim*.
32. G. King, *The Hansie Cronjé Story: An Authorised Biography* (Cape Town: Global Creative, 2005), 56.
33. Interview with Ewie Cronjé, Bloemfontein, 5 September 2008. See also D. Gouws, *... and Nothing but the Truth?* (Cape Town: Zebra Press, 2000), 65–75.
34. A. Donald, *Allan Donald: The Biography: White Lightning* (London: Collins Willow, 2000), 6–9.
35. *Millennium Magazine* (April 1996), 95, 'A Whole New Ball Game'.
36. Interview with Ewie Cronjé, Bloemfontein, 5 September 2008.
37. King, *Cronjé*, 60.
38. Odendaal, 'Turning History on Its Head', 32.

39. *Transvaler*, 5 January 1972 (translated).
40. *SA Protea Cricket Annual*, 1984, 37.
41. Giliomee, *Afrikaners*, 542.
42. R. Bowen, *Cricket: A History of Its Growth and Development Throughout the World* (London: Eyre and Spottiswoode, 1970), 216.
43. *Millennium Magazine* (April 1996), 95, 'A Whole New Ball Game'.
44. *South African Cricketer* (February 1975), 'Krieket, Lekker Krieket'.
45. N. Steyn, *Sesse tot Oorwinning: Suid-Afrika se Kirieketsege, 1966–67* (Johannesburg: Voortrekkerpers, 1967), 9 (translation).
46. R. Hartman, *Ali: The Life of Ali Bacher* (Cape Town: Viking, 2004), 91.
47. P. Pollock and G. Pollock, *Bouncers and Boundaries* (Johannesburg: Sportsman Enterprises, 1968), 154.
48. Bowen, *Cricket*, 216; Archer and Bouillon, *The South African Game*, 88.
49. J. Kaufman and O. Patterson, 'The Cross-National Cultural Diffusion: The Global Spread of Cricket', *American Sociological Review*, 70 (February 2005), 105.
50. B. Majumdar and S. Brown, 'Why Baseball, Why Cricket? Differing Nationalisms, Differing Challenges', *The International Journal of Sports History*, 24, 2 (February 2997), 139–56.
51. Odendaal, 'Turning History on Its Head', 31.
52. B. Murray and C. Merrett, *Caught Behind: Race and Politics in Springbok Cricket* (Johannesburg and Durban: Wits University Press and University of KwaZulu-Natal Press, 2004), 79.
53. L. Alfred, *Lifting the Covers: The Inside Story of South African Cricket* (Cape Town: Spearhead, 2001), 143.
54. E. Griffiths, *Kepler: The Biography* (London: Pelham Books, 1994), 30.
55. Several such stories are recounted in *Volksblad*, 1 November 2000.
56. *Die Burger*, 18 January 2012.

CHAPTER 8

The Education of Bruce Mitchell and the 'Union Babies': History, Accumulation and the Path to Triumph at Lord's, 1924–1935

Dale Slater and Richard Parry

'UNION BABIES': UNION AND OPTIMISM

As South Africa emerged from the depths of the sharp recession of strike-hit 1907, after the bitter years of the South African War and its unquiet aftermath, the country experienced a brief upsurge of optimism.

At the start of this period, negotiations were in train for Union between the historical British colonies and the former Boer Republics. Even after the National Convention had published its conclusions in February 1909 the political situation remained fluid and fast-changing, and therefore all political constituencies were able to retain hopes, if

D. Slater (✉)
Byfleet, UK
e-mail: daleslater@ntlworld.com

R. Parry
London, UK

© The Author(s) 2018
B. Murray et al. (eds.), *Cricket and Society in South Africa, 1910–1971*, Palgrave Studies in Sport and Politics,
https://doi.org/10.1007/978-3-319-93608-6_8

207

not expectations, of future political gains under Union, even where the interests of one contradicted those of another or had no solid, objective basis. Though the tactical effect of Campbell-Bannerman's concession of Responsible government to the former Boer Republics in 1907 had been to drive a potential wedge between elite and rank-and-file, Afrikaners—the white majority despite Milner's efforts to promote mass English immigration—were offered a path to future political power by the Convention's rejection of qualified franchise in favour of 'manhood suffrage'. Despite being thus condemned to perpetual infantilism by their exclusion, Africans seemed at least no worse off, in that the constitutional entrenchment of the Cape's franchise arrangements, though not applied to the country as a whole, still appeared to grant them some sort of political base from which to build, however minimal. Besides, their leadership had not yet lost faith completely in the promises of the Imperial mission, nor was the Land Act yet in sight. Though white English-speakers were split between a 'Progressive' grouping which favoured close imperial ties and those working to cultivate an inclusive (white) nationalism, both sets were sheltered to some degree by Britain's clear interest in peace in South Africa and vigorous political and economic development. Apart from a marginal working class, moreover, the interests of both sets were tightly aligned with those of capital.

The economy was at last showing strong vital signs. Still the largest sector, agriculture was booming as commodity prices recovered from a prolonged slump in world markets. Together with gold and diamond exports, and import substitution to encourage a fledgling manufacturing sector, the balance of trade was pushed into credit. The mining houses too were showing gains. Despite the difficulty of restarting the post-war industry almost from scratch, by 1905 production was back to pre-war levels. Acute labour shortages remained a problem, especially after the defeat of Milner's Chinese labour policy. Nonetheless, the mines continued to resist paying higher wages to African labour. By concerted implementation of policies of recruitment and working conditions, the mines in fact continued to drive down wage levels, shortages notwithstanding. Already down a quarter since 1889, with political connivance of future governments African wages would continue to fall long-term, so that in 1911 they were still 14% higher in real terms than they would be in 1961.[1] As the industrialised nations of Europe geared up for their own war, increased production to meet growing demand leveraged the impact of these cost reductions, yielding profits by 1909 of an order unimaginable back in 1902.[2] Consolidated Goldfields, for example, contrived to pay dividends of 35% that year, and dividends over the decade ending 1914 aggregated 187½% 'free of tax'. Seeking to win support for a plan for diversification into West Africa, Goldfields Chairman Lord Harris told shareholders: 'Mining on the Rand is an absolute certainty. You want a bit of a gamble'.[3]

Nor were shareholders alone in being persuaded of future prospects: the Union-wide census of May 1911 revealed a dividend of a different kind. Buoyed to a degree by an increase in immigration (itself a sign of optimism), the overall population of South Africa had increased since the previous census of April 1904 by over 15%, from 5,175,463 to 5,973,394. Among whites the increase was even more marked. The 1911 census revealed a 19.39% increase in the white birth rate since 1908: the cohort of white children aged four or under stood at 185,572, against 155,430 aged between five and nine.[4]

Among these 'Union babies' was Bruce Mitchell, born on 8 January 1909. Mitchell was the first of a significant cluster of future Springbok cricketers born at this time.[5] He was also the first of five especially gifted batsmen within this cluster. After him in quick succession came H. G. O. 'Tuppy' Owen-Smith, Eric Rowan, Alan Melville and Dudley Nourse, all born before the end of 1910. Between them, these five would aggregate 118 internationals for South Africa, and a combined 219 innings would yield 9542 Test runs at an average of 49.18, with 25 hundreds (three of these doubles) and 51 fifties along the way.

Despite their proximity of birth, the five never once played together in the same side; South Africa might well have wished they had. All five lost their best years to the Second World War but besides that, there was the problem of the class make-up of South African cricket. At practically all levels organised white cricket in South Africa was the possession of an elite of middle-class English-speakers, and the game's development was intimately bound up with the means by which that class reproduced itself: a few dozen elite schools, well-connected and exceptionally well-resourced, that fed the local establishment and, given the extraordinary reach and appetite of Empire and English language culture, sometimes the metropolitan establishment too. For most of these five therefore, serious cricket was only one option among many, and *South African* cricket only one among those. Though Mitchell and Nourse became staples of Springbok sides all the way to the Second World War and beyond, they were exceptions.[6]

The cricketing careers of both Owen-Smith and Alan Melville, for instance, were severely curtailed by considerations of work and status: between them they played only sixteen Tests in total. Despite his great success in the five Tests of 1929 that saw him named among *Wisden's* Cricketers of the Year for 1930, Owen-Smith never played for South Africa again. Studying medicine at Magdalen College, Oxford he earned a triple 'Blue' and stayed to study and work in England so that as, on 4 January 1936, at Newlands South Africa were being bundled out by Grimmett, O'Reilly and Fleetwood-Smith to lose by an innings and 78 runs, Owen-Smith was otherwise engaged, at Twickenham, playing fullback behind the White Russian refugee 'Prince' Obolensky as England famously beat the All Blacks for the first time. Likewise Melville: a Michaelhouse phenomenon, at nineteen he chose a place at Trinity College, Oxford in 1930 rather than tour with the Springboks in 1929. He went on to captain the university, thereafter remaining in England to further his business career and playing for some years as an amateur for Sussex CCC. He returned to South Africa only in 1936, where he took up an appointment at the Johannesburg Stock Exchange, and captained Transvaal and The Wanderers Club. Complementing great elegance and skill as a batsman with a patrician social profile, Melville was irresistible to the South African selectors who appointed him captain on belated debut against Wally Hammond's MCC in 1938/39. Culminating in the back-breaking toil of the Timeless Test, this was a better series in which to bat than bowl. With Mitchell, Nourse, Rowan, Melville and P. G. V. van der Bijl in one corner and Hutton, Gibb, Paynter, Edrich, Ames and Hammond in the other, the two teams aggregated 5930 runs in five Tests at better than 46 runs per wicket, this despite the changed LBW law. South Africa's turf wickets, scarcely a decade old, generously favoured bat over ball, but if ever a series tended to confirm the transformed mental economy that had emerged in cricket since the war, this was it.[7]

But back in January 1910, the bullish Lord Harris might have proved just a touch less complacent, at least from under his MCC Chairman's hat, for cricket's first Golden Age, that era of genius and rare invention over which he had presided, was rapidly approaching its close. Moreover, if South African cricket was then basking in uncommon favour it was mainly at England's expense. The advent of the 'googly quartet' of Schwarz, Faulkner, White and Vogler, and remarkable all-round depth had made South African teams of the period after 1904 formidable combinations.[8] Though weaker now than at their 1907 peak, but with

Faulkner and Vogler still in full cry, South Africa's 1909 incarnation held on 3-2 against Leveson Gower's MCC, Hobbs, Denton, Blythe, Woolley and Wilfred Rhodes notwithstanding. Tight as the series was, England was a little flattered by an easy win in a dead rubber fifth Test over an experimental South African side selected with the forthcoming tour of Australia in mind. But this was South Africa's second successive home win over MCC touring sides, the two victories sandwiching a narrow defeat on English turf in 1907 that even ardent England supporters conceded might with equal justice have gone South Africa's way. With the extraordinary googly bowlers at their cutting edge, the way then seemed clear for a continuation of South Africa's sudden and dramatic ascent into the top ranks of world cricket, a phenomenon that, alongside the country's perceptible political and economic progress, amplified the mood of general optimism.

Yet even before the Great War struck, this flimsy bubble of Union optimism had been burst, in politics as in cricket. Badly beaten successively in Australia in 1910/11, in the Triangular Tournament of 1912, and at home by J. W. H. T. Douglas's 1913/14 MCC, South Africa's cricketing fortunes plummeted. By 1913 the economy too had faltered and the following year plunged into steep depression. Breakneck industrialisation had seen a convergence of urbanisation and proletarianisation that trailed severe social dislocation in its wake. Accompanied by strikes and civil unrest, and met by a militant government response, the depression disclosed fierce and bewilderingly contrary political undercurrents. Though a direct result of downward pressure on wages, the foment reflected the entanglement of Afrikaner nationalism with working-class politics—a blue-collar mirror image of Botha's governing coalition of the mine-owning class with landed Afrikaner notables—as the two constituencies battled to mobilise support around the plight of the increasingly visible urban 'poor white', vulnerable underbelly of capital and the weak point of white privilege.

The Influence of Herby Taylor

Mitchell therefore was born into a period of great upheaval as South Africa, and the wider world, struggled to absorb the shocks of modernity. Straddling the cusp of epochal change, Mitchell was in some things the last of his kind, in others the first. For one thing, he was perhaps the first great cricketer actually born in the Transvaal. There was 'Billy'

Zulch before him, and Quintin McMillan and a handful of others, but Zulch was Lydenburg-born only by the accident of having a pair of gold-prospecting parents, and McMillan retired early and died young.

The son of a doctor, Mitchell was middle-class certainly, though not necessarily as prosperous as that might imply. Since the influx after 1902 of experts come to rebuild the mining industry, Johannesburg was over-stocked with doctors. There was fierce competition for a relatively few full-time posts on the mines themselves; in 1914, only 19 of 63 pro-ducing mines were serviced by full-time medical professionals (10 posts in all), while the other 44 relied on doctors in private practice seeking to augment their income.[9] Each doctor would have to care for all of a given mine's white personnel as well as some 7–8000 African workers, for which they received an annual retainer of around £50. In common with most of the Witwatersrand, doctors were thus reliant on the good will of mine-owners and mine managers, and not keen to trouble them with bad news. The cost structure of the industry meant that mine-own-ers' central abiding article of faith was unremitting downward pressure on working costs per ton. The reef's low-grade ore, averaging only 6.5 dwt gold per ton versus 12 dwt gold per ton in Australia and the USA, necessitated large-scale production for economies of scale, and required a workforce substantially larger than their counterparts. Pre-Great War, the ratio of Africans to white workers was around 7-1, rising to 12-1 among underground workers. It takes no great insight to see where the mine-owners would apply most pressure. African mineworkers, mostly migrants from East Africa on temporary contracts, were housed in appalling squalor, overcrowded and bereft of even rudimentary com-forts. Their diet was starch-rich and protein-poor. Below ground, clad only in loincloths, they were driven hard by white supervisors in unre-lieved physical toil of an extreme nature, and subject to frequent abuse and even assault. Working at great depth, they were by turns hot and then cold. Drinking water was scarce and yet they were constantly sod-den, drenched by waste water, often contaminated by human effluent since there were no underground sanitation facilities. If the drainage was inadequate, so too was the ventilation, designed to prevent pro-duction-threatening fires rather than ensure the health of workers. All the above combined to create a perfect storm of health problems, many of them preventable had mine-owners been prepared to counte-nance investment in well-understood but expensive dust-suppression technologies. Around 80% of African underground workers are believed to have suffered from pneumonia, tuberculosis or phthisis in conditions where the likelihood of effective treatment was vanishingly small.

There are stories of Mitchell as a young boy playing cricket in the shadow of the Ferreira Deep headgear, being bowled to by South Africa's great pre-War wicketkeeper, Ernest Halliwell, who was said to have predicted great things for him, and by his older sister, herself a keen enough cricketer to have won a bat presented by Jack Hobbs in person. It is not inconceivable that Halliwell, a starter at the Johannesburg Turf Club, might indeed have come across the six-year-old Mitchell, but the story smacks a little of the Graces in their orchard at Downend and besides, all great cricketers, first of their type, acquire an origin myth.

Yet such myths survive because they tell us something about the player, or at least his forward projection into the game's future. For Cardus, Grace's connection with Downend imputed a deeper relation between Englishness and the cycle of seasons, both of which Grace bestrode like a natural force, immune to all questions beyond persistence:

> Morning after morning the summer's sun rose for him, and he went forth and trod fresh grass. Every spring-time came and found him ready for cricket; when he was a boy he learned the game in a Gloucestershire orchard white with bloom. He grew in the sunshine and wind and rain; the elements became flesh within him. Why did this natural man ever die?[10]

Mitchell's connection was with a landscape altogether less bucolic: drier, less fertile and less tractable, selected not for natural advantages of location but rather to exploit its subterranean salients; where the connection between depth and surface was thus not patent, and embodied an antagonistic relation that made large-scale industrial intervention necessary to induce the earth to surrender its yield, the mine-dumps looming in the background as a perpetual emblem of the transaction's toxic legacy.[11]

Prior to Mitchell's generation, Transvaal had scaled the peak of South Africa's cricketing pyramid mainly by dint of money spent on talented imports and influence with employers and selectors to advance careers. As George Allsop wrote in 1915:

> ... cricket in the Transvaal ... is on an entirely different footing from
> the older Provinces of South Africa, in that its large towns are of such
> recent growth that it has been impossible for the Transvaal to produce
> its own players in such abundance as the older centres. It must of neces-
> sity be many years before this can be expected. Naturally, also, with
> the growth of a town of such importance as Johannesburg innumera-
> ble cricketers migrated to the Transvaal for business reasons from other
> Provinces. This is only in the natural order of things. Time will remedy
> all this.[12]

Allsop's phlegmatic view of the problem was not shared by the other
provinces, whose best players were regularly whisked away to reappear
in Transvaal blue-and-gold, or to be feted in the Springbok green-and-
gold denied them in the colours of their province of origin. This issue—
or issues, since both were the subject of raucous complaint—had been
a running sore in South African cricket since the 1890s. For decades,
Natal, Eastern Province and Border, three of South Africa's most celebrated cricketing nurseries, had resisted their bluffer, richer neighbours'
propensity regularly to cream off their rising talent, yet the flows towards
the status and job security of Cape Town and Johannesburg continued
unabated, and for every promising cricketer the minnows managed to
retain a couple were lost to the lure of larger prospects. 'Cricketers outside the Transvaal', wrote Herby Taylor in 1927, 'have always felt they
had a very poor chance of being recognised for representative honours.
They felt that such opportunities as were offered were intended more as
a means of elimination than trial'.[13]

Even as Taylor wrote, though, conditions were changing. The embarrassing fiasco of 1924 had forced South African cricket into a long spell
of soul-searching, culminating in its administrative reconstruction and
the introduction of turf wickets in an effort to modernise the game and
reassert itself as—at least potentially—internationally competitive. This
process was not uncomplicated. The reconstruction provoked strong
resistance from interests attached to the game whose attitudes and practices had long been all-pervasive. South African cricket was a deeply
conservative institution. Even its modernisation was motivated in large
measure by reactionary sentiment, its proponents driven as much by nos-
talgic impulses arising out of post-war disenchantment as by any sense of
new social or technical possibilities.[14] Nonetheless, a key goal of reconstruction had been to check Transvaal's automatic dominance of South

African cricket, and Transvaal's new administration was thus forced to reappraise its relationships with other provinces.

Besides, Allsop had finally been proved right. By the mid-twenties Johannesburg's elite schools, augmented by a bevy of professional coaches subsidised by the copious flow of The Wanderers Club money, had at last begun to turn out the 'unfailing supply of young class crick-eters' Allsop had envisaged, and Taylor, a gifted coach and key reformer as well as the sole remaining South African cricketer of unquestioned international status, was quick to recognise the significance of this new phase.[15] Thus, in 1926, after many years leading Natal's battle to resist Transvaal domination, Taylor himself had finally surrendered to per-sistent pressure and permitted Johannesburg's long gilt arm at last to reel him in. With a brief to oversee the ongoing development and inte-gration of this new stream of home-grown talent, Mitchell was soon in Taylor's sights.

Whatever his earlier status, Mitchell's father had evidently made an upward leap from Ferreira Deep, for his son came to Taylor a prodigy from St John's College in the wealthy northern suburb of Houghton. In the previous two seasons, he'd scored over 1600 schoolboy runs and clearly Taylor saw no reason for delay. Mitchell made his debut for Transvaal a mere eleven weeks after his seventeenth birthday. When Taylor, Cyril Vincent and Nupen cried off the final two games of Transvaal's 1925/26 Currie Cup season, both Mitchell and a twen-ty-year-old Port Elizabeth-born 'Jock' Cameron were included in the tour party to the Eastern Cape. Under the watchful eye of captain Hubert 'Nummy' Deane (a former 'Maritzburg boy whom Taylor had known from young), at East London in late March 1926, Transvaal swept Border away by an innings and 50 runs. Bowled out for only 293, Transvaal's margin of victory was due to Alf Hall's six-wicket match, and Mitchell, who bettered his 5/23 in Border's first innings with 6/72 in their second. A week later at St George's Park though he added only one more wicket, Eastern Province were turned over just as decisively and Transvaal stashed a ninth Currie Cup (of 18 in total) into their trophy cabinet. Mitchell's figures were full of promise: 12 wickets at 14 apiece, only one fewer than his aggregate of runs, 13, scored at number ten, not out in both innings, displaying already his obdurate defence.

THE TOUR OF ENGLAND, 1929: 'ANTI-1924'

Mitchell's apprenticeship was clearly destined to be a short one and Taylor, by now a national selector, had soon seen enough. By late December 1928, with only eight Currie Cup matches behind him (plus a bit part against Stanyforth's MCC), he played his way into the 1929 touring party for England with a series of scintillating all-round performances in three Trial matches on Kingsmead's turf wicket. Alongside scores of 23, 79*, 76* and 84 he registered bowling figures of 3/50, 5/29, 5/103, 3/8 and 5/33. No selector on earth could ignore such performances, even from a youth not yet twenty, and especially at a time when they had more reason than usual to be looking to youth.

In the light of South African cricket's recent reconstruction, the tour of England in 1929 was seen as a chance to gauge what ground had been made up since the drubbing of 1924, and what still needed to be done. Thus, it was conceived as a kind of anti-1924, explicitly planned to avoid that tour's most egregious errors, chiefly, an ageing party and a divided one. The tour of 1924 had been undermined by contentious questions of selection arising from a patrician attitude by administrators towards the players, and resulting in a faction-riven party who displayed 'little collective strategy'.[16] The new captain 'Nummy' Deane therefore made it a priority to establish a common purpose. Indeed, this was the rationale behind Deane's own appointment. He was seen as a man capable of welding a team into a whole greater than the sum of its parts: South Africa generally lacked the depth of her opponents and had to make up for it in other ways.[17]

The tour of 1924, fractious and unhappy, had exposed the 'decadence', in the parlance of the time, of South African cricket.[18] Vice-captain Mick Commaille later summed it up as having 'little of summer' about it'.[19] Post-tour reports stated that manager George Allsop 'had a very hard time of it', for reasons never publicly disclosed but to do with marked internal dissension.[20] The tour was preceded by friction at the South African Cricket Association (SACA) over questions of amateur and professional status, with Western Province exercised over a proposal that 20% of tour profits be distributed among the players, a decision passed without demur months previously.[21] Worse, Allan Reid, the Free State delegate, having already insisted on Alf Hall's exclusion (SACA refused to meet Lancashire CC's £130 release fee), now vehemently opposed the selection of Pegler, whom Taylor, recalling his performances in 1912, wanted in.[22] These were not petty matters. They affected the way players would be treated in England, where amateurs and professionals still entered the grounds by different entrances, used separate dressing rooms and luncheon halls, went to and from the wicket by different gates and were accorded a different social status by their hosts. SACA's high-handedness raised bad blood among the party. Pegler, who eventually accompanied the side at his own expense, 'on holiday', played in all five Tests and was, with Bob Catterall, one of the tour's few successes.

Nor was a patrician outlook the selectors'—an unwieldy panel five-man strong plus the SACA chairman, but *not* the captain—sole mistake. In general, one might expect the average touring party to contain a cluster of players between the ages of 27 and 30: experienced enough to understand both the game in general and their own game specifically and yet be in, or close to, their physical prime. In 1924, this was emphatically not the case. Bissett, at 19 the youngest, was one of three tourists 24 or under, alongside Nupen and Catterall. Only one other, Deane, 29, already earmarked as a future leader, was younger than 30. These four aside, not a single member of the party had debuted in South African cricket after 1912. Three players—Nourse (46), Carter (43) and Commaille (41)—were deep in veteran territory; indeed, the inclusion of 42-year old Aubrey Faulkner for the second Test scarcely moved the needle. With half the party 35 or older, the average age was over 33. A tour of England was a plum assignment. South Africa had not toured there since 1912 and was not due again until 1929. One might well conclude that the main principle guiding the process of selection was the recognition of seniority and the sacrifices of war. Even accepting the selectors' hand was forced to some extent by post-war dearth, what is incontestable is that in the quest for experience they had produced a party short on the dynamism, athleticism, endurance and enthusiasm required for a long, arduous tour.

Then in late May, just as the first Test drew near came another sign of ill omen with the sad news of the suicide of 'Billy' Zulch, latest in a cluster of violent or sudden deaths that beset South African cricket, starting with the untimely passing of Jimmy Sinclair, aged 36, in 1913, then Maitland Hathorn, continuing with the war dead (Schwarz and White, Newberry and Ochse, Cook, Lundie and Hands), soon also to consume William Shalders, Tom Campbell, Aubrey Faulkner, Tommy Ward, George Allsop and Gordon Beves, 'Nummy' Deane himself, Neville Quinn, yet another gloveman in 'Jock' Cameron, and Norman Reid.

But the 1924 tour is best remembered for the first Test at Edgbaston where the team froze under the Imperial gaze, its manifold failures seeming to sum up South Africa's diminished state. Though most informed observers agreed captain Taylor was right to put England in, England's total of 438 prompted inevitable questions as to how matting-bred cricketers could be expected to read and respond to the weather-driven vagaries of English turf wickets. The querulous growls grew louder when on a damp pitch Taylor called for the heavy roller that would make the early going harder and bring rewards later on. But with the moisture brought to the surface, South Africa in turn were rolled before the pitch could dry, 30 all out, only 19 off the bat, shot out in only 48 minutes by Gilligan and the debutant Tate. The 'sound defence and dourness' that South African sides had exhibited in the pre-War years was entirely absent, in its place a scrambled technique, bereft of footwork and utterly unsuited to turf wickets and heavy atmospheres.[23] As South Africa's batsmen probed helplessly after the moving ball, one unkind English commentator likened their efforts to 'playing billiards on a round table'.[24] The progress of the series revealed the bowling equally moribund. In the absence of perennially injured fast bowler Bissett, the attack was based almost exclusively on finger-spin. On the good turf wickets of the tour's first—dry—half they 'developed an alarming innocuousness'; on the wet wickets of August they lacked the nous and experience to exploit conditions; in South Africa, one simply bowled, and let the matting do the work.[25] With the last two Tests lost to rain, England's superiority was effortless, as they exactly matched South Africa's series total of 1846 runs, but for the loss of only 31 wickets against South Africa's 74. Winning only eight of 38 matches on tour, the Springboks were judged 'not county strength', compared adversely with the 1923 West Indies and dismissed as a 'complete failure'.[26] Test status was in clear jeopardy.

With this uppermost in their minds, the post-reconstruction selection committee of 1929 (a slimmed-down three-man panel, *plus* captain) therefore took the opposite tack, picking eight tourists younger than 24, and only three—Deane, Catterall and Taylor—who had toured England before.[27] 1929 was to be 'an educational tour'.[28] A strong infusion of youth, more pliant than experience, was therefore necessary. Average age 25, this was, *contra* 1924, the youngest party South Africa had ever sent abroad, and would have been younger still had Melville agreed to tour.

So on 15 June, day one of the Edgbaston Test of 1929, as South Africa took the field with Mitchell among four new caps against an

England side containing, without audible murmur from the tourists, *Duleepsinhji*, the results of South Africa's *Swart Gevaar* election were also announced, disclosing an overall majority for Hertzog's Nationalist Party.[29] Though he deemed it politic to maintain for the time being the Pact with Labour, going forward this majority enabled Hertzog to jettison the working-class elements of his support—at least, those who had not been recruited to capital's advantages by such means as Job Reservation—to clear a way for his next shift in political base: the courtship of capital, essential if he wished to sustain power. Afrikaners had learned well the key lesson of the South African War. Thus by 1933 Smuts, capital's man since 1907, was back in government alongside Hertzog in a new United Party.

The economic 'black year' of 1932 would prove the turning point as, in December, South Africa finally left the Gold Standard, the consequent devaluation raising overnight the price of gold by around a third, and reversing the capital flight which had laid the economy low, threatening even the 1931/32 cricket tour of Australia.[30] By 1935, at least for the white minority, sunlit economic uplands beckoned. Between 1932 and 1939, tax revenues were higher by £110,000,000 than over the previous seven years, 60% of which was due to the gold price windfall.[31] A part of this was used to pay down government debt, but a larger share was dedicated to ideological warfare. Since before the Great War the Union state had been steadily accruing instrumental capacity to extend control of its population and back its developing ideological ambitions. In the war's aftermath, an air force was set up in 1920, a navy in 1922. The Police Force was expanded to take responsibility for rural areas that had previously belonged to specialised mounted units of the army. In 1925, following the defeat of the Rand Revolt bombed and strafed into submission, the Police Force was augmented with a technical support branch featuring expertise in fingerprinting, firearms and crime photography—ironically, a pioneer in the use of colour. Most crucially, the 1927 Native Administration Act gave the Department of Native Affairs powers to make laws by proclamation regulating where Africans could live, with little democratic oversight, negligible representation and minimal safeguards; by segregationist logic, Africans were an administrative problem, not a political one. Africans were already trapped between the rock of the 1913 Land Act that reserved 87% of the country for white occupation, and the hard place of the 1923 Urban Areas Act, that removed their right to reside in urban areas without authorisation, and criminalised infractions. Hitherto the state had lacked the wherewithal to implement these Acts in any rigorous form, but now the newly empowered department began a programme of enforcement.

In Johannesburg, where rapid development had long outrun notions of segregation, from 1932 onwards thousands of African families were removed from inner suburbs. Some Africans were able to escape to 'black spots' such as Sophiatown whose mixed character, despite the squalor of living conditions, promoted a remarkable social vibrancy. Most, however, were removed, often forcibly, to the newly constructed township of Orlando East in the city's distant south-west. The germ of Soweto, the township served to remove Africans from white Johannesburg's line of sight, while keeping them in proximity to service the city's domestic needs and burgeoning manufacturing industry. Ostensibly, the township promoted the principles of public health and slum clearance, for 2 million visitors were expected to the Johannesburg Exhibition of 1936; in actuality it was a latent acknowledgement of the central contradiction about which separate development turned: since white South Africa's economic, social and cultural privileges were dependent on the extraction of African labour, the key to separate development lay in ever tighter economic integration, an ideological circle no segregationist government ever managed to square. Orlando East served as a prototype for the ongoing construction of satellite townships near major cities across the country. Only in one sense was it atypical: in a bid to mop up the tail of the 'poor white' problem, the township was built with exclusively white labour, that raised overall costs and therefore future rents beyond the means of many Africans. Beyond the cities, in rural South Africa, residual African squatters were driven from white demarcated areas into overcrowded and underdeveloped reserves. Kernels of the Verwoerd-era Bantustans, these were dumping grounds for those surplus to white labour requirements, or in the words of the Urban Areas Act, 'the idle and dissolute'.[32] These reserves comprised in total approximately 58,000 square miles and, according to the Census of 1936, supported a population of 3,226,033: almost 49% of the total African population were thus forced to scratch a living by subsistence agriculture or resort to the informal economy, a—literal—reserve army of labour exerting downward pressure on the meagre wages of the employed.[33]

The Edgbaston Test of 1929 was the first of 42 successive Tests for Bruce Mitchell over a period of twenty years. The shaping hand of Deane was in evidence as Mitchell found himself eased out of the attack, bowling only two overs in the match. Evidently Deane was in the same camp as

Mitchell's previous bowling critics, perhaps because of its extreme nature, tossed up so slowly as to pose little threat to a mobile batsman. He bowled fewer than 32 full overs in the series, and henceforth found himself relegated at international level to the ranks of occasional trundlers, though he once achieved a five-wicket innings—against Australia—and he was enough of a bowler to clean bowl Len Hutton in Tests not once, but twice.[34] Instead, at Taylor's prompting, Deane promoted Mitchell to open the batting with Bob Catterall, where they established century partnerships in each innings of the match (119 and 171), the first such instance by South Africans in England. The Test in which 'the South Africans surprised even their best friends' was drawn with England marginally under pressure. Mitchell's share was 88 and 61*.[35]

Alongside these runs, however, another dominant theme of Mitchell's career was introduced, for he occupied an aggregate 575 minutes of the match in making his 149 runs. Edgbaston had, of course, been the scene of the 1924 humiliation. Against an Ashes-winning attack of Larwood, Tate, Fender, Hammond and J. C. White therefore, early caution could be forgiven. There were, moreover, extenuating circumstances for early on the first innings, a bouncer from Larwood had dislocated Mitchell's right thumb, forcing him to rely on his top hand. Swinging his bat pendulum-like, he played on; Mitchell's courage was never in question. Yet at one point he went 80 minutes without adding to his score, and in the fourth innings, with South Africa set an unlikely 304 to win in a little under three hours, as Catterall pushed hard, falling near the end for 98, Mitchell dawdled along at barely one run per over. South African cricket was in a stage of transition. The 'Union Babies' of Mitchell's generation were the last to learn the game on matting, which placed a premium on watchful defence, and relied for scoring predominantly on back-foot play; though they would therefore be the first to benefit from the changeover to turf and the establishment of technical continuity with the broader cricketing world, the shift was yet being managed, and there were a great many cricketing lessons yet to learn. The team of 1929 thus faced the traditional South African problem of adaptation to the different requirements of turf, but on this occasion from a position of technical flux.

Cricket's new 'mental economy', then permeating world cricket from Hammond to Headley to Bradman, was animated by the same technocratic consciousness that, at some remove, had enabled South Africa's belated migration to turf. Diffused—absorbed or retarded—within societies according to a complex network of class interests and class experience, individuals therefore progressed at different rates according to their place within that network, and actual conditions on the ground. As rationalisation articulated against disenchantment, South Africa oscillated between the poles of accumulation, dictated by cricket's economistic turn, and regression to the old ways. Owen-Smith, for instance, versed in turf both at Newlands and at Bishops, demonstrated remarkable progress as the tour went on, playing a number of celebrated innings. Yet as remarkable as his performances was their somewhat misty-eyed reception, especially by the pre-War generation. His hundred before lunch at Leeds, for instance, was rated by Warner, avatar of the Golden Age:

> … an innings we shall never forget. His extreme quickness of foot and his genius in invariably having his feet in the right position for each stroke reminded us in some ways of no less a cricketer than Victor Trumper. This may sound as savouring of exaggeration; but we are not alone in this opinion.[36]

The twenty-year-old Owen-Smith's subsequent loss to South African cricket left it ruefully pondering Robertson-Glasgow's judgement that he was 'an artist … meant by Nature to be remembered, not compared'.[37] It is no disparagement of the twenty-year-old's achievements to observe that his stylish and free-spirited displays evoked in English spectators of a certain age (and class) a nostalgia for their lost pre-War Eden.

More generally, the team displayed customary weaknesses on the front foot, in particular facing English spinners, whose methods were so different from those of most South African spinners; 'even though [South Africa] have been brought up … on slow bowling', commented Frank Mitchell, 'they do not cope with … slow people as well as they do with faster-paced stuff'.[38] They were teased and tormented by R. W. V. Robins and 'Tich' Freeman, who between them chalked up 27 wickets in only three Tests. There were isolated successes, as at Headingly, when Vincent lofted Freeman four times over the long field fence while making 60. But there were also seven stumpings as South African batsmen often sought to combat the leg-spinners by 'lunging forward at the good-length ball spinning away from the bat'.[39] They fared little better when the spinners dropped short of a good length. Anxious to cash in on scoring opportunities given their reluctance to commit to the drive or the sweep, the South Africans were constantly tempted to pull the leg-spinners even where the length was marginal. The shot was a scoring staple on South Africa's matting, since even if the footwork was awry the ball generally rose above stump height but in England, on turf, playing against the turn presented an entirely different risk profile. Again, Frank Mitchell offers us a close-up of the problem:

> [The South Africans] made the most weird strokes, mainly off long-hops. We hear so much about footwork nowadays ... that one was somewhat surprised to see so many bad strokes made in dealing with the short ball. Nine times out of ten the right foot is taken back when hooking the ball, but the error of the South Africans was in standing still and trying to make the stroke, the result being that short leg and mid-on got some simple catches to hold.[40]

As for Mitchell himself, his were mixed reviews: a work-in-progress. No one doubted his value or potential, and his 'quite remarkable defence' was universally acknowledged, especially off the back foot where, it was noted, 'he was able to play back successfully to Tate and have plenty of time to do it in. Most batsmen get into trouble if they play back to Tate on a fast wicket'.[41] His dilatory approach to the scoreboard however was viewed with perplexity. More than one commentator accused him of 'showing little or no initiative...not able to get the ball away at all'.[42] In part this was a technical matter, for it was observed that 'He does not at present force the ball, and there is little or no wrist in his strokes ... He is not stiff in his method, and he is not guilty of a short back-lift, which militates against wrist-work, but he lacks the free swing of the left elbow in playing forward, which gives sting and finish to a stroke'.[43] Here again were matting's effects ingrained in Mitchell's technique. Particularly at The Wanderers the typical front foot drive was little more than an attenuated push, with minimal follow-through, since the orthodox full-blooded drive exposed a batsman to added risks of timing.

However, as the progress of his career would make abundantly clear, there were issues of temperament and sensibility at work here that no amount of technical development would rectify. Mitchell was by all accounts an intensely quiet and private man whom the stress of competition sometimes sent into a meditative bubble where no matter the context only defending the next ball counted. Caught between the contending imperatives of accumulation and withdrawal, Mitchell was sometimes rendered all but shot-less. In his abstracted state he tended to play the game as it was in his head, finding equilibrium in the contest of bat and ball but the scoring of runs was a lowly by-product, and the context of the game a secondary consideration. There are many stories of Mitchell locked in his inner cell while irretrievable points of the game passed him by; not even teammates could penetrate his absolute focus. Thus, it was whispered by critics that however many Tests Mitchell saved for South Africa by his stout defence over his long career, he had cost as many in opportunities unseized. Despite his critical importance to South African cricket between the wars, as the aggressive Republican era drew near the inhibited Mitchell came to be regarded with the air of faint embarrassment that had previously been the lot of Charles Frank and in 1949, despite 99 and 56 in his previous Test, he suffered the same fate.[44]

THE ACME OF ACCUMULATION: BRADMAN IN AUSTRALIA, 1931/32

The 1929 series was finally lost 2-0. Getting on the wrong side of weather and toss were both factors, but that aside South Africa patently lacked England's all-round depth, especially with resources stretched as illness and injury struck key personnel. Still, the fighting nature of their defeat restored South Africa's pride, and their bright cricket showed great promise, winning them 'wide popularity' and 'golden opinions'.[45] Deane's functional approach to team-building that encouraged incremental improvement saw another tradition of South African cricket initiated: the fielding was 'glorious; there is no other word for it. We cannot remember a better fielding side. They all appear to be sprinters and they throw strongly and accurately'.[46] Other countries might be better developed technically, but no team was more gifted physically. Still two years off, commentators began to anticipate with relish South Africa's scheduled clash with Australia.

Both teams had other business beforehand. The England side arriving in South Africa for the return tour of 1930/31 was a chastened one, for they had just come up against Bradman, who in his first full series had altered all calculation of the odds. A near-contemporary of Mitchell (born barely a financial quarter earlier) and having already scored over 3000 runs in the previous two Australian seasons, Bradman held up a mirror to England that demonstrated unequivocally the progressive penetration of cricket by the logic of accumulation. Where in previous ages a batsman might offer a chance having scored sufficient runs Bradman's generation recognised no surfeit. With one hundred, two doubles and the famous 334 at Leeds (then the highest Test innings score), Bradman's limitless capacity for runs confirmed the emergence of the new 'mental economy'. In accounting for Bradman, C. L. R. James adduced a concern with maximum returns for minimal expenditure:

> ... symbolical of the age of J.M. Keynes. After the crisis of World War I and the Depression, Keynes set in motion a systematic and as far as possible scientific use of what existed. He created nothing new. Neither did Bradman ... The thing actually began with Ponsford. But Bradman not only as a batsman set the seal on the incorporation and exploitation of every technique that the game of cricket had invented and which could be adapted to defeating an opponent.[47]

In this judgement, James is undoubtedly correct for the Bradman-like craving for limitless accumulation first made itself incontrovertibly evident in Ponsford's monumental 429 for Victoria as they piled up 1059 against Tasmania in February 1923, to win by a gargantuan innings and 666 runs, and scoring 506 runs on the second day.[48] In December 1927 Ponsford was at it again, surpassing his own record with 437 out of 793 against Queensland. There is also compelling evidence of cricket's new accumulative bent in the paraphernalia of the game's scoring. Essentially unchanged since the nineteenth century when double-entry scoring first granted wickets parity with runs, in the 1920s Bill Ferguson had introduced the wagon wheel, a device that reduced the bewildering torrents of contemporary runs to graphic clarity. Developed to permit the analysis of individual scoring patterns, it soon became an essential requisite of batsmen seeking to improve their game, and of bowlers working out their weaknesses. Aesthetic considerations withered under data's baleful regard. Style, once the individual calling card of a Trumper or a Jessop or a Ranji, was now reduced to something vestigial, a calculus of risk and reward, an index of batting plusses and minuses as keys for exploitation.

Nor, of course, was this instrumental approach an exclusively Australian phenomenon. In his seminal paper 'Cricket and Rational Economic Man', Ian Harriss observes the change in the batting of Hobbs, as similar attitudes to risk and reward seeped into the English game. According to Harriss, 'Hobbs converted only one century out of 42 into a double century in the pre-war period. In the period from 1914 to 1934 however, Hobbs converted 12 centuries into double centuries from a total of 77, or almost one in six', a fact that points towards the ongoing supersession of the aesthetically derived cricketing categories of the Golden Age by a modern concern for purely quantitative validation.[49] Nor, despite the inbuilt limitation on the number of wickets, were bowlers immune to this concern: in the 1928/29 Ashes series in Australia England's left-arm spinner J. C. White had bowled longer and longer spells: only 6.3 six-ball overs in the first Test but then 68 overs in the second, 113.5 overs in the third, 124.5 overs in the fourth and 93.3 in the last. In South Africa on its matting wickets too there were signs of the uptick in expectation: Dave Nourse's 304* for Natal versus Transvaal in a non-Currie Cup match of 1919/20 out of a total of 532 for 8 was the first triple century ever recorded in South African first-class cricket, and, another record, the fifth time Nourse had passed 200.[50]

Bruce Mitchell was perhaps South Africa's nearest thing to a Bradman or a Headley. In 1930/31 versus England two home Tests, at Newlands and Durban, were played on turf for the first time. Mitchell starred in the series with four half-centuries to set alongside his first Test hundred, 123 at Newlands in a South African record opening partnership of 260 with Jack Siedle, in which he was 'steadiness itself, relying for his runs on glancing strokes to third man or long leg. In his 119 he had as many as fifty-nine singles'.[51] (119 was Mitchell's score overnight. The following day he batted another thirty-five minutes to reach 123. Thereafter Taylor and Catterall put on 148 in two hours.) Only Hammond exceeded Mitchell's aggregate of 455 runs at 50.55 as South Africa took a series for the first time since 1909/10.

But at the end of the year, it was South Africa's turn to come under the lash of the white Headley. Where Mitchell, in the defensive South African tradition born of long exposure to matting wickets, was concerned primarily with accumulating time at the crease, Bradman's appetite for runs was overwhelming. Though Mitchell again topped the South African averages, he managed only three half-centuries in the series as the batting folded in the face of the Australian attack. He was unlucky with illness, and there was further mitigation in the number of times South Africa were caught on sticky wickets, at Brisbane and again at Melbourne where, as Ken Viljoen observed from close range, 'The ball would strike the pitch and fly up at the batsman, and … two balls would never go in the same direction if bowled straight'.[52] In the first of these, despite the difficulties, Mitchell displayed all his customary grit. Seventy minutes before getting off the mark, becalmed on 45 for ninety minutes, he was run out for 58 by Bradman's bullet-like return from third man. Yet overall, Australian critics were somewhat disappointed in his performances, observing, 'His form in Australia has been rather surprising, and not at all like that of the batsman who headed the South African averages last year', adding: 'No one would begrudge him a turn of good luck, as he has had little enough of it on the present tour'.[53]

Illness aside—though the illness is suggestive—one issue for Mitchell would have been the Australian crowds. Richard Cashman and others have argued that the raucous and restive nature of Australian crowds, fuelled by alcohol and a long tradition of '[r]owdy, collective behaviour', constitute a specifically Australian mode of sporting consumption.[54] Certainly, South African players of the time would seldom have witnessed their like, either at home or in England. In the game against South Australia, Ken Viljoen reported the crowd, '1100 of them, were like bees' and, recalling the match against Western Australia, he wrote that 'We [South Africans] had our first taste of the barrackers during the afternoon. They say it's nothing to what is coming [at Sydney and Melbourne], so Lord help us'.[55] Clearly the Springboks were intimidated by Australian crowds that would have been swollen by the legions of Bradman-worshippers, for Cashman calculates that Bradman's name on any team-sheet increased the crowd by around 7000. Mitchell, self-deprecating in the approved middle-class way, and embarrassed even by routine interaction with spectators for whom given his persona he was a frequent butt, would most certainly have found their forthright humour and mock-hostility at his expense a trying experience. His preferred method of dealing with crowds was psychic obliteration; even his status as a specialist slip fielder was likely calculated to keep his distance from them. Mitchell, Gideon Haigh judges, preferred 'private places and empty stands' and if he could not find them 'was capable of fortifying them in his own mind'.[56]

The South African batting in general was once again undone by its besetting sin, 'a universal weakness in footwork', especially on the front foot, that rendered them 'incapable of mastering the spin bowling of Grimmett and Ironmonger'.[57] Meanwhile Woodfull, Ponsford, Bradman, Kippax, McCabe and Rigg plundered the South African attack with singular intent. Bradman of course led the charge. Bell, Quinn, Vincent, Morkel and McMillan bowled as well as they ever had;

Bradman himself offered tribute to 'the skill and quality of the South African bowlers who suffered cruel misfortune from missed catches'.[58] Quinn, said Bradman, was a very fine bowler who 'appeared to come off the pitch faster than any medium fast bowler ... with the possible exception of Maurice Tate', and Mailey was impressed enough to compare him with the great English left-armer Frank Foster.[59] 'Sandy' Bell bowled exceptional in-swingers, and 'did an enormous amount of work, and never slackened his energies'.[60] The plan according to Bell was 'to get [Bradman] caught in the slips by bowling short just outside the off-stump': the germ of bodyline hove into view, needing only a change of line and a patrician scorn for the consequences. However, 'We tried for four and a half months', Bell continued, 'but his wonderful placing and command over the ball made life absolutely untenable for gully and point'.[61]

Bradman maintained that the major weakness of the South African attack was that none of the seamers moved the ball away from him. Bell gainsaid this. Quinn in particular moved it a little either way, both in the air and off the pitch. Perhaps Bell had some justification, for in the first Test Bradman might have been LBW first ball but was given the benefit; was missed on 3, skying a pull that Morkel ought to have reached; and was dropped twice in the slips off Quinn before he had reached 20 (by Vincent on 11 and again on 15 by Mitchell, the latter a sitter. Close observers state that Mitchell, a devout and singularly undemonstrative man, swore aloud in disappointment). Yet Bradman was right to cast doubt on South Africa's approach, for the plain fact is that their strategy was ill-suited to prevailing conditions. Cricket's authorities were then considering, in somewhat dilatory fashion, a plan to widen the LBW law by allowing a batsman to be given out to a ball pitching outside off-stump. The original idea was in the face of the worldwide run-glut to reset the balance between bat and ball, but it gained new relevance the following season. Bodyline had dramatically exposed the dangers of a sustained and systematic leg-stump line and administrators needed urgently to offer some incentive to return to an off-stump attack. Had the new LBW law then been in place, the South African tactic—in-swing on or outside off-stump—might have met with more success. Though they managed six LBW decisions in the series only one of these was by a right-handed bowler. South Africa's strategy had the look of one devised by a wicketkeeper.

Whatever the strategy, it was not enough to cope with Bradman. In only five Test innings, he amassed 806 runs at 201.50. When the bowlers were fresh and the ball new, he would score behind the wicket, gliding to leg or cutting between point and third man, seldom risking the drive. As the bowlers tired and the ball grew soft, he would score all round the wicket, scarcely ever hitting in the air or within reach of a fielder. 'He hits the ball just short of cover-point and runs a quick single', Bell observed. 'Cover-point comes in and he then places it just out of reach of his left hand. He does this to every fielder in the team'. Supremely fit, Bradman would run hard for everything so there were relatively few dot balls, and ones were turned into twos. As for the spinners, the Don appeared to view them as little more than an invitation to elevate his scoring rate still further. Such were his 'magnificent exhibitions of foot-work' that he 'never allowed [them] to pitch the ball anywhere near a decent length, but hit it on the full toss all the time'.[62] Five yards down the wicket the direction of turn becomes irrelevant.

The upshot of this method was that Bradman not only made vast numbers of runs, but he made them at a rate nearly twice that of most of his contemporaries. Bradman's Test aggregate of 6996 was accumulated at a rate of 58.64 runs per 100 balls. Given the prevailing over rates, a couple of sessions could put a match beyond opposition reach. In a game of complex simultaneous time-flows, one of Bradman's supreme strengths was his ability to impose his own tempo upon the game and drive it out of his opponents' reach. Mitchell too, on occasions, was capable of this, but his habitual tempo meant that he was better suited to rearguard actions than Bradman-like all-out assaults, and when called upon to raise the rate of scoring he was generally found wanting. Thus his 3471 Test runs, scored off a similar number of deliveries and in exactly the same number of innings (80), were scored at a rate only just better than half of Bradman's, around 31 per 100.[63]

South Africa had its successes though. Despite Bradman's mastery, Quinn's command of left-arm angles and pace off the pitch troubled him more than any bowler since Tate. Though Quinn's were mostly moral victories, in the third Test he tasted the real thing when Cameron's mar-vellous leg-side catch dismissed Bradman for only 2. And left-arm spin-ner Vincent more than once beat Bradman's inside edge, trapping him LBW twice of only four dismissals. And once, in a charity game, Eric Dalton beat him at ping pong.

The 'Union Babies' Grow Up: Triumph at Lord's, 1935

In stark contrast to the Australian tour, where they were mere apprentices to Australia's wizard of accumulation, the next tour proved the apogee of South Africa's cricketing achievement for 50 years. Not only did they win a Test for the first time on English soil, in their fifth full tour, but by drawing the remaining four Tests became the first South African team to win a rubber in England. It was a single bright light in 50 years of cricketing pain.

South Africa's road back from the Bradman-lashing was a hard one. A measure of consolation was achieved with a comfortable win against New Zealand on the way home from Australia but thereafter the long transition from mat to turf was still underway. Moreover, the dire economic depression that had begun in the twenties was now at its height, and cricket was not immune; 1932/33 saw the Currie Cup suspended and players lost to the South African game. Denys Morkel departed to take a position in Nottingham selling motor cars for Sir Julien Cahn and propping up his Sunday side, while 'Jimmy' Christy headed south, down to Queensland to coach. By the time the Currie Cup resumed in 1933/34 however, the worst of the economic crisis was over. During the lull, the balance of cricketing power too had shifted. Natal led by 'Herby' Wade took the trophy outright for the first time since 1913, winning all five games, three outright, and beating hitherto dominant Transvaal by the convincing margin of 309 runs on the strength of hundreds from Jack Siedle and, back in his home province, the evergreen Herby Taylor. Transvaal, having previously complained about the poor standard of the opposition, ended in fifth place. As the economic mood lifted under the stimulus of devaluation and cheap gold, the 1934/35 season was more eagerly awaited than usual, with places in the England tour party up for grabs.

The Currie Cup included some outstanding individual performances and squad names were being inked in: Cameron, Dudley Nourse, Wade, the Erics, Rowan and Dalton, all averaged over 50 with the bat, and Bruce Mitchell just below 50 but his super slow leg-breaks and googlies captured 32 wickets, at an average of less than 15. Dalton meanwhile scored his runs at 69.83 and took 25 wickets at 19.08 apiece, good news given the loss of Morkel's all-round skills. Among the bowlers Bob Crisp was consistently hostile on unresponsive wickets, his emergence making up at least in part for the sad demise of Neville Quinn, then on the edge of greatness. Xenophon Balaskas's bag of tricks earned him 31 wickets at 15.87. In the end the season came down once again to Natal versus Transvaal, where hundreds from Mitchell and Cameron drove Transvaal over 500, and Wade's own hundred proved an insufficient response. In March 1935, before the tour, matting was torn up to lay new grass pitches at The Wanderers, last of South Africa's Test grounds to make the move.

In the end Wade's man management skills and, crucially, his experience of turf wickets while playing two seasons in Yorkshire won him the Springbok captaincy. This freed Jock Cameron to focus on his batting and keeping. The party displayed a satisfying blend of youth and experience. Six of the squad were veterans of the 1929 tour, and seven of the trip to Australasia. Their only obvious weakness was the lack of a quality off-spinner. More, for the first time on an overseas tour all the South African tourists were experienced on turf wickets, even if, like all touring teams to England, adjustments were essential and ongoing as the vagaries of weather and pitches tested to the limit the players' adaptability and technique. With forty games in just over four months the fifteen-strong squad would need all their stamina and spirit. History was against them, and after the Australian drubbing, few gave them any price. Yet by the tour's end, the 'Union Babies'—Mitchell, Balaskas, Nourse the stroke-maker, and Eric Rowan, bristling with transgressive energies—had come of age, losing only two matches and taking home the rubber (Fig. 8.1).

The second Test at Lord's, twentieth game of the tour, turned out to be its key moment. After two months in England, the tourists were fully acclimatised without yet being exhausted, and still undefeated. Rain had washed out the final day in the first Test at Nottingham with South Africa teetering on 17/1 in their follow-on, 147 behind, leaving the MCC, not yet prepared to concede four-day Tests to South Africa, hoist by their own petard.[64]

Moreover, the South Africans' performance in the eighteenth match a week before had given them powerful momentum as a strong Yorkshire side including Sutcliffe, Leyland, Verity and Bowes was beaten by 128 runs. Mitchell, Siedle and Rowan all got runs but the star turn was Cameron with a rapid second innings 100, hitting Hedley Verity, England's most feared bowler, for 30 in an over—4,4,4,6,6,6—and prompting wicketkeeper Arthur Wood's famous comment about Verity having the batsman in two minds, whether to hit him for four or six.[65] Meanwhile the exotically named, and skilled, leg-break and googly

Fig. 8.1 The 1935 South African team was the first to win a Test series in England (standing—left to right): R. J. Williams, K. G. Viljoen, E. A. B. Rowan, D. S. Tomlinson, R. J. Crisp, A. C. B. Langton, A. D. Nourse and X. C. Balaskas; (seated): I. J. Siedle, C. L. Vincent, H. B. Cameron (vice-captain), S. J. Snooke (manager), H. F. Wade (captain), B. Mitchell, A. J. Bell and E. L. Dalton

bowler, 'Bally' Balaskas, who had captured only eight wickets in six first-class matches on tour, was allowed to bowl himself into form, taking 12 wickets including 8/99 in Yorkshire's second innings. Not all the luck ran their way though. A few days before the Test Mitchell was struck over the eye by a ball, while Rowan, another key batsman, was deafened and giddy from drugs taken to combat an ear infection.[66] On the plus side, Wade was able to call upon a full-strength attack of Bell, Crisp, Balaskas and Langton.

By the time the captains walked out for the toss, it was already common knowledge that an attack of 'leatherjackets'—crane fly larvae—had destroyed the grass roots that bound the pitch, producing a dusty surface that would encourage variable bounce and bewildering turn. Clearly the spinners, historically South Africa's nemesis, would be key; but South Africans had had a decade of experience and patient technical development, and their batsmen had laboured to improve their footwork. Besides, as Wade turned from the middle to the players' balcony and gave a thumbs-up, the irony could have been lost on few that the Lord's Test would be played out on a pitch whose action, as far as a grass pitch could, would closely mimic that of a matting wicket. If South Africa had been allowed to produce a turf wicket to order to optimise their chances, minimising their weaknesses and playing to their strengths, this was it. Perhaps this realisation lit some spark in Mitchell, overcoming his habitual reserve and opening some inner channel of optimistic purpose. For once, conditions exactly suited his strengths.

Passing a fitness test and with a large sticking plaster across his stitched eyebrow, Mitchell strode out to bat with Jack Siedle on a sunny Saturday in front of 35,000 spectators. Verity and 'Tommy' Mitchell had first chance to lay down a marker, knowing that England would bat last. 'Tommy' Mitchell's googly defeated Siedle early on, but Mitchell batted patiently for an hour and a half before being adjudged LBW—the first under the new experimental rule—to a Nichols in-swinger, for 30, with the score on 59/2.[67] Dudley Nourse followed early in the afternoon, playing back to Verity, and the balance was slipping England's way at 98/4 when Cameron replaced the dazed Rowan.

Cameron carried on where he had left off against Verity and Yorkshire the previous week, launching a ruthless, even frenzied attack punctuated by occasional moments of staunch defence. Showing how well he had learned the lesson of Bradman—never let a spinner dictate the length—he defied the spin-friendly conditions and wrested the game from England's grip. At one stage when South Africa scored 60 in half an hour Cameron's share was 58. Finally bowled by another Nichols in-swinger for 90 (out of 126 scored while he was at the wicket), with three sixes and six fours, he walked back to a huge ovation. South Africa succumbed soon after for 228, by no means a match-winning total despite the 'leatherjackets'. Cameron had played the innings of his tragically short life. Within a few months he would be dead of enteric fever, contracted on the trip home, aged just 30.

By close of play, England were 75/2 with Balaskas bowling Maurice Leyland with a straight long-hop, much to Leyland's annoyance, especially after he was dismissed in the Yorkshire match with a huge leg-break. When play resumed on the Monday, Balaskas bowled unchanged for two and a quarter hours, with scarcely a bad ball, earning the best figures of his Test career: 32-8-49-5. 'Bally' was known for bowling six different balls an over, often sacrificing control for variety. But his control that day was more crucial than ever since he had no cover for the bad ball; such was Wade's attacking intent that Balaskas bowled for much of his spell to two or three slips, a leg slip and two silly covers. As pressure mounted on the batsmen, his subtle variations of pace, huge turn, and uneven bounce came into play, and England were bowled out with South Africa still a significant 30 runs ahead. Almost every Wade decision paid off. Eric Dalton, given his first bowl for almost a month, promptly bowled Hammond, then had England's captain, Bob Wyatt, well set on 53, superbly caught by Nourse at square-leg.

A Wagnerian thunderstorm was brewing as South Africa's openers came through the Long Room and down the steps to start the second innings. The normally sedate Mitchell drove Nichol's first delivery of the innings for four through the vacant mid-off region, picked up a two and a single off the next two balls, and Siedle drove the last ball wide of cover for another boundary. Again, the lessons of Australia were overt as the two deliberately set out to take the initiative from the off.

But within a few overs, 'Tommy' Mitchell was bowling leg-breaks to three slips, getting sharp turn and irregular bounce. Siedle was quickly caught behind off a leg-break that turned square and Verity's control pushed Mitchell back into his defensive comfort zone, playing out four consecutive maidens. Tension was apparent as Mitchell fidgeted, characteristically plucking at the shirt on his right shoulder, shrugging his shoulders, constantly adjusting his cap. Nonetheless, this was Mitchell in his element, in John Arlott's words 'by nature a man who solves problems, who solves them for himself by himself'.[68]

He ended Verity's run of maidens with a sumptuous straight drive which hurt England twice over, for it forced the chasing Sutcliffe from the field with a strained thigh muscle. Eric Rowan, replacing Siedle, found Mitchell in the middle of a master class, all ease and grace off either front foot or back. He brought up his half-century after 95 minutes, before almost being bowled by a Verity delivery that shot along the ground, but so sound was his matting-moulded defence that he had few other alarms though others found the pitch nigh unplayable. The bloody-minded Rowan played an invaluable supporting role, tempering his own belligerence to suit the circumstances.

Shortly after tea, the partnership of 104 was ended. With Rowan gone for an invaluable 44, Nourse quickly followed, bowled by a Verity scuttler for two, Cameron was caught at deep mid-on for three, and Wade and Dalton both went to Verity without troubling the scorers. The collapse meant South Africa was in danger of losing the advantage that they had fought so hard for, but they were 207 ahead when Mitchell reached an imperious hundred, and Langton, the fourth Transvaal batsman in the line-up, stayed with Mitchell. Stumps saw South Africa at 208/6, with Mitchell in supreme control on 129.

The Mitchell-Langton partnership turned out to be worth more than its weight in runs for next day the weather greatly favoured the overnight batting side. A downpour before start of play softened the uncovered pitch making it easier to bat for the morning session, though it was bound to get more difficult as it dried. Oblivious to the weather, Mitchell moved serenely on, confidently driving through the covers, cutting square and pulling loose balls to the square-leg fence. When Langton was finally caught and bowled by Hammond for a pugnacious 44, Wade declared, giving England 45 minutes batting before lunch and a target of 309 in 285 minutes. Mastery complete, Mitchell had overturned his stereotype. 164 not out, he had made nearly 60% of South Africa's 278/7, the other six batsmen aggregating 114 between them. Herbert Sutcliffe, himself a proven master on spinning wickets, shook his hand, and told him that he had 'just played the finest innings on a wearing wicket I have ever seen'.[69]

Given the state of the wicket 309 looked beyond the England batsmen, yet the South African bowlers had a negative weight of history on their shoulders. Sutcliffe and Wyatt survived until lunch, so the match was in the balance when Balaskas came on from the Nursery End, immediately inducing Wyatt to play on. Then Crisp brought one down the hill through Leyland's defences and England were teetering on 45/2. But Hammond and Sutcliffe were England's best batsmen, and more than capable of thwarting South Africa. Hammond was fluent despite Crisp's pace and Sutcliffe played the shot of the game off Mitchell's looping spin, waiting for the ball and then thudding it backwards past the startled Cameron to the fence, a shot worthy of the Indian Premier League. As the score grew and tension mounted it was 'Chud' Langton who for the second time in the day made a decisive impact, Hammond inside-edging an in-swinger to Cameron, and one run later, Sutcliffe was trapped in front. Holmes was yorked for eight, and Ames dismissed for the same score. Langton's four quick wickets, shrewdly exploiting the new LBW law, had destroyed English resistance. No miracles were forthcoming for England, and Balaskas joined the exultant Langton in wiping out the tail. The last eight wickets had fallen for 62 runs and South Africa had won by 157 runs.

In a fantastic game of Test cricket in which South Africa outplayed their opponents in all areas, Mitchell's innings provided the foundation of victory. Then the highest score by a South African in England, it was made in a game where of the rest only Cameron and Wyatt had crossed 50. It was an innings of patience, determination and intent, exactly suited to the circumstances, the ultimate acceptance of responsibility by a man able to lift his performance and seize the moment. Watching from the pavilion, Douglas Jardine described the innings as 'five hours of mastery', and C. B. Fry acclaimed Mitchell 'the school-master of all the bowlers ever born'.[70] Still this was a triumph built on years of painful defeats. For once South Africa took their chance, and many years would pass before another such chance would come.

THE RETURN HOME

This chapter has sought to map the development of Bruce Mitchell and the 'Union Babies' as cricketers against that of a South Africa grappling with the pangs of modernity.

Modernity was manifest as a dialectic of alienation that unfolded via the articulation of rationalisation and disenchantment. Politically, the country wrestled with issues arising from the contradiction of an aggressive primary nationalism that excluded, even rejected, its own indigenous population, and the gradual evolution of an opposing nationalism of resistance in response. In cricketing terms too, South Africa struggled to adapt to post-war circumstances. Australia—perhaps reflecting its susceptibility to American influence; it was, after all, a Pacific nation as well as a Commonwealth one, as its cricketers' frequent US tours and the popularity of baseball testify—led the game in a transformation dictated by economistic imperatives and technocratic approaches. The age of style, of aura and authenticity had given way to one of pure accumulation, but in South Africa this was complicated by the simultaneous requirements of technical and administrative reconstruction. While the migration to turf resulted in a batting generation of unparalleled technical capabilities therefore, it would take at least a generation more before South African cricket shook off its generally defensive mindset and began to produce cricketers whose self-belief would match their technical ability.

Nonetheless, an economic rebound from sustained depression combined in 1935 with the fruits of cricketing reconstruction to hand South Africa its first series triumph in England. The team, with 'Union Babies' foremost, returned as heroes to a country then engaged in the long-term construction of a grand segregationist edifice designed systematically to privilege its white minority. In the words of Walter Benjamin, cultural accomplishments owe their existence not only to those whom history records as their instigators, but as much to 'the anonymous toil of their contemporaries'. 'There is no document of civilisation' therefore 'which is not at the same time a document of barbarism'.[71] Based, like all white cultural endeavour, on the exploitation of African labour, white South African cricket was thus revealed as a marginal effect of African deprivation: dispossessed, infantilised, obstructed from political or personal development, obscured from social and cultural view.

Thus as they feted their returning heroes, the white cricketing public would have been completely unaware of the accomplishments of Frank Roro, born Kimberley in 1908 and therefore first, perhaps, of the 'Union Babies'. Like all black South Africans, Roro would be denied the opportunity to represent his country, or prove himself against his contemporaries, or even to hand down to posterity a full and lasting record of his achievements and their significance.[72] Nonetheless, despite the handicaps and the lamentable conditions, Roro played on, silently accumulating. Every Springbok team photograph is crowded with invisible faces.

NOTES

1. C. Feinstein, *An Economic History of South Africa: Conquest, Discrimination and Development* (Cambridge: Cambridge University Press, 2005), 66–67.
2. Feinstein records the dramatic scale of reductions in mine-working costs, with the cost in £ per ton of ore milled falling from 1.37 in the period 1902–4 to 0.98 by 1910 (Feinstein, *An Economic History*, 106).
3. The Consolidated Gold Fields of South Africa, Limited, *The Gold Fields 1887–1937* (London: The Consolidated Gold Fields of South Africa, 1937), 80, 85.
4. A. Dale, 'First General Census of the Union of South Africa', *Publications of the American Statistical Association*, 13, 103 (September 1913), 555.
5. 'Tuppy' Owen-Smith came next, in February 1909, then Eric Rowan and Ronnie Grieveson in July and August respectively. In 1910, there were Alan Melville and Ken Viljoen both born in May, Xenophon Balaskas in October, and Dudley Nourse and Len Brown in November 1910. Denis Tomlinson too was born in this period, in Umtali, Rhodesia (September 1910).

6. Besides, Nourse nearly chose football: the relative success of the South African team who criss-crossed the British Isles simultaneously with their cricketing counterparts in 1924 resulted in a steady stream of South Africans following Gordon Hodgson into the English and Scottish professional leagues.

7. I. Harriss, 'Cricket and Rational Economic Man', *Sporting Traditions*, 3, 1, 51–68.

8. Percy Sherwell batted at number 11 in the first Test versus England in 1905/6, his famous last-wicket partnership with Dave Nourse leading South Africa to a one-wicket win. By the first Test of the following series in 1907, Sherwell was opening the batting, scoring 6 and 115 in the drawn match at Lord's. As well as a long batting line-up, South Africa were then formidably equipped with all-rounders, the 1907 side, for instance, featuring no fewer than eight front-line bowlers.

9. E. Katz, 'The Doctors' Dilemma: The Health Care of Workers on the Witwatersrand Gold Mines, 1892–1910', Seminar Paper 8 August 1994, Institute for Advanced Social Research, University of Witwatersrand, accessed at core.ac.uk on 18 February 2018.

10. N. Cardus, 'Old English' in *The Summer Game* (London: Rupert Hart-Davis, 1949), 23.

11. The waste that forms dumps is not only toxic with cyanates and thiocyanates formed by the breakdown of cyanides used in gold extraction, but radioactive too, loaded with radium, uranium and the uranium derivative, radon (*Mail & Guardian*, 19 February 2018).

12. G. Allsop, 'Reminiscences of Cricket' in M. Luckin (ed.), *The History of South African Cricket: Including the Full Scores of All Important Matches Since 1876* (Johannesburg: W. E. Hortor and Co., 1915), 123.

13. H. Taylor, 'How South African Cricket Should Be Built Up', in M. Luckin (ed.), *South African Cricket 1919–27* (Johannesburg: The Author, 1927), 31.

14. Among the motivations for the reconstruction was the desire of certain elements of the South African cricketing establishment to chasten the then-Chairman of SACA, Melbourne-born Reg Fitzgerald, whose attitude to organised labour, whether among professional cricketers or unionised mineworkers, was felt to be too 'Australian' and insufficiently rigorous.

15. M. Susskind, 'A Survey of Transvaal Cricket Since the War' in Luckin (ed.), Ibid., 117.

16. M. Commaille, 'The S.A. Team in England—1924: A Critical Survey of the Tour', in Luckin (ed.), *South African Cricket*, 317.

17. If England chose autocratic captains to lead by 'natural' authority, and Australia democratic ones, to lead by example, then South Africa henceforth would look to technocratic captains, to drive the troops

into the laager. Deane was the first of these technocrats, but a tradition was thereby established of functional captains chosen primarily for their team-building abilities: 'Herby' Wade, Jack Cheetham, Clive van Ryneveld, Trevor Goddard, Peter van der Merwe, Ali Bacher, Clive Rice and Hansie Cronje.

18. Luckin, *South African Cricket 1919–1927*, 18.
19. Commaille, 'S.A. Team in England', 309.
20. SACA Minutes, 2 March 1925.
21. Ibid., 14 February 1924, 19 February 1924, and 25 February 1924.
22. Ibid., 8 February 1924 and 24 March 1924.
23. Commaille, 'S.A. Team in England', 311.
24. *The Cricketer*, vol. 5, 1924–25, 548.
25. Commaille, 'S.A. Team in England', 311.
26. *The Cricketer*, vol. 5, 1924–25, 580.
27. The selection panel of 1924 consisted of 'Tip' Snooke, Tancred, Sherwell, Frank Reid and Kempis with chairman Reg Fitzgerald. As thwarted captain Herby Taylor later pointed out, with a certain bitterness, the chairman had two votes, deliberative and casting, meaning he could single-handedly overturn a split majority vote. 'Why have a Selection Committee at all, if they must have a little bit of string on it?' asked Taylor, quite reasonably (Luckin, *South African Cricket 1919–27*, 32). The make-up of the selection panel and the process by which it was itself selected, were both re-organised in the course of SACA's reconstruction. The 1929 selection committee was only three-strong—Taylor himself, Jack Tandy and T. E. Holmes, with 'Nummy' Deane, whom Taylor knew well, sitting into advise.
28. L. Duffus (compiler), *South African Cricket 1927–1947: Volume III* (Johannesburg: SACA, 1947), 51.
29. The South Africans had already met Duleepsinhji vs. the MCC on 1, 3 and 4 June, where Duleep had played his way into the Test team with 74 and 27*, and a catch to dismiss Taylor described by Frank Mitchell as 'one of the best ever seen at Lord's' (*The Cricketer*, vol. 10, 8 June 1929, 168). Two weeks previously, on 15, 16 and 17 May, the South Africans had beaten by 4 wickets an Oxford University side including the nineteen-year-old Nawab of Pataudi, who scored 5 and 12.
30. C. Chipkin, *Johannesburg Style: Architecture and Society 1880s–1960s* (Cape Town: David Philip, 1993), 93. The price of gold soared from 92 shillings an ounce to 129 shillings an ounce, and in 1934 to 140 shillings an ounce.
31. D. Hobart Houghton and J. Dagut, *Source Material on the South African Economy 1860–1970, Volume Three: 1920–1970* (Cape Town: Oxford University Press, 1973), 114.

32. Quoted in L. Marquard, *The Native in South Africa* (Johannesburg: Wits University Press, 1944), 62.

33. Ibid., 4–5.

34. Mitchell ended with 27 international wickets at 51.11, his best of 5/87 achieved against Australia at Kingsmead in 1936, though his achievement in that match was insignificant next to the 13/173 of Grimmett. In first-class cricket however, he accumulated 249 wickets at 25.63.

35. *The Cricketer*, vol. 10, 22 June 1929, 237.

36. Ibid., 20 July 1929, 364.

37. R. Robertson-Glasgow, *Cricket Prints: Some Batsmen and Bowlers 1920–1940* (London: T. Werner Laurie, 1943), 129.

38. *The Cricketer*, vol. 10, 10 August 1929, 451.

39. Ibid., vol. 10, 15 June 1929, 198.

40. Ibid., vol. 10, 10 August 1929, 451.

41. Ibid., vol. 10, 22 June 1929, 237.

42. Ibid., vol. 10, 8 June 1929, 168.

43. Ibid., vol. 10, 22 June 1929, 237.

44. Pushed out of the Transvaal team in part by Mitchell's emergence, Frank had previously lost his place in the national side for slow scoring. 'He won't go out and fetch it, and when handed to him he sometimes eyes it with suspicion', was Luckin's judgement. Frank too was a complex character: a Transvaal Third League cricketer before the war, under shelling at the Somme he had been buried alive, but when 'unearthed from his temporary grave' elected to fight on, all the way to the armistice. Next to the work of dealing with such psychic damage, batting 518 minutes to save a Test, even against the mighty Australians, must have paled into insignificance. Frank's chanceless 152 was not enough, however; his 'cricketing impotence' was noted, and he 'was not encouraged to continue' (*The Cricketer Annual*, vol. 3, 1922–23, 35).

45. Duffus, *South African Cricket*, 51; *The Cricketer*, vol. 10, 22 June 1929, 524.

46. *The Cricketer*, vol. 10, 29 July 1929, 364.

47. A. Grimshaw (ed.), *CLR James: Cricket* (London: Allison and Busby, 1986), 256.

48. A. Miller (ed.) and R. Webster (compiler), *First-Class Cricket in Australia, Volume 1, 1850–51 to 1941–42* (Victoria: R. Webster, 1991), 595.

49. Harriss, 'Cricket and Rational Economic Man': The quantitative turn was perfectly exemplified by Bill Ferguson's invention at this time of the wagon wheel as an aid to scorers and to players looking to analyse their own—or the opposition's—strengths and weaknesses. Thus, in the winter of 1932, Douglas Jardine holed up in a London hotel with only

Bradman's wagon wheels for company, hatching the plan that would become 'Bodyline'. Based in part on the South African tactic of pushing Bradman on to the back foot, Jardine changed the line of attack from outside off to leg stump to counter Bradman's ferocious cut, and exploit his penchant for glancing behind square early in his innings. Where once style had been an expression of personality and social reach, now it was merely an adjunct of reductive analysis. No episode in the history of cricket so trenchantly illustrates the separation of ends and means as derived from scientific method.

50. In all, Dave Nourse would record 7 scores of 200 or more in his career.
51. M. Turnbull and M. Allom, *The Two Maurices Again: MCC Team in South Africa 1930–1931* (London: E. Allom and Co., 1931), 111.
52. K. Viljoen, B. Bassano, and R. Smith (eds.), *A Springbok Down Under: South Africa on Tour 1931–1932* (Tasmania: Apple Books, 1991), 22.
53. *Launceston Examiner*, 12 January 1932.
54. R. Lynch, 'A Symbolic Patch of Grass: Crowd Disorder and Regulation on the Sydney Cricket Ground Hill', *Crowd Violence at Australian Sport: ASSH Studies in Sports History*, 7 (1992), 10–48; R. Cashman, *'Ave a Go, Yer Mug': Australian Cricket Crowds from Larrikin to Ocker* (Sydney: Collins, 1984).
55. Viljoen, *A Springbok Down Under*, 13, 16.
56. G. Haigh, 'The Contemplative Cricketer', *Cricket Magazine*, 14 February 2006.
57. Duffus, *South African Cricket*, 135.
58. Sir D. Bradman, *The Bradman Albums: Selections from Sir Donald Bradman's Official Collection Volume 1 1925–1934* (London: Macdonald and Co. (Publishers), 1987), 255.
59. D. Bradman, *Farewell to Cricket* (London: Hodder and Stoughton, uncorrected proof), 51.
60. Bradman, *The Bradman Albums*, 279.
61. Ibid., 278–79.
62. Ibid., 279.
63. Robin Isherwood, private communication with Jonty Winch, 18 August 2017.
64. Duffus, *South African Cricket*, 172.
65. L. Duffus, 'Jock Cameron' in Tom Reddick (compiler), *Giants of South African Cricket* (Cape Town: 1971), 36.
66. L. Duffus, *Cricketers of the Veld* (London, 1939), 122. However, in *South African Cricket 1927–1947*, 172, Duffus maintains that the cause of Rowan's problem was being struck on the ear by a ball from Bowes in the Yorkshire game.

67. The new LBW law allowed the ball to pitch outside the off stump provided it continued to hit the batsman in line with the stumps and would have gone on to hit them. Both captain Bob Wyatt and Herbert Sutcliffe were strongly opposed to the new law, and in the match itself there were seven LBWs.

68. Quoted in G. Haigh, 'The Contemplative Cricketer' in *Cricket Magazine*, 14 February 2006.

69. 'Bruce Mitchell: The "Quiet Man" of Cricket' in A. Goldman (ed.), *My Greatest Match* (Pietermaritzburg: CNA, 1955), 136.

70. Ibid.,138.

71. W. Benjamin, 'Theses on the Philosophy of History' in H. Arendt (ed.), *Walter Benjamin: Illuminations* (London: Fontana, 1973), 258.

72. R. Parry, 'African Cricket on the Rand: Piet Gwele, Frank Roro and the Shaping of a Community', in current volume.

CHAPTER 9

'Rejects of the Sporting Whites of the Continent': African Cricket in Rhodesia

Jonty Winch

INTRODUCTION

Sports historians refer to the involvement of the public schools in the administration of empire and the diffusion of ball games, notably cricket and rugby. In many of the colonies, a sharp contrast with cultures emerged as settlers attempted to replicate known values in new and sometimes hostile environments. This was certainly true of the land beyond the Transvaal border when the Pioneer Column of Cecil John Rhodes marched into the northern hinterland in 1890. Cricket and rugby were played *en route*, and very soon the games flourished in a white, male-centred society tied to concepts of British civilisation, culture and imperial power. Lord Hawke's touring side visited Bulawayo in 1898, and cricket and rugby teams entered the Currie Cup, but as the conquered societies of Mashonaland and Matabeleland were not part of the establishment's sporting structures,

J. Winch (✉)
Reading, UK

© The Author(s) 2018
B. Murray et al. (eds.), *Cricket and Society in South Africa, 1910–1971*, Palgrave Studies in Sport and Politics, https://doi.org/10.1007/978-3-319-93608-6_9

243

the myth was created that Africans were not involved in playing the imperial games before independence in 1980. This investigation will endeavour to reconstruct events and demonstrate that Africans did in fact play cricket and in doing so overcame disadvantages presented by successive colonial governments that adhered to a system of segregation and racial inequality. An attempt will also be made to understand the process through which Africans were drawn towards playing cricket and to examine the wider social, political and economic factors that influenced their efforts in developing the game at various levels.

William Milton—Administrator of Southern Rhodesia 1898–1914—and the Mfengu Cricketers

A product of Marlborough College, William Milton arrived in Bulawayo in 1896 in the wake of the Matabele uprising that had taken place against the British South Africa Company administration. He had been invited by Cecil John Rhodes to restructure the civil service at a time when efforts were being made to contact the Matabele who had taken refuge in the Matopos, an area of granite kopjes outside Bulawayo. Progress was slow because British forces were unable to penetrate the stronghold. Eventually, Jan Grootboom—a fearless Mfengu from the Cape—ventured into the hills several times to make communication and clear the way for Rhodes to meet the Matabele and begin the process from which he would extract a promise of peace.[1]

Milton's career in the civil service and as a leading aide to Rhodes at the Cape ran parallel with his involvement in sport where he was the most powerful figure in South African cricket. It was through his prominent position as a cricket administrator and his close links with the Cape government that Milton led the process which prevented 'Krom' Hendricks, a coloured fast bowler, from being chosen for South Africa's first overseas tour in 1894 and for subsequent Test matches. As Milton made his way to Matabeleland, a *Cape Times* editorial referred to the manner in which Hendricks was treated as being 'a deeply flawed course of action'. The editor might have hoped his argument would reach Milton in faraway Rhodesia as the editorial turned to the good service the Mfengu did in quelling the recent Matabeleland Rebellion. 'Coloured readers', he said, 'will debate whether he and his, though good enough to fight side by side with white men, are good enough to play side by side with them. And the answer – NO!'[2]

Rhodes paved the way for Milton to become Administrator of Southern Rhodesia, a colony that was in many respects a north-ward expansion of the Cape. At the same time, Rhodes believed the Mfengu people—who had been loyal to the British and were outstand-ing fighters in the frontier wars—would be useful in the new colony and he took steps to bring up large numbers. They accompanied vari-ous pioneering parties into Rhodesia and according to historian, James Muzondidya, 'saw themselves as an integral part of the fabric of colo-nisation'. An estimated 125 took part in the defence of Bulawayo and were very much 'a distinct social group' who resented being treated as natives.[3] They wanted the same rights and privileges that coloureds were entitled to at the Cape but these did not materialise. It was 'curious', explained Muzondidya, that 'white settlers simultaneously praised and denigrated immigrant blacks for their perceived cultural and intellectual sophistications'.[4]

The Mfengu—of whom there were about 1300 by 1905[5]—were from cricket-playing backgrounds and hoped that their playing the game would enable them to gain a measure of social acceptability. In Cape Town, some 'coloured' cricketers were able to play for white teams but there is no evidence of a similar arrangement occurring in Rhodesia. The Loben Club was established in Bulawayo in 1898 with the committee—F. R. Shelton (captain), D. Faku (vice-captain), R. H. Sioka (secretary) and J. B. Nxahe (treasurer)—reflecting the group's mixed ancestry. In 1901, for example, the club secretary said they played twenty-one matches and won ten. Details of their cricket achievements were not covered in the local white media but reports were forwarded to King William's Town where they were published by an influential Mfengu politician, John Tengo Jabavu, in his newspa-per, *Imvo Zabantsundu*.[6] There were further references to black cricket in the *APO*, the official organ of the African Political Organisation, which referred to matches played in Bulawayo shortly before the First World War by teams such as Ottomans, Pioneers and Californians. They played their fixtures on the Old Scottish ground with W. Pretorius, J. van Eeden, P. Carelse and A. Greeff featuring prominently but, by 1914, they had disappeared from the cricket scene.[7]

Whites were suspicious of the Mfengu, referring to them derogatively as 'Cape Boys', and maintained a social barrier even though the latter were 'the first group of black proletarians ... committed to the open-ing up of the colony to settler capitalism'. Muzondidya said they were viewed as blacks 'alienated from the culture core' who incited problems among local Africans and 'were in touch with and shared many of the radical ideas of black South Africa'.[8] The Rhodesian Africans opposed them because of their support of the white government and their part in the suppression of the rebellions. The Mfengu were able to obtain accommodation in the (Old) Location—later Makokoba—when it was first established in 1894 but many were subsequently driven out and returned to the Cape.[9]

While Rhodesia's indigenous population had no desire to absorb white culture, the administration saw the need to introduce a 'native policy' calculated to produce 'those industrious habits which are so essential to civilisation, without interfering more than absolute necessary with the customs and habits of the natives themselves'.[10] Revisionist writer, Michael O. West, claimed the administration was 'preoccupied with tradition and custom' as a means to oppose 'the rise of an African middle-class because they believed such a social stratum posed a threat to colonial domination'.[11] James Mutambirwa explained in *The Rise of Settler Power 1898–1923*, that a sense of insecurity—'the fear of being swamped by the Africans'—would lead 'Europeans to develop and maintain policies that were intended to keep the Africans at a distance ... The settlers practised politics of exclusion'. He added that 'a political consciousness among the "educated" Africans [did not] make its voice heard in Rhodesian politics ... until the end of World War I'.[12]

EARLY AFRICAN CRICKET IN RHODESIA

There was no thought given to the indigenous population playing cricket either side of the First World War. 'They were still recently conquered people', wrote Richard Bourne, 'with little social intercourse with whites and in no way regarded by them as partners or equals'.[13] A similar view is taken by Richard Gray who thought this state of affairs 'largely conditioned their political ideas and activities'.[14] Education reinforced the existing differences. In shaping the first stage of the country's white education policy up to 1914, the Milton administration advanced the dominant values of the Victorian Public School model and the undoubted appeal of the 'Tom Brown' formula with its focus on sport. In contrast, they were 'wary of giving Africans an education at all', but conscious nevertheless of the need to ensure mobilisation of labour for dominant industries, mining and commercial, as well as domestic service.[15]

As a consequence, the state chose to subsidise mission education and there were no government schools before 1920.

Recreation among blacks was for many years limited to indigenous forms of sport such as stick-fighting, dancing, hunting and an African form of boxing which was, said Richard Parry 'at once solo dancing and competitive sport with its own rules and ideology'.[16] Some of the almost 3000 Southern Rhodesian blacks who served in the First World War were introduced to Western sports, whilst others were able to play games at schools in South Africa. Charles Lobengula, the son of the late Matabele king, played centre half for Zonnebloem College, an elite school set up in the 1850s to educate the children of chiefs. His nephews, Rhodes and Albert, were also educated in South Africa and subsequently active in introducing football to Bulawayo. In 1926, they established the Lions Football Club—later the famous Highlanders—in Bulawayo's Makokoba township.

Shortly before Southern Rhodesia was granted self-government in 1923, a new system of African education was devised by Herbert Keigwin who had played cricket for Cambridge University and W. G. Grace's London County. When serving as a native commissioner, he developed an interest in African education which led to his appointment as Director of Native Development. The keynote of the 'Keigwin Plan' was that education should 'reach the mass, not only the favoured few', and two government schools under Keigwin's direction were established at Domboshawa in the Chinamhora Reserve in Mashonaland and Tjolotjo in the Gwaai Reserve in Matabeleland.[17] Much of the pupils' time was devoted to industrial and agricultural training, although Saturday afternoons at Domboshawa were set aside for football.[18]

It was not until the early 1930s that cricket was promoted at the schools by staff members who encouraged Africans to adopt and assimilate British cultural values. Reports appeared in Bulawayo's *Bantu Mirror*, a newspaper established by the Johannesburg-based B. G. Paver who also ran the South African *Bantu World* on the same mixed black-and-white lines. At Tjolotjo, the cricket season began and ended with a game between pupils and staff. The inspectors attended and the *Bantu Mirror* reported that 'these matches aroused a great deal of enthusiasm and excitement ran high among the pupils as the days for the matches drew near … they set their hearts on winning'. The newspaper reporter was also 'glad to notice the interest taken in cricket at this big Government Training School', adding 'football is not the only good game'.[19]

The main part of Tjolotjo's cricket season was taken up with a competition involving five houses—Coghlan, Jowitt, Keigwin, Jackson and Rhodes—playing for the Harold Jowitt Cup, named after the Director of African Education. The influence of the colonial government in naming the houses was accepted without question, and Joshua Nkomo, who later played a major role in Rhodesian politics, became the Tjolotjo school bugler. He recalled 'proudly sounding reveille in the mornings and hoisting and lowering the Union Jack each morning and evening'.[20] In the face of a dominant white government, Africans absorbed British 'civilisation' whilst the long-serving Prime Minister, Godfrey Huggins, took a locally devised theory of parallel development into party politics.

A March 1936 report on the Mashonaland school noted 'the little cosmopolitan population of Domboshawa witnessed what proved to be a very exciting cricket match between the students and the staff'. The latter included two Rhodesian Africans who had completed their training at Fort Hare and Adams Mission, 'an innovation of considerable significance for the future'.[21] In the cricket match, the staff batsmen were handicapped in that they were made to use baseball bats and 'no fewer than six batsmen failed to defend their wickets against young Mutambiranwa's bowling'. He proved destructive but ultimately experience counted and one of the students, R. S. Khaka, reported: 'Poor fellows couldn't even put up a half of the Staff's score'.[22]

Through reports in the *Bantu Mirror*, it is also learnt that cricket matches were staged on the African Welfare Society's ground at the Salisbury Native Location. A keen rivalry was established between the Drill Hall Demons and the Location Lions, with fixtures played over Saturday afternoons and Sunday mornings, sufficient time to allow both sides to bat twice as scores were not high. The *Bantu Mirror* referred to the teams having 'strong bowling sides' and that 'fielding, generally, was high' but that 'attention should be paid in future to batting practice'. In the second match of the 1937/38 season between the Lions and the Demons, a player recorded simply as 'Peter' returned figures of 7 for 11 and 5 for 20 in helping the latter dismiss their opponents for 39 and 54. It was not, however, a match-winning performance because Demons were bowled out for 28 and 56. Prominent in the Lions' victory by nine runs was Albert Lobengula, the grandson of the late Matabele ruler. He bowled unchanged to take 4 for 15 and 4 for 34.[23]

Demons eventually defeated the Lions for the first time in their fifth contest of the season, played over a rain-affected weekend at Salisbury's

Native Location. The Drill Hall side had scored 43 for 2 when rain stopped play on the Saturday and were eventually dismissed for a total of 100 runs on the Sunday. The *Bantu Mirror* recorded: 'it is a tribute to the Lions wicket-keeper that not a single bye was scored' while 'Mbaiwa (25) and Tennyson (31) for the Demons, set about the bowling with a freedom and a vigour which made their batting a joy to watch'. In reply, the Lions were dismissed for 59.[24]

Efforts were made to start a league as Domboshawa School fielded a side in 1938/39. Practices were arranged on Mondays, Wednesdays and Fridays at the Welfare Ground for all those who were interested. The African Welfare Society strove to promote cricket and hoped 'other centres will adopt the game in order that inter-town matches may be held'.[25] Reports in the *Bantu Mirror* noted the main obstacles to progress were the demands of football, which was being played virtually the whole year round, and the inclement weather. The society bulletins in January and February 1939, for example, recorded weather conditions had made cricket impossible for at least two months during the season.[26]

In the late 1930s, moves were made by Father Alban Winter at St Augustine's Mission, Penhalonga near Umtali, towards transferring the main emphasis of work 'from the traditional function of industrial training to the provision of secondary education'. The government refused to give any support to the Penhalonga enterprise but then realised the danger attached to losing 'the ability to control the structure of the secondary curriculum'.[27] They addressed the problem by establishing Goromonzi School in the Chinyika reserve, fifteen miles from Salisbury, in 1946. It was a school that would in time offer cricket.

While schools and clubs were crucial in encouraging Africans to play games, colonial administrators recognised the advantages attached to extending 'influence over African urban culture by using supervised sport as the vehicle for controlling the social process'.[28] This was already apparent on the mines where the native commissioner at Belingwe said 'the native is intensely imitative, often vain, and always clannish, and all these are qualities which would further "sport" – a parochial spirit of sport, if you like – but one which could forge ties of interest and *esprit de corps* between the labourer and his workplace'. Football was seen as being ideal recreation because 'a patch of ground, a set of goal-posts and a football would not figure largely in the expenditure of a big mine'.[29]

The African Welfare Society was able to provide resources and infrastructure and did much to secure the future of African sport.

In early February 1939, the annual report of the African Welfare Society of Matabeleland followed their Mashonaland counterparts by noting 'arrangements are afloat for the introduction of cricket and tennis in the near future'.[30] Progress had been gradual in Bulawayo, and there was much to be done in improving facilities, coaching and communication. There was even an attack on the *Bantu Mirror* by an unnamed missionary who felt a newspaper should not comment on the games played on Sundays as it was published 'chiefly for people who have been taught at mission stations where the Sabbath is held sacred…'.[31]

THE RISE OF AFRICAN SPORT IN BULAWAYO

An inability to import large quantities of manufactured goods during the War years led to an unprecedented boom in Southern Rhodesian industrial production. The increased demand for supplies of skilled labour could not be satisfied by the European community alone, particularly at a time when many young men were away on military service. As a result, more Africans were able to enter positions of skilled employment; 12,319 African workers were employed by Southern Rhodesia factories in 1938, rising to 18,833 in 1942.[32] Large African townships became 'hostile, fast-changing and overcrowded urban centres'.[33] Bulawayo was granted city status in 1943 and faced two major strikes soon afterwards—the first involving the railway workers and the second a general strike.

In this volatile environment, football played a key role in providing one of the few avenues available to social mobility and improved status. In an article on Southern Rhodesian football, Ossie Stuart reported 'people were obliged to remake their identity' and a football club was 'somewhere to seek solace, support and advice'. The game in Bulawayo was overseen by the African Welfare Society and almost completely African controlled by the outset of the War. Bulawayo's black population grew from 15,000 in 1935 to 35,000 in 1945, and the city's African soccer league became the largest and most popular in the country.[34] The tremendous growth overwhelmed the African Welfare Society, and they were obliged to turn to the white-run City Council to take over the running of their activities. An arrangement was reached but was unpopular because the Council believed the purpose of African football was social control and did not fully comprehend its importance to the people.

In 1947, players and supporters boycotted the first season of Council-run football with no African teams turning up to play. At the beginning of 1948, the Council offered a share of gate takings but received no support and had to accept defeat. An agreement was reached through which the league would be entirely self-supporting and able to use Barbourfields without any definite lease. According to Stuart, the victory achieved represented an important step on the way to modern Zimbabwe.[35]

Football was an integral part of the new expressive culture of Africans in Bulawayo. It was the most popular sport and brought players fame and respectability within their community. A new distinct class was emerging among blacks who had qualified in the areas open to them, and they sought improvement socially and financially. Many of the leading figures were Manyika, the business people from Manicaland in the eastern part of Rhodesia, who started flocking to Bulawayo in 1929. They 'rapidly became the "smart boys" who could throw money around and get beautiful women'.[36] The best African sportsmen in Southern Rhodesia at this time, wrote Peter Alegi in *Laduma!*, 'shared a privileged working-class or elite background' and would be made up of teachers, policemen, craftsmen, welfare workers, drivers, traders and tailors.[37] A number of them made moves towards a process of political mobilisation and improved their positions in colonial society through taking on positions in the trade unions and political movements.

A leading historian on Zimbabwe, Terence Ranger wrote that the two major figures in Bulawayo during the 1950s were Jerry Wilson Vera and Joshua Nkomo, who were both graduates of the Jan Hofmeyr School. They were close friends and travelled overseas together, but were very different in that Vera was an outstanding sports star, 'a glamorous figure, an icon of the adverts, his love-life a constant topic of press speculation'. In contrast, Nkomo was immersed in his work as the first leader of the Railway Trade Union and a rising politician. Vera was content to play an important role in Advisory Board politics, but Nkomo would become president of the militant Southern Rhodesia African National Congress founded in September 1957. According to Ranger, 'Jerry Vera was the undisputed "Mr Bulawayo" in the 1950s while Joshua Nkomo was in waiting to become "Father Zimbabwe"'.[38]

Vera, a Manyika who attended St Augustine's School, played football for Highlanders as well as the Bulawayo representative team, the Red Army, and was chosen as captain of a Southern Rhodesian African side to tour South Africa. *Parade* magazine described him as 'a credit to the city, where he is about the most popular man'.[39] He was very much 'in touch with Bulawayo's high society, controlling functions at Makokoba's Stanley Hall where he was often master of ceremonies at elite weddings, receptions and concerts'. He also became:

> Secretary to the Bulawayo African Football Association, the Bulawayo African Cricket Association, the Bulawayo Committee for the University of Rhodesia and Nyasaland, and the Ibbotson Memorial Fund. He was patron and adviser to the Athletics Society, the Choral society, the Bulawayo and district Pioneers Society. He was on the executive committee of the Inter-racial Club, the Social and Cultural Club, and (along with Simon Muzenda, Joseph Msika and Patrick Rubatika) formed the Sons of Mashonaland Society.[40]

There was the 'Renaissance man' aspect with regard to a number of the men who were not merely footballers or cricketers, a situation which is also true of South Africa's black cricket history. 'Their education', says cricket historian, Dale Slater, 'differentiated them from both the rural population and the proletarian black urban population, yet colour discrimination limited the extent to which they were able to exploit their elite status, or build on their competence'. He pointed out that the all-encompassing nature of the laws legislating segregation frustrated them at every turn, adding:

> ... what you get is a class that networks frantically and expends vast energy seeking out and maximising any opportunities they perceive, inserting themselves into any and every crack they can find in the monolithic wall of discrimination. And, incidentally, often linking their urban interests with their rural roots – which takes us back to Makokoba: the location is the locus where rural and urban aspirations and opportunities meet.[41]

Ranger described Makokoba as 'a little place', for many years accommodating no more than three or four thousand people but, as one of his informants told him, it 'contained a world ... there were people living there from all over central and southern Africa'. It was a vibrant environment where 'many languages were spoken; many different rituals were practised ... Makokoba was constantly a society in the making ...' It was, said Ranger, 'the site of virtually every significant African political event – and most social and cultural ones too – which took place between 1920 and 1960 ...' There were 'concerts and dances and film shows; parades of male dandies; and from the later 1940s parades of female beauties'.[42] Hundreds of people crowded into Stanley Square to watch boxing; many more played soccer in the streets with footballs fashioned out of old rags, tightly wrapped newspaper, discarded stockings and rubber bands, while the elite followed Vera in taking up cricket. The editor of the *African Home News*, Charlton Ngcebetsha—a Mfengu and former footballer of note—gave the clubs his support and was quick to recognise that cricket was another means to open up black middle-class advancement. Leading figures in football such as Jini Ntuta, Gibson Makanda and Canaan Zulu played cricket, as did others who wished to further demonstrate their fitness in adopting and assimilating European culture.

JINI NTUTA AND THE DEVELOPMENT OF MATABELELAND CRICKET

Jean Enock Gwaula 'Jini' Ntuta was born at Tjolotjo on 10 September 1924 and attended St Ninian's, then Tjolotjo during 1939–1944. Two years after leaving school, he set up a leatherwork shop in Bulawayo, before moving into the fish and chip trade.[43] He came under the influence of Benjamin Burombo, a protégé of the South African trade unionist, Clement Kadalie. According to Robert Cary and Diana Mitchell in their *African Nationalist Leaders in Rhodesia—Who's Who*, Burombo showed great qualities of leadership in the course of founding the British African National Voice Association and organising the successful 1948 strike.[44] These events made an impact on Ntuta who developed his administrative skills as vice-secretary and fixture-master of the Bulawayo African Football Association and as a Red Army selector.

It was in cricket, however, where Ntuta made the greatest impression. He founded the Bulawayo African Cricket Association and was for a number of years the Bulawayo CC captain, a player who was described as a 'a first-class batsman and also a most devastating fast bowler'. According to 'a leading African critic of the game' at that time, Ntuta was 'the fastest bowler in this country and that if it were not because of the colour of his skin he would have long been picked to represent Southern Rhodesia'.[45]

African teams were assembled such as Makokoba and Crackers, and these would combine as the Bulawayo CC to play matches against Indian and coloured sides during the early 1950s. Men such as the schoolmasters, Elliott Kupe and Roger Malasalila, and the politicians, Lazarus Nkala and Benjamin Madlela, were prominent personalities in the side. Ngcebetsha's *African Home News* provided articles that invited the local population to watch the matches being played. 'Cricket is an interesting game', it said, and promised to give more information 'so that Africans who like to play cricket may know which clubs to join'.[46]

In the post-War years, black newspapers became an established feature of the Rhodesian Press and contributed—as Ngcebetsha did—to 'more and more Africans taking an active interest in this gentleman's game'.[47] In the first match against the coloured cricket team on their pitch, Ntuta's Africans won by an innings and 55 runs, but they would find the Indians a tougher proposition as they had formed solid cricket structures in Bulawayo and Salisbury.[48]

Ntuta was determined to establish representative cricket for Africans along the lines of that enjoyed by Indians and whites. In late February 1956, he organised the first fixture against Salisbury, very much 'a dark horse in as much as its cricket capabilities are not known at this side of the country'. A sizeable crowd turned out for the game but it was disappointingly one-sided as Bulawayo won by an innings and 171 runs: 'Jean Ntuta and Sister Gumpo were mainly responsible for the defeat of the Salisbury side because of their excellent bowling. Jerry Vera was the best batsman of all'.[49]

The advent of the Central African Federation in 1953 brought change through its 'partnership' ideal between the races, and for the first time, there was a measure of black political participation. It gave reason to believe that mixed-race cricket could be played, particularly as the white Mashonaland Cricket Association changed its constitution to enable Indian teams to participate in their league from 1955/56.[50] Ntuta set about organising a match against whites, a bold initiative as the social exclusivity of the British in the colony had not changed much since the Milton era. Ngcebetsha applauded the arrangement, stating: 'Racial goodwill is on the march in Bulawayo and is resulting in improvement in relations between African and European sportsmen'. There was the additional satisfaction that the match headline should read 'African cricketers beat Europeans at Barbourfields', a consequence of the fact that the white cricketers had 'underestimated the batting and fielding abilities of the African cricketers'. Yet, whilst the white players promised to 'reinforce their side' for the next match, Ngcebetsha dwelt on the significance of the game. He recognised the occasion as a step in the right direction and, aware of sport's potential value for identity-building, stated:

> Perhaps practical and true partnership between the races in the Federation will start seriously in fields of different branches of sport. The European and African cricketers have set the pattern. We suggest that footballers should make the next move.[51]

The value of sport in unifying the races became a recurring theme with regard to cricket during the 1950s. Those administering the game did their best to spread interest, and when the MCC toured in 1956/57, Ngcebetsha recorded African cricket enthusiasts 'felt honoured by being allowed to witness a first-class cricket match ... those who attended sacrificed a florin each day and probably went without a meal or two'.[52] The *Central African Daily News* reported a respect for cricket and said those who witnessed the game at the Queens Ground 'hope to put that first-class batting and bowling which only England could have exhibited into practice next time they play cricket'. Then, when the Australians visited the following year, films were shown at the Bulawayo Location of the fifth Test between South Africa and the tourists.[53] It was mentioned that 'cricket was fast gaining popularity among Africans ... it may soon fill the second place to football'. Reports also indicated tennis, boxing, cycling, football, weightlifting and judo were offered; even a brief reference to P. C. Cragg, an assistant superintendent in the British South Africa Police, holding rugby practices twice a week at a football ground in the Mabvuku 'African township'.[54]

Towards the end of the 1957/58 season, it was observed that 'inter-racial matches have become common' in Bulawayo with Ntuta, assisted by Vera, responsible for the arrangements. Matches that season were played against the Christian Press, Raylton and the Cold Storage Commission, with further 'European' fixtures lined up against 'country sides'. A crowd of 200 watched the Africans defeat the Christian Press by 13 runs, a significant victory because the opposition played in the Bulawayo cricket league. The same season also brought a 15-run defeat at the hands of the coloureds. The match report focused on Ntuta's frustration over the opposition's constant appealing and their captain being unable to control his side. 'If they do not improve their standard of umpires', said Ntuta, 'impartial ones will have to be sought next time by the African side'.[55]

Football and conflict over space continued to pose a problem for the cricketers. The fact that African football in Bulawayo was still busy with its cup fixtures towards Christmas and the New Year cast a serious reflection on the inefficient manner in which the game was organised. Ngcebetsha argued that 'there were enough football grounds throughout the African townships available for general use so that the football season may end on time to give place to cricket which must be developed on a bigger scale than is the case at present'.[56] The only cricket pitch in use for much of the time was at Barbourfields and the Bulawayo African Cricket Association felt there should be another cricket pitch which they could use during the protracted football season.

If cricket was to progress, it also needed to establish a national structure. Ntuta was keen to maintain interest between the 'two well established cricket clubs among Africans – the Bulawayo CC and the Harare CC'. One report claimed interest in the two centres 'is growing year by year' but noted the smaller towns 'do not seem to have taken up the game firmly enough to warrant organisation of a club'.[57]

The Capital's 'African' Cricket

Cricket in Salisbury did not make as great an impression as it had done in Bulawayo. The capital did not have a breeding ground for sport that could match Makokoba, nor did it have a newspaper like the Ngcebetsha-driven *African Home News*. Cricket was seen as an elitist game and, to an extent, inaccessible to the average African. The football administrators not unnaturally capitalised on the popularity of their game and had little sympathy for the cricketers. In one report in 1957 under the heading, 'Football-thirsty Crowds Roam Around [Harare] Township', the argument was put forward 'that football should run for almost the whole of the twelve months of the year'. The *Central African Daily News* interviewed members of the public who pointed out the cricket season might be supported by Europeans, but they, as Africans, 'are still not interested in that game'. One member of the public was quoted as saying 'mockingly' that 'the few [Africans] who had started that game have already given it up'.[58]

In Salisbury, matches were played at the African Welfare Society's Number 5 and 6 Sports Grounds—effectively over a couple of football fields—as well as the Indian and Coloured Morgan High School ground. There were other cricket venues in and around the capital. Chitsere Government School of Harare started cricket in 1956 with boys 'shaping well' under Norman Chitsiga who was coaching them. In 1958, the Harare cricket season opened with the mixed-race University College team playing against Goromonzi. The same year, the Highfield Boys' Club was formed and run by three teachers at various schools in the township. It attracted sixty members and, within a short time, companies and individuals donated second-hand equipment, whilst a cricket pitch and nets were established at Nyandoro School. As a consequence, boys were able to have practices, with the organisers of the club given assistance by 'a European friend who comes out every afternoon to coach boys in the cricket game to get them ready to challenge other teams next season'. Fundraising was undertaken by holding film shows at Cyril Jennings Hall.[59]

In the late 1950s, African cricket was played over a scattered area in Mashonaland with no long-term plans and no clear strategy for its development. African railway employees stationed at Concession, north of Salisbury, were encouraged to play the game for the first time when they received cricket equipment from the African Affairs Department in Salisbury. Whilst press coverage applauded the fact that this was the first station to be issued with cricket equipment, it was also recorded that the employees had actually 'asked for tennis balls and other games for their children'.[60]

Of greater concern for Salisbury's African cricketers was the fact that the Harare CC was regularly beaten by the coloured Central CC and Indian cricket teams such as Starlights, Mayfair, Playfair, the Oriental CC and Waterfalls. There was perhaps a sense of desperation in the fact that they also played teams comprising schoolchildren. They beat a very good side from the Louis Mountbatten School of Salisbury—an Indian team of youngsters of between 10 and 12—by 18 runs and then accounted for the young Javelins team by eight wickets. The report of the match against Lord Mountbatten School noted that 'Harare showed much skill in fielding and bowling', whilst Caephas Hanyani, 'one of the few spin bowlers in the club', was singled out for taking 12 wickets for 58 runs against the Javelins.[61]

The secretary of the Harare CC, the 'wizard wicketkeeper' S. S. Mhlanga remained optimistic, stating that with 'hard practice ... the standard of performance will improve tremendously'. There was certainly interest in the game with D. D. T. Samkange of the well-known family: T. J. Nduna, the chairman, and Philemon Ngwenya, a fine player, conspicuous in reports. Harare CC had just one team but a relatively large squad attended trial fixtures between Revellers and Explorers. Members often went to watch matches played by Europeans, and they also met to discuss progress. After a heavy defeat at the hands of the Mayfair Club, for example, they:

> ... called for a public meeting at Chitsere School on Wednesday night at 7:30 pm to talk the defeat over. They discussed how future fixtures would be affected and the need for more net practices and also more fielding practices. The game served as a pointer to Harare cricketers that fielding is as important in cricket as batting.[62]

Jini Ntuta travelled to Salisbury in order to seek the possibility of a second match between the two centres. He turned out for the Harare CC against Starlights and then invited Salisbury to play a match as part of Bulawayo's Sports Festival in November 1959.[63] Unfortunately, the visitors were again outclassed, beaten at Pelandaba by an innings and 107 runs. Ntuta scored 44 and Kupe 32 in Bulawayo's 216 against which Salisbury made 27 and 82.[64] The one-sided nature of the game was disappointing but staging a match between the two provinces was always an achievement.

The South African Influence

During the 1950s, black cricketers in Rhodesia followed the progress of their South African counterparts. The South African Cricket Board of Control had been formed in 1947 to bring together the governing bodies of the African, coloured, Indian and Malay cricket organisations. Although the race groups were united through the new arrangement, they still maintained their individual identities as the tournaments were played on racial lines. This structure continued until 1958 when a meeting of all affiliate boards of SACBOC was held in Cape Town to discuss the question of racial integration in South African cricket. It is recorded that 'the Rev. B. L. E. Sigamoney proposed that racialism be abolished in "non-European" cricket. This motion was followed by five hours of heated debate before being carried by twelve votes to none (the Malay Board abstained from voting)'.[65]

Bulawayo's African cricket administrators were effectively a step ahead of the South Africans when, in February 1957, they envisaged 'one cricket union for Indians and Africans'. The *Central African Daily News* commented on developments taking place between the two race groups, stating that African cricket enthusiasts felt strongly that amalgamation would be beneficial. The article pointed out that cricket enthusiasts in Bulawayo believed 'the day must come when all non-European cricketers in Bulawayo should be at liberty to join any Non-European cricket club; be it African, Indian or coloured ... by forming a Non-European Cricket Association, it should not be hard to get players joining any of the clubs affiliated to it'. It would mean that the association could 'pick one cricket team from both Indians and Africans in the event of one outside cricket team coming to play a non-European cricket side of Bulawayo'.[66]

It was not until some two-and-a-half years later that Ntuta updated cricket followers on developments taking place among 'fellow rejects of the sporting Whites of the Continent'. In a letter to the *African Home News*, he mentioned African football officials had set their minds on meeting the demands of FIFA membership and established what was initially referred to as an 'African, Coloured and Indian Football Association'. It was seen as an important first step towards merit selection but, as Ntuta conceded, it was an incomplete development. He had been involved in the early negotiations and maintained 'that there is much yet to be done to eradicate the colour outlook of the whole thing'. He praised the Africans—the strongest football group in the country—for promoting this new structure but then asked of the Indians:

> In cricket, here lies the big question. Will the big power of cricket be as reasonable as those of football as to admit the Africans and coloureds into their well-organised cricket and tennis? Surely, they should if they are sincere to the decision arrived at by their fellow sporting body.[67]

It had interested Ntuta and the Rhodesian press that [Ben] Malamba, an African cricketer who proved good enough, was picked to represent South Africa in the 'Tests' against the Kenyans.[68] A similar national non-white team could be established in Rhodesia, although Ntuta appeared to dread the possibility of a negative response from the Indian cricket administrators. He had worked hard over the years to build links with Indians, Africans and coloureds—as well as whites—in a divided country and believed the Indians admire 'good things and they will follow the footballers in all sports'.[69] At the same time, he was impatient for action and masterminded a weekend of cricket in the capital city during which he aimed to demonstrate the strength and organisation of African cricket.

Apart from perennial problems such as the expense of equipment and lack of facilities, a clear indication of the difficulties that Africans faced at that time was emphasised through the obstacles Bulawayo encountered in travelling to Salisbury early in 1960 for the return match. The *Central African Daily News* revealed that the Bulawayo team 'could not raise money for the train fare' in early December 1959.[70] And then when the necessary finance was available, the Harare Cricket Club had difficulties in confirming a venue and making all the arrangements.

Finally, during the weekend of 16/17 January 1960, the Bulawayo CC travelled to Salisbury. On the Saturday, they thrashed 'a less-experienced' Harare CC by an innings and six runs when 'the architects of the easy win were their bowlers Ntuta and Kupe'.[71]

The heavy defeat suffered by the hosts was expected but disappointing because the main purpose of the match was to select the strongest possible Southern Rhodesian African XI to play the Indian XI at Belvedere. It was a historic occasion as the Africans emulated the Indians and whites in forming a national side—a parallel development along the lines of the South African model. White Rhodesians played regularly in the Currie Cup and against international sides whilst the Southern Rhodesian Indian XI had played in an Indian inter-provincial tournament at Cape Town in 1953, as well as the annual Ramabhai Trophy fixture against Northern Rhodesia and more recently against Basil D'Oliveira's South African touring team.

The Southern Rhodesian African XI led by Ntuta was outplayed by the Indians and lost the match by an innings and 14 runs. They crumbled to 37 all out in their first innings during which fifteen-year-old A. S. Bhika claimed 9 for 13, but improved to 108 in their second effort against the Indians' 150. An Indian spokesman said 'cricket matches should be arranged much more often … [and referred to] E Kupe of Bulawayo as a very brilliant and forceful batsman, and J Vera as a batsman who uses a straight bat while Dingani was a good all round cricketer' (Fig. 9.1).[72]

Disappointing as the outcome must have been, the selection of the 'national' team was perhaps the high point of African cricket achievements up to that time. There was also some compensation for the Bulawayo

Indians Dismiss African X1 For 37 Runs In First Innings: 15-Year Old Takes 9 For 13

Africans Lose By An Innings And 14 Runs

SALISBURY, Tuesday.—By dismissing the Southern Rhodesia African Cricket X1 for 37 runs in their first innings; with 15-year-old A. Bhika taking nine wickets for 13 runs, the Indian Cricket X1 paved its way to an easy victory by an innings and 14 runs, at the Belvedere Grounds last Sunday afternoon.

The African X1 won the toss and batted first, but were all out in less than an hour's time, for the total of 37 runs. The Indians replied with a first innings total of 159 runs all out, to gain a comfortable 122 runs lead. The African X1, left with just over two hours in which to force a draw batted their second innings, but were all out before the close of play for 108 runs.

The African X1 opened their first innings with opening batsmen, Kaiza and Vera at the crisses. It however did not take long for them to get into trouble, and Vera was soon bowled out for 1. Mkando came into bat but was out for a duck shortly after.

The African X1's wickets fell in quick succession before some

who each made 22 runs.

SCOREBOARD

African X1 —First Innings: 37
Indian X1—First Innings;
G. Hoosein b Ntuta 4
A. Ebrahim c—b Mothobi 26
Y. Ismail c Chirwa b. Gwaku. .27
A. Vali c Mhlanga b. Mothobi 4
A. Bhika c—b Dingani 5
I. Vali c Chirwa b Gwaku 16
Y. Patel c Kupe b Dingani.... 6
............22

Opening batsmen, J. Vera and Kaiza are seen in the picture entering the pitch to bat.

Fig. 9.1 An article that appeared in the *Central African Daily News* records details of the first match played by a representative Southern Rhodesian African XI. Jerry Vera and Willie Kiaza opened the batting for the African XI

contingent on their return when they defeated the Indian CC by one run at Barbourfields. Peter S. Mahlangu, the noted Ndebele writer, batted number 6 for the Africans in a thrilling match, with Vera (46) and Ntuta (an unbeaten 27 and four wickets) in splendid form. It would mark the end of an era.[73]

THE DECLINE OF AFRICAN CRICKET AND THE RISE OF NATIONALIST POLITICS

African cricket in Bulawayo and Salisbury went into a decline that coincided with the rise of black nationalist politics. The Native Councils Act of 1937 had been amended again in 1957 to ensure a more effective curtailment of opportunity for the advancement of the Africans. At the same time, the Gold Coast became Ghana in 1957 and fuelled the view that the Federation was no longer a viable concept. The idea of 'partnership' that once appeared to offer more than segregation had failed because African leaders were not only disillusioned with the lack of progress that Federation offered them but were wary of white Rhodesians extending their political and economic control northwards.

An African journalist, Lawrence Vambe, believed the banning of the African National Congress in 1959, aroused the African population 'into a political consciousness that had not been seen before'. He claimed the 'five hundred "agitators" put away by the government were replaced by others, some of whom had previously been considered the mildest of Africans'.[74] The Southern Rhodesia African National Congress was banned and then replaced by the National Democratic Party on New Year's Day 1960, and in July of that year, a mass demonstration in Salisbury led to riots with the trouble spreading to Bulawayo.

Ntuta, who was still captain and organiser of the Bulawayo CC, admitted in September 1961, that 'for quite some time now' his club 'had been in the unfortunate position of having no teams to play against'. He made a determined effort to attract membership through the announcement that 'it may have some European members' in the new season, confirming three were 'willing to join the club'. The *Bantu Mirror* supported the innovation and not long afterwards stressed 'even the kids are up in arms against the colour bar in sport … for the first time African and European youths will clash in a friendly soccer encounter'.[75]

Ntuta's plans for a multiracial cricket side did not materialise as politics occupied much of his time. He had been active in both the African National Congress and the National Democratic Party and, when the latter was banned at the beginning of December 1962 by Edgar Whitehead's Southern Rhodesian Government, he joined Nkomo's Zimbabwe African People's Union and then its successor, the People's Caretaker Council, for whom he was chairman of the Barbourfields branch. Later, in 1964, he was detained by Ian Smith's Government at Wha Wha for four months prior to being transferred to the Gonakudzingwa detention camp.[76]

Other key figures were lost to Bulawayo's cricket for different reasons. By 1960, Vera had opened his Happy Valley Hotel ('perched at the edge of Makokoba') and, says Ranger, 'no longer in contact with every sort of African in Bulawayo, he was now limited to the elite activities – tennis and golf'.[77] Benjamin Madlela became the ZAPU representative at their base in Dar es Salaam, where he was described as 'a wizard in organising and administration but died young in exile'.[78] Elliott Kupe, a school principal from Bulawayo, was chosen out of hundreds of applicants to receive a scholarship to attend Carleton University. He spoke of his country as being of 'temperate climate, mostly well-watered for agriculture, with rich mines and great industrial potential', but 'political developments – the rise to power of an illiberal European party – saddened him'.[79] Another useful acquisition to Bulawayo cricket, the Rev. Griffiths Malaba, who had played at Fort Hare, was also lost to education where he would make a major contribution.

Cricket news from the capital was briefly encouraging. The *Central African Daily News* reported in January, 1963, that 'the Harare Cricket Club which was formed in 1956 and had just about died is to start all over again'. The only African club in Salisbury was 'on a membership drive and all those who were interested were requested to meet at the Harare Community Centre'. Practices started and it was hoped to play an Indian cricket side from Belvedere on a Sunday afternoon. In another edition, it was recorded: 'Cricket has been played mostly by one section of the community. It is our wish to have reports of this game from all sections of the community. There are very few African schools where this game is played…'.[80]

Ironically, their appeal came at a time when white cricket was struggling to put its house in order to attract international opponents. In Bulawayo, the local Indian club earned the right to play in the Matabeleland First League but delight turned to dismay when their cricketers were refused permission to play at the Raylton and Bulawayo Athletic Club grounds.[81] When British cricket journalist, Ron Roberts, took advantage of Rhodesia's multiracial sport and brought black Test players to the country in 'Commonwealth' sides during 1961–63, Martin Lee wrote enthusiastically of the progress that the Federation ideal had made. 'We are being watched with real envy from down south', he crowed: 'A few years ago there would have been no question of Pakistanis, West Indians, Indians, a South African "Coloured" as well as Englishmen and Aussies all lining up in one team in Rhodesia'. But then the cricketers were refused permission to play the Bulawayo fixture at Queen's, resorting instead to the Showground 'which sees only horse shows and third-rate soccer in normal circumstances'.[82]

Whites strove to keep the Federation intact with the additional hope of dominion status, but Vambe was critical and believed it better for Africans to assist the northern territories achieve independence so that 'they in turn would assist us to achieve our freedom'.[83] With the Federation's dissolution, Nyasaland gained independence as Malawi in July 1964 and Northern Rhodesia as Zambia in October 1964.

Southern Rhodesia became 'Rhodesia', and Ian Smith's Government declared independence unilaterally in November 1965. White attitudes hardened with the Government determined to restrict social integration, and there was no apparent interest in assisting the Harare CC. The *Sports Herald*, a weekly supplement to the *Rhodesia Herald*, announced in a September 1968 report that the only African cricket club in the Salisbury townships was without a ground and there was no-one within close proximity able to provide much-needed opposition. The club secretary, George Nhari, said that in the past the City Council had made available a pitch, but this was no longer possible as 'all of them were being used for soccer fixtures every weekend'. Practice nets were in a bad state, and the club was unable to secure a place in the league, having been told by the Mashonaland Cricket Association that their application 'arrived too late for inclusion in the present season'. They relied on 'friendlies', beginning with games arranged against Goromonzi School first and second elevens. Reporter, Misheck Mbewe concluded, 'Africans need another sport to turn to in the soccer off-season. And if the City Council can provide the tennis players with courts, surely they could see their way clear to help the cricketers'.[84]

The vice-chairman of the Mashonaland Cricket Association, Alwyn Pichanick, spoke on mixed cricket in the aftermath of a double-wicket tournament that involved the West Indian captain, Garry Sobers, in 1970. In an interview with the *Rhodesia Herald*, he claimed there was 'no colour bar whatsoever in our senior cricket'. He added that 'most of the crowd was white because the Africans generally show no interest in the game'. And while 'our Indian players are considered for representative matches on the same basis as the Europeans', he went back eight years to find an example, singling out leg-spinner Ahmed Suleman who had toured Britain with the Fawns.[85] He might have noted Kish Gokal who had been Rhodesia's star player against the Australian schoolboys in December 1967, scoring 44 and taking 4/47, and overlooked the treatment of Haroon Ismail, who was chosen to attend Rhodesia's annual end-of-year schoolboy cricket trials in December 1969, but could not be selected for the team that would play in South Africa. A *Rhodesia Herald* editorial criticised the country's 'two-faced attitude' of 'welcoming sportsmen of any colour and selecting our best of any colour to play them here' but then playing 'as Lillywhites in South Africa'. It added: 'This means, in effect South Africa picks some of our teams for us … Such teams should not carry the national title unqualified. They should be "White Rhodesian teams"'.[86]

Africans were selected for the country's ill-fated Olympic teams in 1968 and 1972 and were prominent in a 1969 World Cup football qualifier when Rhodesia shocked the Australians by drawing twice before going down in a third encounter. Cricket was nevertheless floundering on the question of race, a situation not helped by its sporting isolation and the South African Cricket Association's rigid adherence to the laws of the land. In Britain, the newly elected Conservative Government worked behind the scenes to end the political deadlock with Rhodesia, and in November 1971, a settlement was reached subject to the Pearce Commission testing public opinion. Bishop Muzorewa's newly formed African National Council successfully opposed the proposals and became increasingly prominent in Rhodesian politics. Ngcebetsha was the party's first Secretary General; Ntuta served on the National Executive; and Nkala later became Organising Secretary. Ngcebetsha maintained that 'top appointments in the new organisation were made by Nkomo from Gonakudzingwa'.[87]

Judith Todd wrote of Ngcebetsha in her book, *Through the Darkness: A life in Zimbabwe*, and mentioned that he was arrested during the Pearce Commission investigation in 1972 and sent to Gonakudzingwa. She recalled that the party's Deputy National Secretary, Arthur Chadzingwa, was …

> … for some time held in a cell with Charlton Ngcebetsha. He helped the time pass by teaching Arthur cricket in a cell with no bat and no ball. Arthur said he got pretty good at shouting 'HOWZAT!' Charlton was quite irrepressible, and somehow, within a short time of his detention, the first edition of the *Gonakudzingwa Home News* hit the streets of Bulawayo.[88]

CONCLUSION

This study has endeavoured to shed light on the appearance of African cricket during the colonial period. The Mfengu immigrants played cricket for almost twenty years from the late nineteenth century whilst matches involving local Africans can be traced from the 1930s when schools and welfare societies encouraged the game. Club cricket after the Second World War paralleled wider developments, with Bulawayo leading the way as the focus progressed from the assimilation process towards cricket becoming a mobilising force for township politics.

Makokoba was central to the progress made, a relatively small township but an important meeting point nevertheless of Africans from various backgrounds. Ngcebetsha's impact was considerable in shaping local developments, as were various other newspapers across the country. The African Press, as it became popularly known—with eight papers—provided 'concrete signs of interracial co-operation' and was an indispensable source for detail on African achievements. Vambe records the Smith Government's ban on the *Central African Daily News* and the subsequent closure of Rhodesia's African Press as 'a tragic loss to the country as a whole, for it left five million blacks without an outlet to reflect their national life and point of view'.[89]

In the 1970s, an escalating civil war enveloped the country and it was not until December 1979 that a settlement was reached with the signing of the Lancaster House agreement in London. The Rhodesian Cricket Union severed ties with South Africa before independence in April 1980 and became involved in development programmes designed to produce players of colour. The cricket played by Africans twenty years earlier had faded from memory but one link from the past was that of the Stragglers CC, established shortly after the Second World War by returning servicemen (Spencer Parker and former England rugby international, Tim Francis) with 'the spirit of cricket at heart'. A junior cricket week was established during the 1960s that would involve players from all races.[90]

The chairman of Stragglers, Spencer Parker—an architect who had played rugby for Rhodesia against the 1938 British Lions—was at the forefront of efforts to encourage cricketers of colour to take up the game. Together with Charles Brockway, he became involved in coaching black players throughout the year. The two gentlemen were described as 'messengers of the Rhodesian cricket authorities' in the late 1970s, supposedly charged with 'unearthing fast bowlers in the mould of West Indian greats such as Andy Roberts and Michael Holding'.[91] The idea sparked interest in the media but their work did have greater responsibilities. 'If we do not encourage African interest in cricket', said Parker at the time, 'the game will die in this country'.[92] The project he began in 1977 catered for coaching young Africans between the ages of 14 and 25; it was so successful, wrote E. W. Swanton that by 1980 '350 young men have been taught the game, the cost of £30,000 having been borne entirely by the [Stragglers] club'.[93]

The scheme catered for Africans from high-density schools and was staged primarily at the Glamis Arena in Salisbury. Lazarus Zizhou, who became a well-known coach, would later state that Parker's practices 'made it possible for most of the current players to be where they are now'. A newspaper journalist, Funny Mashava, who was himself involved in the practices, said the youngsters decided to call themselves 'Strugglers', a play on 'Stragglers', but also a reflection on the hand-to-mouth existence of the boys. He recalled Parker and Brockway would provide lunches that usually consisted of 'a soft drink and a candy cake' whilst 'in the evening, after practice, each player was given 20 cents to help meet their transport costs from home and back'.[94]

In 2014, a leading Zimbabwean cricket writer, Enock Muchinjo, described the 'Strugglers' as 'Rhodesia's first black cricket club'; an indication that the African players of the 1950s and 1960s had indeed become 'forgotten' cricketers.[95] None of the key cricket personalities in an era that popularised sport for Africans in Rhodesia would share in Zimbabwe's involvement in the international sporting sphere after 1980. Nkala, who spent four years in an isolated detention camp with Nkomo and Joseph Msika, was killed in a car accident in 1975, and Ngcebetsha died suddenly two years later. Ranger thought Jerry Vera might 'have become the first mayor of Bulawayo after 1980' but he 'passed into obscurity ... he was to die unremarked in a care home'.[96] Roger Malasalila, a good batsman in the Bulawayo CC team who later taught at Tjolotjo, was killed by the North Korean trained Fifth Brigade in October 1983.

Jini Ntuta was detained at Wha Wha, the largest of Rhodesia's detention centres, in 1978, but two years' later was in Robert Mugabe's first cabinet as his Deputy Minister of Mines. The position was short-lived because Mugabe fired Ntuta, Nkomo, Msika and Josiah Chinamaro for their alleged connection to companies outlawed by the government and the discovery of arms caches on ZAPU properties. Jan Raath of *The Times* described Ntuta as ...

... one of the government's fiercest and most articulate critics, particularly over atrocities committed by security forces against civilians in Matabeleland. Ntuta himself charged that many troops posed as dissidents and then killed civilians.[97]

In November 1984, Ntuta was killed near his home in the southern region of Matabeleland. His killers chased the 60-year-old Ntuta on foot for two and a half miles before 'shooting him to death with automatic rifles'.[98] Judith Todd wrote of '... Jini Ntuta's attempted flight from his pursuers, when he was shot dead like a rabbit'.[99] ZAPU's secretary general, Cephas Msipa stated that Ntuta was murdered: 'The government claimed it was by dissidents, but it was widely believed to be the army ... Why it was necessary for North Koreans to train the army, only God knows'.[100]

Ntuta's life mirrored the tragic Zimbabwean situation over a long period of time. A man of vision in his administration of African cricket, it might be argued that he had by 1960 spearheaded a movement that made greater strides than any other sporting body in bringing the race groups together on a regular basis. In August 1989, Zimbabwe honoured 100 'heroes' with its 'Liberation' decorations: not unexpectedly, Robert Mugabe topped the list, but it also included stalwart members of the Bulawayo CC—Ntuta, Madlela and Nkala—and cricket writer, Ngcebetsha.

NOTES

1. R. Rotberg, *The Founder: Cecil Rhodes and the Pursuit of Power* (New York: Oxford University Press, 1988), 567–69.
2. *Cape Times*, 13 November 1897.
3. J. Muzondidya, 'Towards a Historical Understanding of the Making of the Coloured Community in Zimbabwe 1890–1920', *Identity, Culture and Politics*, CODESRIA, Dakar, 3, 2 (December 2002), 78–79, 84.
4. Muzondidya, 'Towards a Historical Understanding', 79.
5. J. Mutambirwa, *The Rise of Settler Power in Southern Rhodesia (Zimbabwe) 1898–1923* (London: Associated University Presses, 1980), 93–94.
6. *Imvo Zabantsundu*, 4 September 1899 and 2 July 1901; A. Odendaal, *The Story of an African Game: Black Cricketers and the Unmasking of One of Cricket's Greatest Myths, South Africa, 1850–2003* (Cape Town: David Philip, 2003), 59.
7. *APO*, 16 December 1911; A. Odendaal, K. Reddy, C. Merrett, and J. Winch, *Cricket & Conquest: The History of South African Cricket Retold 1795–1914* (Cape Town: HSRC Press, 2016), 375.
8. Muzondidya, 'Towards a Historical Understanding', 79, 84–85. See also T. O. Ranger, *The African Voice in Rhodesia* (London: Heinemann, 1970), 45–63.
9. S. Hyatt, *The Old Transport Road* (London: Melrose, 1914), 31.

10. Lord Grey, then Administrator, to the Martin Commission in C. Summers, *From Civilization to Segregation: Social Ideals and Social Control in Southern Rhodesia, 1890–1934* (Athens: Ohio University Press, 1994), 89.
11. M. West, *The Rise of an African Middle Class: Colonial Zimbabwe 1898–1965* (Bloomington: Indiana University Press, 2002), 13.
12. Mutambirwa, *The Rise of Settler Power*, 74.
13. R. Bourne, *Catastrophe: What Went Wrong in Zimbabwe?* (London: Zed Books, 2011), 29.
14. R. Gray, *The Two Nations: Aspects of the Development of Race Relations in the Rhodesias and Nyasaland* (London: Oxford University Press, 1960), 332.
15. C. van Onselen, *Chibaro: African Mine Labour in Southern Rhodesia 1900–1933* (London: Pluto Press, 1980), 182.
16. R. Parry, 'Birds on a Flat Rock: Black Workers and the Limits of Colonial Power in Salisbury, Rhodesia 1890–1939' (PhD thesis, Queen's University, Kingston, 1988), 431.
17. Rhodesia Resources Committee, Native Development A/3/12/9, 7.
18. C. Zvobgo, *A History of Zimbabwe, 1890–2000 and Postscript Zimbabwe 2001–2008* (Newcastle-upon-Tyne: Cambridge Scholars Publishing, 2009), 43.
19. *Native Mirror (monthly)*, February 1935.
20. J. Nkomo and N. Harman, *The Story of My Life* (London: Methuen, 1984), 25.
21. N. Atkinson, *Teaching Rhodesians: A History of Educational Policy in Rhodesia* (London: Longman, 1972), 118.
22. *Bantu Mirror*, 4 April 1936.
23. Ibid., 11 December 1937.
24. Ibid., 5 February 1938.
25. Ibid., 1 October 1938 and 26 November 1938.
26. See references to Bulletins 5, 6 and 7 of the Mashonaland Native Welfare Society in the *Bantu Mirror*, 10 December 1938, 14 January 1939 and 11 February 1939.
27. Atkinson, *Teaching Rhodesians*, 118–19.
28. Parry, 'Birds on a Flat Rock', 434.
29. Van Onselen, *Chibaro*, 190–91.
30. From the Annual Report of the Matabeleland Native Welfare Society, published in the *Bantu Mirror*, 4 February 1939.
31. *Bantu Mirror*, 14 January 1939.
32. Rhodesia Central Statistics Office MSS, Reports on Census of Industrial Production, 1944, 5.
33. O. Stuart, 'Players, Workers, Protestors: Social Change and Soccer in Colonial Zimbabwe' in J. MacClancy (ed.), *Sport, Identity and Ethnicity* (Oxford: Berg, 1996), 177.

34. Stuart, 'Players, Workers, Protestors', 170, 177.
35. Ibid., 178.
36. P. Shumba, '"Smart Boys" in early business' in *Bulawayo Chronicle*, 31 May, 2014.
37. P. Alegi, *Laduma!: Soccer, Politics and Society in South Africa* (Scottsville: University of KwaZulu-Natal Press, 2004), 100.
38. T. Ranger, *Bulawayo Burning: The Social History of a Southern African City 1893–1960* (Harare: Weaver Press, 2010), 190–91.
39. 'Inside Bulawayo' in *Parade*, February 1956.
40. Ranger, *Bulawayo Burning*, 192–93. Muzenda became Deputy Prime Minister and then Vice-President to Robert Mugabe during 1980–2003.
41. D. Slater to author, 27 January 2018.
42. Ranger, *Bulawayo Burning*, 3–4.
43. D. Mitchell, *Who's Who, 1981–82: Nationalist Leaders in Zimbabwe* (Salisbury: D. Mitchell, 1982), 147.
44. R. Cary and D. Mitchell, *African Nationalist Leaders in Rhodesia— Who's Who* (Bulawayo: Books of Rhodesia, 1977), 5–6.
45. *African Home News*, 21 January 1956.
46. *African Home News*, 30 October 1954.
47. L. Vambe, *An Ill-Fated People: Zimbabwe Before and After Rhodes* (London: Heinemann, 1972), 224; *African Home News*, 14 January 1956.
48. J. Winch, 'Jayanti—A Cricketing Anachronism as Zimbabwe's "Forgotten" Players Make a Fresh Start', *Sport & Society*, 16, 1 (2013), 56–70.
49. *African Home News*, 25 February and 3 March 1956.
50. Winch, 'Jayanti—A Cricketing Anachronism', 59.
51. *African Home News*, 25 January 1958.
52. *African Daily News (Salisbury)*, 22 November 1956.
53. *Central African Daily News*, 1 April 1958.
54. Ibid., 11 January 1958; *African Home News (Salisbury)*, 15 August 1959.
55. *Central African Daily News*, 15 February 1958 and 26 February 1958.
56. *African Home News*, 3 December 1960.
57. *Central African Daily News*, 1 April 1958.
58. Ibid., 4 February 1957.
59. Ibid., 6 January 1959.
60. Ibid., 10 January 1959.
61. Ibid., 28 March 1958, 6 December 1958 and 6 February 1959.
62. Ibid., 2 December 1958.
63. Ibid., 29 November 1958.
64. Ibid., 5 November 1959.

65. J. Winch, *Cricket in Southern Africa: Two Hundred Years of Achievements and Records* (Rosettenville: Windsor Publishers, 1997), 105.
66. *Central African Daily News*, 11 February 1957.
67. *African Home News*, 15 August 1959.
68. *Central African Daily News*, 11 February 1957.
69. *African Home News*, 15 August 1959.
70. *Central African Daily News*, 8 January 1960.
71. Ibid., 18 January 1960.
72. *Central African Daily News*, 19 and 23 January 1960.
73. Ibid., 26 March 1960.
74. Vambe, *An Ill-Fated People*, 282.
75. *Bantu Mirror*, 20 May 1961.
76. Mitchell, *Who's Who, 1981–82*, 147.
77. Ranger, *Bulawayo Burning*, 245.
78. J. Mpofu, *My Life in the Struggle for the Liberation of Zimbabwe* (Bloomington: Author House, 2014), 140.
79. *Ottawa Citizen*, 13 February 1963.
80. *Central Africa Daily News*, 2 and 11 January 1963.
81. *Bulawayo Chronicle*, October 1962.
82. Ibid., 24 February 1962.
83. Vambe, *An Ill-Fated People*, 267.
84. *Sports Herald* (weekly supplement to the *Rhodesia Herald*), 21 September 1968.
85. *Rhodesia Herald*, 30 September 1970. A Rhodesian schoolboy side—the Fawns—toured England in 1962.
86. *Rhodesia Herald*, 17 December 1969.
87. Cary and Mitchell, *African Nationalist Leaders in Rhodesia*, 14.
88. J. Todd, *Through the Darkness: A Life in Zimbabwe* (Cape Town: Zebra Press, 2007), 262.
89. Vambe, *An Ill-Fated People*, 224–25.
90. Annual booklet: Stragglers Cricket Club Winter Season, 1955.
91. F. Mushava in *The Herald*, 22 November 2014.
92. Interview with Spencer Parker, 2 June 1978.
93. E. Swanton in *The Cricketer*, January 1981, 36.
94. Mushava in *The Herald*, 22 November 2014.
95. E. Muchinjo in *Daily News* (Zimbabwe), 25 September 2014.
96. Ranger, *Bulawayo Burning*, 245.
97. J. Raath in *The Times*, 27 November 1984.
98. *New York Times*, 27 November 1984.
99. Todd, *Through the Darkness*, 405.
100. C. Msipa, *In Pursuit of Freedom and Justice: A Memoir* (Harare: Weaver Press, 2015), 112.

PART III

The Politics

Should the West Indies Have Toured South Africa in 1959? C. L. R. James Versus Learie Constantine

Jonty Winch

INTRODUCTION

Frank Worrell's West Indies cricket team was invited to tour South Africa in 1959. They were scheduled to play black sides in a programme that was devised by the non-racial South African Cricket Board of Control. The proposal did not meet with everyone's approval: the newly formed South African Sports Association raised an objection because the tour was arranged within the parameters of the prevailing racial structure and therefore lent credibility to the government's apartheid policy. There was, however, a strong counter-argument that a tour would project weaknesses in the apartheid system, thereby creating serious difficulties

Thanks to Dale Slater for his comments with regard to a number of key issues during this period.

J. Winch (✉)
Reading, UK

© The Author(s) 2018
B. Murray et al. (eds.), *Cricket and Society in South Africa, 1910–1971*, Palgrave Studies in Sport and Politics, https://doi.org/10.1007/978-3-319-93608-6_10

275

and embarrassment for the South African government. The subsequent debate on the merits of the venture included C. L. R. James taking an opposite viewpoint to that of Learie Constantine. Irrespective of who was right, the cancellation of the tour had an immediate impact on the lives of South Africa's black players, some of whom left the country, whilst the West Indians became increasingly curious to find out more about Africa.

The Beginning of the Emancipation of the Coloured Africans as International Cricketers

In the period after World War II, the racially fragmented black cricket bodies came together to form the South African Cricket Board of Control (SACBOC) in 1947. They subsequently organised the Dadabhay Trophy tournaments which were attended by African, coloured, Indian and Malay cricketers. There were some outstanding players, and during the early 1950s, the SACBOC committee sought to create opportunities in the way of international contact. Their first hope was India in 1951 but the South Africans were not in a position to meet the expenses needed to fund the project. Later, when sufficient finance was arranged, an invitation was sent to Pakistan to visit South Africa. 'But', wrote cricket historian, Mogamad Allie, 'just when negotiations had reached a critical stage, the Pakistanis backed out'.[1] It was at that juncture that the ICC agreed to grant membership to the Pakistan cricket authorities.

In 1955, SACBOC made an unsuccessful application to join the Imperial Cricket Conference (ICC) as a full member. It was told to 'prove its ability to conduct tours and also obtain two sponsoring countries', an intriguing step because constitutionally the ICC would have had to consider accommodating two bodies from the same country.[2] SACBOC also entertained hopes of playing a match against the 1956/57 MCC tourists but its request was rejected. This was disappointing as it would have given the players exposure to international competition and an opportunity to play on a turf wicket, an important consideration because cricket under the aegis of SACBOC was staged on matting-over-gravel pitches.

In a divided society, the white South African Cricket Association (SACA) had little sympathy for the plight of their black counterparts. White administrators had the support of the MCC, the governing body of English cricket and an institution committed to preserving traditional links. The MCC valued a tour that Colin Cowdrey described as a 'safari by Rolls Royce' and did not wish to reduce the influence of 'white' nations in the cricket-playing network, especially as Pakistan had just been granted Test status.[3] England off-spinner, Jim Laker, wrote of the MCC's priorities when touring South Africa in 1956/57. 'Before we left England', he said, 'we were given the usual preliminary briefing by the President of MCC. He reminded us of South Africa's problems, and told us that colour, as a topic of conversation, was strictly out. It was something never to be mentioned'.[4]

Basil D'Oliveira was a particularly outstanding cricketer of colour. When the Springboks were creating headline news in an absorbing series in England in 1955, reference was made to his deeds in *The Cricketer*. In the June issue, there was mention of the Dadabhay Trophy tournament at Johannesburg during which D'Oliveira scored 153 in ninety-five minutes for the South African Coloureds against the South African Malays. A month later, there was a report on the South African Coloured Tournament at which D'Oliveira recorded scores of 155 not out and 112 for Western Province.

Cricket presented challenges, enjoyment and opportunities for players of colour to demonstrate their skills. D'Oliveira wrote of 'non-white' South Africans being passionate about the game and 'extremely proud' of what they had achieved.[5] They might not have had the benefit of the facilities and coaching of the white community but, whenever possible, they would walk to Newlands where they used to sit in the segregated part of the ground and watch players from overseas with particular interest: 'There has never been a crowd as studious, or as hungry for knowledge and instruction', said Peter Oborne. They were 'stealing with their eyes', often envious of the talented stars playing on a magnificent ground.[6]

The Cape youngsters longed for 'some contact with these players from overseas … we would wait outside the hotels in the hope of seeing and speaking to them'. D'Oliveira and his friends did meet the Australian journalist, Ray Robinson, who watched them play and wrote an article on 'coloured' cricketers at the Cape, entitled 'The darker side of cricket'.[7] The need to be noticed by the international press was essential for black cricketers denied the opportunity to compete for 'Test' places. Ironically, when overseas attention focused on South Africa, journalists were not looking to dwell on the great interest black people had for an imperial game. D'Oliveira complained, 'As a non-white African I am depressed and often angry at the distorted and shabby picture which is shown to the outside world by film, television, newspapers and photographs as being typical of non-white life in South Africa'.[8]

SACBOC's efforts to arrange international competition for their players were rewarded in the 1956/57 season when their 'non-white' cricketers were matched against a Kenyan team that included several players with first-class experience, notably Shakoor Ahmed who had toured England with the first Pakistan team in 1954. Arrangements were in accordance with government policy but the tour progressed smoothly; the visitors thrashing Northern Districts, Natal, Eastern Province and Western Province in an impressive run-up to the first 'Test'. D'Oliveira contributed 70 and 36 not out to lead his side to victory by six wickets in the opening clash between the two countries. The second encounter featured a century by 'Laam' Raziet and was won by 39 runs but the rain-ruined third match was drawn.

The Kenyans asked the South Africans to make a reciprocal tour in 1958, an invitation that was gratefully accepted by SACBOC. 'When we left Jan Smuts Airport in the Alitalia 'plane on Monday, 4 August', recalled D'Oliveira, 'I am sure that, in our new blazers, ties and with official travelling bags, we were the proudest team ever to leave any country'. They won the two representative matches convincingly, with skipper D'Oliveira scoring 139 in the first 'Test' and Eric Petersen bowling to great effect. A seven-wicket victory against an East African XI further enhanced their tour record, D'Oliveira plundering a rapid 96. It was a memorable trip for the South Africans. 'We all hoped it was to be the first of many tours', said D'Oliveira who saw it as 'the beginning of the emancipation of the coloured Africans as international cricketers'.[9]

Such was the success of these early tours that plans were put into motion to invite the West Indies to South Africa—the primary purpose being to demonstrate that South Africa possessed black cricketers good enough to play 'Test' cricket. Transvaal officials of SACBOC—notably Rashid Varachia, A.M. 'Checker' Jassat and 'Bree' Bulbulia—arranged for a West Indian team led by Frank Worrell to tour in November and December 1959. Varachia contacted the Minister of the Interior, Dr. Eben Donges, in order to obtain permission and in early January 1959, he was able to announce that he had received a letter from the minister stating that he had 'agreed in principle to the admission of the West Indies cricket team'. Varachia made it clear from the outset that arrangements were made strictly in accordance with government requirements. 'The West Indies', he said, 'are fully acquainted with the conditions here and are prepared to accept them'. He explained that 'they are keen to encourage non-white cricket in South Africa'.[10]

Worrell was at Manchester University studying towards a B.A. Administration that featured social anthropology. The West Indian star was drawn into playing for the staff cricket side by a South African, Professor Max Gluckman, who had founded the University's school of anthropology and was a noted political activist. Worrell's biographer, Ivo Tennant, refers to Gluckman's 'liberal leanings' but there is no evidence to suggest that he tried to influence the SACBOC project. It was essentially a 'private' venture, and Tennant noted a promise that 'matches would be arranged against multi-racial teams'. Worrell fully supported the tour—'he had readily accepted, feeling it would help to break down apartheid'.[11] Jassat travelled to London to confirm arrangements, later recalling the emergence of a 'strange twist'. Worrell, he said, wanted 'to bring the best West Indian team and that meant it would be all black'.[12] It suggested no restrictions were placed on Worrell in his choice of players. It was also a revealing reflection of West Indian cricket rather than a racial issue—Worrell was said to have more white than coloured friends.[13]

According to Tennant, Worrell not only organised the side for South Africa but had ties made—in mauve, green and blue (the colours of the Vic Lewis 'showbiz' eleven that he liked to represent in England)—and ordered long- and short-sleeve sweaters.[14] Worrell was also in a position to assemble a powerful combination that was expected to include Tom Dewdney, Andy Ganteaume, Conrad Hunte, Frank King, Ralph Legall, Ivan Madray, Sonny Ramadhin, Donald Ramsamooj, 'Collie' Smith, Garry Sobers, Alf Valentine, Chester Watson and Everton Weekes. It was thought that they would have been favoured to beat the white South Africans but—officially—were scheduled to play only teams affiliated to the South African Cricket Board of Control. A report that the West Indians might visit Rhodesia where the local union would choose a representative team of Indians and whites to play the tourists seems to have been a little optimistic.[15]

'As far as SACBOC was concerned', wrote Allie, 'the tour was in the bag: visas had been applied for and issued; the South African government had given its approval ... the badges and ties had been made and the programme drawn up'. It was 'just a case of waiting for Worrell's team to arrive'.[16] The organisers attended to every detail, which included securing Newlands, the Wanderers and Kingsmead for the matches, and raising £5000 to guarantee expenses. Travel was to be by air, coaches and private cars; there were to be sight-seeing trips including a game reserve and, where suitable high-class hotels were not available, then the tourists would stay in private homes. SACBOC also hoped to make provision for separate seating so that whites could attend all matches.[17]

D'Oliveira and his team were thrilled to be given the opportunity to play arguably the world's most exciting side. 'Excitedly, we talked long into the night', said D'Oliveira, 'about asking Frank to "throw" one of the games, so that the publicity about our victory would reach a wider audience'.[18] Good performances by players at this level would thrust them into the international limelight.

'It was sheer bad luck for D'Oliveira and his cricket team', wrote Oborne, 'that the forthcoming West Indies tour was announced at a moment when Brutus was badly in need of an issue to establish his authority'.[19]

The Emergence of Dennis Brutus

Dennis Brutus was a teacher who believed in 'a single, simple principle: that all South Africans should be allowed to represent their country – if they are good enough'.[20] In 1955, he went so far as to found the Coordinating Committee for International Recognition of Sport, an organisation that aimed to persuade South Africa's non-racial bodies to affiliate to international sports federations. He took up the issue 'not as a tactic to attack the apartheid system but because of the personal harm the policy was doing to athletes'.[21]

His new organisation barely lasted a year but did serve as a warning to whites that they could no longer pretend that black sportsmen did not exist. When the International Table Tennis Federation granted affiliation to the black South African Table Tennis Board ahead of its white counterpart in June 1956, it had immediate repercussions. Apartheid sport had been challenged, and the Minister of the Interior, Dr. Eben Donges, was obliged to issue the first major policy statement on the subject of sport, noting that 'non-whites' could compete against 'non-white' teams from overseas in South Africa but, should they wish to seek international recognition, they would have to do this through the recognised white organisation within a particular sport. Donges wanted to curb any hopes that black sporting bodies had of gaining international recognition alongside or in place of white organisations.[22]

Brutus was determined to build on his initial progress and formed the South African Sports Association (SASA) in 1958. The organisation aimed to overcome problems that existed in black sport because of the lack of coordination that stemmed from separate African, coloured and Indian groups. The likes of Dennis Brutus, G. K. Rangasamy, George Singh, William Herbert and Ramhori Lutchman were named as those seeking to fight for the complete elimination of racial discrimination in sport in South Africa. It was said they were able to speak on behalf of 70,000 black sportsmen representing athletics, baseball, tennis, cricket, cycling, netball, softball, table tennis, football and weightlifting.

Brutus was not concerned by SACBOC's aspirations, nor was he bothered by the timing of his intrusion. SASA believed the black population had no recognised means in which to pursue political protest and therefore turned to sport which had already been politicised by the Nationalist Government. According to Jon Gemmell, SASA viewed sport 'as central to South African psyche and as such was a "legitimate target"'.[23]

There have been those who queried the new body's credentials. In his book, *Critical Perspectives on Dennis Brutus*, Craig W. McLuckie says that he interviewed his subject on the support that SASA supposedly commanded. Brutus replied: 'David Evans, a reporter from the *Evening Post* said privately to me, "as you know Dennis, it really consists of about two people" and that's nearly true, half a dozen at most. But we became tremendously effective'.[24] Randolph Vigne, writing in *The Independent*, also questioned the SASA operation. He pointed out that 'Dennis Brutus was the S.A. Sports Association', and whilst 'running on small donations, the photocopier of a local liberal NGO, no office and no staff, he took on the deeply embedded racially discriminatory South African sports establishment'.

Vigne further noted that Brutus 'constructed a committee of which he was secretary, but which scarcely ever met'. There was also a reluctance to be linked to an established organisation. Vigne believed that Brutus's 'independence of the ANC in his sports-campaigning years sidelined him … In his teaching job he kept clear of the [organisation] and its multi-racial allies, the Liberal Party and the Trotskyites, certain that he could run his own campaign more effectively independent of them'. Running the risk of being considered a loose cannon,

Brutus nevertheless attracted favourable comment as an ambitious and resourceful anti-apartheid campaigner. His objective was 'to open up South African sport, at home and abroad, to spectators, administrators, and media people of all races, and in the process to bring the anti-apartheid struggle before millions scarcely aware of it'.[25]

Ronnie Govender, sports editor of *The Leader*, appreciated the difficulties that SASA faced in their quest 'to awaken the consciences of and mobilise the victims of apartheid sport'. In implying that Brutus had to stir the people into action, Govender suggested that they were not ready for the events about to take place: 'With meagre resources, an unsympathetic establishment press and an apathetic, beleaguered audience with the more pressing problems of the ravages of poverty to contend with, the task was not easy'.

Govender remembered 'the positive deluge of press releases that Brutus sent around the country, an exercise that was not only costly but certainly labour intensive'. It upset Govender that the all-white South African sports teams enjoyed competition against the rest of the world as if everything was normal. 'They were not referred to as "white" teams', he said, 'and the exclusion of "non-whites" was taken for granted, even among the "non-whites" themselves'. With the launching of SASA, Govender believed 'an intensive campaign was initiated to expose naked racism in sports in the country'.[26]

There was support from the British organisation, Campaign Against Race Discrimination in Sport, which was initiated by Father Trevor Huddleston, who wrote 'white South Africa is obsessed by sport' and advocated 'a policy of boycott ... isolation would shake its self-assurance very severely'.[27] The new organisation announced their opposition to Springbok teams being selected on the basis of racial discrimination and challenged the all-white South African and Rhodesian squads that participated in the 1958 Cardiff Empire and Commonwealth Games.

In South Africa, Brutus observed a change of direction in SACBOC's sports policy. All affiliate boards of the parent body held a meeting in Cape Town in 1958 to discuss the question of racial integration in South African cricket. It was led by the Rev Bernard Sigamoney, who called for a system of integrated provincialism which would result in racialism being abolished in 'non-white' cricket. Fragmentation of sides into Bantu, coloureds, Indians and Malays weakened black sport and played into the hands of pro-apartheid white bodies, yet few black cricket followers at the time had given much thought to the significance of such matters. Segregation in cricket was, after all, normal practice in many of the British colonies. As a result, five hours of heated debate ensued before the motion was eventually carried by twelve votes to none (the Malay Board abstained from voting).

It was the success of this meeting that gave Brutus the idea to target the West Indian tour. He objected to the restricted visas granted to the visitors, but the whole question went much deeper. Brutus believed such a tour was tacit acceptance of apartheid. He was fighting for black sportsmen and women to be given the opportunity to be chosen for Springbok teams. If they accepted the West Indian tour, he thought they would lose credibility in their fight for a unified, non-racial cricket body in South Africa. It would be a backward step after the unification of the four 'non-white' cricket bodies.

Brutus wrote a number of letters to those involved in the tour. In writing to Rashid Varachia, he criticised SACBOC for not looking towards achieving genuine Test cricket.[28] He justified the allegation by arguing that the cricket body accepted a system which 'allowed South Africa's whites [as the country's official national representatives] to play against England, Australia and New Zealand, while South Africa's blacks [simply as blacks] would play Kenya, Uganda, Guyana, Jamaica and other black nations'.[29] He was largely correct in his assessment insofar as the Government's intentions were concerned, but he missed the significance of South Africa's black cricketers playing the West Indies. The opposition was a quality side from a Test-playing member of the ICC, the body which had rejected SACBOC's earlier application for membership. The tour would pose awkward questions for cricket's unsympathetic white authorities at both the ICC and SACA.

ALAN PATON, LEARIE CONSTANTINE AND THE LINK WITH JACKIE GRANT

Brutus was prepared to do the hard work but he needed the assistance of an international figure to promote the ideals of his organisation. The person he turned to was Alan Paton, the world-famous author of *Cry the Beloved Country*. Paton accepted the position of patron when SASA was formed, and it was he who wrote the first letter in a series of communications aimed at the cancellation of the scheduled West Indies tour to South Africa in 1959.

Paton's involvement in sport was surprising but, conscious of his position, he told the inaugural meeting of SASA in 1959 that he was thought 'to have some knowledge of fair play'.[30] In this regard, he saw apartheid in sport as having harmed the very 'spirit of fair play that should underlie all sport'.[31] He was also a close friend of Jackie Grant who had captained the West Indies cricket team in the 1930s. Paton would write the foreword to Grant's autobiography, and in the course of their friendship, they would almost certainly have discussed cricket and politics. Grant's wife, Ida, joined Paton's Liberal Party and, at one stage, was invited to stand for Parliament.

Grant and Paton shared concerns about the colour question. When the former was first selected for the West Indies, he was chosen as captain of the tour to Australia and was immediately aware of the fact that he, 'as a white man, had advantages which a black man was unable to have'.[32] In March 1935, when injured and forced to leave the field during the fifth Test against England in Jamaica, Grant made an important decision in asking Learie Constantine to take over the captaincy. It was 'the first time that a non-white cricketer had captained a West Indies side' and, said Grant, 'well do I remember the smile of approval given me by George Headley'.[33]

More than twenty years later, Constantine as a cabinet minister in Trinidad, was instrumental in offering Grant the position of Director of Education, although the latter was unable to accept because he was on his way to Southern Rhodesia as a career missionary. At that stage, the National Party Government closed down Adams College in Natal where Grant had been Principal.[34] He and his wife were informed that they were 'considered to be undesirable residents of, or visitors to' South Africa.

Of greater encouragement to Grant—if he was indeed aware of it—was that Worrell was twice offered the captaincy of the West Indies. But, despite pressure to accept the responsibility, Worrell turned down offers at home against Pakistan in 1957/58 and then against India and Pakistan in their countries in 1958/59.[35] The development was not widely known, and as a consequence, the captaincy situation remained a 'potent source of social division'.[36] Although concern over the issue still persisted through 1959, there was a brief period when the controversy was overshadowed by the proposed South African tour. Grant's friends, Learie Constantine and Alan Paton, were key figures in deciding its fate.

C. L. R. JAMES, LEARIE CONSTANTINE AND THE SOUTH AFRICAN TOUR

Dennis Brutus is reported as stating: '[C. L. R.] James argued that if [Frank] Worrell had successfully captained a team in South Africa, pressure would have been put on the West Indian selectors to appoint him captain of the official Test side'.[37] This is not true: Brutus seems to have had difficulty accepting the fact that James was very much in favour of the visit to South Africa. In the course of writing about the SACBOC invitation in both *The Nation* and *Beyond the Boundary*, James did not mix the captaincy issue with that of the tour. Moreover, he had for many years shown an interest in South Africa and wrote authoritatively about matters pertaining to the country.

In South Africa, the Treason Trial had in 1958 disrupted the struggle's leadership and Robert Sobukwe chose the time to break from the ANC and form the Pan Africanist Congress (PAC). 'At stake', said Dale Slater, 'was the important question of leadership and strategy of the struggle for liberation: would the ANC's "broad church" alliance prevail, or had momentum shifted too far towards Africanism?' In Port of Spain, in response to the ANC's calls for international support, the Trinidad Waterfront Dockers Union began a boycott of South African shipping. There is evidence to suggest 'the ANC sent people to lobby Constantine to firm up the boycott' and it's quite possible, even likely that they brought up the issue of the cricket tour.[38] If it took place, it would probably be represented by the PAC as a vindication of Africanist exclusionism. Seen from this standpoint, said Slater, James and Constantine 'were not really talking about cricket at all, but were proxies for the PAC and ANC in this wider strategic debate'.[39]

James returned to the Caribbean in December 1958 to take up the editorship of *The Nation*. He did so in answer to a personal request from Eric Williams who wanted the eminent writer to build and promote the socialist People's National Movement. Not long after arriving in Trinidad, and with the tour in mind, James said it was not the first time he had questioned the ability of the West Indian cricket administration 'to understand the age in which it was living'. He referred to an earlier case of two South Africans, Roy McLean and Johnny Waite, being prepared to visit the West Indies with an invitation team. He stressed '*they were ready to break the barrier. We should have been ready to accept*'.

He believed West Indians would have taken to the Springboks: 'one hook off his face by McLean would have made him a favourite of the crowd'.[40]

In early 1959, Learie Constantine contacted James with regard to a letter he had received from Canon John Collins, Canon of St Paul's Cathedral. James published the letter in *The Nation*:

> My Dear Learie
>
> I have been asked by Alan Paton to try to persuade Worrell not to take his team to South Africa on the terms at present agreed. Alan Paton and many others who are working for better race relations in South Africa, feel that a visit by the West Indies team under such terms would seem to be an acceptance of the policy of apartheid, and would certainly be taken as such by the South African Government and the African National Congress. They believe, therefore that the visit would do great harm.
>
> If you agree with this judgement – as I do – would you very kindly do anything you feel might be useful in the matter.
>
> Yours ever
>
> J. C.

James did not agree with the argument presented by Collins but admitted it was 'not an easy question to decide'. As a consequence, he invited readers to participate in the debate that he would describe as 'wide and acute'.[41] James saw it as 'a free discussion', one in which people from different backgrounds could respond to his view which was an emphatic 'BY ALL MEANS GO'.[42] A number of letters were published in the newspaper's 'People's Forum' over a period of several weeks. James thought that the ordinary West Indians listened to and trusted his argument because they knew he was on their side.[43] Most were in favour of the tour, generally believing it supported international solidarity among African people and those of African descent. One West Indian player who was a strong candidate to go to South Africa, Andy Ganteaume, thought the 'venture could possibly open a way for bigger opportunities to the African in future'. The trip was also an education for players which 'would provide us with an opportunity for seeing things in that country at first hand'. He said the invitation had come from a recognised black cricket body and that 'while we all deplore apartheid, I don't think that by going we are subscribing to it'.[44]

L. G. Richards of Irois Forest, Trinidad, believed the West Indians were obliged to become involved in the South African struggle. 'The policy of apartheid', he said, 'is a challenge not only to the South African negro but the negroes all over the world'. The writer thought that 'the worthy, noble and courageous opponent does not side-step but accepts the challenge and proceeds to deal with it by way of counter'. He pointed to the power of the game of cricket to shape people's lives and the moral effect that it would have on 'the South African negro under the gloomy cloud of apartheid'. He suggested that the West Indian players who had 'enjoyed equality among all men' would bring 'that equality' to their South African opponents.[45]

There were opposing viewpoints as to the direction the tour captain should take. P. Philip, a member of the Hyads Club in Belmont, felt strongly that Worrell had a moral duty to make contact with the oppressed of South Africa. He cited examples whereby ministers of religion or experts in the field of medicine were expected to assist people in need. In the case of the South African cricketers, he argued, 'the call is for spiritual, social and scientific assistance. Why shouldn't [Worrell] go?'

George C. Ramdial from San Fernando was against Worrell taking on the task. He stated at the beginning of a lengthy piece that he had come to accept Worrell as 'a god and that is the truly liberal sense of my cricket ideology'. There was an acceptance that Worrell could do 'no wrong' but 'his purpose of letting his unfortunate brothers see for themselves that their own are on par with the rest of the world, could be lost in the dark clouds of racial antagonism'. The writer recognised the difficulties attached to breaking down racial barriers and feared Worrell might fail as a leader because the task was not confined to simply dictating tactics on the cricket field. If Worrell could succeed in the realm of race relations 'then by all means – go!' said the nervous Ramdial. 'But will it be that easy?' He concluded by conceding that Worrell was perhaps mortal: 'If Gandhi failed in South Africa, I cannot see how Worrell will succeed'.[46]

Constantine, who was by then Trinidad's Minister of Communications, Works and Utilities, entered the debate in *The Nation*. His main concern with the proposed tour was that it fell within the scope and influence of South Africa's racial policy. He thought it was the intention of the apartheid regime to convince 'world opinion that the negro can live a "full" life in his ghetto'. But, said Constantine, whatever good might be achieved by the cricket tour, was nullified by the government laying down certain conditions. He noted the private arrangements for transporting players and the separate seating accommodations on the grounds. Constantine saw such discrimination as emphasising the fact that 'all the restrictions operating in South Africa are placed on the negro and they affect the whites only in their relations with blacks'. He did not think that the tour would provide the suggested 'uplift both psychological and real' for South Africa's blacks, nor would 'it help them in their battle to defeat apartheid'.

With reference to attempts being made to block South Africa's participation in international sport, Constantine said it was obvious world opinion was being 'mobilised against these destroyers of the human personality'. He concluded his argument by referring to an article written by Ronald Segal, editor of the journal, *Africa South*. It claimed the anniversary of the Zulu defeat on 16 December 1838 was being used to inspire the Afrikaners once again to stand firm against an enemy determined to destroy them. Constantine called upon Worrell and his team not to 'be party to postponing the day of reckoning'.[47]

In opposing Constantine's argument, James said he was not impressed by those who opposed the tour—'Canon Collins, Alan Paton and others of that way of thought'. He hoped Constantine would not mind if he said that they were 'political persons' of a type he knew well. He wrote, 'They are dominated by opposition to the South African government and apartheid. That struggle they want to keep pure'. Then, to reinforce his argument he opined, 'They are holding high a banner of principle. This means more to them than the living struggle of living people'.[48]

James thought the tour would change South Africa by providing both its black and white populations with a new experience, something out of the ordinary for a country ravaged by apartheid. 'With the subtle historical imagination of a dialectician', explained Dale Slater, it was possible for James to project the tour 'as a lever to shift entrenched attitudes … a union of Africa and Diaspora [that] would revolutionise relations not only of white to black but of blacks to themselves and hence also to whites'.[49] African cricketers, said James, were 'stifling in a prison', a situation they wanted to escape. The tour, he argued, would produce changes in the consciousness of the people and enable them to perceive the world differently.

Out of this experience, James also recognised advantages that would accrue for black cricketers to demonstrate their talents, play cricket at the highest standard and provide effective models that would ensure the next generation operated with a new set of givens, not least the new-found status of playing against a Test nation. 'They want to know exactly how good they are', said James; 'they want to make contact with Test cricketers, so that they and the world may judge. For me, here as everywhere else, that is what comes first'. He thought it was 'to assume a heavy responsibility to deny this desire on their part'.

The extent to which the tour might have transformed South Africa is of course debatable in the light of the Government's strength and the barriers it was able to establish. It would nevertheless have forced people to focus on South Africa, its cricket and apartheid's contradictions. '[The tour] has not yet taken place', said James, 'and look at the stir it has created. The whole world is talking about it'. He knew that the publicity could only favour the oppressed. 'People say the South African government is in favour of it. Are they?'[50] James believed the apartheid government had been forced to agree to the tour but had then laid down rigorous apartheid conditions in the hope that it would be cancelled.

He spelt out his reasoned argument in *The Nation*, later repeating his concern in *Beyond a Boundary* where he said 'apartheid sought the isolation of the Africans not only from whites but from free blacks'. After the tour had been cancelled he was able to stress more forcefully 'there might have been incidents. So much the better'.[51] It was a tour that had the potential to expose the numerous disparities that prevailed in a racist system, thereby presenting the people with opportunities and the government with a new challenge in weakened circumstances.

James did not differ from Brutus in that he also wanted Africans to be recognised as candidates for an 'All South Africa' team. He hoped 'to see an African make a century in the first Test, a bowler bowl Sobers and Kanhai for 0 in the same over ... It will be for a good cause'. He thought the cricket would 'hit the headlines in Pakistan, in England, in Australia, in the West Indies, and in South Africa too'. His aim was clear: 'Think of what it will mean to the African masses, their pride, their joy, their contact with the world outside, and their anger at the first proof, before the whole world, of the shameful suppression to which they are subjected ... Will this strengthen apartheid?'

James concluded that the South African Government would live to curse the day that a West Indian side toured the country. It was 'a political bombshell ... I want it to go on exploding and exploding. The only people who can be hurt are the South African jailers ... My personal belief is that they will try to stop the tour without coming out openly and saying so'.[52]

THE SOUTH AFRICAN DEBATE

Significant support for the tour came from a leading African sportswriter, Theo Mtembu. In an article in the *Golden City Post*, Mtembu—the sports editor—reacted sharply to news that Brutus had written to Worrell in protest against the tour. 'The SA Cricket Board of Control', said Mtembu, 'is the only truly national body in South Africa. It has gone a long way to stamp out racialism in cricket'. He believed SASA fared poorly in comparison and had no right to pass judgement on the activities of the cricketers. Whilst accepting there was 'a crying need for a coordinating body in South African non-white sport', Mtembu was critical of the manner in which Brutus had formed his new organisation. He wrote:

> The undignified haste with which the Association was brought into being, without giving the national bodies time to ponder its aims and objectives, its hopes and aspirations, its policies and politics, betrays the motives of its prime-movers. Is it not obvious, then, that the indirect representation at the conference – the inaugural meeting of SASA – reflects total disinterestedness on the part of the major national bodies?[53]

Mtembu, who would in later years be honoured for his contribution to non-racial sport by being the recipient of the President's Award (Silver) from Nelson Mandela, pointed out that cricket and rugby were not represented at the conference whilst 'most of the bodies who affiliated at the inaugural meeting of SASA can hardly claim to be national in character and/or their scope of activity while others exist on paper only'. He was forthright in his comments and highlighted his criticism of the recent SASA conference with the question: '*Does it not strike you to note that of the 29 delegates present, 24 were Natal Indians?*' He went further in his examination of the 'architects of the Sports Association' by declaring that nineteen had 'entrenched themselves by electing each other into the position of vice-president'.

The Natalians were 'the only SA Indian Cricket Union unit to oppose the tour'.[54] They were also backed by *Indian Opinion* which drew attention to the fact that black sportsmen had 'a somewhat bitter choice' between 'the opportunity of wider world recognition' and being able 'to refuse to play Verwoerd's game'.[55]

In Johannesburg, the *Sunday Times* entered the debate by featuring a discussion between two of the country's best-known white sport journalists: Richard 'Dick' Whitington, a former South Australian batsman, who was accompanied by Viv Granger, better known for his involvement in soccer.[56] Whitington appeared the most comfortable, not least because he was a relatively well-travelled cricket writer who had been to the West Indies. He thought that white cricket-lovers of Johannesburg were hoping that the tour would take place. He said that they wanted 'to stage a match between the best white cricketers of South Africa and Frank Worrell, Everton Weekes and company …. Why? Simply because they want South Africa to see the greatest stroke players that cricket owns today'.[57]

As Worrell was thought in some quarters to have been promised multiracial fixtures and the *Sunday Times* believed whites would become involved, it seemed as if government policy was not clearly understood. Interracial fixtures had and would continue to be played in South Africa, but they were rare events invariably accompanied by an element of risk. There again, speculation also existed as to where the team would stay. 'I even know', announced Whitington, 'that several leading cricket "barons" in Johannesburg are prepared to have Worrell and his men stay in their homes, so that unfortunate accidents will not occur'. Then, drawing upon references to the cricket he had seen in the West Indies, Whitington said he could 'assure whites that they will find no finer or more charming gentlemen than Frank Worrell and Everton Weekes'.

Whitington's opening remarks contrasted with those of Granger, whose comments might well have reflected the mood of white South African sports followers at that time. Whilst claiming to agree with his fellow journalist that the tour should take place at the end of the year, Granger thought it necessary to emphasise that 'if there is any trouble next season, it will come from the blacks – not from the whites'. It bothered him that 'the blacks are not quite ready yet for full development', before diplomatically conceding, 'They're on the way ….'.

Whitington made a half-hearted attempt to distance himself from his colleague's remarks at that juncture of the debate. 'Having watched the antics and behaviour of some of *your* coloured enclosures at cricket matches', he told Granger, 'I think you are possibly right'. But he was quick to address such racial bias by declaring he had 'mixed with coloured crowds in the West Indies and they have been as sporting crowds as I've seen in the world'. He drove home his point by adding, 'I believe it is *your* colour prejudice that causes *your* coloured spectators to forget sportsmanship and make them back visiting teams, instead of their own South African sides'.

Granger shrugged off Whitington's argument by maintaining that such an attitude did not help the black cause. He believed that most people put their support of opposition sides down 'to a lack of appreciation of the finer points of sport' and that unless the West Indies 'met one or two white teams … the tour will be a horrible flop'. He argued that 'the coloureds simply haven't had the experience to cope with players like Worrell and Weekes'.

Whitington agreed before concluding: 'But let's have the West Indies … and give the darkies of this country a chance to prove that they are sportsmen'.[58]

WHAT NEXT FOR SOUTH AFRICA?

The tour did not take place. Aviston D. Downes, a lecturer at the University of the West Indies, referred to Worrell's letter to Brutus which stated 'this tour will be of inestimable benefit to the coloured people', before noting the West Indian captain and his Board made a 'cautious decision to call off the tour'.[59] Tennant lists those who tried to dissuade Worrell from touring but came to the conclusion that 'the strictures of [Vic] Lewis, who had been in South Africa with his band, made more of an impression'. *The Independent* described Lewis as 'a man driven compulsively to make claims that seemed like braggadocio but often, when checked out, turned out to be true'. In the case of Worrell, the band leader recalled: 'I think when Frank had heard several stories of mine, he was persuaded not to go. The country was in a mess when I was there …'.[60]

Brutus said it took SASA almost a year to turn opinion against the visit by Worrell's team. Through pressure, perseverance and threats, he eventually forced SACBOC to succumb to his demands. He paid tribute to 'the future Rivonia trialist, Ahmed Kathrada [who] came to me and promised that the ANC would call out its Youth League to take part in pitch invasions if the tour was allowed to go ahead'.[61] He later put forward the idea that Essop Pahad, a minister in Thabo Mbeki's post-apartheid cabinet, had said 'if the West Indies team comes we're going to set the stadium on fire'.[62] Jassat claimed Nelson Mandela, Walter Sisulu and Dr. A. B. Kazi of the Indian Congress had visited and voiced opposition but that he remained 'determined to show off the talented black players to the world'.[63]

Brutus admitted the decision to cancel the tour 'not only caused unhappiness among many cricketers and officials in South Africa', but was also 'bitterly criticised in some significant quarters in the West Indies'.[64] At a time when they had so little going for them anyway, black South African cricketers were forced to suffer again through sport being exploited for political purposes. D'Oliveira wrote of 'the heartbreak of the cancellation of the West Indies tour to South Africa. ... [it] so upset me that I decided to finish with cricket'. He was of the opinion that if black politicians 'were to deny teams from the West Indies, India or Pakistan the chance to come to South Africa, then there was no point in devoting my life to the game'.[65]

D'Oliveira did, of course, play on and ultimately achieved remarkable success, but stressed that he was never 'able to understand the political argument which cancelled Sir Frank Worrell's 1959 tour'. He reasoned: 'Even if the coloured politicians were right in saying that it would have appeared to condone the abhorrent policy of apartheid, their attitude still denied to the coloured Africans contact and communication with people from another country'. D'Oliveira said he found it hard to understand who had 'gained anything by denying this advancement'.[66]

Comment from those involved in the game at that time generally reflected disappointment in the cancellation of the tour. The official 'non-white' cricket annual described the development as 'a sad blow for South African cricket'. The captain of the Springbok cricket team during the latter part of the 1950s, Clive van Ryneveld, said that the proposed tour had raised issues with regard to black cricket 'in a significant way. It was a pity that it didn't go ahead; it would have brought our coloured cricketers to the attention of white cricketers and the white public'.[67]

Historian, Bruce Murray, wrote of black cricket going 'into a shallow decline in the 1960s'.[68] International contact had ended and there was no alternative plan. Jassat went to India, where he was told an invitation would be forwarded to SACBOC, and Pakistan, where it was suggested that a team be entered into an associate members' tournament with the then Ceylon, Canada and Holland.[69] On his return, he discovered the SACBOC committee was unwilling to take on the politicians again. Moreover, black cricketers would soon discover that it was necessary for them to travel overseas if they were to have a chance of succeeding at the game. Obviously that would weaken the playing strength within South Africa. 'It is paradoxical', wrote Oborne, 'that Dennis Brutus's first major achievement was not to secure, but to deny, black cricketers the opportunity to play in an international sporting contest. Even today, with the benefit of hindsight, the issue does not appear clear-cut'.[70]

Brutus proceeded to confront SACA about their 1960 tour to England. He aimed to have non-white players chosen for the team and received written support from the Campaign Against Race Discrimination in Sport, stating that it knew 'of at least two Non-European cricketers in the Union who are first rate'. In the context of selecting a team for an overseas tour, it was a naïve statement in that it lacked supporting evidence such as a significant innings that D'Oliveira might well have played against the West Indies. But the tour did not happen; mixed trials were not permissible; and white cricket officials could with justification ignore the statistics of matches in Kenya some eighteen months earlier. It was obviously a tragic situation because D'Oliveira would have been a most exciting acquisition for an ordinary team.

Brutus received little joy from the white officials he met: 'Whereas SACBOC had conceded', wrote Murray, 'SACA was totally dismissive'. It could be argued that Brutus did not adequately research developments in the country's cricket. His threat that he might persuade the MCC to take action against South Africa invited a 'Go ahead and try' response from Arthur Coy, the president of SACA.[71] The tour went ahead with an anticipated boycott amounting to little more than the cricketers being greeted by pickets at the airport and their London hotel. It would take time for the sports boycott to make an impression and in an active year for white South Africans, their rugby side entertained Scotland and the All Blacks and then spent four months in Britain, Ireland and France, whilst an all-white team was sent to the Olympic Games. Pete Suzman, vice-chairman of the South African Olympic and British Empire Games Association, was unsuccessful in his bid to have the coloured weightlifter, Precious McKenzie, included in the Olympic team. 'One black sportsman in the march-past at Rome', he had informed the committee, 'can do more for South Africa than all else'.[72]

The Sharpeville massacre on 21 March 1960 dramatically affected international opinion and was instrumental in generating a campaign to isolate South Africa that would have the unwavering support of newly independent African countries. The Anti-Apartheid Movement, which had been promoting a 'consumer boycott', committed itself to campaigning for the total isolation of apartheid South Africa. Its secretary, Abdul Minty, worked closely with Brutus in orchestrating a sports boycott. On 7 October 1962 at the initiative of SASA, the South African Non-Racial Olympic Committee (SAN-ROC) was formed, with the new organisation drawing attention to the first 'Fundamental Principle' of the Olympic Games which prohibited discrimination 'against any country or person on grounds of race, religion or political affiliations'.[73] South Africa was subsequently barred from the Tokyo 1964 Olympic Games, the year the Football Association of South Africa was suspended by FIFA. The International Olympic Committee was still prepared to read-mit South Africa to the 1968 Mexico City Games, but the invitation was withdrawn in the face of a threatened boycott by forty countries.

During this period, the white South African cricket team contin-ued to play against England, Australia and New Zealand. It would take D'Oliveira's selection for England to turn cricket opinion against his country of birth and allow the boycott movement to gather in breadth and impetus. Even then D'Oliveira found it difficult to comprehend the stance that Brutus and the Anti-Apartheid Movement continued to take with regard to the black cricketers in South Africa. More than once they endeavoured to prevent him from returning home to coach non-white players. SAN-ROC argued that he should 'not coach only the non-whites because that would be showing public approval of the South African government, who were denying the non-whites contact with the white cricketer'. D'Oliveira was adamant that he would not accept a sit-uation whereby young men, who had been given hope by what he had achieved, should be 'denied *by their own people* the means to help them achieve the same thing'.[74]

Coloured South Africans would prove they were good cricket-ers, perhaps the hard way because of the intervention of Brutus. 'Dik' Abed believed D'Oliveira opened doors for many of his former team-mates: 'He proved that cricketers from our communities could com-pete with the best in the world – and more than hold their own'.[75] John Arlott agreed: 'Before him, the non-white cricket of his country was barely regarded. Now because of him, it is recognised as a source of talent ...'.[76] A number of players did travel to England and performed with varying success in league cricket. Dale Slater records in an article in the *Picador Book of Cricket* that 'Dik' Abed, Cecil Abrahams, John Neethling, Desmond February, Rushdi Magiet, Owen Williams and Dik's brother, Goolam participated in the Lancashire League. Although D'Oliveira saw Dik Abed as 'a potential Test player', Slater commented that it was not so easy for those who followed the 'trailblazer' ... as 'the romance had faded with the novelty'.[77]

WHAT NEXT?—WEST INDIANS

Caribbean and African territories shared a period of de-colonisation and great possibilities despite pessimism voiced by some metropolitan and imperialist critics. James embraced pan-Africanism and saw cricket as 'not simply a building block for empire but also a vehicle for forging an anti-imperialist consciousness'.[78] Assisting South Africa's black cricketers might well have been a missed opportunity in 1959 but West Indian cricketers were conscious of their African origins and their curiosity had been aroused by the discourse that had taken place. Although a tour to South Africa was ruled out, Rhodesia posed an interesting option. Jackie Grant had settled there in the late 1950s happy that the Central African Federation was in existence with a policy of 'partnership' between races.[79] Cricket-wise, Rhodesia could offer opposition of a good standard as the national team played in the Currie Cup and fielded a number of players who were or were about to become Springboks.

A former West Indian captain, Gerry Gomez, said their cricketers had no objection to playing in southern Africa at that time. The team was invited to Rhodesia in 1960/61 after their successful tour of Australia, but then it was discovered that some players had to return to England because of county and league commitments. 'Otherwise', said Gomez, 'we would certainly have gone'.[80] With the Southern Rhodesian Government publicising the racial character of its sport, a cricket journalist, Ron Roberts, seized the opportunity to arrange a tour in February–March 1962. He selected a star-studded team that included two West Indian players who had earlier hoped to visit South Africa—Everton Weekes and Sonny Ramadhin—as well as Basil D'Oliveira and leading cricketers from India, Pakistan, Australia and England. It was the first time black cricketers had been allowed to play first-class cricket in southern Africa.[81]

The Queens Sports Club, Bulawayo, refused the cricket authorities permission to use their facilities but the Showground provided a sufficiently good wicket. At the end of a thrilling contest in which runs flowed freely, the Commonwealth XI secured victory over Rhodesia by six wickets with just five minutes of scheduled play remaining. On his thirty-seventh birthday, Everton Weekes won the game 'with a glorious straight drive off [Joe] Partridge for four'. Splashed across the sports page of the *Bulawayo Chronicle* was the headline, 'BIRTHDAY BOY A WINNER', with the newspaper recording that 'one had the unique sight of seeing a former West Indian star walk straight across to former South African opening bat Tony Pithey and shake hands on the field'.[82]

The euphoria of the moment was dampened somewhat by a front-page story in the next edition of the newspaper. Weekes was refused a drink at the Midlands Hotel, Gwelo, on his way to the tour party's fixture at Que Que. It was mistakenly thought that he was a 'freedom sitter'.[83] According to Roberts in a letter to his friend, E. W. Swanton, there were 'a few incidents of Europeans refusing to serve our non-Europeans – Ramadhin a hair-cut, Weekes a drink – but these little set-backs have been accepted philosophically'.[84] They were, nevertheless, both a reminder that Rhodesia had some way to go in order to fulfil its 'partnership' ideal and an indication of the sort of embarrassing moments that James had envisaged happening in South Africa if the 1959 tour had taken place.

Oborne, who was reliant on D'Oliveira's account, thought that Roberts made a 'potentially catastrophic mistake' in taking a tour to Rhodesia. It is not clear whether Oborne was aware that Roberts arranged a second tour in which he included West Indians, Wesley Hall, Rohan Kanhai and Chester Watson, alongside D'Oliveira and players from India, Pakistan, England and South Africa. With reference to the latter trip, D'Oliveira said that Kanhai was upset by incidents and wanted to fly home, but 'by this time, it was getting laughable, so Rohan decided to see the funny side of it and called off his decision'.[85] D'Oliveira was conscious of the way everyone reacted and noted: 'It was particularly difficult for the West Indies players who had never suffered this form of segregation'.[86]

When Barbados became independent in 1966, they (along with Guyana) agreed to join international action against links with South Africa. But the Barbadians were also keen to compare respective cricket strengths, and in March 1967, they arranged to host a Rest of the World cricket team that included the Pollock brothers and Colin Bland. Trevor Marshall, a lecturer in History at the Barbados Community College, said the invitation to the South Africans offended the island's Caribbean neighbours and 'after strong protests from the Barbados Workers Union and the People's Progressive Party (a small Marxist party), the invitation was withdrawn'.[87]

Rothmans optimistically hoped to capitalise on the interest that existed in the two most exciting teams on the international stage by sponsoring two Tests between them in England in 1968. The West

Indies Cricket Board of Control objected but their captain, Garry Sobers—another West Indian who would have toured South Africa in 1959—visited Rhodesia in September 1970 for an internationally publicised double-wicket competition. On his arrival, Asian well-wishers placed a garland of red and white flowers around his neck, and at the end of the weekend's cricket, the mixed crowd of 7000 fans 'gave him a standing ovation and sang "For he's a jolly good fellow"'. By coincidence, one of the West Indian prime ministers was in Gambia talking to their leader who complained: 'How can we be blood brothers when one of your greatest ambassadors is having tea with Ian Smith and telling the world how good he is?' When Sobers returned to Barbados a few days later he was informed, he 'would not be welcomed in various of our islands'. The politicians sought to assert themselves, beginning with Frank Walcott, general secretary of the Barbados Workers' Union. 'He was extremely critical', wrote Sobers, '... it gave him the sort of national and international platform he had never before experienced'. Forbes Burnham followed, then Michael Manley (Fig. 10.1).

Sobers was made aware of the extent to which political opinion on southern Africa had hardened. Events of the 1960s had seen the region become world sport's pariah. 'For two and a half months', said Sobers of

Fig. 10.1   Garry Sobers chats to the Prime Minister of Rhodesia, Ian Smith, during his controversial appearance at the Mashonaland Cricket Association's double-wicket competition at the Police Ground, Salisbury in 1970. They are flanked by cricket officials, Alwyn Pichanick and Jock Holden

his ordeal, 'it was front-page news, back-page news and the main topic for radio phone-ins … it could have carried on because I did not feel that it warranted an apology from me'. The islands were divided as Sobers had his supporters, notably his Prime Minister, Errol Barrow, who said he would write a letter to the president of the Guyana Cricket Board. It produced 'a happy compromise', explained Sobers, as 'it appeared others were keener to extricate themselves from this mess than I was!' Jamaica's soon-to-be prime minister, Michael Manley, probably summed up the situation best when he told Sobers 'he was so sorry … the other party were making gain from the situation so he had to use it too'.[88]

CONCLUSION

Much had happened since Canon John Collins sent off a letter to say that a tour by the West Indies cricket team to South Africa in 1959 'would do great harm'. That the tour should be cancelled had ramifications for black cricket, challenged the structure of apartheid and served as a starting point for Brutus' fledgling Anti-Apartheid Movement. For many years thereafter, Collins 'kept the exiled SAN-ROC organisation in London in pocket with an annual subsidy of eventually £12,000'.[89] In turn, SAN-ROC was able to coordinate a successful boycott at international level. and by 1970, the ruling bodies of over twenty sports, including the IOC and FIFA, had expelled South Africa.[90] The same year, the 'Stop The Seventy Tour' campaign contributed to cricket's isolation.

There were intermittent attempts by South Africa's cricket authorities to create opportunities to play international cricket. In 1977, Rashid Varachia, an organiser of the West Indies tour in 1959, aimed 'to break our isolation and re-enter the international arena' through merging SACBOC with SACA and the S.A. African Cricket Board to form the South African Cricket Union (SACU).[91] However, the desire to establish 'normal' cricket was short-lived, countered by Hassan Howa's South African Cricket Board and the slogan 'no normal sport in an abnormal society'. Howa's organisation affiliated to the South African Council on Sport (SACOS) which had formed a partnership with SAN-ROC and adopted a policy of non-collaboration towards those involved in racist sport.

West Indian 'rebel' teams visited South Africa as SACU endeavoured to combat isolation. The Caribbean players earned 'life bans', whilst the tours evoked comparisons with the cancelled 1959 venture.

Commentator, Tony Cozier, pointed out that 'in Barbados, the majority view, expressed in letters to the press and on radio call-in programmes, was that the players were professionals with the right to earn a living wherever they could'. But he also singled out disparities that James had anticipated, notably the ejection of Colin Croft from the 'whites only' section of a train out of Johannesburg.[92] The *Daily News* (Natal) chose to publish an interview with 'Checker' Jassat who thought the 'rebel' tours were 'wrong and immoral', but that circumstances were different from the project in which he had been involved. He believed that if Worrell's team had toured, it 'might have changed white attitudes earlier and provided incentives to black players'.[93]

With apartheid crumbling in the 1980s, pressure grew for fundamental change and the perception emerged that SACOS lacked a broad base and was unable to mobilise support from within the townships. There was also criticism of the organisation's rigid policies, not least the use of the double standards resolution and the way it was used against oppressed people. 'The sole objective of the international community's boycott was to integrate South African sport', wrote sports historian, Douglas Booth, but 'SACOS turned the boycott into a strategy against apartheid *per se*'.[94] Mluleki George, a serving member, said their approach was adversely affecting hopes of normalising sport in South Africa: 'We started the debate within SACOS in 1984 ... We had to do something to normalise sport. SACOS policy meant that it did not come out with any position. You went to a meeting, condemned apartheid and waited for the next meeting. There was no real drive to do something'.[95]

'Black sports officials with the support of the ANC', wrote John Nauright, 'sought to place sport at the forefront of negotiations for non-racial society in the late 1980s ...'.[96] A cultural desk was established by the ANC in Lusaka, with Barbara Masekela taking on a position that included overseeing sport. She recalled: 'We started to rethink our tactics. The boycott had also disadvantaged the oppressed. It therefore became necessary to prepare people inside South Africa to cope with the post-liberation period'.[97] The decision was taken in May 1987 by the ANC president, Oliver Tambo, in his Canon Collins Memorial Lecture:

Indeed the moment is upon us when we shall have to deal with alternative structures that our people have created and are creating through struggle and sacrifice as the genuine representatives of these masses in all fields of human activity. Not only should these not be boycotted, but more, they should be supported, encouraged and treated as the democratic counterparts within South Africa of similar institutions and organisations internationally ...[98]

The National Sports Congress—led by Mluleki George and 'dubbed the ANC in tracksuits'[99]—became the most powerful of the non-racial movements and paved the way for South Africa's return to Test cricket in April, 1992 when they played against the West Indies at Bridgetown, Barbados. The return to international sport—and particularly the Barcelona 1992 Olympic Games—did not meet with the approval of Dennis Brutus who had returned to South Africa and 'was marginalised because of his identification with SACOS, whose patron he had become'.[100] Steve Tshwete, the leading figure in the sports unity negotiations, warned Brutus that 'he must not think in terms of imposing his own ideas because there are people who have been working here who are better acquainted with the situation ... He would do well to listen to them'.[101]

Today, South Africa's cricketers of colour are recognised as being among the best in the world. Many more might have become household names if it had not been for the discriminatory policies of successive governments since the 1890s. They might also have made an impression in 1959 if the tour had not been sacrificed because it conformed to the sporting structure imposed by the apartheid system. Was Brutus too impulsive, too keen to create an impact for his new organisation? One does not doubt his motives in opposing the inequalities perpetrated by the policy of apartheid. And he has never suggested that the cancellation was a mistake; he simply stated that he and James 'were fighting racism, but coming from different angles'.[102]

Brutus later wrote that he was 'at a conference in Havana with the intellectuals of the world ... CLR was hopping mad at me. We disagreed instantly, and in fact we never managed to agree'.[103]

James never changed his mind about a tour in which 'a pitiless light would have been thrown on the irrationality and stupidity of apartheid'. He made this clear in his celebrated *Beyond a Boundary*, stating: 'From the beginning I was certain that, whatever the South African government might say, it did not want this tour. Racialists do not ever want the eyes of the world on their crimes'.[104]

Notes

1. M. Allie, *More Than a Game: History of the Western Province Cricket Board 1959–1991* (Cape Town: The Western Province Cricket Association, 2000), 17.
2. K. Sandiford and B. Stoddart, *The Imperial Game: Cricket, Culture and Society* (Manchester: Manchester University Press, 1998), 100.
3. C. Cowdrey, *MCC: The Autobiography of a Cricketer* (London: Hodder and Stoughton, 1976), 111.
4. J. Laker, *Over to Me* (London: Frederick Muller, 1961), 90–91.
5. B. D'Oliveira, *The D'Oliveira Affair* (London: Collins, 1969), 39.
6. P. Oborne, *Basil D'Oliveira: Cricket and Conspiracy; The Untold Story* (London, Time Warner Books, 2006), 41.
7. D'Oliveira, *The D'Oliveira Affair*, 33–34.
8. Ibid, 39–40.
9. D'Oliveira, *The D'Oliveira Affair*, 36.
10. *Daily Gleaner*, 25 November 1958 and 7 January 1959.
11. I. Tennant, *Frank Worrell: A Biography* (Cambridge: Lutterworth Press, 1987), 47.
12. Interview with Ameen Akhalwaya, *The Daily News*, 14 February 1983.
13. Tennant, *Frank Worrell*, 36.
14. Ibid, 47. L. Alfred (*Mail and Guardian*, 19 December 2014) notes that a Fordsburg (Johannesburg) tailor made up the tie, blazer badge and bow tie.
15. *Rhodesia Herald*, 24 November 1958.
16. Allie, *More Than a Game*, 18.
17. *Daily Gleaner*, 25 November 1958.
18. B. D'Oliveira, *Time to Declare: An Autobiography* (London: J. M. Dent and Sons, 1980), 5.
19. Oborne, *Basil D'Oliveira: Cricket and Conspiracy*, 58.
20. P. Alegi, The 17th Alan Paton Memorial Lecture, *Soccer and Human Rights: Chief Luthuli, Alan Paton, Dennis Brutus and the 2010 World Cup*, University of Kwazulu-Natal, Pietermaritzburg Campus, 14 May 2010.
21. *New York Times*, 2 January 2010.
22. *Die Burger*, 27 June 1956.
23. J. Gemmell, *The Politics of South African Cricket* (London: Routledge, 2004), 90.
24. C. McLuckie and P. Colbert (eds.), *Critical Perspectives on Dennis Brutus* (Colorado Springs: Three Continents Press, 1995), 7.
25. R. Vigne, 'Dennis Brutus: Activist Whose Efforts Helped Bring About the End of Apartheid' in *The Independent*, 1 January 2010.

26. *The Leader*, 15 May 1959.
27. T. Huddleston, *Naught for Your Comfort* (New York: Doubleday, 1956), 197–99.
28. Dennis Brutus to Rashid Varachia, 28 February 1959, in the Brutus Papers, Borthwick Institute, University of York.
29. Allie, *More Than a Game*, 19.
30. See Peter Alegi, The 17th Alan Paton Memorial Lecture.
31. Alan Paton: keynote address at the inaugural meeting of the SA Sports Association at the Tamil Vedic Hall, Carlisle Street, Durban in 1959.
32. J. Grant, *Jack Grant's Story: Educator, Cricketer, Missionary* (Guildford: Lutterworth Press, 1980), 30–31.
33. Ibid, 179–80.
34. Ibid, 111. Adams College, opened in 1853, was the second-oldest school in South Africa to educate Africans.
35. Tennant, *Frank Worrell*, 49. Worrell placed the completion of his studies before the captaincy.
36. G. Trevelyn referred to it as such in the *English Social History* (London: Longmans, 1946), 246.
37. Allie, *More Than a Game*, 19–20.
38. Correspondence with Dale Slater; M. O'Callaghan, 'Mandela the Extraordinary', *Africa Speaks*, 16 December 2013.
39. Correspondence with Dale Slater.
40. C. James, *Beyond a Boundary* (London: Serpent's Tail, 1994), 236–37.
41. James, *Beyond a Boundary*, 236–37.
42. *The Nation*, 28 February 1959.
43. James, *Beyond a Boundary*, 237.
44. Ganteaume, who scored 112 in his only Test innings, produced his auto-biography, *My Story: The Other Side of the Coin*, in 2007. In it, he is critical of 'the colonial cricket establishment'.
45. *The Nation*, 27 March 1959.
46. Ibid., 20 March 1959.
47. Ibid., 24 April 1959.
48. Ibid., 15 May 1959; C. James, *Cricket* (London: Allison & Busby, 1986), 89–90.
49. Correspondence with Dale Slater.
50. *The Nation*, 15 May 1959; James, *Cricket*, 89.
51. James, *Beyond a Boundary*, 237.
52. *The Nation*, 15 May 1959; James, *Cricket*, 89–90
53. *Golden City Post*, 8 February 1959.
54. A. Desai, V. Padayachee, K. Reddy, and G. Vahed, *Blacks in Whites: A Century of Cricket Struggles in Kwazulu-Natal* (Pietermaritzburg: University of Natal Press, 2002), 221.

55. *Indian Opinion*, 19 June 1959.
56. Granger is the author of *The World Game Comes to South Africa* (Cape Town: Howard Timmins, 1961).
57. *Sunday Times*, 15 March 1959.
58. Ibid.
59. A. Downes, 'Forging Africa-Caribbean Solidarity Within the Commonwealth? Sport and Diplomacy During the Anti-Apartheid Campaign' in H. L. Dichter and A. L. John (eds.), *Diplomatic Games: Sport, Statecraft and International Relations Since 1945* (Lexington, KT: University Press of Kentucky, 2014), 122.
60. Tennant, *Frank Worrell*, 47; *The Independent*, 25 February 2009.
61. Allie, *More Than a Game*, 19.
62. L. Sustar and A. Karim (eds.), *Poetry and Protest: A Dennis Brutus Reader* (Chicago: Haymarket Books, 2006), 130–31.
63. *The Daily News*, 15 February 1983.
64. Allie, *More Than a Game*, 19.
65. D'Oliveira, *The D'Oliveira Affair*, 40.
66. Ibid., 38.
67. Clive van Ryneveld to author, 12 October, 2012.
68. B. Murray and C. Merrett, *Caught Behind: Race and Politics in Springbok Cricket* (Johannesburg and Pietermaritzburg: Wits University Press and University of KwaZulu-Natal Press), 86.
69. *The Daily News*, 15 February 1983.
70. Oborne, *Basil D'Oliveira*, 58.
71. Murray and Merrett, *Caught Behind*, 74.
72. A. Joubert (ed.), *The History of Inter-Varsity Sport in South Africa: Looking Back with Pete Suzman* (Johannesburg: SA Universities Athletics Association, 1985), 77.
73. *The Olympic Games: Fundamental Principles, Rules and Regulations* (Lausanne: IOC, 1962), 9.
74. D'Oliveira, *The D'Oliveira Affair*, 38–39.
75. Allie, *More Than a Game*, 55–56.
76. B. D'Oliveira, *D'Oliveira: An Autobiography* (London: Sportsmans Book Club, 1969), 14.
77. D. Slater, 'Abed and Apartheid' in Ramachandra Guha (ed.), *The Picador Book of Cricket* (Witney: Past Times, 2002), 268–73.
78. K. Malik, Book Review: F. Dhondy, 'C. L. R. James: The Caribbean and World Revolution', *New Statesman*, 30 July 2001.
79. The Federation of Rhodesia and Nyasaland—also known as the Central African Federation—existed from 1953 to 1963.
80. *Rhodesia Herald*, 15 September 1970.

81. The work of Krish Reddy and André Odendaal in recent years has attended to 'statistical injustices' with regarded to matches played outside the whites-only SACA.
82. *Bulawayo Chronicle*, 27 February 1962.
83. Ibid., 28 February 1962.
84. Ron Roberts letter, 'Missionary at Work' in E. Swanton, *As I Said at the Time: A Lifetime of Cricket* (London: Unwin Paperbacks, 1986), 492–93.
85. D'Oliveira, *Time to Declare*, 20. An intriguing development occurred when Kanhai helped Transvaal to their only first-class SACBOC title in 1974/75. He would depart in unfortunate circumstances, when he refused to continue batting on a dangerous wicket. After his appeal to the umpires was turned down, he left the field and, on this occasion, carried out his threat to go home by flying to London the same evening (Allie, *More Than a Game*, 101).
86. D'Oliveira, *D'Oliveira Affair*, 68.
87. T. Marshall, 'The Anti-Apartheid Movement in the Caribbean' in A. G. Cobley and A. Thompson (eds.), *The African-Caribbean Connection: Historical and Cultural Perspectives* (Bridgetown: University of the West Indies, 1990), 102–03. Jon Gemmell notes that the sponsors, Banks Breweries, attributed the withdrawal of invitations to a statement that South Africa's Minister of the Interior, Peter le Roux, had made with regard to D'Oliveira (Gemmell, *The Politics of South African Cricket*, 147).
88. G. Sobers, *Garry Sobers: My Autobiography* (London: Headline Book Publishing, 2002), 226–30; *Rhodesia Herald*, 14 September 1970.
89. D. Herbstein, *White Lies: Canon Collins and the Secret War Against Apartheid* (Cape Town: HSRC Press, 2004), 155.
90. R. Nixon, 'Apartheid on the Run: The South African Sports Boycott' in *Transition* (University of Indiana Press), No. 58 (1992), 66–68.
91. Murray and Merrett, *Caught Behind*, 180.
92. T. Cozier, 'Forgotten Men', *SA Cricket*, June–August (2013), 117–18.
93. *The Daily News*, 15 February 1983.
94. D. Booth, 'The South African Council on Sport and the Political Antimonies of the Sports Boycott', *Journal of Southern African Studies*, 23, 1, March (1997), 54.
95. Mluleki George to author 17 February 2000; M. Bose, *Sporting Colours: Sport and Politics in South Africa* (London: Robson Books, 1994), 158.
96. J. Nauright, *Sport, Cultures and Identities in South Africa* (London: Leicester University Press, 1997), 156.
97. Barbara Masekela to author, 3 February 2000.
98. Canon Collins Memorial Lecture, May 1987.
99. Mthobi Tyamzashe, NSC secretary, to author, 18 November 1999.

100. *The Telegraph*, 5 March 2010.
101. William C. Rhoden, 'Brutus Returns to the Scene of His Crimes Against Racism' in *The New York Times*, 12 May 1991.
102. Allie, *More Than a Game*, 20.
103. Sustar and Karim, *Poetry and Protest*, 131.
104. James, *Beyond a Boundary*, 237.

CHAPTER 11

The D'Oliveira Affair: The End of an Era

Bruce Murray

INTRODUCTION

The most significant event in South African cricket in the period covered by this volume was undoubtedly the D'Oliveira Affair of 1968, when John Vorster's National Party Government refused to allow Basil D'Oliveira, the South African-born coloured cricketer who played for England, to tour South Africa with the MCC team.[1] That refusal led not only to the cancellation of the MCC tour but ultimately to South Africa's exclusion from all Test match cricket for some 22 years. The crass racism and blatant political interventionism of Vorster's ban on D'Oliveira caused outrage in Britain, galvanising opposition to apartheid in sport and enabling anti-apartheid activists to mobilise the formidable militant opposition to the projected 1970 tour by South Africa to England that forced its cancellation. Protest from below, including the threat to physically disrupt games, likewise forced the cancellation of the 1971/72 South African tour of Australia, and with that secured South Africa's effective expulsion from Test cricket. This represented a major landmark in the campaign to impose a sports boycott on apartheid

B. Murray (✉)
University of the Witwatersrand, Johannesburg, South Africa
e-mail: bruce.murray@wits.ac.za

© The Author(s) 2018
B. Murray et al. (eds.), *Cricket and Society in South Africa, 1910–1971*, Palgrave Studies in Sport and Politics,
https://doi.org/10.1007/978-3-319-93608-6_11

South Africa—for the first time South Africa's bilateral relations with 'traditional' opponents had been disrupted—and it likewise constituted a major victory for the radical new methods of popular protest employed to prevent tours abroad by South African teams. The D'Oliveira Affair was also a watershed event for the relationship between politics and sport in negotiating apartheid sport, with the notion that sport was somehow autonomous of politics, that politics and sport did not mix, being swept away. From start to finish, and in its consequences, the D'Oliveira Affair was intensely political.

The notoriety of the D'Oliveira Affair derives not only from Vorster's ban, but also from the initial decision of the English selectors to leave D'Oliveira out of the team to tour South Africa in 1968/69. This caused a massive outcry in Britain that MCC and its selectors had capitulated to pressure from the apartheid Government to exclude him. Then Tom Cartwright, a bowler, dropped out of the team, and D'Oliveira, who the selectors had announced had been considered purely as a batsman, was hastily drafted in to replace him. This, Vorster announced, was clearly a case of MCC capitulating to anti-apartheid political pressure—how, otherwise, could a batsman replace a bowler?—and he duly announced that he would not allow the team of the anti-apartheid movement into South Africa.

Had D'Oliveira been selected in the first instance, Vorster told the British ambassador, he would have accepted him as a cricketing choice, even though his presence would have caused him a good many headaches, but he could not accept his selection as the outcome of a politically motivated agitation.[2] That was a lie; Vorster never had any intention of accepting D'Oliveira. Before the team was selected the Cabinet had resolved that if D'Oliveira was included the tour would be off, and Frank Waring, the Minister of Sport and Recreation, had already prepared his statement announcing the Government's decision not to allow D'Oliveira into the country as a member of the MCC team.[3] More than that, as critics of the apartheid regime suspected, massive pressure was put on the MCC and its selectors not to include D'Oliveira.

D'Oliveira

D'Oliveira was one of the finest cricketers produced by South Africa in the last century—he was one of the world's leading all-rounders of the 1960s—but he also stands as the iconic symbol of all that was wrong with South African cricket under the apartheid regime. Because of his colour, he could not play for South Africa—he could not represent the country of his birth—so in 1960 he emigrated to England and qualified to play for the country of his adoption. Altogether he played in 44 Tests for England, scoring 2484 runs, including five centuries, at an average of 40.06, and took 47 wickets at an average of 39.55. It was a formidable record established against all the Test playing nations of the world, except one. The one country that he never played against was South Africa. Politics prevented him from playing for South Africa; politics also prevented him from playing against South Africa.

D'Oliveira himself was most anxious to play against South Africa—he was dying for the opportunity to prove his worth against the Springboks—but Vorster flatly refused to allow him that opportunity, with calamitous consequences for the Springboks in Test cricket. In the contemporary assessment of Louis Duffus, the post-war doyen of cricket writers in South Africa, D'Oliveira's role was that of 'a dagger directed at the heart of South African cricket'. 'Posterity will surely marvel', he wrote, 'how a player, helped to go overseas by the charitable gesture of white contemporaries, could be the cause of sending the cricket of his benefactors crashing into ruins'.[4]

Posterity has indeed marvelled at D'Oliveira's central role in stirring the conscience of South Africa's traditional cricketing rivals, England, Australia and New Zealand, over their collaboration with apartheid cricket, leading ultimately to their refusal to continue playing against apartheid teams. The irony is that, despite the aspersions of Duffus, D'Oliveira himself never wished isolation on South African cricket. He would much have preferred to have played against South Africa and scored a century at Newlands, where he first watched international cricket as a youngster. But his dream was the apartheid regime's nightmare. The dagger that pierced it, and that condemned white South African cricket to the wilderness, was wielded by the South African Prime Minister, B. J. Vorster.

D'Oliveira's formal cricketing career began in Cape Town at the end of the Second World War at a juncture when segregation in South African cricket was at its height. It was not simply that whites and blacks did not play with or against one another, but that black cricket itself was thoroughly divided along ethnic and religious lines. Africans, Indians, coloureds and Malays all had their own leagues and competitions. In the 1950s the newly formed South African Cricket Board of

Control (SACBOC), an umbrella body of black cricketing bodies, organised national competitions along multiracial lines, and D'Oliveira excelled as the captain of the South African Coloured Cricket Association team. 'I loved playing for the coloureds against the Malays, the Indians and the Bantus in national tournaments', he later recalled.[5] In 1956, he played a historic role in captaining the first ever non-racial 'non-white' South African team against the touring Kenyan Asians, and in 1958 he captained the SACBOC team that successfully toured East Africa and Rhodesia.

Such was D'Oliveira's prowess as a batting all-rounder that it was suggested to the South African Cricket Association (SACA) that he was one of a couple of black cricketers who should be considered for inclusion in the Springbok tour of England in 1960.[6] Unwilling even to contemplate challenging the National Party Government's apartheid policy, SACA ignored the suggestion. Instead of touring England, D'Oliveira emigrated there with the help of John Arlott, the strongly anti-apartheid BBC commentator. He began by playing Lancashire League cricket, and such was the form he struck after a hesitant start that the African magazine *Drum* suggested that Jackie McGlew's struggling touring Springboks should recruit him: 'The Springbok cricketers have done badly against England, even against ordinary counties. Their bowlers are being overworked. D'Oliveira is right there in England getting runs and taking wickets. He should be invited to play for S. Africa. It would be a fine sporting gesture that would win the hearts of the British public, and show there is no racial feeling between sportsmen. It would pay dividends too'.[7] The Springboks remained oblivious to D'Oliveira.

But not for very much longer. In 1964, D'Oliveira was signed by Worcestershire, qualifying thereafter both as a Worcester player in the county championship and as a British citizen. In 1966, he made his debut for England against the touring West Indies and enjoyed a highly successful series. The question that arose immediately was what would happen if he was included in the MCC team to tour South Africa in 1968/69?

Vorster and D'Oliveira

That was a prospect that Vorster, who in 1966 succeeded the assassinated Dr. H. F. Verwoerd as Prime Minister, contemplated with dread. At that juncture South Africa was facing the threat of sporting isolation because of its segregationist practices in sport—in 1961 South African soccer was suspended by FIFA and in 1964 South Africa was excluded from the Olympics. In rugby and cricket bilateral relations with 'traditional' national opponents were threatened because of the Government's continued insistence that visiting touring teams had to respect apartheid principles, that they themselves had to be all white. In 1966, New Zealand cancelled its scheduled rugby tour of South Africa because Verwoerd had declared Maori players unwelcome. Intent on reversing this slide into sporting isolation, Vorster announced a new sports policy in 1967 whereby, among other things, visiting teams might include black players.[8] When commenting in August 1968 on the 'injustice' British authorities inflicted on Colin Bland, the Rhodesian cricketer who played for South Africa, in turning him back from London Airport because he carried a Rhodesian passport, the *Glasgow Herald* asked: 'What would be the reaction in this country were Basil D'Oliveira included in next winter's MCC side to tour South Africa and refused entry by the South African authorities, as could have happened at one time before the South African government liberalised their attitude to non-white sportsmen playing in South Africa'?[9]

The *Herald* failed to appreciate the limits of Vorster's 'liberalisation'. Politically there was one category of black player he could never allow, and that was for a South African-born black to return as a member of a visiting team and flaunt his talents in front of South African crowds. That was the challenge posed by D'Oliveira. As it was, the right wing of Vorster's party was hostile to his new sports policy; to allow D'Oliveira in would invite a revolt. At the same time, Vorster appreciated that a formal ban on D'Oliveira would sabotage his new sports policy at the outset and hasten the onset of sporting isolation. What he required was a strategy to ensure that no such ban became necessary and in this endeavour he worked in close collaboration with SACA. Behind the scenes, they worked hand-in-glove to secure D'Oliveira's omission, either by engineering his non-selection or his non-availability. The 'unofficial' message that was sent to the MCC through various emissaries was that the MCC could select anyone they liked, except D'Oliveira. A plan was also hatched, in Vorster's office, to bribe D'Oliveira to make himself unavailable by offering him a lucrative coaching job in South Africa (Fig. 11.1).[10]

Although a founder member of the Imperial Cricket Conference (ICC), along with England and Australia, South Africa had automatically forfeited its membership in 1961 when the country became a

Fig. 11.1   Shortly after playing in his first Test series against the West Indies in 1966, Basil D'Oliveira was pictured wearing his England colours whilst coaching young players in Cape Town

Republic and left the Commonwealth, thereby rendering precarious its status in international cricket. Subsequently, South Africa became heavily dependent on the operation of the imperial old boy network, headed by the MCC, to protect its position in international cricket, with the MCC insisting that England, Australia and New Zealand remained free to pursue their traditional rivalries with South Africa. In 1966, D'Oliveira loomed as a threat to this arrangement at its potentially most vulnerable point, the South African veto over the racial composition of touring teams. Following the cancellation of the New Zealand rugby tour of South Africa because of the ban on Maori players, Billy Griffith, the MCC secretary, advised that if the MCC ever found itself in a similar situation, it would likewise cancel.[11] In January 1967 Dennis Howell, the minister responsible for sport in the Labour Government, informed the House of Commons that after consultation with the General-Purposes Sub-Committee of the MCC he could give the assurance 'that the team to tour South Africa will be chosen on merit and in this respect any preconditions that the host country lays down will be totally disregarded'. If any player chosen by the MCC was rejected by the host country 'then there would be no question that the MCC would find such a condition wholly unacceptable and the projected tour would be abandoned'.[12]

On 5 January 1968, at the instigation of Howell, the MCC made a formal request to SACA for assurances that no preconditions would be laid down regarding their choice of players to tour South Africa.[13] For Vorster, this represented a blatant attempt to embarrass him politically and no satisfactory formal reply was sent. That the MCC did not insist on one was due to the intervention of another politician, Sir Alec Douglas-Home, the former British Prime Minister, the current Conservative Party shadow minister for foreign affairs, and a member of the MCC Committee. His intervention was central to the way in which the D'Oliveira Affair unfolded. Prior to it, Jack Cheetham, the SACA Vice-President, was convinced after a visit to Lord's that 'MCC compromised themselves to such an extent with the Labour Government in their statement read in the House of Commons last year that no Selection Committee, which has a majority of MCC members, would dare not select the person concerned, despite loss of form'.[14]

Douglas-Home met Vorster in Cape Town on 22 February primarily to enlist Vorster's support for sanctions against Rhodesia, which had declared its unilateral independence of Britain. On behalf of the MCC Committee, he also raised the question of D'Oliveira touring and reached the conclusion that if he pressed Vorster for advance assurances the answer would be 'no'. On his return to Britain, Douglas-Home advised the MCC Committee to drop its request for assurances and to proceed on the assumption that there would be 'more chance of the selected team being accepted if we waited until the selection was actually made'.[15] His advice as a seasoned politician was accepted unanimously and the decision to proceed was never formally reconsidered, despite evidence to the contrary filtering into Lord's. The politically charged question of D'Oliveira's selection was consequently left for the selectors themselves to decide. As Doug Insole, the chairman of selectors, reputedly remarked, 'Thanks for leaving everything to the selectors'.

On 12 March Vorster saw Lord Cobham, a former MCC President, in Cape Town, and told him 'quite categorically' that D'Oliveira would not be acceptable. As Cobham later recalled in a letter to Sir de Villiers Graaff, the leader of the United Party, 'As I remember, he said that a

Cape Coloured, alone of all races, castes and creeds, would be likely to provide a catalyst to the potentially explosive — or possibly one should say tricky – Cape Coloured situation'. In April Lord Cobham duly conveyed this information to Billy Griffith when he saw him at Lord's and was told that Sir Alec had also seen Vorster and that he was 'the obvious person to advise the Committee on this issue'.[16] Griffith thereafter consulted with the two leading members of the MCC hierarchy, Arthur Gilligan, president, and 'Gubby' Allen, treasurer, and the trio agreed not to pass on Cobham's message to the MCC Committee as it ran contrary to the advice they had received from Sir Alec and 'in order not to embarrass the two selectors who formed part of it'.[17] Cobham, for his part, assumed that Sir Alec had conveyed basically the same message and reckoned that 'MCC was gambling, <u>not</u> that Vorster would change his mind, but that D'Oliveira would not be selected'.[18]

Within SACA a subcommittee of three, E. R. Hammond, as president, Jack Cheetham and Arthur Coy, who was in regular contact with Vorster, was set up to deal with the D'Oliveira question 'on a confidential basis'. In June Coy was sent over to England in time for the second Ashes Test at Lord's to 'privately' warn MCC officials of the perils of selecting D'Oliveira and also to try and secure his 'non-availability'. Before departing Coy met Vorster to brief the Prime Minister about 'our plans, possible solution and alternatives'.[19]

MCC SELECTORS AND D'OLIVEIRA

A 'Cassandra-like' Coy duly arrived at Lord's, as the guest of Lord Cobham, to convey his warnings and according to Cobham 'was more or less summarily told to "shut up"' by Billy Griffith.[20] Nonetheless, a spurt of activity accompanied Coy's visit to Lord's. At the pre-match dinner to celebrate the two hundredth Test between England and Australia D'Oliveira was approached by Griffith himself with the advice 'that the only way the tour could be saved would be if I announced I was unavailable for England but would like to play for South Africa'. D'Oliveira 'angrily refused' and said 'Either you respect me as an England player or you don't'. The next day an 'eminent cricket writer' evidently E. W. Swanton of the *Daily Telegraph* put the same proposal to D'Oliveira.[21] For the Test itself, D'Oliveira found himself relegated to twelfth man. A surprise inclusion for the first Test, given his disappointing form in the recent tour of the West Indies, he was now a surprise omission as he had top-scored with 87 not out in England's second innings in a losing cause. The selectors ascribed England's defeat to an 'unbalanced' bowling attack and replaced D'Oliveira with the bowling all-rounder Barry Knight, who promptly took 3 for 16 as Australia were bundled out for 78 in their first innings in a rain-affected draw. During the Test Wilf Isaacs, the Johannesburg property tycoon and cricket benefactor visited D'Oliveira in the English dressing room in the company of Doug Insole, the chairman of selectors, and told him how he was looking forward to watching him play in South Africa. On his return to South Africa, Isaacs informed the Johannesburg *Sunday Times* that on the basis of discussions with various officials and players he reckoned that D'Oliveira was not on the shortlist for South Africa.[22]

When the selectors met on 26 July, during the fourth Test, to draw up their shortlist of thirty D'Oliveira was not included. Nor, for that matter, did the major cricket correspondents include him in their projected touring teams; his form in county cricket was generally unremarkable. His best prospect for going out to South Africa, it seemed, would be to accept the lucrative coaching offer being made by 'Tienie' Oosthuizen, head of the London office of the Carreras Tobacco Company, part of the tobacco empire of the South African entrepreneur, Anton Rupert, a good friend of John Vorster. A condition of the contract was that D'Oliveira declared himself unavailable for the MCC tour.

What transformed the situation was D'Oliveira's last-minute recall for the fifth Test at The Oval. Roger Prideaux, an opening batsman, dropped out through illness and D'Oliveira was drafted into the team by the captain, Colin Cowdrey, who reckoned that The Oval pitch was ideally suited to D'Oliveira's medium-paced bowling. D'Oliveira made his lasting mark as a batsman, with his match-winning 158 in the first innings enabling England to square the series. In response 'Tienie' Oosthuizen phoned the secretary at The Oval, Geoffrey Howard, from the Prime Minister's office in Pretoria to convey to the selectors that 'if today's centurion is picked, the tour will be off'. The message was duly passed on to Doug Insole as chairman of selectors.[23]

On the evening of 27 August, immediately after The Oval Test, the selectors met at Lord's to choose the team for South Africa. The meeting comprised the regular selection committee of Doug Insole, chairman, Peter May, Alec Bedser and Don Kenyon together with Colin Cowdrey, as England captain, Leslie Ames, as tour manager, and two office-holders of the MCC, Arthur Gilligan as president and 'Gubby' Allen as treasurer, whose official task was to rule on the acceptability as tourists of those considered for selection. Billy Griffith and Donald Carr were also present as part of the MCC administration.

To widespread disbelief in the wake of his Oval feats, D'Oliveira was not included in the team selected after a five-and-a-half hour meeting. 'No-one of open mind', John Arlott charged, 'will believe that he was left out for valid cricket reasons'. The general accusation was that the selectors had succumbed to pressure from the apartheid regime, an accusation the selectors always strenuously denied. In their own perception, they had omitted D'Oliveira for purely cricketing reasons.

The issue of D'Oliveira's non-selection for the South African tour remains a substantial debating point, open to speculation, but with the evidence now available it is possible to provide a credible reconstruction of what transpired at that fatal meeting at Lord's. First, it is clear that the selectors were fully informed as to the consequences that would follow on D'Oliveira's selection; 'Tienie' Oosthuizen's phone call to The Oval had seen to that. Second, despite denials at the time, it is also evident that 'political' issues were raised at the meeting. The two MCC office-holders Gilligan and Allen, for long aware that D'Oliveira would be unacceptable to the South African Government, started the meeting by speculating whether there was any point in going ahead with the selection of a team to South Africa, and the meeting seemed to be going round in circles until Insole suggested that to get away from political considerations they should imagine they were selecting a team to go to Australia.[24] On the basis of that fiction, they proceeded to select the team without D'Oliveira in it.

Two sets of cricketing considerations led directly to D'Oliveira's exclusion. The one was to view him purely as a batsman, and not as an all-rounder. According to Hugo Young of the London *Sunday Times*, who received his information from 'one of those present' (evidently Insole) the first 'cricketing' decision taken by the committee was to select seven batsmen, and the second was that D'Oliveira would be considered purely as a batsman. 'It was at this point', Young commented, 'that the reasoning got, to an outsider, almost unintelligibly contorted'. D'Oliveira had been drafted by Cowdrey into the England squad for The Oval Test primarily for his medium-paced bowling, but for overseas conditions his bowling was considered of no account.[25] As a batsman he, along with Colin Milburn, was not considered to be one of England's top seven and was consequently left out. The all-rounder spot went to Tom Cartwright, a fine bowler, when fit, who could bat a little.

The other cricketing factor that counted against D'Oliveira was that, following the West Indies tour, he was deemed a 'bad tourist' who did not adjust well to overseas conditions, spent much of his time partying, and generally detracted from team morale. That had been the report of Ames as tour manager.

In the final analysis, the selectors proved unwilling to revise their plans, at the risk of jeopardising the tour, and even South Africa's place in international cricket, in the light of D'Oliveira's Oval innings. He had not been on their shortlist prior to The Oval—he had not been part of their plans for South Africa—and evidently one century was not sufficient to persuade them to change their plans. As Peter May explained in his autobiography: 'After Basil had made 158 at The Oval, we reconsidered the position but, as he had been dropped twice early on, came to the conclusion that his innings, valuable though it had been in its context, did not alter the judgements made over the cricket of the past year'.[26] Evidently, only one selector, Don Kenyon, D'Oliveira's former captain at Worcester, put the case for D'Oliveira. Crucially, according to Insole, neither Cowdrey as captain nor Ames as manager urged the inclusion of D'Oliveira. Rather, they had been disappointed by D'Oliveira's performance and behaviour during the previous season's tour of the West Indies and were reluctant to risk a repeat. Had they insisted on D'Oliveira, he would likely have been selected.[27]

At one point, Arthur Coy had wondered whether 'for the sake of one man would they [the MCC] jeopardise the success and harmony of a tour?'. He seemingly now had his answer. When the team was announced Vorster phoned Coy to congratulate him on the satisfactory resolution of 'our respective problems'. Coy wrote back: 'The inside story of the two final meetings held by MCC, I hope to have the privilege of telling you when the opportunity presents itself. My information is that "he" was still available and had not withdrawn'.[28]

The truly intriguing role in this whole intrigue was that played by Cowdrey.[29] It was at Cowdrey's instigation that D'Oliveira was recalled for the final Ashes Test against Australia. During the Test, he told D'Oliveira: 'I want you in South Africa. If anyone at the Tour selection meeting asks me if I am prepared to accept responsibility for anything which might happen on tour should you be selected, I shall say I am prepared to do so'.[30] After the Test Cowdrey confided to Jack Bailey, the MCC assistant secretary: 'It's good to have beaten the Aussies. It looks as though we shall have problems with South Africa, though. They can't leave Basil out of the team. Not now'.[31] Yet in the selectors meeting, he evidently spoke out against D'Oliveira and supported instead the inclusion of Cartwright. As he recounts in his autobiography, he had gathered from Bill Lawry, the Australian captain, that South African pitches were now a 'seamer's paradise', ideally suited to Tom Cartwright and Barry Knight, whereas D'Oliveira was more 'a batsman who could bowl well'.[32] After the team was announced, Mrs. Cowdrey sent a bouquet of flowers to Mrs. D'Oliveira. D'Oliveira himself was convinced Cowdrey had voted for him.

Cowdrey's role did not end there. On the morning of Monday 16 September, the day the selection committee was due to meet to name reserves, Tom Cartwright took the train from Birmingham to London to consult Bill Tucker, the orthopaedic surgeon, on his shoulder injury. After discussing the matter at Lord's with Insole, Billy Griffith and Donald Carr, Cartwright then withdrew from the tour. At four o'clock that afternoon the selection committee duly met and decided that Cartwright's replacement would be D'Oliveira, but at some point Cowdrey phoned Cartwright's home to ask: 'Will you agree at least to start the tour? When you get out there, if things go wrong, there are people out there who are coaching, like Don Wilson, who we could bring in'. D'Oliveira was not mentioned. Cartwright said 'no' and Cowdrey said 'OK, fine'.[33] A curious call, but one that suggests that Cowdrey, at least, was desperate to avoid the selection of D'Oliveira.

Cowdrey, the evidence suggests, was thoroughly under the influence of Sir Alec Douglas-Home, who had all along been anxious not to provoke Vorster. A firm opponent of boycotts in dealing with South Africa, and a firm proponent of 'bridge-building', Douglas-Home had a long discussion with Cowdrey during the first Ashes Test at Trent Bridge, urging that Cowdrey as captain and as a selector, should not be 'misled by the press or swayed by public opinion', but should 'pick the strongest team, whether it included D'Oliveira or not'. He explained the advice he had given to the MCC Committee, and made it clear that in meeting Vorster he had been anxious not to place undue pressure on him: 'We wanted relationships kept as warm as possible in the current climate'. He added that the 'moral issue was not Britain's to go into' and that 'He was certain that to break off cricket relations with South Africa would have no effect on her attitude to apartheid, however long we refused to play against them'. Cowdrey found these words 'very reassuring' and claimed that they 'sustained him greatly' in dealing thereafter with the D'Oliveira issue.[34] The coded message was that it was not the MCC's brief to force a confrontation with Vorster and apartheid sport, and that it should not allow itself be stampeded into provoking one. The behind-the-scenes influence of Douglas-Home, on the MCC Committee and on Cowdrey, was central to the making of the D'Oliveira Affair.

CANCELLATION AND AFTERMATH

With D'Oliveira's selection as the replacement for Cartwright, and Vorster's refusal to accept it, MCC duly cancelled its tour of South Africa, but in the face of internal opposition still sought to preserve playing relations with South Africa, beginning with the Springbok tour of England in 1970. In this situation, Cowdrey was again in contact with Douglas-Home over D'Oliveira, evidently in an effort to ensure that D'Oliveira supported the tour and agreed to play against the Springboks. On 4 December 1968, the day before the special general meeting of the MCC to consider future relations with South Africa, Cowdrey took D'Oliveira to see Douglas-Home at his London flat. As recalled by D'Oliveira, Douglas-Home was 'particularly worried that the Springbok tour scheduled for the UK in 1970 was in danger of being called off'. The advice he gave D'Oliveira was: 'Keep doing it out on the cricket field, that's your job. Other forces can look after events off the field'.[35] The next day Cowdrey wrote to Douglas-Home: 'Thank you so much for giving time to see Basil and I [sic] yesterday. What a problem! But you helped him enormously and when the time is right, he will reiterate what he has said all the way through'.[36] D'Oliveira's decision to make himself available against the Springboks opened up a serious breach between him and the anti-apartheid campaign, but ultimately did nothing to save the tour.

Designed to disrupt games, the direct action tactics adopted by the Stop the Seventy Tour campaign, launched in September 1969, threatened that the Springbok tour, if it went ahead, would be played under siege conditions. In spite of this, the Cricket Council, the successor to MCC as the governing body of English cricket, decided at an emergency meeting on 18 May 1970 to proceed with the tour, but also reached the decision that effectively condemned South Africa to a prolonged period in the wilderness. In a seemingly desperate effort to avert large-scale disruption of the tour, and in a signal to SACA that it could no longer hold the ring for apartheid cricket, it announced that 'no further Test tours will take place between South Africa and this country until such time as Test cricket is played and tours are selected on a multiracial basis in South Africa'.[37] Four days later the Cricket Council finally called off the tour, due to begin on 1 June, after the Labour Government departed from tradition and formally requested the cancellation of the tour 'on grounds of broad public policy'. Thereafter, in the estimate of the cricket journalist, Christopher Martin-Jenkins, politicians in Britain proved more powerful than sportsmen in determining sporting relations with South Africa.[38]

After the cancellation, the *Rand Daily Mail* reported that several members of the Cricket Council had become thoroughly exasperated at their South African counterparts for their patent failure to assist themselves by taking forceful steps against racialism in South African cricket. A member of the Cricket Council was quoted as saying that 'we thought they could have helped us a bit more'.[39] SACA's leadership was still intent on working with, rather than against, government. At the annual general meeting of SACA on 28 September 1968 Clive van Ryneveld, the former Springbok captain and Progressive Party MP, proposed that SACA disassociate itself strongly from the Government's decision not to admit an MCC side that included D'Oliveira, but got nowhere, with Cheetham 'not persuaded'.[40] Following his visit to Lord's in late November 1969, when the 'seriousness of the situation' was impressed on him, Cheetham announced that in future South African teams would be selected 'on merit' alone 'irrespective of colour considerations', and was promptly slapped down by Vorster for making 'futile promises'. Pressure thereafter from the Cricket Council was for SACA to at least issue a major statement against apartheid in sport, but none was forthcoming. 'It will amaze and disgust future generations of South Africans when they come to read of this phase of our cricket history', Donald Woods' *Daily Dispatch* asserted, 'to find that the prevailing response from our officials and cricketers in the game's great hour of need was: "No comment"'.[41]

In Australia, the Campaign Against Racism in Sport, founded in 1969, followed the British example by embarking on a militant campaign to prevent the projected Springbok cricket tour of 1971/72. To outflank the protestors, and salvage the tour, Sir Donald Bradman, the chairman of the Australian Cricket Board (ACB), advised SACA to include two black players in the touring team as that would 'effectively counter the protests from organisations which insist that the South African Team is selected from only 18% of the population'.[42] SACA consequently urged the Government to permit the inclusion of two 'non-whites', but Vorster would have none of it. The team, he insisted, would remain all white. In response to the Government's veto, South Africa's top white cricketers staged a celebrated walk-off at Newlands on 3 April 1971, issuing the statement: 'We cricketers feel that the time has come for an expression of our views. We fully support the South African Cricket Association's application to include non-whites on the tour of Australia if good enough and, furthermore, subscribe to merit being the only criterion on the cricket field'.[43] White South African cricketers had mounted their first political protest against apartheid in sport, but it was not enough to save their tour of Australia or the future of the Springboks in official international cricket.

Unlike Britain, there was no formal government pressure on the ACB to cancel. The official position of the Liberal Government of William McMahon was that politics had no place in sport, and that 'the business of selecting sporting teams and arranging their visits should be left to sporting bodies themselves'.[44] Bradman, who consulted widely, found himself 'constantly fobbed off' in his attempts to speak to the Prime Minister.[45] In the end, contact was established and McMahon advised that the view of his Government had turned against the tour. Bradman also established contact with Vorster, who indicated that his Government preferred to see the tour cancelled than allow blacks to represent South Africa.[46]

On 8 September 1971, Bradman announced that the ACB had unanimously agreed to cancel the tour. Having himself witnessed the mayhem caused by demonstrators at the rugby Test between Australia and South Africa in Sydney on 17 July, he had concluded that it was impossible to mount a cricket tour under such conditions.[47] Nonetheless, in explaining the decision for cancellation Bradman gave as the underlying cause 'the widespread disapproval of the South African Government's racial policy which restricted selection of South Africa's teams'. Had Vorster allowed two 'coloured' players to join the Springbok cricketers, Bradman allegedly told the journalist Jack Fingleton, the tour would not have been cancelled. Vorster responded by accusing Bradman of talking through his hat and of capitulating to the 'riff-raff' elements in Australia.[48]

Nationalists later conceded that Vorster's ban on D'Oliveira had been a huge political blunder. At the time the party faithful reckoned that Vorster's hardline stand in dealing with D'Oliveira and South African cricket had been tactically astute, ensuring that the party's split over the Government's new sports policy was largely contained. The secession in September 1969 to form the Herstigte Nasionale Party was limited to a handful of MPs, and in the general election of April 1970, the new party was roundly defeated. But the ban proved totally counterproductive to the whole purpose of the new sports policy; it greatly accelerated the progress of the sports boycott in isolating South African sport, casting Springbok cricket into the wilderness almost overnight, and ushered in new forms of militant protest that rendered it highly impolitic for South African teams to be invited to tour abroad, even after South Africa began 'normalising' its sport in the effort to regain international acceptance. This was a lesson New Zealand learnt to its cost when the Springbok rugby team toured in 1981. No matter what their sympathies towards Springbok cricket, the English cricket authorities were never prepared to risk a repeat of 1970.

NOTES

1. For previous analyses of the D'Oliveira Affair see B. D'Oliveira, *The D'Oliveira Affair* (London: Collins, 1969); B. Murray, 'Politics and Cricket: The D'Oliveira Affair of 1968', *Journal of Southern African Studies*, 27, 4 (2001), 667–84; J. Williams, *Cricket and Race* (Oxford: Berg, 2001), chapter 3; P. Oborne, *Basil D'Oliveira—Cricket and Conspiracy: The Untold Story* (London: Little, Brown, 2004), chapters 10–12; B. Murray and C. Merrett, *Caught Behind: Race and Politics in South African Cricket* (Johannesburg: Wits University Press, 2005), chapter 5; R. Steen, 'Dolly Mixture', *The Wisden Cricketer*, July 2008, 38–42.
2. The National Archive (TNA) FCO 25/709, Sir John Nicholls to Commonwealth Office, 17 September 1968.
3. South African National Archives (SANA) MEM 1/647, 138/2, Proposed statement to be issued in the event of D'Oliveira being selected for MCC to tour South Africa, 28 August 1968.
4. L. Duffus, *Play Abandoned* (Cape Town: Howard Timmins, 1969), chapter 29.
5. B. D'Oliveira, *Time to Declare: An Autobiography* (London: Dent, 1980), 5.
6. South African Cricket Association (SACA) correspondence, 'Non-White Cricket' files, Campaign Against Race Discrimination in Sport to SACA, 23 July 1959.

 7. *Drum*, August 1960.
 8. *House of Assembly Debates*, 20, 11 April 1967, cols. 3952–96.
 9. I am grateful to Jonty Winch for the reference.
10. SANA MEM 1/647, 138/2. Arthur Coy to Vorster, 27 March 1969.
11. Murray and Merrett, *Caught Behind*, 66.
12. *Parliamentary Debates (Hansard)*, 5th Series, 740, 30 January 1967.
13. SANA MEM 1/647, 138/2, S. C. Griffith, MCC Secretary, to D. C. Bursnall, SACA Honorary Secretary, 5 January 1968.
14. SANA MEM 1/647, 138/2, Coy to Vorster, 27 March 1968.
15. MCC minutes, 21 March 1968.
16. Cobham Papers (CP), Lord Cobham to Sir de Villiers Graaff, 13 April 1969.
17. MCC minutes, 16 April 1969.
18. CP, Cobham to Graaff, 13 April 1969.
19. SANA MEM 1/647, 138/2, Coy to Vorster, 20 May 1968.
20. CP, Cobham to Graaff, 13 April 1969.
21. D'Oliveira, *Autobiography*, 64; Oborne, *D'Oliveira*, 157–60.
22. Ibid., 194–95.
23. S. Chalke, *At the Heart of English Cricket: The Life and Times of Geoffrey Howard* (Bath: Fairfield, 2001), 206.
24. Interview with Doug Insole, Cape Town, 4 January 2000.
25. *Sunday Times*, 1 September 1968.
26. P. May, *A Game Enjoyed* (London: Stanley Paul, 1985), 191.
27. Oborne, *D'Oliveira*, 200–1.
28. SANA MEM 1/647, 138/2, Coy to Cheetham, 1 March 1968; Coy to Vorster, 4 September 1968.
29. For analyses of Cowdrey's role see M. Peel, *The Last Roman: A Biography of Colin Cowdrey* (London: André Deutsch, 1999), 152–55; Oborne, *D'Oliveira*, 191–93 and 200–1.
30. D'Oliveira, *D'Oliveira Affair*, 138.
31. J. Bailey, *Conflicts in Cricket* (London: Heinemann, 1989), 52.
32. C. Cowdrey, *MCC: The Autobiography of a Cricketer* (London: Hodder & Staughton, 1976), 201.
33. S. Chalke, *Tom Cartwright: The Flame Still Burns* (Bath: Fairfield, 2007), 152–53.
34. Cowdrey, *MCC*, 195–96.
35. D'Oliveira, *Autobiography*, 73–5.
36. Lord Home of Hersel Papers, Cowdrey to Douglas-Home, 5 December 1968.
37. Minutes of the emergency meeting of the Cricket Council, 18 May 1970.
38. C. Martin-Jenkins, *Twenty Years On: Cricket's Years of Change 1963 to 1993* (London: Willow, 1994), chapter 8.

39. *Rand Daily Mail*, 25 May 1970.
40. SACA minutes, 28 September 1968; Clive van Ryneveld, *20th Century All-rounder* (Cape Town, 2011), 169.
41. Murray and Merrett, *Caught Behind*, 141–43.
42. Ibid., 156.
43. Ibid., 156–58.
44. National Archives of Australia A1838/264, 201/10/10/3 Part 1, Item on 'Apartheid' prepared for Prime Minister, 12 April 1971.
45. SANA Department of Sport and Recreation MSO MS6/5/9, South African ambassador's report on conversation with Sir Donald Bradman, June 1972.
46. G. Haigh and D. Frith, *Inside Story: Unlocking Australian Cricket's Archives* (Melbourne: News Custom, 2007), 156–57.
47. Interview with Sir Donald Bradman, Adelaide, 2 February 1998.
48. Murray and Merrett, *Caught Behind*, 153–54.

CHAPTER 12

'Who Are We ... to Tell the South Africans How to Run Their Country?' The Women's Cricket Association and the Aftermath of the D'Oliveira Affair, 1968/69

Rafaelle Nicholson

INTRODUCTION

In September 1968, the planned MCC tour to South Africa was cancelled by the MCC in the wake of the South African Government's rejection of the belated inclusion of the coloured cricketer Basil D'Oliveira in the touring squad. The D'Oliveira Affair, as it became known, marked the beginning of the isolation of South Africa from international men's cricket and has probably been analysed more than any other single event in the history of Anglo-South African cricketing relations.[1] Yet its most immediate impact was actually felt within the women's cricket community. The England women's cricket team had organised a stopover in South Africa on their way to Australia and New Zealand, scheduled for December 1968. But in the wake of the D'Oliveira Affair, the UK Government, suddenly alert to the now potent issue of continued sporting contact with

R. Nicholson (✉)
Queen Mary University, London, UK

© The Author(s) 2018
B. Murray et al. (eds.), *Cricket and Society in South Africa, 1910–1971*, Palgrave Studies in Sport and Politics,
https://doi.org/10.1007/978-3-319-93608-6_12

325

South Africa, placed pressure on the British Women's Cricket Association (WCA) to cancel the visit.

The fact that this incident has until now gone almost unmentioned in the extensive literature on the D'Oliveira Affair is symptomatic of the chronic lack of research into women's cricket history in both England and South Africa. This extends to accounts of Anglo-South African cricketing relationships. Generally, cricketing women have been totally absent from the literature on colonial and postcolonial cricket; where they have been mentioned, it has been as a brief counterpoint to accounts which focus on sporting masculinity. The assumption, as Adair, Nauright and Phillips have explicitly argued, is that women's sport did not provide the same opportunities as male sport did to reaffirm or reject cultural connections with Britain.[2]

Yet an examination of the reaction of female cricketers in Britain and South Africa to the D'Oliveira Affair highlights how flawed this assumption is. By the time of D'Oliveira's selection for the MCC tour of South Africa, the British Women's Cricket Association had been in existence for 42 years, having been founded in 1926, and had formed a close relationship with the South Africa and Rhodesian Women's Cricket Association (SARWCA) since its formation in 1952. This relationship mirrored that of the MCC with the male South African Cricket Association (SACA); it is unsurprising, therefore, that in 1968 the WCA displayed a similar reluctance to the MCC to break their imperial bond with a nation whose cricketing development they had so strongly encouraged. In fact, the WCA felt just as firmly as the MCC did that sport and politics should be kept separate, and that, as England captain Rachael Heyhoe-Flint expressed in her autobiography: 'Who are we ... to tell the South Africans how to run their country?'[3]

The following pages use the cancellation of the intended 1968 stopover as a way to shed light on Anglo-South African relationships within women's cricket. Firstly, the close, imperial relationship between the WCA and the SARWCA in the years leading up to 1968 is examined in some depth, in order to provide some context to the incident. The second section considers the rationale behind the intended 1968 stopover in South Africa, the reasons for its subsequent cancellation and the WCA's reaction to the incident. Lastly, there is an analysis of the aftermath of the cancellation and the ways in which both the British and the South African WCAs reacted to South Africa's increasing international isolation. Throughout, the chapter draws on WCA archival material which has previously gone untouched by historians to give a new insight into the evolving attitude of the UK Government towards continued sporting contact with South Africa in the wake of the D'Oliveira Affair. Overall, it is argued that a study of women's cricket provides a crucial component of our understanding of Anglo-South African cricketing relations.

ANGLO-SOUTH AFRICAN WOMEN'S CRICKET, 1952–1968

While the British Women's Cricket Association had formed prior to the Second World War, in 1926, its South African counterpart was not founded until 1952.[4] André Odendaal has briefly outlined its origins— beginning with a league in Johannesburg and the dispatch of two Southern Transvaal teams to play against Rhodesia in 1947. In 1952, the SARWCA was established, and the first inter-provincial tournament was held in December that year. By 1956, an estimated 400 females were playing cricket in South Africa.[5]

What of the relationship between the British WCA and the new SARWCA? Generally, elements of the old colonial relationship were present in the WCA's dealings with all other national governing bod-ies of women's cricket, which at this time encompassed the Australian Women's Cricket Council (AWCC, formed in 1931) and the New Zealand Women's Cricket Council (NZWCC, formed in 1934), as well as SARWCA. From 1945, WCA rules dictated that 'A Council or Association now or hereafter formed in any part of the world outside Great Britain desiring to be affiliated shall submit a copy of its rules for the approval of the Women's Cricket Association'.[6] The WCA, as the oldest governing body, evidently saw its role as a paternalistic one, head of what we might term the female cricketing Commonwealth.

Attempts were made by the WCA from the outset to exercise influ-ence over the conduct of women's cricket in South Africa. In 1951, Netta Rheinberg, the WCA's Secretary, wrote to Mrs. Louise Goodall of the Southern Transvaal:

> I am receiving frequent reports of cricket activities in your country and think that possibly the time for the formation of a South African Women's Cricket Association might have arrived.

Fig. 12.1 Front-page coverage was given to the women's inter-provincial tournament at Liesbeek Park, Cape Town, in February 1954

As you may know, the Women's Cricket Association is the parent body for women's cricket in much the same way as the MCC acts for the men, and should a South African W.C.A. be formed we should most sincerely welcome its affiliation to us in the same way as Australia and New Zealand are affiliated.

From what you say in your letter I doubt whether you have drawn up any sort of constitution, but in case you or any other authority can draw together all your groups of enthusiasts into an association, I enclose a copy of our own, which might conceivably act as a basis.[7]

Evidently, though, the South Africans failed to take heed of this. When the Southern Transvaal sent a copy of their constitution in 1952, Vera Cox (Secretary and co-founder of the WCA) 'reported that having read their Constitution she did not consider this body ready for affiliation yet'.[8] Only in 1953 when a revised constitution was sent was their application for affiliation accepted, and then only on the basis that the WCA 'reserve[d] the right to request South Africa to conform to WCA dress regulations if a South African team ever visited England' (Fig. 12.1).[9]

A South African tour of England did not eventuate prior to the D'Oliveira Affair, but the WCA's threat was carried out in the case of New Zealand, who were requested not to wear caps during their 1954 visit to England.[10] Australia, too, were not immune from criticism. In 1950, the WCA sent a letter to the AWCC objecting to the passing of a resolution which enabled trophies to be presented to individual players, on the grounds that 'as an affiliated body of the WCA this ruling was not in accordance with our principles'.[11] Two years later, this rule was rescinded by the AWCC, possibly due to pressure from the WCA during the 1951 Australian tour.

The conduct of international tours in these years suggests that the WCA subscribed to the same moral code of cricket as the MCC espoused and considered itself the true bearer of these standards. In 1956, Rheinberg wrote that the upcoming tour of Australia and New Zealand would have:

a far-reaching influence on the conduct and standard of the game; tourists naturally benefit greatly themselves, but by passing on their knowledge and experience they help all players and the game as a whole.[12]

A key part of the consolidation of cricket's status as imperial sport *par excellence* was the staging of international tours. Landmark tours like Australia's 1878 tour of England and the MCC tour of India in 1926/27 were seen by the MCC as opportunities to spread the 'spirit of cricket' and assert their physical and cultural superiority over the colonies.[13] As time progressed and teams improved and nations gained independence from Britain, the MCC remained convinced of its own cultural (if no longer cricketing) superiority. This seems to have been the case for the WCA as well.

The first women's cricket tour had taken place in 1934/35 when England went to Australia and New Zealand, with Australia returning the visit in 1937. International tours were an integral part of women's cricket as they displayed female prowess on the world stage, attracted relatively large amounts of media coverage and raised levels of public interest in the sport. Netta Rheinberg's tour diaries during her time as England manager on their tours to Australia and New Zealand in 1948/49 and 1957/58 suggest that ideas of British supremacy remained potent for some female cricketers during this period. In 1949, she wrote:

> We have tried our best here to instil into the Aussies the advantage of playing cricket merely for the love of the game, as it is done in England, and not for points altogether as is the case throughout Australia. This competitive spirit leads to jealousy and rivalries and personal animosities which are unknown in England. It will be interesting to see what influence we have had.[14]

In her 1957/58 diary, she critiqued both the Australian attitude and the 'New Zealand mentality'; the majority of matches ended in draws, and in Rheinberg's view, this was due to the lack of sporting declarations by the opposing captains, Rona McKenzie and Una Paisley. Rheinberg wrote: 'Remarks made by various members of England team in dressing room are unrepeatable ... I'd suggest a change of captaincy – as whatever Rona learnt in England she must have forgotten'.[15] The idea that touring teams to England could 'learn' the correct way to play there is a deeply imperialist sentiment, but evidently remained part of Rheinberg's mentality by the late 1950s.

The WCA were thus keen to arrange tours with South Africa in order to facilitate the development of cricket there and to reaffirm the imperial bond which existed between the two nations. In Rheinberg's letter to Louise Goodall of the Southern Transvaal, she stated:

I have been interviewed several times by representatives of the South African Press who wish to know when a South African touring team may be visiting England, or when we might be visiting South Africa!

Naturally, if something of this sort could be arranged between us and a South African WCA, it would be a splendid innovation.[16]

By 1960 there was 'a steady trickle of South African recruits to [the WCA's] leading clubs'.[17] The WCA consequently enthusiastically accepted when, in 1956, South Africa requested England to tour during the English winter of 1960/61.[18] The tour, which was the first ever international women's cricket tour South Africa had ever participated in, subsequently took place, with four Tests being played, all on large, good-quality men's Test grounds. For England, it was an opportunity to reinforce their own cricketing superiority over the South Africans; three of the Tests ended in draws, but the third was won by England, by 8 wickets. One of the England team, writing in *The Times*, reported during the tour that:

Crowds have been good, interest is lively, and the efficient, graceful fielding of the English girls has caused much comment. Members of the touring team are coaching South Africans at each of the centres they visit and, undoubtedly, South African women's cricket will benefit considerably from the tour.[19]

English cricket was clearly seen to be helping develop its South African counterpart during the tour.

However, by 1960, the apartheid regime was already becoming firmly entrenched within South Africa, and the English touring team were well aware of the difficult political situation. Before the team arrived, they were given a briefing on the 'correct' way to behave while on tour by a member of the Executive Committee, Elspeth Jackson, who had reportedly 'obtained information from friends in South Africa'.[20] One member of the team recalled this in an oral history interview:

we were given a little lecture at the beginning to say, I can't remember what the Afrikaans was, but you had to know, even if you went into the park for instance, there were seats that the blacks were allowed to sit in, and those that the whites were expected to sit in ... And so we had a quick lesson on that, as to, we had to understand entrances into shops, all sorts of things like that. And we stuck to the rules, because we were guests. And so although we didn't like this, at all, it was totally foreign to us, we did what we were told. We were guests. And so we'd go in the right entrance to the shop, sit on the right benches … And no, we didn't like it. But as I said we were guests and we did as we were told.[21]

All coaching undertaken during the tour was within exclusively white schools, and the black population were forbidden to enter the grounds where the women's matches were taking place. Yet the tour did not engender any qualms whatsoever about continuing cricketing contact with South Africa. 'I found it strange and sad', wrote Heyhoe-Flint, 'but retained the view that it was their country, and hardly the place of any English people to criticise'.[22] Indeed, the WCA Executive Committee reported that the tour had 'engendered…goodwill' between the two governing bodies.[23]

The WCA remained keen to support the inclusion of the South Africans in the touring schedule throughout the 1960s. This schedule was now mediated by the International Women's Cricket Council, which had been formed in 1958. Rheinberg claimed that the rationale behind its formation was as follows:

> Up to the present time, overseas Associations and Councils have affiliated to the WCA which acted as the parent body. Now that they are all recognised and well established it is felt that they should be on equal terms within a main Association.[24]

This reeks of imperial sentiment, and it was also glossing over the facts. It does not seem that the WCA had any particular desire to form an international organisation. However, in November 1954 at an Executive Committee meeting, Vera Cox, the WCA's Chairman, reported that:

> the Australians had some international organisation in mind, but [she] thought it would be advisable for the WCA to send a definite proposal first on this matter. She therefore put forward the following proposition:
>
> There should be formed an organisation to be known as the International Women's Cricket Council. Each country would pay an annual affiliation fee, the sum to be determined between the member countries. The Council's function would be to discuss all matters pertaining to international women's cricket and future tours.[25]

The WCA thus quickly latched onto the idea: 'The inauguration of any world-wide organisation is an opportunity for aiding the ideals of international peace and happiness', wrote Vera Cox in 1958. Nonetheless, the real appeal seems to have been that the organisation was viewed as a way in which the WCA could continue to exert their influence over other bodies of women's cricket in a more structured way.

In truth, of course, the IWCC in 1958 was not the worldwide organisation Vera Cox had described: just as the Commonwealth had been up to 1948, it was an organisation of the former white Dominions. Four of the founder members were England, Australia, New Zealand and South Africa, and at the 1960 meeting, it was agreed to write to Canada and Ireland to encourage them to join—despite the fact that women's cricket in both these countries was almost non-existent.[26] All founder members seem to have initially respected the WCA's leadership of the IWCC; while Ruth Preddy of the AWCC took the chair at the inaugural meeting, held in Melbourne in 1958 during England's tour of Australia, Rheinberg reported that:

> I guided her along ... It was very gratifying to note the respect with which England's delegates were held, and it was possible to give a lead in many directions ...[27]

The WCA's keenness to continue to embrace the SARWCA in the international women's cricket community, and include the South Africans in the touring schedule throughout the 1960s, was therefore initially respected by the other former Dominions. The onset of apartheid did not go undiscussed by the IWCC; the minutes of the 1958 meeting state:

> During discussion of possible future tours to other countries, the question of colour bar arose. Miss Robison (South Africa) explained that the South African team would be unable to visit Pakistan for instance, owing to political drawbacks which all the sporting bodies in South Africa very much regretted.
>
> Mrs Poulter (New Zealand) expressed very strong sentiments on this question, fearing embarrassment should a Maori be included in any team to South Africa. Miss Robison stressed that everything possible would be done to ensure the smooth running of the tour. Miss Rheinberg (England) pointed out that politics should not enter a Council such as the IWCC,

and Miss Preddy (Australia) endorsed this remark and said the Council should keep a dignified attitude and players would have to bear with the country who had these laws.[28]

Rheinberg's more personalised account describes this as 'a rather anxious moment … this question obviously arouses the deepest feeling and has to be handled with utmost care'.[29] Yet despite the hesitance of the New Zealanders, England's suggested tour schedule—which would see New Zealand visit South Africa in 1966, and South Africa visit Australia and New Zealand in 1975/76—was adopted by the meeting. Indeed, the South African representative, Miss Robison, stated that attending the meeting was 'a proud moment for South Africa' and that 'they would do everything in their power to keep up the goodwill' felt within the community towards her country.[30]

South Africa continued to be welcomed into the international fold throughout the 1960s. The second meeting of the IWCC was hosted by the SARWCA in Durban in December 1960, during England's tour there, and at the next meeting in 1963, Miss Robison of South Africa was elected as the new IWCC President.[31] And when the AWCC postponed a scheduled tour by South Africa to Australia in 1966, reportedly due to financial constraints, the other members of the IWCC reacted strongly against this decision:

> Miss Whitehorn advised she had received no correspondence from Miss Verco on the subject and South Africa stated that they had received no communication from Australia on the subject of a further postponement.
>
> The meeting deplore the apparent discourtesy on the part of the Australian Council in not advising the interested parties concerned …
>
> the Acting Secretary was instructed to write to Australia requesting them to reconsider their decision …[32]

The decision was not reconsidered, but the Australians did agree to the continued inclusion of South Africa in the tour schedule. While a cleavage had begun to emerge from the late 1950s in the ICC, with India, Pakistan and West Indies all questioning the position of white South Africa within the organisation, the lack of 'non-white' members of the IWCC meant that a similar process did not take place within the Women's Council.[33] If anything, in the build-up to the D'Oliveira Affair, it was the women's cricket community who continued to wholeheartedly embrace South Africa, over and above their male counterparts.

Women's Cricket and the D'Oliveira Affair

The D'Oliveira Affair brought the matter of continued contact with apartheid South Africa to a head within the men's cricketing community. The public outcry surrounding D'Oliveira's initial non-selection by the MCC for their scheduled 1968/69 tour of the country, in the wake of his 158 at The Oval in the last Test of the 1968 summer, reflected the suspicion (later proved true) that, behind the scenes, it had been made clear by the South African Government that a team which included D'Oliveira would not be able to tour. The protests surrounding his non-selection, however, were too vocal for even the imperialist MCC to ignore. He was subsequently called up to the squad and, on 24 September 1968, the MCC cancelled the tour after the South African Government refused to accept D'Oliveira.

This was to have unanticipated repercussions within the women's cricket community. It had long been decided that the England Women's cricket team would tour Australia and New Zealand in 1968/69. But in April 1967, during the planning of their touring schedule, it was agreed by the WCA Executive Committee that they would include a ten-day stopover in South Africa en route to Australasia, as a way to partially acclimatise to the differing conditions.[34] Thus, at some point later that year, the WCA Executive Committee, independently and without consultation, went ahead and purchased plane tickets incorporating the stopover in South Africa.

It was a point of pride for the WCA that they had always organised their affairs totally separately from the governing bodies of men's cricket: in 1950, when discussing the role of men within the Association, the WCA's Executive Committee concluded that 'of the fundamental principles on which the WCA was founded, one of the most important ... was that women should run every aspect of it'.[35] This was all well and good, but there was a new consideration which did not seem to factor into their thinking: the England team were due to be the recipients of government grant aid for the 1968/69 tour.

Involvement by the UK Government in sport greatly increased during the 1960s, the result of a growing public demand for an expansion of opportunities for sport and recreation within an economic context of a new affluence, as well as a fresh interest in the pursuit of excellence due to Britain's perceived 'decline' in international sport in comparison with the successes of East Germany and the USSR.[36] The Wolfenden Committee, assembled to investigate the position of sport within British society and to which the WCA supplied a written statement, had also placed pressure on the government when it recommended in its 1960 Report that increased government funding be given to governing bodies of sport, and that a Sports Development Council be established to distribute these funds. In 1959, just £165,000 was given by the Ministry of Education to national voluntary sporting bodies to spend on coaching; by 1965, the total grants offered were worth £457,000 and involved 58 governing bodies of sport, including the All England Netball Association and the All England Women's Hockey Association.[37] The WCA was one of the first women's governing bodies of sport to benefit from these increased investments when, following secretary Miss Riley's application to the Ministry of Education in June 1962, the WCA was awarded an initial grant towards coaching costs of £200, for the year 1962/63.[38] Liaison was maintained, and an HM Inspector came to watch one of the England–Australia Test matches in 1963; the following year, the WCA's grant was increased to £600.[39]

After a Sports Council was set up by the Wilson Government in 1965, as recommended by Wolfenden, the ability to award grants was transferred to this organisation, and the total amount was vastly expanded, rising from £195,922 in the financial year 1960–61 to £1.27 million in 1970–71.[40] The WCA Executive Committee reported in 1965 that they 'welcomed the formation of the Council' and that their initial request for grant aid had been successful, with £600 being made available in the first year of the Council's existence.[41] In 1967, the Council provided grant aid for the Young England team's visit to Holland, and in May 1968, it was confirmed that the Council would provide £2000 towards the travelling costs of the WCA's 1968/69 tour to Australia and New Zealand.[42] Naturally, this was welcomed by the WCA Executive Committee. Yet it was to have severe consequences for the WCA's touring plans.

Precisely how or when the Sports Council discovered the WCA's plan for a stopover in South Africa is not clear. What is apparent is that at some point between 24 September, the date that the MCC announced the cancellation of their tour of South Africa, and 7 October, when the UK press broke the story, the WCA Chairman wrote to WCA members announcing the cancellation of the South African leg of the forthcoming tour.[43] On 7 October 1968, *The Times* reported:

> The England women's cricket team have cancelled the South African part
> of their winter tour. They were due to visit South Africa for 10 days at the
> end of November on their way to Australia and New Zealand, but the
> party will now travel direct to Australia on December 3.
>
> Miss Audrey Collins, chairman of the Women's Cricket Association,
> said: 'It was an independent decision by our executive committee. I have
> no further comment'.[44]

Minister of Sport Denis Howell was quoted as welcoming the decision:
'This is a right decision and has been taken quite independently. It would
have been incongruous for them to play in South Africa because of the
MCC cancellation. You can't play cricket where apartheid applies without in some measure condoning it, even if you don't want to'.[45] Howell
thus clearly linked the WCA's actions in the minds of the public to the
MCC's cancellation of their own planned tour to South Africa.

It is interesting that both the WCA and Howell were keen to stress
publicly that the decision to cancel the stopover in South Africa had
been taken independently. In fact, oral history interviews have made
it clear that there was enormous pressure placed on the WCA by the
Government to cancel the stopover; privately, Howell threatened to
withdraw the entire travel grant of £2000 unless the WCA altered their
plans. England wicketkeeper on the 1968/69 tour of Australia and New
Zealand, Shirley Hodges, recalled:

> The government said if we went we would no longer get any grants what-
> soever ... they just said, 'you're not to go. You can't go.' ... It was a gun
> to our head.[46]

Given that the WCA was an entirely amateur organisation and the
tour could not have gone ahead at all without Sports Council funding,
Howell's threat effectively forced the WCA to cancel the South Africa
leg of the tour. The public outcry surrounding the D'Oliveira Affair had
evidently made it apparent that the Council could not, as a public body,
be seen to be funding a tour to South Africa when public opinion was
beginning to turn against sporting contact with the apartheid regime.

Indeed, in the wake of the whole affair, the Sports Council felt compelled to clarify their policy with regard to grant-aided tours, as the
Guardian reported:

The cancelled tour shows up one loophole in the Government's policy of sports promotion which is now being investigated. The grant of £2000 to the women's team was made to contribute to their Australian and New Zealand cost, not to help them go to South Africa, and it is understood that there was indignation when tickets were bought which took them on the detour.

The Sports Council ... now has a subcommittee investigating how in future the Government can be sure that it is not helping to subsidise trips to South Africa.[47]

Sports Council minutes show that the issue of visits to South Africa was discussed at several meetings in the wake of the WCA incident. On 18 December 1968, the Council concluded that they 'should not be involved in considering the rights or wrongs of visits and matches against South African teams, and that governing bodies should be advised that a decision in these matters rested with them'. But it became clear that this was insufficient, as governing bodies continued to approach the Council for advice as to whether they should arrange matches against South African teams, presumably concerned that they too might have funding withdrawn were they to do so. Finally, on 16 April 1969, at the suggestion of Howell, it was agreed that 'in future the International Committee should refuse to offer grant assistance to international teams for tours which included a visit to South Africa'.[48] This statement solidified the beginning of the almost total isolation of South Africa from international sport, confirmed by the Gleneagles Agreement eight years later.

The WCA, though, were clearly extremely dissatisfied with the position in which they had been placed and were not slow to express such sentiments publicly. The Chairman, Audrey Collins, was reported to have stated: 'One is always disappointed when matters beyond one's control affect amateur sport. It is the only way to promote friendliness and it seems such a pity that it is not to happen'.[49] Collins later suggested that several members of the Executive Committee had wanted to go ahead with the stopover in spite of Howell's threat, but had been outvoted.[50] Presumably, this included England captain Heyhoe-Flint, who told *The Times* that she was 'very disappointed'.[51] She later wrote in her autobiography, published in 1978, that:

I deplored this intrusion ... [if] the British Government consider it their duty to register their disapproval of South African policies I suggest they cut off every contact with them, including banking and trading links. For, as things stand, sport is merely being used as a political lever. Who are we, in any case, to tell the South Africans how to run their country?[52]

The view that sport and politics were separate arenas and that one should not influence the other appears to have been held by many within the WCA (as it was by the majority of MCC members).

What of the South African response? Although the President of the WCA had written personally to the President of the SARWCA to convey the cancellation, she actually discovered the news when it was broadcast by the South African media, the letter arriving late due to a postal delay.[53] Given the lack of archival research which has been conducted into South African women's cricket to date, it is hard to gauge the SARWCA's immediate reaction. Nonetheless, some insight can be gained from both the IWCC and the WCA Executive Committee minutes in the months following the departure. The first IWCC meeting after the incident was held in February 1969 in Wellington, during England's tour of New Zealand, and the SARWCA representative used the opportunity to express their anger and concern over the incident. She stated:

> Cricket in South Africa was at present kept alive through international tours. Their Government was helpful to teams both coming and going overseas ... They urged the IWCC to step up the tour programme, as they felt that without the international competition, better competition could not be obtained, and brighter cricket and greater interest would result from such tours.[54]

The following month, the SARWCA wrote directly to the British Prime Minister, Harold Wilson, to express their dissatisfaction at the decision and to enquire 'whether the cancellation of the proposed stop-over on the outward journey to Australia had been brought about by any pressure on the WCA by the Foreign and Commonwealth Office [FCO] or by the Sports Council'. The reply, sent by the FCO and approved by the WCA's President Amy Bull, stated that 'the WCA had taken an independent decision after reviewing the proposed itinerary in the light of the events leading to the cancellation of the MCC Tour to South

Africa'.[55] As outlined above, the idea that the WCA had taken an independent decision was in fact false, but this was the official government line, and it seems that the WCA felt obliged to adhere to it in their communications with SARWCA. While the South Africans would have to have been extraordinarily naive not to realise what was actually going on behind the scenes, it is likely that the incident did damage the relationship between the English and South African associations, at least in the short term.

Both the WCA and the MCC were strongly in support of continued cricketing links with South Africa during and in the wake of the D'Oliveira Affair. In December 1968, an Extraordinary General Meeting of the MCC rejected a proposal to end cricketing contact with South Africa; the reaction to the cancellation of their 1968 stop-over suggests that, had a corresponding meeting of the WCA been held, a similar result would have eventuated. The WCA, though, did not have that option open to them. What becomes clear from the incident described here is that they were acting under severe government pressure; as an amateur organisation reliant on Sports Council grant aid to enable them to go ahead with the 1968/69 tour of Australasia, the government had much greater control over their actions than they had over the independent, private members' club that was the MCC. In fact, then, the MCC's actions surrounding Basil D'Oliveira actually affected female cricketers more immediately and more intensely than their male counterparts.

The Aftermath: South Africa's Isolation from International Women's Cricket

The outcry surrounding D'Oliveira's initial non-selection made the MCC's perusal of continued tours from the country an increasingly problematic one, due to the perceived threat to national security. This was made plain by the response to South Africa's planned visit to England in 1970, which sparked off a virulent 'Stop the Seventy Tour' campaign and saw the Labour and Liberal parties, some Conservatives, the trade unions and even the royal family publicly come out against the tour. It was ultimately cancelled, but only when the Home Secretary James Callaghan formally requested it two weeks before it was due to go ahead. The government pressure which had so strongly impacted on the

WCA's tour plans was finally being brought to bear on their male counterparts, and this combined with the influence of the newer members of the ICC (India and West Indies from 1926, and Pakistan from 1952) ensured that by the end of 1971, after the cancellation of the South African tour to Australia, a full cricketing boycott of South Africa was instituted.

South Africa's isolation from the women's game was not quite so complete. While the SACA had lost representation at the male International Cricket Conference in 1961 due to their departure from the Commonwealth, by contrast the SARWCA continued to send representatives to IWCC meetings until the early 1980s. They also, even in the wake of the D'Oliveira Affair, continued to be included in the tour schedule: at the 1969 IWCC meeting, it was agreed that South Africa would visit England and Holland in 1972 and that Australia would visit South Africa in 1974/75. In 1973, in the wake of the inaugural World Cup in England, the IWCC voted in favour of hosting the second such tournament in South Africa in 1977/78.[56] The English WCA continued to be a major proponent of embracing South Africa internationally.

Yet there were two factors which made this position increasingly difficult for the WCA to sustain. The first was continued pressure from the UK Government, who as we have seen hardened their position with regard to sporting contact with South Africa in the wake of the D'Oliveira Affair. Following the 1969 meeting of the IWCC, the WCA advised the Foreign Office that the agreed touring schedule provided for an invitation to the SARWCA to tour England in 1972. By October 1969, they had received a reply which expressed in no uncertain terms 'that no invitation should be sent at the present time'.[57] It was subsequently agreed at the July 1970 meeting of the Executive Committee that 'it would not be possible to invite South Africa to tour in 1972'—though, in keeping with the WCA's desire to include the South Africans in the touring schedule, this was only done 'most reluctantly' and was evidently a decision made as a result of government pressure rather than any kind of reversal of opinion within the WCA, regarding contact with South Africa. The WCA continued to express their hopes that circumstances would alter at a later date, but must surely have recognised that they were unlikely to do so.[58]

The second factor also made it unlikely that circumstances regarding South African tours would alter in the foreseeable future: the widening membership of the IWCC from the early 1970s. The formation of the Women's Cricket Association of India (WCAI) and the Caribbean

Women's Cricket Federation in 1973, and their admission to membership of the IWCC at the 1973 and 1976 meetings respectively, was deeply significant for women's cricket.[59] Importantly, it had been agreed at the first ever IWCC meeting, and entrenched in the constitution, that each member country would be entitled to two voting delegates, and as such 'each member should have equal power in the Council'.[60] Thus, the influence of the newer members could immediately be brought to bear on the South African question.

Firstly, while the South Africans were not invited to participate in the 1973 World Cup directly, the International XI which competed alongside teams from England, Australia, New Zealand, Jamaica and Trinidad and Tobago appears to have been conceived as a way of including SARWCA players in the tournament without taking the controversial step of issuing them with a direct invitation; five South African players were personally invited to participate. Yet at the last minute, the WCA was forced to withdraw the invitations to the South African players, in order to ensure the participation of other countries in the competition—namely the two Caribbean nations. Heyhoe-Flint wrote of her disappointment at this decision in her autobiography:

> Unhappily, politics won again. The West Indian teams threatened to withdraw if any South Africans played, and we were advised that it would be an unwise and potentially disruptive move, so the WCA were forced to back down.[61]

While government advice regarding the issue of national security did help dictate the WCA's decision to 'uninvite' the South Africa players, it was pressure from their fellow IWCC members that forced their hand.

This pressure would only increase as the 1970s progressed and the WCA's imperial influence within the IWCC continued to decline. At the 1976 IWCC meeting, held in London, discussion on the next planned World Cup tournament in 1977 again took place. This time around, though, it was recognised by all members that it would be impossible for the South Africans to stage the event, despite their wish to do so. The minutes state that members 'expressed sympathy' with the plight of the South Africans, but:

as all Associations were involved with politics – because of financial grant-aid, etc. – they were unfortunately bound by government regulations. As an international body our first concern was cricket, but regrettably powers outside our control were affecting the situation.[62]

It is interesting, too, that there was a 'nucleus of acceptances from the members' of the suggestion by the WCAI at the 1976 meeting that they would be willing to serve as an alternative host for this next World Cup tournament. As it was obvious that the South Africans would not be able to take part in a World Cup in India, the agreement in fact served to completely exclude South Africa from the future international schedule, for the first time in the IWCC's history. Their isolation would increase progressively thereafter: after 1982, they did not send any representative to IWCC meetings, and no further official women's tours by or to South Africa took place until 1997, well after the ending of apartheid. The cancellation of the planned stopover by the WCA in 1968, therefore, ultimately put paid to the WCA's last chance of official contact with the South Africans for several decades.

CONCLUSION

The D'Oliveira Affair was a key turning point for Anglo-South African cricketing relationships, within both the men's and the women's games. The public reaction to the initial non-selection of D'Oliveira, which was front-page news in England, showed up for the first time the strength of feeling against continued sporting contact with the apartheid regime. It would become increasingly difficult in the wake of this for either the MCC or the WCA to continue to embrace South Africa. Additionally, the issue highlighted the loss of influence of both organisations within the international cricketing community; both the ICC and the IWCC would eventually reject the former, imperial-based leadership of Britain and elect to exercise their own preferences regarding tours by and to South Africa.

Nonetheless, this chapter has highlighted the importance of studying the women's cricket community in conjunction with the MCC, SACA and ICC. As Netta Rheinberg stated at the inaugural meeting of the IWCC in 1958, 'the women's associations did not necessarily follow the men's lead'.[63] As independent organisations, their interactions are highly informative about the varying ways in which South Africa was regarded by female cricketers internationally and are worthy of study in their own right.

In fact, the last official cricket tour of South Africa to take place during apartheid was the three-Test tour by New Zealand Women in early 1972, a fact which is often overlooked in histories of South African cricket. Furthermore, the pressures acting on female cricketers were often different to those acting on their male counterparts: in the WCA's case, it was the pressure from the UK Government which could be brought to bear upon them as an amateur, publicly funded governing body of sport which forced the cancellation of their planned 1968 stopover in South Africa. The MCC simply did not face the same overt government pressure.

There is a great deal more research to be conducted into women's cricket, in South Africa and internationally; the WCA, SARWCA and IWCC as organisations are all ripe for future study. This chapter has shown that continuing to ignore the relationships between the WCA and SARWCA, and within the IWCC more generally, overlooks a key component of the story of cricket and apartheid South Africa. Indeed, historians who continue to make assertion about 'the cricketing world' without featuring discussion of the women's game do so at their peril.

NOTES

1. For accounts of the D'Oliveira Affair, see J. Williams, *Cricket and Race* (Oxford: Berg, 2001), 57–59; C. Merrett and J. Nauright, 'South Africa' in Stoddart and Sandiford (eds.), *The Imperial Game: Cricket, Culture and Society* (Manchester: Manchester University Press, 1998). See also *Wisden*, 1969; B. Murray, 'Politics and Cricket: The D'Oliveira Affair of 1968', *Journal of South African Studies*, 27, 4 (2001), 667–84.
2. See, for example, D. Adair, J. Nauright, and M. Phillips, 'Playing Fields Through to Battle Fields: The Development of Australian Sporting Manhood in Its Imperial Context, c.1850–1918', *Journal of Australian Studies*, 22 (1998), 51. See also P. McDevitt, *May the Best Man Win: Sport, Masculinity, and Nationalism in Great Britain and the Empire, 1880–1935* (New York: Palgrave Macmillan, 2004).
3. R. Heyhoe-Flint, *Heyhoe! The Autobiography of Rachael Heyhoe-Flint* (London: Pelham, 1978), 74.
4. For an account of the formation of the WCA, see J. Williams, *Cricket and England: A Social and Cultural History of the Interwar Years* (London: Frank Cass, 1999), chapter 5.
5. A. Odendaal, '"Neither Cricketers Nor Ladies": Towards a History of Women and Cricket in South Africa, 1860s–2000s', *International Journal of the History of Sport*, 28, 1 (2001), 124–25.

6. 'WCA Rules', WCA Yearbook, 1945, http://www.womenscrickethistory. org, accessed 1 July 2014.
7. http://www.stgeorgespark.nmmu.ac.za/content/women/displayarticle. asp?artid=wom_009, accessed 20 July 2014.
8. WCA Archive, Lancashire, Executive Committee minutes, 18 April 1952.
9. Ibid., 21 November 1953.
10. Ibid., 19 February 1954.
11. Ibid., 7 July 1950.
12. *Women's Cricket*, 3 May 1957.
13. See J. Bradley, 'Inventing Australians and Constructing Englishness: Cricket and the Creation of National Consciousness', *Sporting Traditions*, 11, 2 (1995), 35–60; R. Guha, *A Corner of a Foreign Field: The Indian History of a British Sport* (London: Picador, 2002), 323–30.
14. WCA Archive, Netta Rheinberg Tour Diary, 17 February 1949.
15. Ibid., 5 and 6 November 1957, 10 and 11 March 1958.
16. Letter from Netta Rheinberg to Mrs. Louise Goodall, 13 November 1951, http://www.stgeorgespark.nmmu.ac.za/content/women/displa-yarticle.asp?artid=wom_009, accessed 20 July 2014.
17. *The Times*, 1 December 1960.
18. WCA Archive, Executive Committee minutes, 22 June 1956.
19. *The Times*, 1 December 1960.
20. WCA Archive, Executive Committee minutes, 22 July 1960.
21. Interview with Mollie Buckland (nee Hunt), 18 June 2014.
22. Heyhoe-Flint, *Heyhoe!*, 66.
23. WCA Archive, Executive Committee minutes, 29 July 1961.
24. *Women's Cricket*, 30 August 1957.
25. WCA Archive, Executive Committee minutes, 5 November 1954.
26. Private Collection, Surrey, IWCC minutes, 28 December 1960. Women's cricket associations did not form in West Indies and India until 1973. The fifth founder member, was the Netherlands, which complicates things somewhat. However, the Netherlands tended not to send a representative to meetings, and was therefore not a particularly influential member of the organisation in its early years. The point about the organisation being entirely 'white', of course, still stands.
27. WCA Archive, Netta Rheinberg tour diary, 19 February 1958.
28. Private collection, Surrey, IWCC minutes, 20 February 1958.
29. WCA Archive, Netta Rheinberg tour diary, 20 February 1958.
30. Private collection, Surrey, IWCC minutes, 19 February 1958.
31. Unlike the ICC, whose presidents were nominated by the MCC, it was agreed from the outset that IWCC officers be elected by all member associations, and that Council officers 'shall not be drawn from the same country in succession'. See IWCC minutes, 19 February 1958.

32. Private collection, Surrey, IWCC minutes, 4 August 1966.
33. See Merrett and Nauright, 'South Africa', 68.
34. WCA Archive, Executive Committee minutes, 22 April 1967.
35. Ibid., 19 May 1950.
36. B. Houlihan, *The Government and Politics of Sport* (London: Routledge, 1991), 27.
37. The National Archives, Kew (TNA), T 227/2416.
38. TNA, ED 169/79.
39. By comparison, the AEWHA received £1750 for the financial year 1963–64. See TNA, ED 169/79.
40. TNA, AT 30/15.
41. WCA Archive, Executive Committee minutes, 26 March and 10 September 1965.
42. Ibid., 26 May 1968.
43. Ibid., 26 October 1968.
44. *The Times*, 7 October 1968.
45. *The Guardian*, 7 October 1968.
46. Interview with Shirley Hodges, 5 June 2014.
47. *The Guardian*, 7 October 1968.
48. TNA, ED 249/1, Sports Council meeting minutes, 18 December 1968, 12 February 1969 and 16 April 1969.
49. *The Guardian*, 7 October 1968.
50. WCA Archive, Executive Committee minutes, 26 October 1968.
51. *The Times*, 7 October 1968.
52. Heyhoe-Flint, *Heyhoe!*, 74.
53. WCA Archive, Executive Committee minutes, 26 October 1968.
54. Private collection, Surrey, IWCC minutes, 19 February 1969.
55. WCA Archive, Executive Committee minutes, 15 March 1969.
56. Private collection, Surrey, IWCC minutes, 19 February 1969 and 1 and 2 August 1973.
57. WCA Archive, Executive Committee minutes, 15 March 1969 and 11 October 1969.
58. Ibid., 17 July 1970 and 10 October 1970.
59. Private collection, Surrey, IWCC minutes, 1 and 2 August 1973 and 9 August 1976.
60. Ibid., IWCC minutes, 19 February 1958.
61. Heyhoe-Flint, *Heyhoe!*, 119.
62. Private collection, Surrey, IWCC minutes, 9 August 1976.
63. Private collection, Surrey, IWCC minutes, 20 February 1958.

CHAPTER 13

Newlands 'Walk-Off': Politics and Players

Patrick Ferriday

INTRODUCTION

It is difficult, if not impossible, to establish exactly when the exclusion of South Africa from international cricket became inevitable. The 1652 landing of Jan van Riebeeck at Table Bay might be pushing a point, but that was the first step towards 1948, when Malan's Nationalists finally unseated the United Party with a promise of enshrining racial segregation in intractable law—a promise it kept—or maybe March 1960, when police fired on an unarmed group of black protesters at Sharpeville, killing 69, and woke the world to the reality of South African internal affairs.

In the safe haven of Lord's, the MCC were much more concerned by the declaration of republic status in 1961 and South Africa's consequent ineligibility for the Imperial Cricket Conference (ICC). Even the MCC were required to take action eight years later, however, when Basil D'Oliveira's inclusion in the team to tour South Africa was rejected by the South African Government. The cancellation of the tour was an important development in the course of the sporting boycott and, although not evident until 1970, effectively ended the republic's

P. Ferriday (✉)
Norwich, UK
e-mail: p.ferriday@gmx.com

© The Author(s) 2018   347
B. Murray et al. (eds.), *Cricket and Society in South
Africa, 1910–1971*, Palgrave Studies in Sport and Politics,
https://doi.org/10.1007/978-3-319-93608-6_13

cricketing relations with England. It left just New Zealand and Australia as potential cricketing opponents and it was the prospect of touring Australia in 1971/72 which caused white South African players and officials suddenly to behave wildly out of character.

A 'GOLDEN AGE' OF SOUTH AFRICAN CRICKET

The first eighty years of South African Test cricket was largely dominated by defeats at the hands of England and Australia, although there were several series victories over the former. It was not until the 1950s that two real fast bowlers and a top-class spinner gave cause for optimism that consistent success could be achieved. But, even with Neil Adcock, Peter Heine and Hugh Tayfield, results were ultimately disappointing, as the national team fell backwards to the degree that they were held to a drawn series against New Zealand at home over five Tests in 1961/62. Names such as Peter Pollock, Eddie Barlow and Colin Bland gave hope for a brighter future, although it remained to be proved that this would not be the latest in a long line of false dawns. But when a second Pollock joined the side, along with Denis Lindsay and Tony Pithey, and Trevor Goddard continued to make an invaluable all-round contribution, they achieved parity with the nations against which they competed.

At this point, the normal course of events would have been the break-up of the team through injury and business commitments followed by a further decade of rebuilding. Fortunately, the structure behind this new generation of players was radically different. Professionalism within South Africa was still years away, but generous sponsorship and government assistance became possible through the 1960s economic boom. South Africa's elite schools had long nurtured sporting excellence, with Lord Nuffield's bequest in 1939 ensuring a week-long festival for the leading schoolboy cricketers, followed by a match against the host province's senior team for the best eleven schoolboys. Such was the quality of these junior teams that they sometimes beat their seniors and were able to mark themselves out as future Test players. It is no coincidence that South Africa's strength in cricket terms dates from the period when these erstwhile schoolboys began to make their presence felt. Teams such as the Fezelas (with Barlow, Bland, Lindsay, Peter Pollock and Peter van der Merwe) in 1961 and the South African schoolboys (with Barry Richards as captain and Mike Procter as vice-captain) in 1963 were sent abroad to gain experience of foreign conditions. These initiatives, together with Nuffield Week and an increased Afrikaner interest, were factors that raised the game to a new level.

In time increasing criticism of the country's politics drove Afrikaner and English speakers together in the face of a common enemy in the anti-apartheid movement and its supposed links to communism. The upshot in cricketing terms was that Afrikaners were more likely to see the game as South African rather than as English. Afrikaners at schools such as the bilingual Grey College in Bloemfontein were offered a grounding equal to any English speaker, particularly as their economic and political influence had grown rapidly during the decades after the Second World War. The appointment to the captaincy of Anglo-Afrikaner Peter van der Merwe was symptomatic of the shifting balance, and with it came further success which in turn begat greater enthusiasm for the game across all sections of white South Africa. It was no great surprise when England were beaten 1-0 in 1965 and that Graeme Pollock should be considered the only batsman in the world to rival Garry Sobers. The team was full of confidence and with considerable talent to follow. When South Africa faced Gloucestershire on that 1965 tour, two young-sters—Richards and Procter—put on 116 for the home side. To put matters into context, though, the following English summer saw the West Indies defeat England 3-1 in the Test series with one match drawn.

In 1966/67, the sixth Australian team in South Africa were in for a rude awakening. A strength in depth was revealed in young batsmen, Ali Bacher and Tiger Lance, whilst Lindsay morphed into the best wicketkeeper-batsman in the world. Procter shared the new ball with Peter Pollock in a powerful attack, with Trevor Goddard a key performer in taking 26 wickets. Barlow continued to be the inspirational figure in the side, a development that had begun on the 1963/64 Australian tour when he was noted for the 'abounding confidence and aggressive manner in which he set the initial tempo of an innings'.[1] This was a team to take on the best, particularly as Barry Richards and Lee Irvine had not yet joined the side. They were an all-white side with South Africa's cricket relatively unaffected at that stage with regard to the sporting boycott. There was nevertheless an unfortunate episode whereby the Australian Cricket Board had been required to show photographs of their part American-Indian player Grahame Thomas to the South African ambassador in order that the player be allowed to tour South Africa in 1966/67. It was subsequently concluded that his appearance was not really 'negroid' despite his dark skin tone.[2]

England defeated the West Indies in the Caribbean in 1967/68 and drew the Ashes series 1-1 with the visiting Australians in 1968, thanks to an exciting fifth Test win at The Oval. They were South Africa's next scheduled opponents in 1968/69 until an astonishing combination of Basil D'Oliveira, inexplicable MCC selectorial decisions and the unyielding National Party put paid to any hope of a further testing ground. This left one last throw of the dice when in 1970 Australia arrived in South Africa for four Tests on the back of a 3-1 series win in India. On paper the visitors could boast a fine side, notably batsmen Bill Lawry, Ian Chappell and Doug Walters, pace-bowler Graham McKenzie, and the 'mystery' spinner, John Gleeson. The reality was little more than a mismatch, as the shattered Australians stumbled forlornly from defeat to defeat. The figures were dismal: beaten 4-0, with Procter and Pollock sharing 41 wickets at 14.40, and Richards and Pollock scoring 1025 runs at 73.21. McKenzie recorded 1/333 and Chappell, lauded by his skipper as the world's best batsman on all wickets, made just 92 runs in eight innings.

The visitors were noted as being affected by their earlier Indian tour but the series was, nonetheless, astonishingly one-sided. In retrospectively applying the current rating system, the ICC ranked South Africa as cricket's top side by the end of 1969. Yet, within months, that team was gone for over twenty years and only John Traicos would ever play Test cricket again. The arrival a couple of years later of Greg Chappell, Rod Marsh and Dennis Lillee would have ensured a thrilling contest between Australia and South Africa, but as things stood in early 1970—and with England having beaten the West Indies again in the previous year—there was no doubt about the best team in the world, and by some margin. This was the team and these were the players that assembled at Newlands in April 1971, with the world at their feet and the devil at their shoulder.

CRICKETING POLITICS

In February 1960, Harold Macmillan made his 'wind of change' speech at Cape Town and could well have influenced the South African whites who were to vote in a referendum on whether to become a republic. The referendum took place on 30 October 1960 and South Africa was officially constituted as a republic on 31 May 1961. Quitting the Commonwealth on becoming a republic was not an automatic consequence but was a decision made by the National Party Government. South Africa therefore forced its own exit from the ICC and with that, theoretically, wasn't entitled to play official Test matches. The series against New Zealand in 1961/62 was deemed unofficial and the matches played over four days. When both countries quite simply treated the matches as the real thing (they certainly looked like it), then so did everyone else, including the ICC. This lack of resolution of the governing body in response to its own rules highlighted the anachronistic and paternalistic nature of the way the game was run.

A further extension of this was the old watchword 'there is no place for politics in sport', harking back to the supposed glorious days when men knew their place in society. This absurdity was echoed even in South Africa where politics decided who could vote, who could play sport with whom, where they could do it and who could represent which team under what circumstances. But to the average, entitled white South African, a group that included all international cricketers, this was not political. It was just the way it was, and the vast majority was wholly convinced it was the right way. As late as 1968, with the D'Oliveira Affair in full swing, newspaper editor Donald Woods was asked to give the main address at a public banquet attended by South African players: he later recorded that when he said 'the cricketers themselves should speak up in favour of non-racial cricket there was an uproar in the audience'.[3] He was accused of dragging politics into sport and one of the players walked out. Afterwards, Trevor Goddard spoke for the would-be liberals when he admitted privately that he agreed with much that Woods had said but claimed the players could not speak out and were 'in a difficult position'.[4] His reaction was understandable (although Woods was distinctly unsympathetic)—as he faced sanctions from his own cricket board.

After the cancellation of MCC's tour of South Africa in 1968/69, the possibility of further cricket ties between two countries came under close scrutiny. Trouble in terms of protests and damage to cricket grounds surrounded a Wilf Isaacs-sponsored tour of England in 1969 and there were mass demonstrations with thousands protesting against and disrupting Springbok rugby matches in Britain and Ireland during 1969/70. The success of the direct action strategy of the Stop the Seventy Tour campaign threatened the projected 1970 Springbok cricket tour of England. Fixtures in the latter tour could only be staged where sufficient protection was guaranteed and the projected itinerary was cut by 28 matches to 11. Eventually, Harold Wilson's Labour Government intervened and the Home Secretary, James Callaghan, requested the Cricket Council withdraw its invitation to South Africa. The 1970 tour was consequently abandoned 'on grounds of broad public policy', and a sum of £75,054 was paid by the Government in compensation. The response amongst players in South Africa was almost immediate: Peter Pollock went so far as to tell the Johannesburg *Sunday Times* that: 'Sports isolation stares South Africa in the face, and to creep back into the laager is no answer. Sportsmen who genuinely believe there should be multi-racial sport should say so'.[5]

Even the most stubborn South African players and officials could see where this was going. If Australasia were to follow the English lead then South Africa was alone, with no obvious way back. Against this background, powerful voices within the South Africa Cricket Association (SACA) decided that action was necessary. The SACA president and ex-Test captain, Jack Cheetham, had attempted to salvage the 1970 tour of England by announcing that all future Springbok sides would be selected on merit, irrespective of colour. This was, predictably, rubbished by his Government. Cheetham's next move came in response to warnings from Sir Donald Bradman, the chairman of the Australian Board of Control, that the tour to Australia was in jeopardy if South Africa insisted on sending an all-white side. It was therefore proposed that a mixed trial match be staged 'so that the best and strongest Springbok team could be chosen on merit'. This proposal was given equally short, and secret, shrift. The final throw was carefully timed. In March 1971, shortly before a much-publicised trial match at the Newlands ground in Cape Town, an official request was made to include two 'non-white' players in the squad to tour Australia. This appeared to be born of desperation, but Cheetham had been in contact with the Government in the previous month and had been given grounds to believe that his suggestion might receive a 'favourable hearing'.[6]

Up to this point, Cheetham had been campaigning in secret. Vorster maintained the secrecy when he forwarded his Government's response directly to the SACA president on the 26 March.[7] As a consequence, neither the players nor the press were aware of the request that had been made and that the Government had rejected the idea of including two 'non-white' players in the South African touring team to visit Australia. News of Cheetham's 'deep disappointment' that his initiative had been rejected by the Government was to be made public on the opening day of the Van Riebeeck festival match between the Currie Cup champions, Transvaal and the Rest of South Africa on 3, 5 and 6 April 1971. When it was arranged that Cheetham should fly to London on that day, the announcement was moved forward to 2 April.[8]

THE FESTIVAL MATCH AT NEWLANDS

The Van Riebeeck festival was established to mark the anniversary of the arrival of the Dutch in South Africa, and in 1971 also served to celebrate the tenth anniversary of the republic. The cricket match was significant in that it acted as a final trial for the forthcoming Australian trip. As if that were not enough, the match also attracted attention because Mike Procter and Barry Richards were the first South African cricketers to be officially sponsored. Richards had flown back from Australia after an astonishing season in which he scored 1538 runs and averaged 109.85, whilst Procter was on the cusp of a world record, having scored six consecutive centuries leading up to this match. Enthusiastic newspaper previews on the morning of 3 April assured readers that the game would be fully competitive and that the only danger was that the 'Rest' side would outclass the opposition, especially as the mighty Graeme Pollock would be sporting his new glasses. The touring squad was still undecided insofar as some eight players had realistic hopes of joining the ten certainties in the 15-man group and all but one would be playing for the five available places.

The Government's rejection of the SACA request required a response from the players who were standing in the front line. Both national captain, Ali Bacher—'his medical practice was keeping him busy'[9]—and vice-captain, Eddie Barlow, who was in New Zealand on business, were absent so the onus shifted onto the senior men. Peter Pollock was the elder statesman and he 'strongly believed the time had come to make a stand'. At dinner that evening he discussed a possible protest with his brother Graeme, Procter and Lindsay. An initial plan to boycott the match altogether was formulated. As luck would have it, commentator, friend and sage Charles Fortune was sitting nearby and was invited into a discussion that would also include Barry Richards. Fortune was initially shocked at the proposal and persuaded the players to adopt some other form of protest as it was essential to maintain public support—leaving a sold-out holiday crowd high and dry would not be a positive move.

A symbolic gesture was required. A draft statement was prepared by the core group and finalised by Fortune and Peter Pollock, himself a journalist. It was decided that the South African team, captained by Graeme Pollock, had to field first in order to ensure that the four players who had initially discussed taking action were able to lead the symbolic 'walk-off'.[10]

Don Mackay-Coghill, as captain of Transvaal in Bacher's absence, was brought into the group as a conduit to the other dressing room. He was crucial to arrangements as the protest could not come from just one side. Not all the Transvaal players were happy with the idea of a protest but, despite expressed misgivings, no one refused to participate. Transvaal opening batsman, and ex-Oxford University captain, Fred Goldstein, made his position clear at the players' meeting, stating: 'If this is just an attempt to save the Springbok tour to Australia, I'm not interested. But, if it is a genuine effort to promote equality on the sporting field, then count me in all the way'. Goldstein was clearly convinced by what he heard. The decision was kept in the dressing room away from the ears of those such as the Transvaal manager, Johnny Waite, who the players believed would have been quick to sabotage the process.

The match commenced with Barry Richards, who was a 'guest' player in the Transvaal team, taking guard, whist Procter paced out his gargantuan run. The crowd settled back in the expectation of watching arguably the world's 'fastest' bowler attacking the world's most 'thrilling' batsman. But after one ball had been bowled and pushed for a single (thus earning Richards two Rand), the thirteen players walked off the field (Fig. 13.1).

Confusion then reigned. Spectators arriving at the ground were greeted by an empty field; those who had been there at the start wondered why the players had trooped off. No loudspeaker explanations followed, but four bemused cabinet ministers gradually became aware of the reasons behind what they had just witnessed. It remained a 'silent protest' as Ron Delport, manager of the 'Rest', handed a statement to the press, after which the game restarted:

> We cricketers feel that the time has come for an expression of our views. We fully support the South African Cricket Association's application to include non-whites on the tour of Australia if good enough and, furthermore, subscribe to merit being the only criteria on the cricket field.

Fig. 13.1 The Pollock brothers, Peter and Graeme, lead the 'walk-off' at Newlands in 1971

The wording was short, succinct and hardly revolutionary, but this was 1971 in apartheid South Africa. To a government unpractised in compromise, it was a declaration of war. But this was not a group of black demonstrators who could be restrained with batons, tear gas and bullets; this was an elite group of privileged white males interrogating the very foundations of their sport, and through that their society. As a sporting elite, they were role models and national heroes. Worse still, it was not confined to a few hotheads and malcontents; it was almost all the players who were pledging support to an action that had already been rejected at the highest government level. Eric Rowan, one of the selectors, sought out Mackay-Coghill in the erroneous conclusion that the Transvaal captain was the ringleader, and vindictively informed him, 'You've just done your dash'.[11] From a strong candidate for the tour party he had now become a pariah, at least to the selectors.

For the rest of the day, the cricket meandered along with Barry Richards scoring a century so restrained that he was slow-handclapped for probably the first time in his career. Grahame Chevalier ensured his place in the tour team by taking seven wickets. Mackay-Coghill recalled that as captain of the batting side, he spent the day ensconced in the library fielding calls from all corners of the globe.[12] Even without social media the word had spread to Britain, Australia and, curiously, the USA. The following morning cricket was all over the domestic front pages, but in a very political way.

'The walk-off', Peter Pollock recalled, 'was a huge event for the times, shaking both the government and the cricket administration'. It had been the right time to make the stand in that 'most of the leading players had been brought together by the game' but it did not prevent Pollock, along with the others, being 'accused of trying to preserve their own skins in international cricket'. Such an accusation might well be tempered by the fact that their actions 'landed them in political deep waters at home'.[13]

THE AFTERMATH

The Government in South Africa was furious. Vorster said he would worry about the 'blerrie cricketers' after his round of golf, and with that he cancelled plans to visit the match. The four cabinet ministers in attendance left the ground and Frank Waring, the Minister of Sport, cancelled a *braaivleis* (barbeque) that he was hosting for the players. In the next day's press, Waring accused Cheetham of embarrassing the Government by publicly announcing that they had rejected his request that blacks be included in a touring cricket side. He denounced Cheetham's idea—with some justification—as 'merely a gesture for local and particularly foreign consumption',[14] and pointed to the fact that SACA had not even consulted the South African Cricket Board of Control (SACBOC) which was the governing body for 'non-white' cricketers.

Ironically, the identity of the likely coloured candidates, Dik Abed and Owen Williams, became irrelevant because the SACBOC President, Hassan Howa, opposed their selection. *The Star* reported that Howa did not believe that SACBOC could agree to 'Mr Cheetham's suggestion because the two non-white players would have been included, not because of merit, but because of expediency'.[15] The forthright cricket administrator praised the cricketers for their protest and stressed that they had supported everything he had asked for over a long period of time—'selection on merit is the crux of the matter'—but he informed the Cape Town representative of the *Sunday Times* that he regarded Cheetham's proposal as the 'greatest affront' to his cricketers. It was a case, said Howa, of parading 'token non-whites like dummies in a shop window'.[16]

Amidst the drama, the trial match ambled through to its dull conclusion. When the touring squad was announced without fanfare after the match, most of the expected names appeared. As an aid to the selectors, the game had been relatively meaningless. Graeme Pollock, Richards and Chevalier performed well, but all three were certain to tour anyway. There was also the feeling that most if not all the players had probably been decided before the game. Certainly none of the fringe players that were included had performed particularly well and one, Dassie Biggs, had not even played. Vintcent van der Bijl remembered standing in the shadow of the Newlands pavilion after the match:

> I felt relief at having made the side, but we knew then it would be no more than another ghost team, and that clouded the moment. Two days later I received a letter from my father, advising me not to harbour any hopes of the tour taking place.[17]

Mackay-Coghill did not regret his actions, later saying 'conscience-wise I never sacrificed my principles', but he did express regret that 'the players waited far too long to make our voices heard'.[18] It is unknown whether he was excluded on the grounds which had been outlined by Rowan but what is certain is that the possible scapegoating of Peter Pollock did bring all protesters together and the selectors did not carry out their threat to exclude him. They realised that first his brother and then the others would bring the house of cards crashing down. Pollock had been correctly assumed to be the ringleader as both the senior player and a man from a liberal background. His father was the editor of the *Eastern Province Herald* with 'his friends being Donald Woods and Laurence Gandar, fellow editors who were passionate in their disapproval of "that regime"'. In his book, *Peter Pollock: God's Fast Bowler*, there is also a reference to his being a member of the Progressive Party and addressing a couple of meetings.[19]

The Nationalist press was disgusted with regard to the 'walk-off', predictably so, branding the players 'unpatriotic' and lampooning them as 'long-haired hippies' indulging in a 'childish and laughable demonstration'.[20] In contrast, the white 'liberal' press was genuinely impressed. The Durban *Sunday Tribune* was fully behind the players who 'have been pushed around long enough by racially-obsessed politicians'.[21] Johannesburg *Sunday Times* reporters emphasised the significance of the action: Barry Glasspool thought the walk-off 'has sparked a split in the country's thinking on the colour issue in sport'[22] whilst Kevin Craig wrote that 'the cricketers have now courageously stood up and the world – and free-thinking South Africans – are counting. What are the rest of our sportsmen doing to break the stranglehold of sports apartheid?'[23] The *Star* called it a 'dramatic and gallant demonstration of feeling', a view echoed in a *Cape Times* editorial:

> The fact is that the Government has made politics so central to the whole sports issue that sportsmen and administrators alike can hardly keep out of political controversy. We believe that the cricketers' frustrations are echoed over a wide cross-section of South African public opinion as the destructive tentacles of ideological apartheid grasp at every corner of life.[24]

Support was forthcoming from the liberal opposition parties. 'Good for them; it's nice to see they are coming along so well', remarked Helen Suzman, the Progressive Party's lone voice in Parliament, whilst the leader of the United Party, Sir de Villiers Graaff, accused the Government of dragging sport into politics. The latter party's spokesman on sport added 'the anger and frustration of our leading cricketers has boiled to the surface'.[25] Absent from reports, however, were any quotes from the players involved. They stuck together behind the press release, partly because the captain and vice-captain had not been there, but also because two of the outraged selectors, Arthur Coy and Rowan, were conducting an inquest into who initiated the protest. Above all, the players were aware that, with the predators circling, the greatest safety was with the pack.

The *Cape Times* editorial described the actions of the players as 'the wishes, not of budding politicians, but of ordinary sportsmen prepared to take on all-comers in a competition'. Almost all of them were 'ill at ease in political controversy', but there was relatively little evidence of differing levels of commitment.[26] Evidently, Bacher and Barlow were initially 'sceptical of what had happened – they asked "what have you done?", but then came on board'.[27] There was the suggestion that had they been there at the time, the protest might not have occurred but both did go on to offer their full support for the players—Bacher stating that 'this gesture displays the feelings of the top cricketers in South Africa at the moment'.[28] SACA president Cheetham claimed to have had no notice of the demonstration but called it a natural extension of the failed attempt to have two 'non-whites' in the tour party in order 'to do all we can to foster our international relations'.

If Vorster hoped that the protest would go away quietly he was wrong, as Waring immediately went onto the attack in a dramatic attempt to steal the players' thunder. Sensing that SACA had made a mess of things, Waring confronted them with an astonishing proposal born of the confidence of a man who thought he knew his country and how deeply entrenched was its racism. In a blatant attempt to divide opinion amongst white cricketers (divide and rule being the *modus operandi* of the Government), he stated that it was not an issue that could 'be solved by a gesture at top level'. It required the cricket authorities to state clearly where they stood on multiracial play. He continued:

> When they come to me and talk for the clubs, and for the cricketers at all levels, then I will listen carefully ... Do South Africa's cricketers want multi-racial cricket or don't they? If the cricket authorities come to me and state that this is the position, then I am fully prepared to take it to the Cabinet.[29]

The initial response in South Africa was one of confusion. Convener of selectors Arthur Coy, a man who had long defended segregated cricket, rightly called it a 'radical change of view'.[30] This it was, bearing in mind that Vorster had said in 1967 that 'no mixed sports between whites and non-whites will be practised locally irrespective of the standard of proficiency of the participants'.[31] Former South African captain, Clive van Ryneveld, termed it a 'red herring'[32] and journalist Stanley Uys, reporting from Cape Town, saw through the sham, stating that Waring was intent 'on exploiting the undoubted white racial prejudice which exists at the lower levels of South African sport to frustrate multi-racialism at the higher levels. This shows how determined the Government is to maintain apartheid in sport'.[33]

John Arlott, writing in the *Guardian*, was equally unconvinced:

> Since the social structure of South Africa is based on a strict colour bar, it would be a violent reversal of pattern if non-whites were admitted into the social-cum-sporting setting of the cricket club. If this were to be done, the Government would be at least extremely embarrassed, at worst all but routed, and the South African cricketers would have achieved an almost immeasurable moral victory in the eyes of the world.[34]

With extraordinary speed, the heads of the cricket unions of Border, Eastern Province, Natal and Transvaal all said they personally supported the move towards multiracial cricket at all levels. In a unique show of accidental solidarity, the president of SACBOC, Hassan Howa, called for SACA to take up the gauntlet thrown down so carelessly by Waring.[35]

At the same time, he reiterated SACBOC's stance by stating that they did 'not ask to play together at club level as suggested by Mr Waring. We merely ask for South African teams to be chosen on merit'.[36]

A few days later, the headline in the Johannesburg *Sunday Times* screamed out, 'Waring's Big Blunder!' He was caught on the hop as his bluff was called, and when the Argus newspaper group released the result of a poll seeking the views of white cricketers, he realised that he had been outmanoeuvred. Five newspapers in the country's five largest cities canvassed 292 first-league cricketers with the question 'Are you prepared to play with or against non-Whites at league level?' The answers were that six were unsure, 10 said 'no' and an astonishing 276 were in favour of what would be a radical change to club cricket, and a fundamental challenge to segregation in sport. Oddly enough, *The Star* reported that Bacher refused to answer the question but, despite this, Waring had clearly misjudged the mood of the sportsmen he was 'representing'.

AUSTRALIA AND THE ISOLATION OF SOUTH AFRICAN CRICKET

In Australia, there was a significant shift in opinion against the tour after it was made known that Vorster had rejected the proposal that two black players accompany the South African touring team. Only a month earlier a poll had shown Australians as being hugely in favour of the tour going ahead, but then the storm broke. Labour governments in West and South Australia announced they would make 'no facilities available' and the Council of Trade Unions, led by Bob Hawke and with 1.8 million members, threatened mass disruption. The Catholic Archbishop of Brisbane said there was little point protesting as the South African Government would not listen although other church leaders were slightly more dynamic in their suggestions. With the possibility of India, Pakistan and the West Indies refusing to play against Australia and the fear of exclusion from the upcoming Munich Olympics, a tour that had 'hung like a gossamer thread' since the start of the year became ever more tenuous. Australian captain Ian Chappell remained immune, branding himself 'unaffected by anti-apartheid protests over the tour'. This was not an uncommon view; the Australian Board of Control secretary Alan Barnes said 'what they are doing is their own business', and New South Wales Cricket Association president Alan Davidson offered the thought that 'as cricketers we will play against anyone'. Former captain Ian Johnson argued on ABC television that a boycott would do more harm than good, but retired Australian all-rounder Tom Veivers, who had toured South Africa in 1966/67, took the opposite view, calling for the immediate cancellation of the tour.[37]

A clash between Australia's cricket authorities and the South African Government was inevitable. The former had sent a clear message in late 1970 that there should be players of colour in the side. Vorster in response was not prepared to veer from his position of April 1967 when he made it clear that he would rather accept South Africa's sporting isolation than capitulate to the ultimatum 'that our Springbok team would not be welcome unless it included all race groups'.[38] Just as had been the case in Britain with the D'Oliveira Affair, South African politicians forced themselves into Australian households through sport and via the media. This left many unsure how to respond. The Labor Party's boycott policy was clear enough but an editorial in the *Sydney Morning Herald* on 8 April 1971 was symptomatic of more complex responses. The message was that the Australian Government should only apply pressure on the Cricket Board of Control if 'clear, immediate and transcendent issues of national interest were involved', an approach accompanied by a call for all sportsmen to support the players' protest in Cape Town. What was not specified was the form this 'support' should take.

During the course of the Australian winter of 1971, Bradman's mind and that of McMahon's Government were changed by events on the rugby field where large-scale protests followed the touring Springboks all over the country. Equally effective was union action ensuring maximum discomfort for players and spectators alike. It rapidly became clear that the cricket tour which was scheduled to follow in just a few months would be unmanageable, certainly if the South Africans sent an all-white team. Bradman needed assistance from South Africa but it was not forthcoming. In a bid to salvage the tour, he telephoned Vorster, but found the Prime Minister completely intractable; he would rather the tour was cancelled than allow two 'non-whites' to participate in it.[39] In July 1971, the Australian ambassador in Pretoria reported that McMahon was still in favour of the tour, but by August the Australian Government had adopted a position of neutrality. The decision was left to the Board of Control which met on 9 September and thereafter announced 'with great regret' that the invitation had been withdrawn. It also noted that it was hoped the South African Government would 'so relax its laws that the cricketers of South Africa may once again take their places as full participants in the international field'.[40]

CRICKET AND THE DEVELOPMENT OF A POLITICAL CONSCIENCE

Was Newlands, then, less of radical expression of a new generation of liberal South African thinking than a cynical *volte face* by sportsmen seeking to defend if not feather a nest? Certainly there were those who thought so, in addition to some whites who were furious that these privileged young men were rocking the boat. There were even conspiracy-theory suggestions that the Australian authorities had masterminded the whole event in order to deflect criticism of the upcoming tour. In fact the combination of the refusal to select 'non-whites' and the walk-off had drawn attention to problems in South Africa and effectively mobilised Australian public opinion. The inclusion of the two 'non-whites' would of course have depended on their agreement and Howa's approval. One of the two players, Owen Williams, said that he wanted to be selected on merit and was not prepared to be 'a glorified baggage-master', whilst Howa would emerge from the situation as a major figure in South African cricket and able to capitalise on divisions in sport in order to create a platform for wider action.

The Newlands protest was a symptom of developments taking place and reflected the opinion of leading white players who were desperate to ensure that South Africa continued to play cricket at an international level. The occasion could be seen as another in the series of shocks going under the umbrella name of the 'Sports Boycott' that were being delivered to apartheid society, of which the 1969/70 'Demo' Springbok rugby tour might be described as 'a truly seismic one and the walk-off a relative after-tremor'. The fact that the players stood up as a united group was important in that 'apartheid's naked underbelly became visible, and people who had previously regarded the apartheid state as an unassailable monolith began to understand that it could be opposed'.[41] What thereafter happened in Australia was outside their control but what occurred in South Africa was undoubtedly of great significance—it gave heart to those who wanted to see change. The South African Tennis Union called the protest 'a wonderful thing'—they had experienced apartheid in sport first-hand in trying to obtain a visa for the African American Arthur Ashe.

Despite the support that the cricketers received in their call for merit selection, there were many who viewed the action with a sense of cynicism. A critical view was trenchantly put by the coloured player, Tiefie Barnes:

They [the Test team] were so happy and contented that they never gave black South Africans a second thought. But when it all started crumbling around them what did they do? They started showing concern, not for us, but for themselves ... according to Dr Bacher this was done to show the outside world of the whites' sincerity. Are they sincere? I say not.[42]

Most illuminating, or damning, of all are the words of some of the leading protagonists themselves when they later considered the motivation behind their actions. Barry Richards has since stated the protest may have been 'sensationalistic' and probably 'futile' driven by 'the real possibility of being cast out from the Test scene'.[43] Mike Procter later freely admitted the whole idea was to 'pacify international opinion' and confesses that it now seems like '...tokenism, a patronising decision that amounted to window-dressing'.[44] Vintcent van der Bijl agreed this was true 'to an extent' but it was 'also a plea for equality in sport...a spontaneous reaction of a frustrated group'.[45] Eddie Barlow was deeply impressed by the action of his fellow players: 'This was earth-shattering stuff in a time when it was considered almost treasonable to oppose the Government, but at least those cricketers who had the courage of their convictions can look back on the protest with some pride'.[46] Lee Irvine, who was overseas on business at the time, felt it important to make clear how the land lay: 'We did what we could. Not enough perhaps but those bleating about half-measures weren't in our shoes', adding, 'I can tell you of that 1970 team there wasn't a single man in the team who voted for the Nats [National Party] and apartheid'.[47]

Vorster's plan of apparent compromise was quick to appear, less than three weeks after the walk-off. He had made use of the Broederbond in formulating a strategy. He hoped in doing so that he would not only satisfy international opinion but would avoid antagonising his right wing. The proposal, which effectively meant that he would not be deviating from the Government's policy of separate development', was announced in the House of Assembly on the 22 April. It was to open sport to a multinational system whereby black, coloured, Indian and white teams might play against each other 'under certain circumstances' but not at club or provincial level. This was categorically not the interracial reform sought by his opponents, not least because it largely bypassed the complexities of mixed changing rooms, Pass Laws, white-only facilities and other such obstacles. Vorster certainly understood the sense of what would become Hassan Howa's battle cry: 'No normal sport in an abnormal society'.

The post-Newlands debate continued as the issue of sport and race became central to the question of how sport and society were organised. Under international pressure, changes were enforced slowly but surely over the next decade but they were all too little and too late. To refer to some examples, College Old Boys, a leading 'non-white' cricket club side, announced its application to join the Transvaal Premier League; tennis player Cliff Drysdale and, belatedly, golfer Gary Player felt newly emboldened to press for multiracial competition; and the public were confident enough to heckle Frank Waring as he presented the South African Open tennis runner's-up medal to Evonne Goolagong at Ellis Park, as 90% of white tennis players declared themselves in favour of multiracial games at all levels. Meanwhile any wild hopes of a reversal of South Africa's exclusion from the Olympic movement were fast disappearing from view.

It is easy to approach the events of 1970/71 with the wisdom of hindsight and forget how bewildering many of the situations were to those living in South Africa and not fully aware of mounting opposition overseas. Insubordination from such a source as a sporting team was unheard of and the Newlands affair was a notable event within wider issues concerning the 'sporting boycott' and the structure of sport in South Africa. The plea that teams be selected on merit was ignored and, as time went on, it became clear that it would be increasingly difficult to end South Africa's cricket crisis whilst apartheid was in place. Within five years, the focus of attention had turned to the entire system of apartheid and not how it was or was not practised in cricket. As Howa pointed out, black players could not be expected to play 'normal' sport for a day and then return to their 'abnormal' lives for the rest of the week. The debate became more urgent, and with that urgency came a real recognition that the system in place was not only unsustainable but also morally bankrupt.

NOTES

1. E. W. Swanton, *Barclays World of Cricket: The Game from A to Z* (London: Collins, 1980), 236.
2. G. Haigh and D. Frith, *Inside Story* (Southbank: News Custom Publishing, 2007), 154.
3. D. Woods, *Asking for Trouble: Autobiography of a Banned Journalist* (London: Gollancz, 1980), 194.
4. Mihir Bose, *Sporting Colours* (London: Robson Books, 1994), 80.

5. P. Hain, *Outside In* (London: Biteback, 2012), 37.
6. *The Star*, 5 April 1971.
7. G. Chettle, *South African Cricket Annual*, 1971, 51.
8. *Sunday Times*, 4 April 1971; Chettle, *South African Cricket Annual*, 1971.
9. R. Hartman, *Ali: The Life of Ali Bacher* (Johannesburg: Viking, 2004), 133.
10. B. Murray interviews with Peter Pollock, September 2015; Mike Procter, August/September 2015 and Barry Richards, September 2015.
11. J. Winch correspondence with Don Mackay-Coghill, January 2015.
12. Ibid., January 2015.
13. Murray interview with Peter Pollock.
14. *Observer*, 4 April 1971.
15. *The Star*, 5 April 1971.
16. *Sunday Times*, 4 April 1971.
17. V. van der Bijl, *Cricket in the Shadows* (Pietermaritzburg, 1984), 29.
18. Correspondence, Mackay-Coghill.
19. P. Pollock, *Peter Pollock: God's Fast Bowler* (Vereeniging: Christian Art Publishers, 2001).
20. *Sunday Times*, 11 April 1971.
21. *Sunday Tribune*, 4 April 1971.
22. *Sunday Times*, 25 April, 1971.
23. Ibid., 18 April 1971.
24. *Cape Times*, 5 April 1971.
25. *Daily Star*, 4 April 1971.
26. *Cape Times*, 5 April 1971.
27. B. Murray interviews with Peter and Graeme Pollock, August/September 2015.
28. *Sunday Times*, 4 April 1971.
29. *The Times*, 6 April 1971.
30. *Sunday Times* (SA), 11 April 1971.
31. Address to House of Assembly, 11 April 1967.
32. *Sunday Times* (SA), 11 April 1971.
33. *Guardian*, 5 April 1971.
34. Ibid., 5 April 1971.
35. *Cape Times*, 13 April 1971.
36. Mogamad Allie, *More Than a Game: History of the Western Province Cricket Board 1959–1991* (Cape Town: Cape Argus, 2000), 93.
37. *Guardian*, 5 April 1971.
38. Address to House of Assembly, 11 April 1967.
39. Haigh and Frith, *Inside Story* 2007, 156–57.
40. B. Murray and C. Merrett, *Caught Behind: Race and Politics in Springbok Cricket* (Johannesburg: Wits University Press; Scottsville: University of KwaZulu-Natal Press, 2004), 154.

41. Email correspondence with D. Slater, February 2018.
42. A. Odendaal, *Cricket in Isolation* (Stellenbosch: The Author, 1977), 221.
43. B. Richards, *The Barry Richards Story* (London: Faber & Faber, 1978), 121.
44. M. Procter, *South Africa, The Years of Isolation and the Return to International Cricket* (London: Queen Anne Press, 1994), 23.
45. Van der Bijl, *Cricket in the Shadows*, 30.
46. E. Barlow, *The Autobiography* (Cape Town, 2006), 118–19.
47. A Murtagh, *Sundial in the Shade: The Story of Barry Richards; the Genius Lost to Test Cricket* (Pitch Publishing, 2015), 99.

INDEX

© The Editor(s) (if applicable) and The Author(s) 2018
B. Murray et al. (eds.), *Cricket and Society in South Africa, 1910–1971*, Palgrave Studies in Sport and Politics,
https://doi.org/10.1007/978-3-319-93608-6